M000101077

MARKETS AND MARKETING

Monographs in Economic Anthropology, No. 4

Edited by

Stuart Plattner

Society for
Economic
Anthropology

UNIVERSITY
PRESS OF
AMERICA

Lanham • New York • London

Copyright © 1985 by the
Society for Economic Anthropology

University Press of America®, Inc.

4720 Boston Way
Lanham, Maryland 20706

3 Henrietta Street
London WC2E 8LU England

All rights reserved
Printed in the United States of America
British Cataloging in Publication Information Available

Co-published by arrangement with
the Society for Economic Anthropology

Library of Congress Cataloging-in-Publication Data

Society for Economic Anthropology (U.S.).   Meeting (1984 : Davis, Calif.)
   Markets and marketing / Society for Economic Anthropology,
edited by Stuart Plattner. – Lanham : University Press of America, c1985.
xx, 418 p. : maps ; 23 cm. – (Monographs in economic anthropology ; no. 4)
   Bibliography: p. 411-416.
   1. Economic anthropology–Congresses.   2. Markets–Congresses.
   3. Marketing–Developing countries–Congresses.   I. Plattner, Stuart.
   II. Title.   III. Series.
   GN448.S63   1984
   306'.3–dc19   85–3302
   ISBN 0–8191–4604–8 (alk. paper)
   ISBN 0–8191–4605–6 (pbk. : alk. paper)

 The paper used in this publication meets the minimum requirements of
American National Standard for Information Sciences—Permanence
of Paper for Printed Library Materials, ANSI Z39.48–1984.

Acknowledgments

The papers in this volume were presented on April 6 & 7, 1984 at the fourth annual meeting of the Society for Economic Anthropology. William Davis, of the Department of Anthropology, University of California at Davis was the host of the two day meeting held at the University Center. The program committee included Frances Berdan, Norbert Dannhaeuser, Lillian Trager and Stuart Plattner, chair. Mrs. Sue Bording, Anthropology Department Secretary, The University of Missouri at St. Louis, was in charge of word processing and manuscript preparation. The editor would like to thank all those named above, as well as the volume contributors, for helping to bring this book into existence so soon after the conference.

SEA MONOGRAPHS

Monographs of the Society for Economic Anthropology are conference proceedings of the annual meetings of the Society.

1. Ortiz, Sutti (editor), Economic Anthropology: Topics and Theories. Monographs in Economic Anthropology, No. 1. 1983. Lanham, MD. University Press of America and Society for Economic Anthropology.

2. Greenfield, Sidney and Arnold Strickon (editors), Entrepreneurship and Social Change. Monographs in Economic Anthropology, No. 2. In press, Lanham, MD. University Press of America and Society for Economic Anthropology.

3. Maclachlan, Morgan (editor), Household Economies and their Transformations. Monographs in Economic Anthropology, No. 3. In press, Lanham, MD. University Press of America and Society for Economic Anthropology.

CONTENTS

I. INTRODUCTION

Stuart Plattner

Economic anthropology has had a conflicted view of markets and marketing in the past. In the early days when the role of the subfield was defined as the natural history of tribal and band economic activities, markets were usually seen as irrelevant. The obvious local effects of market activities (steel tools, manufactured cloth, and such) were easily dismissed as intrusive, i.e., directly related to Western/capitalist/industrialized economic activities that were by definition (at the time) not relevant to the function of native economies.

Bohannan and Dalton's fourfold classification of African societies by whether "the market principle" ("...the determination of prices of labor, resources, and outputs by the forces of supply and demand regardless of the site of transactions.") was dominant or peripheral, in independent relationship to whether market places are present or absent, is a good example of this point of view.(1965:2) The articles in their collection were heavily descriptive for the most part, and the book, though widely read, did not significantly influence the theoretical development of the field.[1]

We now know that "the market", in the sense of the macro- economic interactions between the European capitalist economies and other societies, was an active determinant of many features of "native" life. Wolf's book on the history of relationships between Europe and the societies of people "without history" in Africa, Asia, and America exemplifies this point of view within anthropology (1982). Modern studies of exotic economic systems can ignore the history of local interaction with exogenous markets only if they concentrate on the most microlevel issues of individual behavior.

This does not mean that market analyses pertinent to large, wealthy, industrialized, developed economies can simply be applied without change to small, poor, agrarian and developing societies. People in exotic cultures may buy and sell many things in ways that can be described with terms drawn from Western market theory. Whether such description adds understanding or hides ignorance is always an open question. Herskovits'

(1940) pioneering survey of economic anthropology was justly criticised for confusing the application of terms from capitalist markets for an explanation of process and function in exotic economic systems.

An anthropological economic analysis should, almost by definition, be grounded in broad knowledge of local context. This is a valuable lesson to be learned from the "formalist-substantivist" debates of the sixties (although it is hard to say that the price, in divisiveness, was worth it.) The writers here are more eclectic than the participants in that polemic. In explaining economic behavior people draw ideas as befits the need from formal economic theory, economic geography, political economy and economic history as well as from cultural anthropology.

1. A Note on Terminology

The term "market" will be used to denote the social institution, meaning any domain of economic interactions where prices exist which are responsive to the supply and demand of the items exchanged. A "marketplace" contains these interactions confined in a specified time and place. "Marketing" denotes buying or selling in any market, not necessarily in a marketplace.

All the societies described here (except China) are integrated by capitalist markets. This means individuals own and invest private capital, economic functions are specialized into various productive and distributive roles, and of course currency is used. The term "mass market" is used to mean the production, distribution and consumption of industrially mass- produced goods for family consumption.

II. ECONOMIC ANTHROPOLOGY AND ECONOMICS

Another development underlying a concern with markets is the expansion of the field of interest of economic anthropology to agrarian, developing and industrialized societies. This meant that the economic activities studied were seen increasingly in a market context. As more economic anthropologists focused upon these societies, and fewer upon the economics of band and tribal societies, the pretense that theories of markets and marketing were irrelevant became less viable.

Economic anthropology will not therefore wither away into a corner of economics. The traditional anthropological need to view human behavior and institutions as dealing with whole persons - involving as it does the importance of field work, the concern with the family, the household, and the community - is a point of view that is becoming more relevant in economics (e.g., Akerloff 1976; Becker 1974a, 1974b; Ben-Porath 1980).

This interdisciplinary interest is one of the more exciting developments of modern economic anthropology. When economists try to analyze economic behavior directly observable in the real world, as anthropologists do, they confront the same issues that anthropologists deal with. It is not so easy to dismiss a serious interest in local context as "butterfly collecting". As more anthropologists become familiar with modern economic theory, they give up the "knee -jerk" rejection of all economic theory as irrelevant to an explanation of observed human behavior. This convergence of interest should yield some significant new work.

In addition to changes in theoretical economics, the field of economic development has changed during the past twenty years. The anthropological viewpoint is commonly included in project planning and implementation. Anthropologists may complain that their holistic ideas are given more lip-service than real authority in such projects, but the concerns are no longer just ignored. Thus in applied work, as well as in theoretical economics, an anthropological point of view is no longer considered relevant only to the disappearing "primitives".

III. THE ECONOMIC ANTHROPOLOGY OF MARKETS AND MARKETING

What is the anthropological point of view in the economic anthropology of markets and marketing? This volume includes papers on the central place theory analysis of marketplace systems; microeconomic studies of the role of information and of communication on individual behavior in markets; studies of marketing in economic development; work on the place of markets, marketers, and marketing in the informal sector; and papers on the function and structure of markets in primitive states and empires.

The work presented here represents several streams of significant research, but does not claim to offer a comprehensive picture of the economic anthropology of markets and marketing. This is not achievable in a publication of this short length. The papers included here represent about half of those on the meeting program, for example. We tried to include work that was significant, exciting, and in line with the traditional interests of economic anthropology, but inevitably have left out some excellent papers.

1. Central Place Studies

The first section includes work that has been a major development in this field in the past twenty years: the central place theory analysis of marketplace systems. This formal model was introduced into the economic anthropology literature by G. W. Skinner (1964), and had a tremendous impact upon students of agrarian marketplaces.

The formal model, as such, was a powerful help in organizing the complex reality of marketplaces observed "in the field". Central place theory gave students of complex market systems the ability to precisely analyze functions and processes. They did this by describing the system in terms of the central place model, and then analyzing the pattern of real-world deviations from the model's predictions. Skinner's (1964) analysis, using figures showing a Chinese marketing system at several stages of abstraction from a map to a geometric central place model was revolutionary.

For example, Smith expected a priori to find the Indian marketplaces she classified as rural bulking centers both more numerous and situated differently in the Guatemalan landscape. In several papers Smith showed precisely how the market system under study differed from the standard central place pattern, and explained this deviation by pointing to specific differences between the social, political and economic context (and infrastructure) and the assumptions that the formal model was built on. Her work on the market system of Western Guatemala has been extraordinary in this regard. (references in C.A. Smith, this volume)

Appleby's contribution here analyzes the market system in the Gambia River basin. He shows the heuristic power of the central place model, used as a "conceptual and methodological tool kit" developed in economic anthropology, to analyze the relation between the contemporary marketing system and the earlier export economies.

2. Individuals in Markets

The papers in Part II change from the macroeconomic concerns with systems of marketplaces in Part I to the microeconomic behavior of individuals in markets. The papers in this section can be read as dealing with the question, how do working people with very limited knowledge and resources act as they face real economic risk? While the focus is on the reasoning and causality behind individual economic decisions, this does not mean that the decisions are simply defined as maximizing. (Schneider 1974, Plattner 1974) The current view sees individual economic behavior as the outcome of a multicausal, goal-driven decision procedure, where the actor is operating in relative ignorance and uncertainty, with complex goals and constraints. (e.g., Barlett 1980, Gladwin 1979, Ortiz 1983)[2] The significant issues often focus on information and trust. Acheson shows how the Maine lobster fishermen are prisoners of faulty information caused by the nature of their industry. They can't trust their dealers, yet they must enter into trusting relationships with them. Acheson's analysis of the role of pricing information in this situation is grounded in his expert fieldworker's knowledge of the fishery, yet is generalizable to any other economic situation with similar informational constraints.

Plattner's paper analyzes the conditions under which individuals in a market will enter into reciprocal long-term relationships. His paper shows the general, abstract issues so concretely presented in Acheson's work, and explains why people in markets all over the world willingly enter into regular trade relationships with others whom they characterize as (in the

Maine fisherman's's words,) "misarble fuckin bahstids".

Byrne's paper in this section focuses on one aspect of regular market relationships: that of market "niches". He demonstrates quantitatively that fresh produce vendors in a public marketplace offer consistent product clusters, which vary significantly from each other. This may seem obvious on casual inspection to a market shopper, but it is also obvious that market merchants should take advantage of daily special deals and handle any produce they can buy cheaply and sell expensively. The value of Byrne's sort of analysis is to demonstrate which, of more than one "intuitively obvious" pattern, exists in any real world situation.

3. Markets in Economic Development

Part III contains market studies in economic development. Each of the papers deals, in one way or another, with the fact that the world is becoming one vast multinational market. Most of the "dual economy" issues of the 1960's, portraying "traditional" cultures confronting modern markets, are irrelevant in a world with a global mass market for industrial consumer goods. When the "natives" own Singer sewing machines and TV sets and negotiate for their own bottled beer and soft drink distribution routes, then the important questions on the institutional level include the nature of distributive channels, and how these are suited to the service requirements of different goods; community level issues deal with how groups make use of, or are victimized by political issues which affect their economic security; an interesting question on the individual level is how persons use the human capital they developed in the traditional marketing system in the new distribution system for mass manufactured consumer goods.

These papers essentially deal with the shift in production from the developed countries to the less developed hinterlands of the world market. As central cities extend their control and influence out further into their peripheries, retailing in general becomes more integrated; and the movement of people with generalized agrarian marketing and production skills from agricultural villages to cities increases in pace and volume. Young persons newly arrived in the cities work under novel conditions of personal independence and control over cash income. The enormous growth of the world mass market for popular consumer goods like soft drinks, bottled beer, cheap electronics goods and the like, coupled with the internationalization of production, is a major development in the economic system of the world.

Dannhaeuser compares the urban market channels in a town in India with one in the Philippines. The aggressive vertical integration of retailing in the Philippines is related to the influence of the U.S. market and the higher standard of living there; while the more passive approach to retailing in an Indian city is largely explained by the chronic shortages in key goods, which create a seller's market. The few examples of aggressive marketing in the Indian town are by fully integrated retailers, whose businesses are wholly owned and managed by the manufacturers. Dannhaeuser stresses the importance of understanding the nature of wholesale suppliers in explanations of retail trade.

McGee deals with some of the same issues as Dannhaeuser, and shows how the aggressive control of distribution channels in Malaysia has led to the growth of a mass consumption-oriented market in Malaysia. McGee presents statistical data to show that this market has grown explosively in urban areas recently, and points out that it is related to far-reaching changes in popular culture. The most obvious implications are a growth in the urban, nuclear family based middle and upper classes.

Cook analyzes the crafts industry in a Mexican city and shows how the fate of traditional craft industries becomes problematic as local regions integrate with national markets. The owners of the local capital and entrepreneurial skills, who used to control the crafts industries, find more rewarding occupations as new opportunities for urban business expand. The worldwide shift of semi-skilled and unskilled manufacturing from more to less developed countries seems to be replicated within developing countries by a shift of crafts manufacturing from more to less urban settings. The underlying

causes are the same: the out-of-pocket costs of
small-scale production become too high as markets
become more integrated, while the opportunity cost
increases with the growth of opportunities
connected with the public sector and with large,
vertically integrated enterprises. Cook describes
how the piece-wage system operates in
merchant-operated businesses in the city as well
as in the countryside. He shows that urban male
pieceworkers in various lines of production are
relatively better paid than rural female
pieceworkers in the embroidery industry. He
explains this difference as reflecting the
contrasting life situations of laborers in the
urban and rural sectors of the regional economy
together with the contrasting operating and market
conditions confronting merchant capital.

The next set of three papers deals with urban
markets in developing countries as part of an
informal sector. The concept of an informal
sector was embraced by ethnographically oriented
observers in the 1970's. It seemed to give
analytic clarity to the economic behavior urban
fieldworkers in developing countries were so
familiar with. This concept partially solved the
problem of how to approach the analysis of urban
marketers, who looked just like the rural
marketers described in the literature, yet who
occupied different economic and class positions.
The questions dealt with in the papers by Trager,
Babb and Lessinger concern the nature of economic
differentiation within the informal sector, and
the variety of political relations between the
informal sector and the government and the close,
symbiotic relationship between the formal and
informal sectors.

Trager shows how the skills learned in the
traditional market of a Nigerian city are used by
individuals to take advantage of opportunities
opened up in the retailing of mass manufactured
consumer goods - beer and soft drinks in this
case. She shows that earlier uses of the informal
sector concept were overly simplistic, in that
they refused to admit significant class variation
in the informal sector. Her paper gives a good
example of the mutual dependence of the formal and
informal sectors.

Babb focuses on the working poor in a highland

city in Peru. She describes the increasing
number of marketers and street vendors in the past
few years and compares the traders to petty
commodity producers. Babb shows how the role
they play in the local economy changes as the
economic conditions in the country change, and
suggests that the municipal government seems bent
on using them as scapegoats for problems created
by others who are more able to defend themselves.

Lessinger presents a similar case of urban
marketers in the Indian city of Madras. The India
marketers were highly organized and involved in
local politics, to the point where different
market organizations were clients of different
political parties. The marketer population
studied by Lessinger seemed to include much more
heavily capitalized firms than Babb's cases, which
may explain the relative powerlessness of the
latter (although the different history of
political repression in the two countries is also
an important cause). These two papers show the
need for a comparative study in the urban
sociology of marketers, with specific focus on the
marketers' access to political institutions.

It is interesting to note that the papers here
took a more supply-side approach to marketing
systems. Dannhaeuser, Trager, and to some extent,
McGgee looked at how the trade strategies of large
suppliers shaped the system. This is different
than the demand-side approach taken by the papers
in the first section. Skinner, Smith and Appleby
were more concerned with the effects of the demand
attributes of a population in a landscape. Of
course, the role of government policies may be
crucial no matter which point of view is taken.

5. Markets in History

The final section deals with the role of
markets in early states and empires. It adds to a
lively literature which questions whether the
markets described for states like the Aztec
performed integrating functions similar to modern
markets (Berdan 1983, Blanton 1983, Carrasco
1983). The issues dealt with here include the
social and economic preconditions for capitalist
markets; the nature and variety of preconquest
markets in the Aztec state; and the function of
markets in the prehispanic Inca state.

Berdan discusses the complex nature of markets in the preconquest Aztec state. While most chroniclers focused on major urban marketplaces such as the one at Tlatelolco (now in Mexico City), she shows that there is considerable information on a wide variety of smaller, distinctive marketplaces. She defines four different types of marketplaces in distinct economic - political niches of the Aztec empire. Analyzing these latter markets shows the complex spatial and political structure of the Aztec economy, in a far more precise manner than simple extrapolation from the major central market would allow.

Earle discusses the role of market exchange in the preconquest Andean Inca state. He asks a simple question: "Did markets distribute commodities in the prehispanic Inca State?", and goes on to present concepts and data to deal with the issue. The answer, in a nutshell, is 'not much', and he discusses the way such a highly organized state could function without an integrated market system.

Blanton questions the importance of markets for state formation. He notes the increasing commercialization of late Postclassic Highland Mexican society, and wonders whether this commercial orientation could have produced an independent development of European-style capitalism. He compares the general situation of China, as a case of a commercial society which did not develop an indigenous capitalism, with Mesoamerica. By comparing the political economy of early Europe, China, and Mesoamerica, Blanton concludes that Mesoamerica, like China, had a market system whose very strength impeded the development of capitalism.

The underlying message from these papers is that generalization from the physical existence of marketplaces in a preconquest society to the full array of integrative market functions observed in modern capitalist states is simplistic and probably wrong. Exchange existed within and without marketplaces, and marketplaces served some integrative functions, but understanding of the precise nature of the social and economic systems in early states must come from a solid knowledge of rural production and regional distribution.

6. Summary

How can such a diverse set of papers be summarized? In terms of level of social integration, the interests of the scholars represented here range from the regional, macro-level economic and political studies of the central place and the early state papers, through the institutional and class concerns of the development and informal sector works, to a focus on the individual behavior of market participants. In terms of style of analysis, the papers range from the quantitative analysis of observed and recorded behavioral data to the abstract theoretical discussion of fundamental issues in interpersonal market transactions and the development of capitalism. In traditional anthropological style, they blend the virtues of intensive investigation of the single case with the vice of generalization from small samples.

The underlying theme that unifies the papers is a commitment to theoretical analysis based on careful description. The willingness to become familiar with the assumptions and concepts of allied fields such as economics (in all its branches), geography, and marketing coupled with the commitment to detailed, solid empirical description and the holistic view of human behavior is producing some exciting work.

It should be noted that the old polemics about formalism and substantivism that characterized economic anthropology in the 1960's are absent here. While no attempt was made to explicitly balance points of view in this volume, readers will see issues of political economy, institutional and formal analysis. The Society for Economic Anthropology was founded on the assumption that our common concern to stimulate research is best served by the full exchange of analytic ideas instead of polemics.

REFERENCES CITED

Akerloff, George
1976   The Economics of Caste and of the Rat Race and Other Woeful tales. Quarterly Journal of Economics, 90:599-617.

Barlett, Peggy
    1980   Agricultural Decision Making:Anthropological Contributions to Rural Development. New York: Academic Press.

Becker, Gary
    1974a   A Theory of Social Interactions. Journal of Political Economy, 82:1063-1093.

    1974b   A Theory of Marriage. In Economics of the Family: Marriage, Children and Human Capital. ed. T. W. Schultz. A Conference Report of the National Bureau of Economic Research. Chicago and London: University of Chicago Press.

Ben-Porath, Yoram
    1980   The F-Connection: Families, Friends, and Firms in The Organization of Exchange. Population and Development Review, 6:1-30.

Berdan, Frances
    1983   The Reconstruction of Ancient Economies: Perspectives from Archaeology and Ethnohistory. in Economic Anthropology. Monographs in Economic Anthropology No. 1. Sutti Ortiz, ed. Lanham, MD: University Press of America and the Society for Economic Anthropology. pp. 83-95.

Blanton, Richard
    1983   Factors Underlying the Origin and Evolution of Market Systems. in Economic Anthropology. Monographs in Economic Anthropology No. 1. Sutti Ortiz, ed. Lanham, MD: University Press of America and the Society for Economic Anthropology. pp. 51-66.

Bohannan, Paul and George Dalton
    1965   Markets in Africa: Eight Subsistence Economies in transition. (selections, with revised introduction, from 1962 volume of same title published by Northwestern University Press). Garden City, New York: Doubleday.

Cancian, Frank
    1974   Economic Man and Economic Development. in Rethinking Modernization: Anthropological Perspectives. John Poggie Jr. & Robert Lynch, eds. Westport, CT.: Greenwood Press.

Carrasco, Pedro
    1983   Some Theoretical Considerations About the
            Role of the Market in Ancient Mexico. in
            Economic Anthropology. Monographs in
            Economic Anthropology No. 1. Sutti Ortiz,
            ed. Lanham, MD: University Press of America
            and the Society for Economic Anthropology.
            pp. 67-82.

Cooper, Eugene
    1984   Mode of Production and Anthropology of Work.
            Journal of Anthropological Research, 40:257-
            270.

Douglas, Mary
    1965   The Lele - Resistance to Change. in Markets
            in Africa. P. Bohannan & G. Dalton, eds.,
            Garden City, New York: Doubleday. pp. 183-
            213. (also in 1962 volume of same title
            published by Northwestern University Press).

Gladwin, Christina
    1980   A Theory of Real Life Choice: Applications
            to Agricultural Decision Making.   In
            Agricultural Decision Making, P. Barlett,
            ed. New York: Academic Press.

    1979   Production Functions and Decision Models:
            Complementary Models. American Ethnologist,
            6:653-674.

Herskovits, Melville
    1940   The Economic Life of Primitive Peoples. New
            York: Knopf.

Ortiz, Sutti
    1983   What is Decision Analysis About? The
            Problems of Formal Representations. in
            Economic Anthropology. Monographs in
            Economic Anthropology No. 1. Sutti Ortiz,
            ed. Lanham, MD: University Press of America
            and the Society for Economic Anthropology.
            pp. 249-297.

Plattner, Stuart
    1984   Economic Decision Making of Marketplace
            Merchants: An Ethnographic Model. Human
            Organization, 43:252-264.

    1983   Economic Custom in a Competitive Market-
            place. American Anthropologist, 84:848-858.

1974   Formal Models and Formalist Economic
            Anthropology: The Problem of Maximization.
            <u>Reviews</u> <u>in</u> <u>Anthropology</u>, 1:572-582.

Schneider, Harold
    1974   <u>Economic</u> <u>Man</u>. New York: Free Press.

Skinner, G. William
    1964   Marketing and Social Structure in Rural
            China, Parts I & II. <u>Journal</u> <u>of</u> <u>Asian</u>
            <u>Studies</u>, 24:3-43, 24:195-228.

Smith, Carol
    1976   Markets in Oaxaca: Are They Really Unique?
            <u>Reviews</u> <u>in</u> <u>Anthropology</u>, 3:386-400.

Wolf, Eric
    1982   <u>Europe</u> <u>and</u> <u>the</u> <u>People</u> <u>Without</u> <u>History</u>.
            Berkeley: U. California Press.

NOTES

1. Although I must note the publication in this
   volume of Mary Douglas' (1965) superb analysis of
   the differences in economic productivity between
   the Lele and the Bushong tribes, the paper has
   nothing to do with markets or marketing.

2. This complexity should be viewed as a challenge to
   analysis rather than referred to as an excuse for
   mere description. Cancian 1974 discussed the
   general issues with respect to "economic man";
   Gladwin 1980 showed how to analyze complex
   production decisions with a formal ethnographic
   model; and Plattner 1984 gives an example of an
   analysis of market decisions.

PART ONE

CENTRAL PLACE ANALYSES
OF MARKETPLACE SYSTEMS

PART ONE

CENTRAL PLACE ANALYSIS OF MARKETPLACE SYSTEMS
Stuart Plattner

When people complain that social science
knowledge is not cumulative, and does not advance, but
instead merely follows the dictates of current
intellectual style, I mention the impact of
central- place studies of agrarian marketplace
systems. Introduced into the anthropological
literature by G. W. Skinner in a truly seminal
series of articles in the Journal of Asian
Studies, (1964, 1965) this theory of the structure and
function of marketplace systems revolutionized our
knowledge. Cultural anthropologists at that time
were looking for ways to formalize their theories.
The elegant model presented by Skinner to analyze
the traditional Chinese marketplace system was
impressive in its reliance upon explicit
functional relations of well- specified variables.
His sequence of figures going from a detailed map of a
portion of the Chinese landscape to an abstract
geometric model of the locational pattern of markets in
the area was breathtaking to graduate students.
Skinner's work inspired several students, most notably
Carol Smith and the authors in her influential volumes
on Regional Analysis(1976).

Skinner's contribution to this volume reviews the
analysis he published 20 years ago of the Chinese rural
marketing system, and brings it up to date. He begins
by pointing out the variability of marketing systems
instituted in different macroregions, and discussing
the changes over time in the pre-revolutionary period.
Then Skinner reviews the impact of government policies
upon the marketing system during the Maoist era. The
ideology of the time was rabidly anti-market, and he
shows how the government methodically undermined the
marketing system by attacking its hierarchical links.
Then he traces the reversal in Chinese policy towards
markets since 1977. At present the market system is
growing, new marketplaces are appearing and old ones
increasing their periodicity. Using his original
analysis, Skinner shows how the capitalist development
of the marketing system will eventually destroy its
traditional periodicity, as trade grows to fill the
available time.

In her paper Smith traces the steps she went through

3

to create her analysis of the marketing system of Western highland Guatemala. Her publications on this topic were the first to use central- place theory with data from a field study in a non-Western society. Smith points out that the bi-ethnic nature of Guatemala was a key principle in the function of the market system. On the most basic level, Ladinos (Spanish-speaking, non-Indian Guatemalans, including the elite classes) live in towns and need to buy their household food from marketplaces, but rarely need to sell in them since they control the other merchandising channels in the country. Indians produce most of the goods sold in marketplaces, and buy in them as well. Smith developed a simple characterization of marketplaces using a trichotomous measure composed of the proportions of seller types: long- distance traders, producer-sellers, and local middlemen. The distribution of marketplaces which she got from this measure led her to create her analysis of market subsystems and to distinguish two functional categories of marketplaces, the rural bulking centers and Ladino market towns. This innovative method is simple, flexible, and basic to the understanding of market sytems in such agrarian societies.

Appleby is an economic anthropologist with field experience in several agrarian marketplace systems. In this paper he shows how the general issues dealt with by central-place theory orient the analyst to allow a quick understanding of a marketplace system. He studies the markets in two areas of the Gambia River basin in West Africa: southern Senegal Oriental, and the Upper River Division in Gambia. There is an apparent paradox of marketplace development in these two areas. The Upper River division has more and denser population and a greater production of cash crops than southern Senegal Oriental, yet the latter area has more and older markets than the former. Appleby explains this by examining the history of settlement in each area, finding roughly similar development of population, commercialization and transport. The key difference lies in the nature of the peanut trading channel in the Gambia River area. The companies who bought peanuts also operated retail general stores. Thus the cash earned by selling peanuts was spent in the same store, and rural marketplaces never had the chance to develop. When the colonial firms lost their privileged position in the peanut trade, they closed their branch stores in the interior, opening the way for a system of marketplaces to develop. Appleby notes that his rapid

4

understanding of the market system rests on the "conceptual and methodological tool kit developed for marketplace study by anthropologists that provided the hypotheses and the means for honing in on the answers".

REFERENCES

Skinner, G. W.
  1964,   Marketing and Social Structure in Rural
  1965   China, Part I, Part II, Part III. Journal
          of Asian Studies, 24:3-43, 24:195-228,
          24:363-399.

Smith, Carol (editor)
  1976   Regional Analysis, Volumes 1 & 2, New York:
          Academic Press.

RURAL MARKETING IN CHINA: REVIVAL AND REAPPRAISAL

G. William Skinner, Stanford University

Twenty years have elapsed since the publication of my three-part article "Marketing and Social Structure in Rural China" (Skinner 1964, 1965a, 1965b). On the occasion of this "revisit," I should like to contextualize the phenomenon of Chinese marketing in ways not open to me in 1964 and to bring the story up to date. The paper has five parts. Part I points to certain ways in which premodern Chinese marketing was exceptional in comparative perspective and suggests possible explanations. Parts II and III contextualize premodern rural marketing by examining variation in regional space and historical time, respectively. Part IV summarizes the vicissitudes of rural marketing during the Maoist era, and Part V treats the revival of marketing since 1977 and discusses its significance.

I. CHINESE MARKETING IN PERSPECTIVE

The outpouring of comparative research on rural markets during the past two decades (see Smith 1979-80) has made Chinese marketing appear even more exceptional than when I first analyzed it. In pre-Communist China we see the state playing a distinctly minor role in founding and regulating rural markets, and we find that a strictly economic location theory holds up remarkably well. The functional hierarchy of marketplaces is unusually clearcut in China, as is the integration of periodic marketing with urban commercial institutions. The Chinese case stands out, too, for the overwhelming significance of marketing in shaping other aspects of rural life.

In these and other ways, Chinese marketing is exceptional, and most of the reasons, in my view, stem from China's extraordinary scale and longevity as a unified sociopolitical system. A major argument here is that growth of the Chinese empire to a scale unprecedented elsewhere in the world forced a withdrawal of government from the regulation of local commerce. As late as the eighth century, when China's population was less than 70 million, the Tang state maintained an elaborate apparatus for regulating the commercial activities of the empire. Markets were effectively limited to administrative centers, and the director of each market, a bureaucrat, was charged with

7

responsibility for the quality of money, the accuracy of weights and measures, the prevention of unfair business practices, the registration and surveillance of brokers, and the control of prices (Twitchett 1966). A millennium later China's population was at least five times larger, but for some reason the territorial field administration of the bureaucratic state had hardly grown at all. In fact, the record shows a remarkable stability in the number of county-level units throughout imperial history. As new counties were being founded at the expanding frontiers of the empire, counties in the earlier settled areas were consolidated so that the total never surpassed a "forbidden" threshold around 1,500 (Skinner 1977a: 17-19).

Why? To have maintained bureaucratic field administration at the intensity that obtained in the early eighth century would have meant a field administration in the mid-nineteenth century of over 8,000 subprovincial yamens. My argument is that such growth in the scale of field administration, involving not only a proliferation of yamens but also a massive expansion of the ranked bureaucracy and of subbureaucratic personnel, would have taxed communication facilities to the breaking point and posed problems of coordination and control beyond the capabilities of any premodern agrarian state. Moreover, the enlarged officialdom could only have been supported by raising the extraction rate in the form of extralegal exactions as well as agricultural and business taxes. Higher extraction rates across the board would have served not only to depress peasant living standards but also to reduce the take of local gentry and traders. And problems of controlling the consequent disaffection at the local level would doubtless have been the undoing of any ruling house. On this reading, then, a unified empire could be maintained on into the late imperial era only by systematically reducing the scope of basic-level administrative functions and countenancing a decline in the effectiveness of bureaucratic government within local systems (Skinner 1977a: 20-21). In due course it became the accepted view in Chinese statecraft that "since markets could neither be suppressed nor adequately controlled, regulation had best be abandoned and commerce exploited as a source of revenue" (Twitchett 1968:80). For most of the middle and late imperial period, then, the wraps were off and local marketing evolved with little effective governmental restrictions or regulations. This is the major reason why economic principles of commercial capitalism had

8

such free play in China -- and, in particular, on the one hand, why Christaller's K=3 marketing principle had such clear expression in the cores of China's regional systems and, on the other, his K=7 administrative principle has left barely a trace on the Chinese landscape.

It is worth emphasizing that this retrenchment, forced by the growing scale of empire, involved a radical decline in official involvement not only in marketing and commerce at the local-system level but also in social regulation and administration itself. It was not just commerce that "spilled out of capital cities," but all kinds of central functions and services -- for the simple reason that new capitals were not created "as needed." In fact, one could argue that the level of intensity of "central functions" held more or less steady throughout the imperial era, the really significant change being the steady retrenchment of the bureaucratic government's role in all of those functions -- administrative and social as well as economic. This is the essential historical background to the finding that in late imperial and Republican times low-level marketing systems in rural China were at once parapolitical and social systems, dominated by local gentrymen and traders rather than by bureaucrats (Skinner 1977a: 24-26; 1977c: 336-339).

The scale of the Chinese empire and its unity throughout most of the medieval and late imperial era also help us understand how market towns in China came to be so well integrated into the various macroregional urban systems. The contrast with Europe is instructive. The development of an integrated regional economy and of a single urban system within the basin of the Danube or of the Rhine, say, was hindered throughout most of European history by the subdivision of these physiographic macroregions among the jurisdictions of several, often antagonistic states. But in China, international frontiers, with their potential for obstructing trade and sociopolitical transactions, almost never cut across physiographic regions [1].

II. MARKETS IN REGIONAL SPACE

This contrast raises the question of how rural market towns were positioned within China's spatial structure. In my 1964 article I emphasized the importance of demand density in determining the size of marketing systems and argued that the three functional

9

levels of market towns -- standard, intermediate, and
central -- were but the lower reaches of a single
economic hierarchy that included cities. I soon
realized that there was nowhere to take these findings
short of a full-scale regional analysis. In my 1977
book The City in Late Imperial China, I attempted to
deal systematically with departures from the
unrealistic assumptions of location theory so as to
develop an empirically sound model of Chinese spatial
structure and of settlement patterns (Skinner 1977c:
276-288). Naturally, I cannot repeat that analysis
here, but I do wish to point up its relevance for
variation in rural marketing.

    I have identified, as of the twentieth century, ten
macroregional economies in agrarian China [2]. The key
fact is that, with one exception, each of these
economic systems took shape in and was wholly contained
within a physiographic macroregion that can be defined
in terms of drainage basins. Each was characterized by
the concentration in a central area of resources of all
kinds -- above all, in an agrarian society, arable
land, but also, of course, population and capital
investments -- and by the thinning out of resources
toward the periphery. An indication of where regional
resources were concentrated is given on Map 0, where
each macroregion's area of highest population density
is shaded.

    It will be noted that, with the exception of Yungui,
these regional "cores" are river-valley lowlands. In a
traditional agrarian society it is virtually axiomatic
that population density is a close function of
agricultural productivity per unit of area, and it
follows that a higher proportion of land was arable in
the cores of regions than in the peripheries and that
arable land in the former was generally the more
fertile. Ecological processes, such as the transfer of
fertility through erosion and the use of fertilizer,
boosted agricultural productivity in the lowland cores.
The level of capital investment in drainage,
reclamation, irrigation, and flood control was also far
higher per unit of arable land in cores than in
peripheries.

    In addition, regional cores had major transport
advantages vis-à-vis peripheral areas. Because of the
low unit cost of water as against land transport,
navigable waterways dominated traffic flows in all
regions except Yungui and the Northwest; and even where
rivers were unnavigable their valleys typically

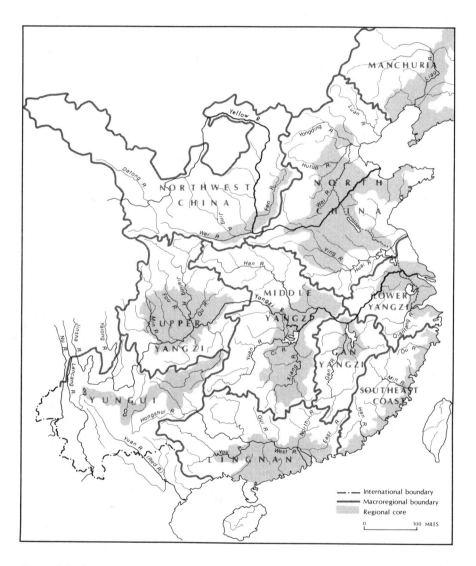

Map 0. Macroregional Systems of Agrarian China, Showing
Major Rivers and Regional Cores (shaded).

11

afforded the most efficient overland routes. Thus the transport network of each region climaxed in the lowland core, where most of the transport nodes were situated. River systems aside, the less rugged terrain of the core areas made it relatively inexpensive to build roads and canals. Moreover, investment in transport infrastructure was relatively high in regional cores precisely because their dense population meant low average cost per capita.

Finally, because regional cores were more urbanized and boasted a denser transport net, the local economies of core areas were consistently more commercialized than those of peripheral areas, both in the sense that more commercial crops and handicrafts were produced for the market and in the sense that households were more dependent on the market for consumer goods.

In my book (Skinner 1977b: 217ff.) I argue that each macroregional economy developed a distinct semi-autarkic urban system -- a hierarchy of central places whose base was the standard market town and whose apex was the central metropolis of the entire macroregional system. Let us see how it worked out in the case of a single macroregion [3].

Map 1 presents an overview of the upper levels of the economic system within the Upper Yangzi macroregion. The regional core, shown shaded, included the major navigable stretches of the Upper Yangzi river system and, as one might expect, coincided rather closely with the Red Basin. The population density of the core as a whole was over six times the mean for the inclusive periphery. Note that most of the region's high-ranking economic centers were situated in the core: both metropolises, five of the six regional cities, and 16 of the 21 greater cities. The dotted line bisecting the macroregion separates the economic sphere of Chengdu (Chengtu) from that of Chongqing (Chungking) and defines the limits of the macroregion's two metropolitan trading areas.

Map 1 also shows the approximate boundaries of the Upper Yangzi's eight regional-city trading systems. Three points are worthy of notice here. First, around the periphery of the region, the limits of trading systems almost without exception followed the mountain ridges separating basins of tributary river systems. Second, whereas in peripheral areas local and greater cities were oriented to single higher-level centers, in the more central areas a number of cities were oriented

12

to two or more regional-city trading systems; no fewer
than four greater cities and 21 local cities are shown
at the boundaries of trading systems, reflecting their
economic dependence on two or more of the eight nodes
of regional-city trading systems.   Third, with the
exception of the system centered on Guangyuan (Kuang-
yuan) which lay entirely in the regional periphery,
each of the regional-city trading systems included core
as well as peripheral areas.   The general structure,
then, was one in which regional-city trading systems
tended to be discrete around the periphery and
interdigitated within the core.

It is apparent that economic centers were sited on
navigable waterways whenever possible, a preference
that was general throughout China.   In the Upper
Yangzi, 27 of the 29 greater- and higher-level cities
were served for at least part of the year by river
junks. Major roads, not mapped here, had the effect of
compensating for deficiencies of the river system in
linking those cities.

Map 2 shows greater-city trading systems, the next
level below the regional-city trading systems shown in
Map 1.   In general, the pattern noted in Map 1 is
recapitulated for the hinterlands of greater cities.
System boundaries in the periphery were relatively
impermeable, following mountain ridges that limited
intercourse between cities in the various drainage
basins, whereas those in the core passed through
numerous local cities that were members of two or more
greater-city trading systems.

Two of the most important ways in which transport
systematically distorts the regularity of the central-
place hierarchy were apparent in the Upper Yangzi, as
in most other regions of late imperial China.   First
major transport routes of all types foster linearity by
attracting (as it were) central places that would
otherwise be sited on a triangular lattice.   This
effect is evident in the siting of two local cities
(rather than one) between higher-level cities along
major rivers. A second distorting effect, wholly
expectable in a regional system whose basic transport
network is a river system, is the tendency for cities
to be situated within their hinterlands off-center in
the downstream direction.

Map 3, which continues the progression down the
hierarchy of nested economic systems, is necessarily
limited to a small portion of the region, namely the

13

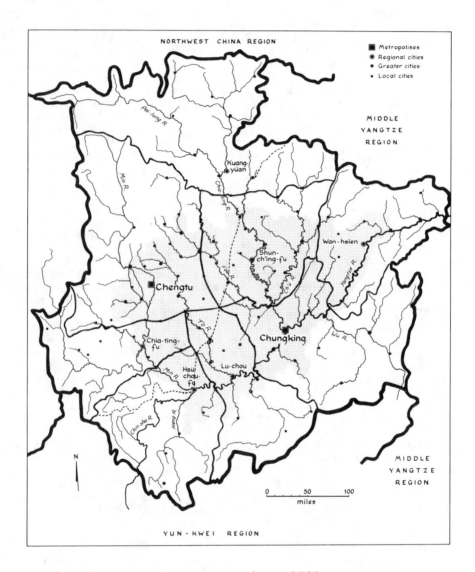

Map 1.   The Upper Yangtze Region, 1893.

14

Map 2.   The Upper Yangtze Region, 1893.

15

area in the vicinity of Chengdu enclosed by the dotted
rectangle on Map 2.   The upper-left frame of Map 3,
like Map 2, shows greater-city trading systems, thereby
conveying a feel for the sharp increase in scale.   Each
of the other three frames of Map 3 takes us a step
lower in the economic hierarchy.   The upper-right frame
shows local-city trading systems and central places
down to the central market town; the lower-left frame
shows central marketing systems and central places down
to the intermediate market town; and the lower-right
panel shows intermediate marketing systems and central
places down to the standard market town.   In each case,
system boundaries at the next higher level are
indicated by wide shaded lines, thereby dramatizing the
manner in which economic centers and hinterlands at
each level were related spatially to those at adjacent
levels in the hierarchy.   In conjunction, they
illustrate a general feature of the hierarchy of local
economic systems, namely that whereas higher-level
systems completely enveloped only one system at the
next lower level (the one with the same node), they
enveloped several systems at the level below that.   We
also see at each level the interstitial placement of
orders that is characteristic of a regular central-
place hierarchy: note in particular that the great
majority of intermediate market towns fell at the
borders of central marketing systems, i.e., were
oriented economically to two or more central market
towns, and that the great majority of standard market
towns were similarly situated with respect to
intermediate marketing systems.

Map 4 completes the progression down the hierarchy
of local economic systems.   It is limited to a still
smaller portion of the landscape, namely that enclosed
by the dotted rectangle shown in the lower-right frame
of Map 3.   To ensure visual continuity, the left frame
of Map 4 repeats at the larger scale what is shown
within the dotted rectangle of Map 3.   The right frame
of Map 4 makes clear that nodes of standard marketing
sytems were not limited to standard market towns, but
also included intermediate market towns, central market
towns, and local cities.   It shows that standard market
towns were normally situated interstitially between
higher-level towns and that standard marketing systems
were invariably split between intermediate marketing
systems.   It was these spatial features, all predicted
by central-place theory, which, through replication at
successively higher levels, integrated local economic
systems into the complex interlocking network of
higher-order trading systems.

16

Let me now suggest how marketing systems varied through the core-periphery structure of these macroregional economies. Four factors are of primary importance in accounting for variation in the size of marketing areas: population density, commercialization, transport efficiency, and ruggedness of terrain [4]. The first two are conjoined in the concept of demand density: purchasing power per unit of land. Demand density rises with an increase in the density of households on the land and/or an increase in the degree of household participation in the marketing process. It should be clear that marketing areas are inversely related to demand density: a high density of demand means small marketing areas, and a low density means large marketing areas.

This contingency alone accounts for much of the gross variation within regional systems. It follows from our operational definitions that demand density was relatively high in the regional cores and quite low in regional peripheries. Insofar as ruggedness of terrain has an independent effect, it would intensify that of demand density, for areas of rugged terrain are generally inaccessible and little commercialized. The difference in this regard was, in fact, quite marked in pre-Communist China. I have developed empirically based estimates for each macroregion separately, and in all cases the average size of standard marketing systems in the periphery was at least twice that in the core, even though the average population was considerably larger in the core systems. For agrarian China as a whole in 1893, the mean standard marketing system in regional peripheries covered approximately 120 sq. kilometers and included some 1,800 households. The corresponding figures for regional cores were 45 sq. kilometers and 2,200 households.

A standard marketing system of 120 sq. kilometers implies that the most disadvantaged villager must travel slightly less than 7 kilometers to market, a round trip that is easily managed in a day. Since these are average figures for regional peripheries, it should be clear that in the mountainous far peripheries of China's internal macroregions, standard marketing systems were far larger in area. As demand density drops off and the terrain becomes increasingly rugged, a point is reached where the standard market is no longer viable. A situation near that threshold was described by Fei Xiaotong and Zhang Zhiyi for Yicun, a village in the periphery of the Yungui macroregion (Fei and Chang 1945: 170-172). Its standard market town was

17

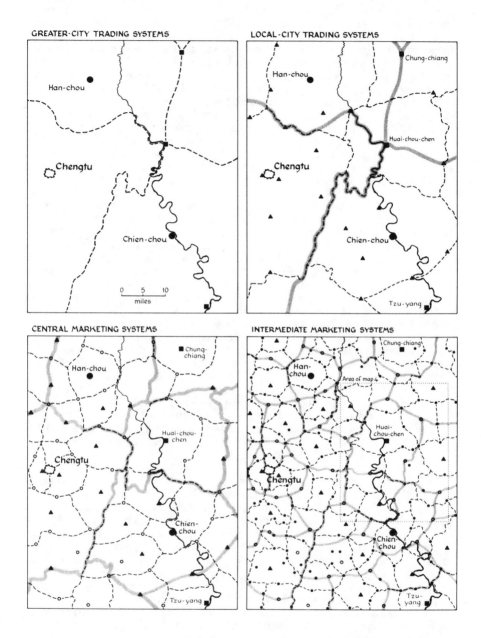

Map 3.   A Small Portion of the Upper Yangtze Region, 1893.

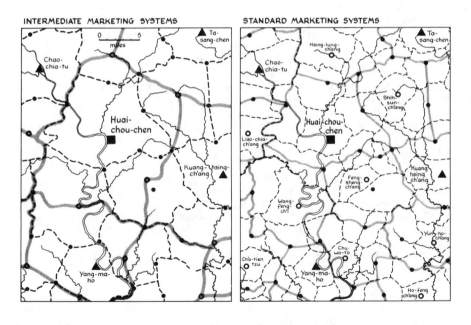

INTERMEDIATE MARKETING SYSTEMS

STANDARD MARKETING SYSTEMS

Map 4. A Still Smaller Portion of the Upper Yangtze
Region, 1893.

16 kilometers distant, implying a standard marketing area of at least 665 sq. kilometers. In this situation, few villagers went to market regularly, and when the round trip was made in only one day their stay at the market was necessarily short; consequently, those who brought their own products for sale were unable to wait for individual buyers and so had to sell at wholesale. A trip to Yicun's intermediate market, some 48 kilometers distant, required an overnight stop. In still less favorable environments, periodic marketing gave way to peddling: the few essential exogenous needs of peasant households were obtained from peddlers, whose circuits took them to isolated hamlets only a few times a year.

In regional cores we again see considerable variation around the mean size of marketing areas. However, the patterns of variation are rather more complex, and in explaining them we must introduce transport efficiency, the last of the four determinants of marketing-area size. I have already called attention to the critical nexus, namely, that transport efficiency has an effect on the size of economic hinterlands that countervails that of demand density. High demand density favors small hinterlands, whereas efficient transport -- typically found only in regional cores, where demand density is high -- favors large hinterlands. Prior to mechanization, the crucial distinction was that between overland and waterborne transport, the latter being not only markedly cheaper per ton/kilometer but usually faster as well. Focusing on standard marketing systems, then, a crucial question becomes the relative importance of boat traffic. In regional peripheries boat traffic was everywhere negligible so that it was possible to explain variation without specific reference to the transport variable. In regional cores, however, we see an extremely wide range in transport efficiency. One would expect to find the smallest marketing areas on landscapes where demand density was high but peasants did little marketing by boat. The extreme case in this regard was probably the central area of the Chengdu Plain in the Upper Yangzi's inner core, where standard marketing systems occupied less than 15 sq. kilometers on the average.

When we look at the one Chinese macroregion in which boat transport was widespread and efficient, namely the Lower Yangzi, one sees a clearcut curvilinear pattern: marketing areas decreased in size as one moved from the far to the near periphery and on to the outer core, but at a decreasing rate; as one approached the inner core, decline gave way to no change and eventually to an increase. The effect of the marked increase in transport efficiency was that marketing areas were larger in the inner than in the outer core. In the Upper Yangzi and Northwest China, where little peasant marketing was done by boat, the modest increases in transport efficiency encountered as one moved through regional space toward the inner core had the effect of decelerating but never stopping the decline. In other regions, the curvilinear pattern was to some degree apparent in that pockets of the inner core where peasant marketing involved considerable boat traffic had larger marketing areas than did surrounding portions of the core.

Only in the Lower Yangzi, however, was the curvilinear pattern pronounced and the area of "enlarged" marketing systems extensive. Moreover, marketing data for the Lower Yangzi core reveal an anomaly not found elsewhere: In one area at the heart of Kiangnan's "golden triangle," basic-level marketing sytems were approximately three times larger than predicted by the values of the four determinants of marketing-area size. It was as if, in moving through regional space toward the center, one passed a threshold in the ever increasing proportion of waterborne marketing, at which point there occurred a quantum jump in the size of basic-level marketing areas. Indeed, on my analysis this anomalous inner-core area lacked standard markets altogether, the standard marketing system being obviated by institutional arrangements made possible only by an exceptionally fine-grained net of navigable waterways.

The threshold is just this: as virtually all economic actors become directly accessible to one another by relatively inexpensive water transport, it pays for economic specialists to perform all aspects of peasant marketing. Peasants did not themselves travel to market to sell their products or buy their daily consumption needs; these tasks were performed for them by itinerant retailers and commission agents. How the system worked in one intermediate marketing system, that of Zhenzezhen, has been carefully described by Fei Xiaotong (1939: chap. 14); his analysis pertains to the 1930s, but there is no reason to believe that much had changed since late imperial times: the water transport tying this system together was still unmechanized, and evidence is presented that the agent boat, kingpin of the system, was a hoary institution. Where peasants did

21

not themselves go to market, where peasant marketing was conducted by economic specialists, the standard market -- the peasants' market par excellence -- was obviated. Thus in the area under discussion, intermediate marketing systems formed the base of the economic hierarchy. Since the K=3 mode of stacking prevailed in this core area, such systems were approximately three times the size standard marketing systems would have been.

Thus, as it turns out, standard markets were not quite "standard" everywhere. They were phased out at the two ecological extremes of regional systems. In the far peripheries of interior macroregions, demand density was so low that the standard market gave way to peddling. In the inner core of the macroregion most favored by navigable waterways, the standard market was obviated, its economic functions being performed by waterborne agents who tied peasant households to firms in intermediate and higher-level market towns.

III. MARKETS AND HISTORICAL CHANGE

With respect to variation through time, the critical point to make about premodern eras is that temporal structure is specific to particular regional systems. That is, we are dealing here with spatial-cum-temporal systems, and historical patterns emerge with any clarity only when the analysis is limited to and specified for the pertinent system. For instance, the Upper Yangzi macroregional economy experienced three macrocycles of economic development and decline during medieval and late imperial times. The first, which peaked out in the Southern Song, was brought to an end by the protracted Mongol conquest and associated epidemics in the mid-thirteenth century. Repopulation of the region was slow and development was weak during the second cycle, which was cut short in the mid-seventeenth century by warfare and massacres associated with the struggle for dynastic succession during the Ming-Qing transition. The third cycle of development got under way only in the 1680s after the region was pacified by Qing troops. This time, repopulation from neighboring regions, actively promoted by the court, was rapid, and economic development proceeded at a brisk rate throughout the eighteenth and early nineteenth century. In the case of each cycle, the founding of new markets and the development of an integrated marketing system paced the developmental upswing. The growth of the marketing system during the

22

third cycle can be shown to have accorded quite closely with the models of market intensification set out in Skinner 1965a.

If exogenous catastrophes were prominent in shaping the developmental cycles of the Upper Yangzi, in other regions the contours of development were primarily determined by the court's changing policies toward foreign trade, or by the relocation of the imperial capital, and/or by consequences stemming from the dialectical sequences of dynastic rule. It is for these reasons, among others, that the various regional cycles of development were only occasionally synchronized. One can also identify cyclical episodes that are shorter and less dramatic than the centuries-long pulsations of the macroregional economies -- epicycles, if you will, along the trajectory of the long waves. And of particular relevance here, the historical rhythm of alternating good and bad times, of economic growth and decline, of social order and social breakdown were equally characteristic of lower-order regional economies -- of regional-city trading systems within macroregions, and of the greater-city trading systems at the next lower level.

One example must suffice. The Zhangquan region, a subsystem of the Southeast Coast macroregional economy, experienced a century-long upswing of economic development beginning in 1522, when Portuguese traders began holding markets on offshore islands near the region's major port. After the Portuguese discovery of Japan in 1542, a triangular trade developed. The founding of Manila by the Spaniards in 1571 and the subsequent initiation of shipments of Mexican silver led to an expanded trade by Zhangquan merchants with the Philippines. Without attempting to provide a rounded picture of the impact of trade expansion in the Zhangquan region, let me simply note that new rural markets were established throughout the regional economy. Their number, in a major portion of the region for which we have documentation, increased from 11 near the end of the fifteenth century to 65 in 1628, near the upper turning point of the developmental cycle in question (Rawski 1972: 88-94). In the subsequent depression many of these rural markets were closed, as agriculture saw a shift from cash-cropping to subsistence farming.

Students of Chinese economic history are only now coming to recognize that such topics as the emergence of capitalism, changes in land tenure, and the

23

commercialization of agriculture are best studied in the framework of specific cyclical episodes within particular regional systems rather than in a scheme of progressive, sequential, absolutely dated stages applied to China as a whole (cf. Skinner 1985). The facts of rural marketing development have been instrumental in stimulating this reorientation.

IV. MARKETS DURING THE MAOIST ERA

Rural markets and peasant marketing did not fare well during the Maoist era, which extended from well before the consolidation of Communist power in China to the triumphal return of Deng Xiaoping as the central political figure in 1977. Maoist radicals, who in broad perspective may be said to have held the political initiative throughout the era, can be fairly characterized as having an anti-market mentality. While this set of attitudes derives in part from Marxism, it is also rooted in the ideological preconceptions of late-imperial Confucian bureaucrats. The Maoist elite in the People's Republic and the traditional bureaucratic elite of the late empire were equally unhappy with market exchange, and both showed a preference for redistribution.

Much of the opposition to the market on the part of both elites stemmed, it seems to me, from the fact that the market mechanism is disruptive of community and tends to diminish collectivity orientation. Price-setting markets mean haggling, and haggling means contention; furthermore, markets disrupt solidarity by introducing competition and envy through stimulating the mobility aspirations of all and fulfilling them for only some. The market in effect invites each participant to maximize the economic interests of his household, which focuses collectivity orientation at the lowest level. Moreover, by their very nature, markets flout self-sufficiency, an ideal for inclusive collectivities espoused by Maoists no less than Confucian bureaucrats. Finally, the market is seen as tempting members of the collectivity into deviance: the marketplace attracts ne'er-do-wells and breeds shysters and bullies. The traditional vision of Datong, the Great Togetherness of harmony and solidarity -- the strain toward pure undifferentiated community and toward selfless service to the collectivity -- this vision, resonating unmistakably within the Maoist world view, was ill served by market exchange.

24

To these considerations we must add the inequalities, injustices and antisocial consequences of an uncontrolled free market -- features viewed somewhat differently but no less disparagingly by the two elites. As Samuelson notes in his classic economics text (1964:621), a perfect market "does not mean that the people who are deemed by various religious or ethical observers to be most worthy, most deserving, or most needy will necessarily get their ethically best share of goods and services." There is no way by which the market mechanism can ensure that widows and cripples will not starve or that temples will be restored, or even that all households of the community will be supplied with coffins for their dead. This way of putting it points up one reason why redistribution commended itself to both elites: Redistribution can be a means to ideological, ethical, collective, normative ends.

As it happened, the ideological aversion to markets that characterized the premodern bureaucratic elite had little scope for practical expression and almost negligible impact on marketing systems. For one reason, as we have seen, problems of bureaucratic control constrained the court to maintain a small bureaucracy and a shallow field administration that penetrated society no deeper than the county; it simply lacked the manpower and organization to attempt control of events in subcounty local systems. No doubt the primitive communications and unmechanized transport of the day would have rendered such an attempt logistically impossible in any case. Moreover, as with other agrarian civilizations, the state was preoccupied most of the time with revenue, defense, and internal security -- that is, with economic and order goals to the neglect of ideological goals. Finally, the anti-market mentality of the bureaucratic elite was not shared by the populace at large or even by the local elite who dominated the affairs of villages, marketing communities, and other local systems. Community prosperity was, understandably enough, a far more salient goal for the local populace than for the court.

The situation of the Maoist elite was, by the mid-1950s, very different from that of its imperial predecessors. The bureaucracy had been increased to the point where state cadres, who numbered in the tens of millions, penetrated virtually every basic-level marketing system. Modern communications and transport meant that central coordination and control of localities were no longer infeasible. With societal

25

transformation high on the regime's agenda, ideological goals were stressed as never before, and local resistance to them was muted by the cooptation of local leaders into the lower ranks of bureaucratically organized cadremen.

Thus, the Maoists were in fact able, at least in the short run, to implement a program that diverted rural trade to supply and marketing cooperatives and state trading companies, reduced the number of markets, and closely regulated marketing activity. However, as we understand well enough in retrospect, while the Maoists generally dominated the political scene so long as Mao himself lived, their policies were contested throughout the era within the leadership councils of the Communist Party itself. Perhaps the most concrete historical expression of this political struggle was the persistent phenomenon of policy cycling.

My colleague Edwin A. Winckler and I have identified and analyzed eleven policy cycles during the years 1949-77 [5]. That the political initiative generally lay with the Maoists during that era is evident from the fact that each cycle was set off by a Maoist radicalization of policy -- for instance, the radicalizations of 1958 and 1966 that inaugurated the Great Leap Forward and the Cultural Revolution, respectively. In each cycle the initial radical phase led, in dialectical fashion, to a crisis phase, followed in turn by a liberal phase, which was brought to an end by a new radicalization. To oversimplify, one may say that the Maoists allowed liberal policies to come to the fore only when necessary to consolidate socialist advances, to contain disaffection of the masses, and to avoid serious threats to the political system they dominated.

It goes without saying that progress away from capitalist institutions and practices toward more socialist arrangements occurred during the eleven radical phases of the era. The collectivization of agriculture was completed during the successive radical phases of the 1950s. With the three-tiered structure of team, brigade and commune in place, policy cycling thereafter focused on the level of accounting, private plots, and private sideline production. During the liberal phases of all cycles from 1960 to 1977, the level of accounting was firmly lodged in the team (which is to say that collective agricultural production was controlled and organized by the smallest of the collectivized units), the use of private plots

26

was guaranteed to all agricultural households, and private sideline production was tolerated if not encouraged. The radical phases of the same cycles, by contrast, inevitably produced rhetoric concerning the socialist virtue of raising the accounting level and the capitalist dangers of private plots and uncollectivized sidelines. And wherever and whenever accounting levels were raised, private plots reduced or reclaimed, and sidelines recollectivized, these developments occurred during radical phases.

Turning now to markets per se, it should be stated explicitly that at no time from 1954 to the end of the Maoist era were China's rural markets ever unregulated or their trade ever genuinely free (cf. Bucknall 1979). It would have been politically untenable to suggest that rural markets were something other than an expedient of "the present stage," and liberals, too, found it necessary to deplore and contain speculation and profiteering. Liberal support for market controls, one may infer from liberal-phase editorials, rests on the realization that the very real advantages of relatively free trade would be jeopardized by capitalist excesses. Thus, even during the most relaxed of the liberal phases, the commodities that might be traded were restricted, prices were controlled, peddlers and brokers were licensed and their movements monitored, and the "discipline of the market" was maintained by market-control committees or supply and marketing cooperatives.

What was distinctive about market controls during the radical phases, apart from their greater severity, is that they had the effect of disrupting the hierarchy of marketing systems. The standard market of pre-Communist times, in addition to serving the horizontal exchange among peasant households, was the conduit for peasant products moving up the marketing hierarchy and the retail outlet for exogenous goods that had moved down the hierarchy from higher-order central places. This hierarchical marketing system, with standard markets at its base, was manifested as the inter-level flow of goods and services, money and credit, economic intelligence, and persons in their various economic roles. But it was precisely the flows connecting levels which, in the Maoist scheme, should be monopolized by supply and marketing cooperatives and state companies. In their approach to rural marketing, then, ultraleftist Maoists were prepared to tolerate only its horizontal-exchange function. Vertical exchange through the structure of standard,

27

intermediate, and central market towns was to be disrupted and impeded so as to facilitate its cooptation by official channels.

It is in this light that one must interpret radical-phase prohibitions against peddlars operating beyond the confines of a single county and against peasants or teams attending markets other than their local standard market. Another common restriction was to allow peasants to market only what they could transport under their own power (carrying poles, wheelbarrows, bicycles). The use of trucks and tractors for transport by teams was denounced as a mechanism for reviving capitalism. Peddlers and brokers who came from any distance were taxed more heavily than those from nearby localities, and in general the transport of commodities between distant marketplaces was forbidden (Weiss 1978: 658; Chan and Unger 1982:459; Bucknall 1979: 71; Sun Deshan 1981; He Jingpei 1981).

The economic articulation between market towns and cities was seriously disrupted by radical policies that 1) prohibited peasants from marketing their produce within cities proper, 2) limited peasant attendance at periurban rural markets to those households situated within the boundaries of the municipality or the metropolitan county in question, and 3) closed the traditional markets at city gates. In general, Maoist planners attempted to contain or constrain the interlocked network of natural marketing systems within the bounds of discrete administrative units and to direct commodity flows in conformity with the administrative hierarchy (Skinner 1965c: 374-75). I have emphasized elsewhere (Skinner 1964: 31; Skinner 1977c: 340-342) the distinction between administration and marketing in mode of articulation: Whereas administrative units are discrete throughout the hierarchy, each lower-level unit belonging to only one unit at each ascending level, marketing systems are indiscrete at all levels except that of the standard market. Thus, it is generally uneconomic if not infeasible to redesign marketing systems along administrative lines. Nonetheless, radical-phase policies typically attempted to do so, with costly consequences that were revealed only in subsequent liberal-phase reforms designed to restore a modicum of economic efficiency in commodity flows.

Perhaps the most telling of radical practices in this regard was the enforced synchronization of market schedules. A brief recapitulation of the pre-Communist

28

situation in this regard will highlight the significance of such an interventionist policy. As demonstrated in Skinner 1964, the periodic schedules of standard markets were typically set so as to minimize conflict with the schedules of the higher-level markets to which they are oriented. Thus, to illustrate with an example in an area where five-day marketing weeks were customary, if a standard market were oriented to two intermediate markets meeting on 1-6 and 4-9 schedules, respectively, one of the possible nonconflicting schedules (say 2-7 or 3-8) would have been selected for its market days. I should perhaps emphasize here, since I did not do so in 1964, that such coordinated scheduling also characterized most central marketing systems and indeed underlay the efficiency of hierarchical commodity flows within them. A well analyzed case in point (Shiba 1977: 428-30) is the western sector of the Ningbo Plain (Zhejiang province), in the 1870s, three central market towns coordinated the collection and distribution of commercial goods. One, Maimianchiao, dominated the direct canal route to Ningbo's west gate. Another, Shiqi, held the corresponding position vis-à-vis the city's south gate. The third, Huanggonglin, lay equidistant from the other two on canals linking it with both. All other market towns between the city and the western hills held standard or intermediate markets commercially oriented to one or more of these three central markets. The notable fact is that every one of the lower-level markets within each of these three central marketing systems maintained a schedule that dovetailed with that of the central market in question. Since, as it happened, the schedules of all three central market towns included the 3d of each xun, not a single lower-level market on the western plains was held on that date. Economic specialists of all kinds benefited from this intrasystemic synchronization, including purchasing agents, itinerant traders, shopkeepers ordering stock from wholesalers, and such marketplace professionals as brokers, measurers and weighers, and even revenue agents.

Now, from 1959 on, radical officials not infrequently required all the markets within a county to adhere to the same uniform schedule (e.g., RMRB, 19 Sept. 1979: 3; Chan and Unger 1982: 457; Ni and You 1984), which had the effect of crippling the systems of markets centered on intermediate and central market towns. I have located no central directives urging this practice upon local cadres, and the synchronization policy was given virtually no media

29

notice at the time, but its overall consistency with other anti-market elements of the radical policy bundle is apparent. More often than not, when officials moved to synchronize all peasant marketing within a county, they took the occasion to reduce the frequency of market schedules as well. The most usual frequencies in pre-Communist days were two-per-xun (that is two market days per ten-day segment of the lunar month), or three-per-xun, and the least frequent of the usual schedules was one-per-xun. In some instances, radical officials decreed one-per-xun schedules throughout a county where two- or three-per-xun had been customary, and in a number of reported cases the mandated schedule was one-per-fortnight, an infrequent market periodicity that was seldom encountered in pre-Communist China. In conjunction with other radical-phase policies, this practice served to channel peasant products increasingly to official purchasing depots. It also served to force greater self-sufficiency on local units, a perennial Maoist objective, but all too often at the cost of reduced living standards. In particular, perishable foodstuffs were difficult to obtain on a regular basis when markets convened only every ten or fifteen days.

In a sense, closing down a rural market altogether is simply the ultimate reduction in periodicity. And indeed, one gets the impression that under the pressure of anti-market policy signals from the center, local cadres would close markets if they judged official channels to be adequate, but otherwise would merely reduce schedule frequencies. Many localities experienced both market closures and frequency reductions in the course of recurrent radicalizations. An instructive case in point is Changli county (Hebei province), in the northeastern sector of North China's inner periphery. In 1933 the county boasted 31 markets including Changtuo, a central market (and apparently the only one in the county). Changtuo's market met daily, and, at the other extreme, two of the most remote standard markets followed an infrequent one-per-xun schedule (i.e., had ten-day marketing weeks); all other markets in the county followed two-per-xun schedules (Tao Ningqi 1933). After closure during the Great Leap, only 23 of the 31 original markets were reopened prior to the initial radicalization of the Cultural Revolution, and by 1976 the number had been further reduced to ten. Moreover as of the latter date, all markets had been synchronized on a fortnightly schedule (RMRB, 19 Sept. 1979: 3). In sum, whereas in 1933 the county's markets were convening

30

over 200 times each month, by 1976 the number of market meetings had been reduced to 20 per month.

Unfortunately, particular examples of this kind are too few to help in estimating the number of market closures at the national level, much less the average frequencies of their schedules. As for the number of markets, we have apparently reliable figures to go on for only two points in time. The total number of rural markets China-wide is cited in official sources as 37,000 just prior to the Cultural Revolution in 1965 and as 33,300 in 1978 [6]. Available evidence (cf. Skinner n.d.) suggests that most of the implied 3,700 market closures occurred during 1969-70 (i.e., the radical phase of the ninth cycle in Winckler's and my analysis).

For an overview of the Maoist era, we must put these post-Leap data together with what is known about rural markets in the earlier periods. In Republican times and on into the early 1950s, two distinct processes affected the number of rural markets. On the one hand, as population grew and commercialization increased, the rise of demand density triggered the establishment of new standard markets in localities where they had never before existed, for the most part in the peripheries of economic macroregions. On the other hand, as transport modernization proceeded in the densely populated, relatively urbanized cores of those macroregions, standard markets were obviated and closed as their clientele were drawn to newly accessible higher-order markets. On my analysis, the decrement arising from the second process was small by comparison with the increment arising from the first, at least to 1937, when the number of rural markets throughout China may be estimated at 45,000. During the Sino-Japanese war, Japanese authorities in many of the counties they occupied reduced the number of markets for security reasons. While most of the closed markets would have been restored within a few years of the Japanese withdrawal, by the 1950s the modernization of transport had progressed to the point, I would judge, where the demise of standard markets in core areas came to balance and then countervail their proliferation in the periphery. On the eve of the Great Leap in 1958, the number of rural markets may be estimated as 42,000 (plus or minus 2,000).

The disastrously premature closing of rural markets in 1958 and the painful process of restoration during subsequent liberalphases was described in detail in

31

Skinner 1965c. We know that even higher-order markets were in some cases not revived until 1960 or 1961, and thousands of standard markets were never reopened before the radicalization of the Cultural Revolution. Thereafter the prevailing radical tone of central policy meant that few new markets were permitted to open in response to rising demand density, even during the liberal phases of the policy cycle.

The big picture then, is one of marked decline during the Maoist era in the capacity of periodic markets to serve the needs of the rural population. As of 1953 there were approximately 45,000 rural markets serving a rural population of roughly 507 million. By 1965 the number of markets was down to 37,000, while the rural population had grown to 583 million. By 1978 the number of markets had declined further to 33,300, even as the rural population had ballooned to 775 million [7]. Thus, each rural market had to service, on average, a population that was more than twice as large in 1978 as in 1953. We have seen, moreover, that many of the 1978 markets had been forced to follow reduced schedules, and when the decline in schedule frequency is also taken into account the number of markets per capita per unit of time in 1978 could have amounted to no more than a third of what it had been in the early 1950s.

The replacement of periodic marketing in rural China by an efficient modern distributional infrastructure is a perfectly reasonable policy objective. The fundamental error of the radical program for rural commodity distribution during the Maoist era was the persistent attempt to restrict, impair or eliminate rural periodic markets before a viable modern infrastructure was in place.

V.   THE POST-MAO REVIVAL OF MARKETS

In 1977 the political initiative in China passed to liberal pragmatists, led by Deng Xiaoping, and such radicalizations as can be identified in the years since, three in all, appear as carefully controlled and contained campaigns designed to neutralize critics from the right while disarming Maoists on the left [8]. In any case, for present purposes the years since 1977 may be viewed as a steady and methodical deradicalization.

A consistent feature of radical policies in the Maoist era had been the general restriction on individual and household autonomy. There remained little scope for direct action by the household to increase its income and to secure its economic well-being and, in fact, radical policies specifically limited such action. By contrast, the policy bundle that evolved during the liberal phases of the Maoist era had expanded the scope for direct action by households to maximize income and economic security and, moreover, explicitly permitted such action. But it was only after 1977 that the liberal program could be carried to its logical conclusions. Dengist reforms have, within a period of eight years, secured unprecedented economic autonomy for persons and households throughout rural China and succeeded in creating an institutional framework and incentive structure that favor entrepreneurial initiative and agricultural productivity. The revival of rural marketing is a critical element of these reforms.

To appreciate the significance of that revival, however, we must first review the dramatic changes in agriculture since 1977 [9]. The very organization of agricultural production has been transformed through a gradual but thoroughgoing decollectivization. Communes have been converted (and sometimes subdivided) into xiang, which are strictly administrative townships, and brigades no longer play a significant role in agricultural production. The collectively held land is managed by teams, many of which have been reduced in size through subdivision in recent years. Even so, few teams cultivate their landholdings as a single productive unit; rather parcels of land are contracted (leased) out to work groups, households in partnership, or individual households within the team. Initially such contracts were for one year or less, but the trend has been toward longer-term contracts that would increase incentives for investment.

Decollectivization under the responsibility system has been accompanied by an increase in the size of private plots. The portion of cultivated area allocated for private plots, set at 7 percent in 1978, was raised to 15 percent in 1981. In the most common form of the responsibility system, there is no practical difference between the private plot and the leased collective land managed by the household. Many high-income teams, especially those situated in the inner core of macroregional economies, have maintained collective production at the level of the team or work group, but throughout regional peripheries, and among lower-income teams generally, agricultural production has largely devolved to the household level. In most

33

of rural China, then, family farms have been reborn as tenants of the landholding team.

This fundamental reorganization of agricultural production has been accompanied by a relaxation of controls over what may be grown and marketed, by price changes favorable to farmers, and by policies encouraging specialization. Maoist policies that aimed to maximize local self-sufficiency in grain were repudiated early on, and by 1980 restrictions on the use of private plots were largely removed. The commercialization of agriculture has been encouraged not only by higher purchase prices for agricultural products, but also by the expanded scope for over-quota sales and increased grain sales by the state to rural areas. Specialization has been further facilitated by state commitments of external grain supplies for specialized producers of such crops as sugarcane and cotton.

Turning now to marketing per se, the pro-market leanings of Deng's regime were first heralded in January 1978, when People's Daily carefully explained just why rural markets should not be considered capitalistic (RMRB, 31 Jan. 1978). Later that year, in December, the Third Plenum of the Eleventh Party Congress set the stage for the liberal rural reform to follow; its communique (RMRB, 23 Dec. 1978) declared:

> The private plots of commune members, the family sideline occupations, and the trade in rural collective markets are necessary supplements to the socialist economy. Nobody is allowed to interfere with them arbitrarily.

While the directives emanating from the Third Plenum fully legitimized rural markets, they retained virtually all of the trade controls that had characterized Maoist-era liberal phases. Shortly thereafter, however, relaxation of the inherited restrictions got under way. Permission was granted early in 1979 to hold free markets within municipal boundaries (RMRB, 19 Feb. 1979). Later that year it became possible to trade in draft animals at rural markets, a relaxation that necessarily accompanied a reform allowing peasant households to own and breed such animals (He Jingpei 1981). Practice in various provinces had already departed from central guidelines well before the most onerous of the restrictions were formally dropped in new regulations approved by the Twelfth Party Congress in September 1982. Officially

34

promulgated in January 1983, the new rules legalized what had previously been stigmatized as trafficking in goods (i.e., buying goods in one locality for sale in another), allowed private ownership of mechanized vehicles for use in transporting goods to market, removed restrictions on the destination of private goods, and permitted resumption of wholesale trade in rural markets [10]. As of 1983, trade in China's rural markets was less restricted then at any time since 1953.

The political legitimation of rural markets and the liberalization of policy concerning them led to a remarkable increase in their number nationwide, as shown in Table 1. By the end of 1980 the number of markets had surpassed the total in 1966, on the eve of the Cultural Revolution, and by the end of 1983 the number was at least equal to the total in 1958, on the eve of the Great Leap. Overall, the number of markets increased by over 30 percent in five years.

In the second of my earlier articles (Skinner 1965b: 209), I argued that an increase in demand density may stimulate any or all of three contingent responses: an increase in market size (as indicated by the number of participants or the turnover of trade per market day), an increase in the frequency of marketing (i.e., the addition of new market days to the traditional schedules), and an increase in the number of markets. The data in Table 2 show that the total turnover of trade in rural markets has increased far more rapidly than the number of markets (162.4 percent in five years as against 30.6 percent). Average turnover per market, 375,000 yuan in 1978, increased in five years to 750,000 yuan. The many case studies available make it clear that this increase reflects greater market frequency as well as larger turnover per market day.

Two illustrations must suffice [11]. In the 1920s, Ciyutuo, a standard market town in Liaozhong county (Liaoning), held its market on a three-per-xun schedule and attracted an average of some 3,000 persons each market day (Xu Weihuai 1930). As of 1976, all the markets of the county were convening on a uniform, reduced one-per-xun schedule. Between 1977 and 1981, Ciyutuo's marketing schedule was first doubled and then further increased to a three-per-xun schedule (the same schedule as in the 1920s). And then, in 1982 its market frequency was increased again to every-other-day. These schedule changes were, of course, prompted by a rapid growth in trade volume -- an increase of 55

35

TABLE 1:   NUMBER OF "FREE MARKETS," I.E., MARKET
            SITES, 1978-83.

	Total	Rural	Urban
1978	33,302	33,302	--
1979	38,993	36,767	2,226
1980	40,809	37,890	2,919
1981	43,013	39,715	3,298
1982	44,775	41,184	3,591
1983	48,000	43,500	4,500

Source: 1978-82: Zhongguo Guojia Tongji, ed.,
           Zhongguo Tongji Nianjian [Chinese
           Statistical Yearbook] 1983, p. 386.

           1983: Turnover of Peasant Markets Up in
           1983. Xinhua (Beijing), 11 Feb. 1984. In
           JPRS-CAG-84-008, 16 March 1984.

TABLE 2: FREE MARKET SALES (BILLIONS OF YUAN)

	Total	Rural markets	Urban markets	To urban residents
1978	12.5	12.5	--	3.11
1979	18.3	17.1	1.2	4.75
1980	23.5	21.1	2.4	6.90
1981	28.7	25.3	3.4	8.94
1982	32.8	28.7	4.1	11.08
1983	37.9	32.8	5.1	--

Source: 1978-82: Zhongguo Guojia Tongji, ed.,
           Zhongguo Tongji Nianjian [Chinese
           Statistical Yearbook] 1983, pp. 386-87.

           1983: Turnover of Peasant Markets Up in
           1983. Xinhua (Beijing), 11 Feb. 1984. In
           JPRS-CAG-84-008, 16 March 1984.

percent between 1979 and 1982 alone -- but despite the increased frequency of market days, the number of participants per market day had also grown -- surpassing 15,000 as of 1984 (Ni nd You 1984).

The second illustrative case is that of Changli county (Hebei), whose marketing history to 1976 was sketched out in the preceding section. It will be recalled that at the end of the Maoist era the county's markets had been reduced to ten in number, all following a uniform fortnightly schedule. In 1978, the markets were permitted to increase schedules to the two-per-xun frequency that had been traditional in the area, but market days were still synchronized throughout the county. Within a year, however, as marketplaces previously closed were reopened, all markets within the county were permitted to resume their traditional dovetailed schedules. Changtuo, the central market town in 1933, had resumed its daily schedule and by 1981 was attracting 78,000 participants per day (RMRB, 19 Sept. 1979: 3; 14 Oct. 1981: 2).

The cyclical theory of marketing intensification developed for traditional China (Skinner 1965a: 195-211) retains a paradoxical relevance for the present period. The repression of marketing during the Maoist era meant in effect that by 1977 demand density had far outstripped the capacity of the diminished and deformed system of markets, and, moreover, with the rapid commercialization of the post-1977 period, demand density was growing at an accelerating pace. In consequence, the response to rising demand density has been telescoped. Even during the upswing of regional development cycles in traditional times, the doubling periods for market frequencies and for trade volume per market day typically exceeded half a century. In the present period of reconstruction, many localities have seen both market frequency and market size double in a matter of years.

As the pressure to maintain reduced and synchronized schedules was lifted after 1977 and the restrictions on long-distance trade were relaxed, functional differentiation among markets has reasserted itself and the marketing hierarchy has reemerged. Many if not most of the pre-Communist intermediate and central market towns have by now resumed their higher-order functions. Changtuo, the central market town described above, is a case in point. At the same time, the emerging hierarchy has not simply replicated that of the 1950s for, with the extension of China's modern rail and road network during the Maoist era, locational advantage has shifted appreciably in many areas. With artificial political constraints removed, standard market towns advantaged by an altered transport grid could be expected to assume higher-order central functions after 1977. The rapid rise of Ciyutuo, discussed above, owed much to its location on a major highway built to connect Shenyang, the regional metropolis of the Manchurian regional economy, with its hinterland to the southwest. Ciyutuo, a standard market town as late as 1976, had by 1984 become a central market town with important wholesaling functions.

At the time of the 1982 census some 2,664 important towns and smaller cities were officially designated as zhen, which are to be distinguished from 236 shi, the municipalities in which China's major cities are situated (Li Chengrui 1982). In terms of place in the functional economic hierarchy, most zhen count as central market towns or local cities, so that newly designated zhen are likely to be towns that have moved up the hierarchy to at least the central-market level. In this respect, it is notable that reports are increasing of market towns (many of them former commune centers) applying for zhen status. For instance, in Shaodong, a county in Hunan recently favored by the completion of a major railroad through it, six of the thirty periodic market towns requested zhen status in 1982 (Zhongguo jingji nianjian 1983: IV-129). In a general summary, Xinhua News Agency reported (Beijing, 9 Jan. 1984. Transl. in JPRS-CEA-84-007, 30 Jan. 1984) that "in many places, periodic markets have become daily markets: morning and noon markets now last the whole day. New towns have grown out of some rural marketplaces." Clearly the transformation of higher-level periodic market towns into modern trading centers, described in my 1965 article as having begun in China after 1895 in the cores of China's most advanced regions, is under way once again. Even as traditional dynamics are playing themselves out in the reconstitution of marketing systems and in their further extension into regional peripheries, modern change is at work in the cores of the more developed regions.

As might be expected, Deng's regime has repudiated radical efforts to contain marketing within administrative units, to force commodity flows to follow the administrative hierarchy, and to isolate cities from the rural marketing system. Current

39

policies aim to rationalize economic networks so that commodities may be transferred from production sites to the point of consumption "along the shortest route with the fewest links and at the lowest cost," and to "integrate the economic activities in large, medium-sized, and small cities of various types with the economic activities in rural townships" (Ma, Yuan, and Wei 1982:9,12). From 1979 free markets were permitted in cities, as we have seen, and initial restrictions on their location, hours, and supply were soon relaxed. As shown in the rightmost column of Table 2, free market sales of rural produce to urban residents have steadily increased since 1978 (both absolutely and proportionately), accounting in 1982 for one-third of total free market sales. Moreover, economic planners now recognize and capitalize on the key role of regional metropolises within their respective regional economies (Ma, Yuan, and Wei 1982:15). For instance, planners no longer speak of Wuhan as a provincial center; it is now seen as the economic center of its maximal hinterland, the Middle Yangzi macroregion: "We must break up the artificial barriers and organize within the economic region a commodity circulation network" and "set up a regional financial network with Wuhan as its center" (Li Chonghai 1983: 14, 19).

Meanwhile it is clear that the revival of rural marketing has not yet run its course. For one thing, political resistance to free markets has hampered the revival in various localities and regions [12], and its effects continue to the present. A meeting of Shaanxi commercial administrators held in April 1984 focused inter alia on "eliminating leftist ideological influence and promoting the development of markets" (Xi'an Mandarin broadcast, 15 April 1984. Transl. in JPRS-CAG-84-013, 4 May 1984). In neighboring Shanxi province, the revival of markets has been desultory -- as of 1982 each of its operating rural markets had to service some 30,000 rural residents, as against approximately 20,000 in the other three provinces of the Northwest [13] -- and leftist intransigence may well be a major reason. Rural cadres in Shanxi had once taken great pride in Dazhai's early success in closing all markets, and in fact the county in which Dazhai is located, Xiyang, delayed reopening any markets until 1980. On the assumption that rural cadremen in such areas will eventually be brought around to the Dengist line, we are likely to see significant further increases in the number of markets.

In addition, there are indications that the

extension of marketing networks in the far periphery of
several regions is still under way. It appears that in
many mountainous and minority areas markets began to
reopen only in 1980 (Sun Deshan 1981). An account in a
Canton newspaper (Nanfang Ribao, 18 Dec. 1982)
describes mountainous areas in the periphery of Lingnan
in which peasants are still dependent on peddlers for
their marketing needs. A recent report on Shaanxi (Han
Wen 1984) notes that in mountainous and hilly areas
"many districts and townships are still without
markets," and the conference of commercial
administrators mentioned above called on cadres in
rural districts that had not yet done so, to establish
markets to "fill in the gaps."

Finally, of course, with agricultural productivity,
economic diversification, and incomes still rising in
the countryside, it is likely that increasing demand
density will continue to foster further intensification
of the marketing network, especially in the outer cores
of regional systems. But both proliferation and
intensification have their built in limits, and in
accordance with the dialectic emphasized in my analysis
of twenty years ago, the demise of obviated standard
markets in the developed cores of macroregional
economies cannot but countervail and eventually halt
the increase of rural marketplaces. In my view, their
number is likely to peak out in the low 50,000s.

It is apparent that the dramatic revival of
marketing is integral to the larger liberating reform
of the rural economy -- both responding to and
stimulating in turn the increases in specialization and
productivity. The entire episode may be viewed as a
kind of historical catch-up. It is almost as if
China's pragmatic leaders were letting commercial
capitalism run its course in the countryside, bringing
the economy very quickly to where it would have been
had the Maoist experiments not intervened. Perhaps by
way of excusing how far they have traveled along the
capitalist road, the liberal pragmatists tell us that
socialism cannot be built on the backs of an
impoverished peasantry. It remains to be seen whether
that is but an epitaph for the Maoist era or the
promise of a renewed effort to build socialsm when the
economy has caught up.

Eitherway, the beginning of the end of traditional
periodic marketing is at hand.   The very logic of
market periodicity assumes inefficient transport and
weak demand density -- valid assumptions for most of

41

China in the late 1940s but only for peripheral areas in the mid-1980s. The volume of trade in "free markets" is growing so fast that a majority may already be operating on a daily schedule. Major efforts are under way to construct permanent facilities in marketplaces that are now open continually, and today many if not most higher-order markets have regular bus service. The number of "free markets" may be expanding, but a growing proportion of them are no longer either traditional or periodic. The historical role of periodic marketing in China's social and economic development is likely to end with the present century.

NOTES

1. Even during the period of division from 1127 to 1280, the Southern Song empire consisted essentially of six intact macroregions -- Lingnan, the Southeast Coast, and the four Yangzi regions.

2. My original regionalization, as set out in Skinner 1977b:211-216, divided agrarian China into nine units. In a subsequent refinement and revision, I have detached the Gan basin in central China from the Middle Yangzi macroregion to which it had been assigned to form a separate macroregion: Gan Yangzi. The revised regionalization is shown in Map 1. Maps 2-3 were drawn prior to the revision and hence the Upper Yangzi macroregional boundaries differ somewhat from those shown in Map 1. The discrepancies, all in the far periphery, have no relevance to the points being made in Maps 2-5.

3. This analysis of the Upper Yangzi macroregion rests primarily on data culled from 60-odd county and prefectural-level gazetteers spanning the century from the 1830s to the 1930s. For citations of the Western-language sources used, see Skinner 1977c:728(n.20).

4. These factors are the major determinants of the size of marketing and trading systems at all levels of the economic hierarchy. The regression equation I arrived at for the size of such systems is:

$$y = ax + b + c/x$$

where y is the size of the marketing or trading area, x is population density, a is an index of average transport efficiency, b is a factor measuring the ruggedness of the prevailing topography, and c is a measure of household self-sufficiency or reliance on the market.

5. The overall scheme and the dating of the first seven cycles are set out in Skinner and Winckler 1969. For an updating of the cycles to the end of the Maoist era, see G. W. Skinner n.d.

6. The figure for 1965 is cited in He Jingpei 1981 and in various yearbooks. For the source of the 1978 datum see Table 1. I have located two other estimates of the number of rural markets China-wide, but I consider neither to be valid. Guan Datong (1961) gives 40,000 without specifying source or date; I surmise that it is a round figure for the total prior to the Great Leap. In their book on rural markets (1957), Chu Qing, Zhu Zhongjian, and Wang Zhiming give a total of 36,710, presumably for 1956; that the figure is an undercount is clear from the description of procedures followed in collecting and aggregating the data.

7. These estimates of the rural population are derived from the annual series for total and urban populations in Banister 1984.

8. The mini-radicalizations began, respectively, in early 1979, spring 1981, and summer 1983. Only the second had discernable impact on rural economic policy.

9. This paragraph and the next two are based on general retrospective China-watching and a considerable secondary literature. I have relied in particular on Travers 1984.

10. The regulations were issued by the Central Committee of the Chinese Communist Party as Document No. 1 for 1983. Transl. in FBIS Daily Report, 18 April 1983, pp. K1-K13.

11. I am grateful to Carol Benedict for calling these cases to my attention.

12. Interesting reports of early resistance appeared in Guangming Ribao, 18 Aug. 1978 (transl. in FBIS

Daily Report, CHI-78-170) and in RMRB, 28 Mar. 1979.

13.   Provincial rural populations were extrapolated from the ten-percent sample of 1982 census data. Province totals of rural markets in 1982 have been pieced together from Zhongguo jingji nianjian [Almanac of the Chinese Economy] 1981, 1982, 1983, and from JPRS China: Economic Reports during 1983.

REFERENCES CITED

Banister, Judith
    1984   An Analysis of Recent Data on the Population of China. Population and Development Review 10:241-271.

Bucknall, Kevin
    1979   Capitalism and Chinese Agriculture, 1960-66. Australian Journal of Chinese Affairs 1:69-90.

Chan, Anita, and Jonathan Unger
    1982   Grey and Black: The Hidden Economy of Rural China. Pacific Afairs 5:452-471.

Chu Qing, Zhu Zhongjian, and Wang Zhiming
    1957   Woguo nongcun shichang di gaizu [The Reorganization of Rural Markets in China]. Beijing: Caizheng Jingji Chubanshe.

Domes, Jürgen
    1982   New Policies in the Communes: Notes on Rural Societal Structures in China, 1976-1981. Journal of Asian Studies 41:253-267.

Fei, Hsiao-tung
    1939   Peasant Life in China: A Field Study of Country Life in the Yangtze Valley. London: Routledge & Kegan Paul.

Fei, Hsiao-tung, and Chih-i Chang
    1945   Earthbound China: A Study of Rural Economy in Yunnan. Chicago: University of Chicago Press.

Guan Datong
    1961   Guanyu nongcun jishi maoyi [On Trade in Rural Markets]. Hongqi [Red Flag] 18:16-22.

44

Han Wen
1984   Foster the Establishment of Markets, Promote
        Circulation of Commodities. Shaanxi Ribao
        [Shaanxi Daily], 23 Apr. Transl. in JPRS-
        CEA-84-053:110-111.

He Jingpei
1981   Vigorously Promote the Healthy Development
        of Trade in Urban and Rural Markets. Jingji
        Guanli [Economic Administration] 5 (15 May):
        12-14. Transl. in JPRS-CEA-78-562:48-52.

Li Chengrui
1982   Cong renkou pucha gongbao kan Zhongguo
        renkou de xianzhuang [The Chinese Population
        as Shown by the Population Census
        Communique]. Jingji Yanjiu [Economic
        Research] 12:31-32.

Li Chonghai
1983   Take Off on Two Wings and Build Wuhan into
        an Economic Center. Wuhan Daxue Xuebao
        [Wuhan University Journal] 6 (28 Nov.): 71-
        78. Transl. in JPRS-CEA-84-052:5-21.

Ma Ye, Yuan Ganwu, and Wei Bingkun
1982   On Economic Networks. Tianjin Ribao
        [Tianjin Daily], 27 July:3.

Ni Di and You Xi
1984   Guanyu Ciyutuo di jishi di xingwang gei
        chengshi fuzhuang ye di qishi [Regarding the
        Inspiration Given to Ciyutuo's Textile
        Industry by the Prosperity of the Town's
        Market]. Jingji Guanli [Economic
        Administration] (Mar.):46-47.

Rawski, Evelyn S.
1972   Agricultural Change and the Peasant Economy
        of South China. Cambridge: Harvard
        University Press.

RMRB (Renmin Ribao) [People's Daily], Beijing.

Samuelson, Paul A.
1964   Economics: An Introductory Analysis, 6th ed.
        New York: McGraw-Hill.

Shiba Yoshinobu
1977   Ningpo and its Hinterland. In The City in
        Late Imperial China, G. W. Skinner, ed. pp.

45

391-439.   Stanford: Stanford   University
Press.

Skinner, G. William
    1964   Marketing and Social Structure in Rural
              China, Part I. Journal of Asian Studies
              24:3-43.

    1965a   Marketing and Social Structure in Rural
              China, Part II. Journal of Asian Studies
              24:195-228.

    1965b   Marketing and Social Structure in Rural
              China, Part III. Journal of Asian Studies
              24:363-399.

    1977a   Urban Development in Imperial China. In The
              City in Late Imperial China, G. W. Skinner,
              ed.   pp.   3-31.   Stanford: Stanford
              University Press.

    1977b   Regional Urbanization in Nineteenth-Century
              China. In The City in Late Imperial China,
              G. W. Skinner, ed. pp. 211-249. Stanford:
              Stanford University Press.

    1977c   Cities and the Hierarchy of Local Systems.
              In The City in Late Imperial China, G. W.
              Skinner,   ed.   pp.   275-351.   Stanford:
              Stanford University Press.

    1985   The Structure of Chinese History. Journal
              of Asian Studies 44(2).

    n.d.   Rural   Marketing   and   Agricultural
              Modernization in China.   Santa Barbara:
              University of Californa, Modernization of
              China Project, forthcoming.

Skinner, G. William, and Edwin A. Winckler
    1969   Compliance Succession in Rural Communist
              China: A Cyclical Theory. In A Sociological
              Reader on Complex Organization, 2d ed.
              Amitai Etzioni, ed. pp. 410-438. New York:
              Holt, Rinehart, and Winston.

Smith, Robert H. T.
    1979-80   Periodic   Market-places   and   Periodic
              Marketing: Review and Prospect, Parts I and
              II.   Progress in Human Geography 3:471-505;
              4:1-31.

46

Sun Deshan
    1981   Active Village Markets and Flourishing Rural
            Economies. Zhongguo Caimao Bao [Chinese
            Financial and Trade News], 22 Sept.:3.
            Transl. in JPRS-CEA-79-762:45-48.

Tao Ningqi, comp.
    1933   Changli xianzhi [Changli County Gazetteer].
            Taipei: Chengwen Chuban She, 1968 (reissue).

Travers, Lee
    1984   Post-1978 Rural Economic Policy and Peasant
            Income in China. China Quarterly 98:241-259.

Twitchett, Denis
    1966   The T'ang Market System. Asia Major 12:202-
            243.

    1968   Merchant, Trade, and Government in Late
            T'ang. Asia Major 14:63-95.

Weiss, Udo
    1978   China's Rural Marketing Structure. World
            Development 6:647-662.

Xu Weihuai, comp.
    1930   Liaozhong xianzhi [Liaozhong County
            Gazetteer]. Taipei: Chengwen Chuban She,
            1974 (reissue).

HOW TO COUNT ONIONS: METHODS FOR A REGIONAL ANALYSIS OF MARKETING [1]

Carol A. Smith, Duke University

Marketplaces in agrarian societies are usually large, crowded, noisy, and very busy affairs. Without systematic observations and methods, it is difficult to understand what is happening in one market center, much less to see systemic relations among many market centers in a large regional market economy, such as that of western Guatemala. Yet if one concentrates on certain economic elements within marketplaces--in particular, (1) diversity of commodities, (2) types of vendors, (3) types of economic transaction (wholesale versus retail), and (4) general demographic settings of the marketplaces--it is possible to reduce the confusion of market activity to certain economic patterns through which one can see how a complex commodity economy is integrated. In this essay I describe how I developed measures of these four market elements in order to make sense of the regional marketing system of western Guatemala.

I carried out my field study of western Guatemala's marketing system more than a decade ago and have published a number of articles that discuss my findings. But I have nowhere described how I arrived at my findings--how I went from counting onions in more than 200 diverse market centers to describing the articulation of different kinds of market centers in a region with two distinct producing and consuming economies. Since the methodological problems I encountered in my study are ones that most students of agrarian marketing systems would run into, I think it is worth recounting how I solved some of them. Many of the problems were solved by using the procedures developed by geographers for analyzing central-place systems (especially the procedures detailed by Marshall, 1969). G. William Skinner (1964, 1965) introduced this way of looking at agrarian economies in an early series of articles on traditional Chinese marketing systems. But Skinner, like me, described the results of his analysis, not his procedures. And it is important to recognize that in certain respects studies of rural marketing cannot replicate the methodology designed to explain urban central-place systems. How to deal, methodologically, with the difference between rural marketing systems and urban central-place systems is the focus of my discussion here.

49

Before that discussion, however, let me briefly describe how basic central-place measurement procedures can order one's economic data on a regional marketing economy to answer many different kinds of questions-- not just questions of locational relationships. They can tell one which marketplaces are most important in regional trade and why, how rural market centers relate to urban market centers, how specialized and well integrated a marketing economy is, and how various contradictory practices can be encompassed by a single, unified marketing economy. In other words, central- place measurement procedures can help one find the patterns and functions of regional marketing systems in a systematic way, whether that system is rural or urban, permanent or periodic. What they help one see is the hierarchical organization of market trade, a pattern of organization that varies in accordance with the complexity of a particular commodity economy, but a pattern of organization that is basic to all commodity- based economies.

I. DETERMINING BOUNDARIES AND LEVELS IN A REGIONAL MARKETING SYSTEM

To carry out a central-place analysis, one must first determine the boundaries of a regional marketing system. This is not as easy as it sounds, since economic regions in market economies are diverse rather than homogeneous, inasmuch as they rest upon a division of labor. In the case of western Guatemala, for example, one cannot understand market exchange without understanding the interdependence of the peasant highlands and the plantation lowlands. A regional study that isolated a group of highland marketplaces (or a group of lowland marketplaces) would miss the basic economic dynamic of market exchange in Guatemala, a dynamic created by the shortage of domestic commodities in the plantation area (food, clothing, household utensils) and the shortage of income or cash in the highland area. The market economy functions largely to arbitrage these shortages. Yet the definition of region used by most scholars would isolate homogeneous areas rather than functionally diverse ones. The methodology of central-place studies helps one define a functional region, much more useful for marketplace studies.

How does the methodology of central-place theory help one see an economic phenomenon as general as a regional division of labor? It does so by defining regions by the reach of high-level market centers, the

50

places that organize hierarchically and articulate
spatially complex divisions of labor. One may define a
large or small economic region by chosing a large or
small central place to delimit the region.   One then
finds the limits or boundaries to the system by looking
at the range of downward distribution from that central
place. But whatever the size of region one selects by
defining it on the basis of a central place, functional
diversity will always exist within it.   In the case of
western Guatemala, for example, one could define a
"provincial" region in the highlands by picking a
provincial market town as one's center.   Here the
diversity would be that between a town center and a
rural hinterland, the division of labor that between
rural and urban producers.   Or one could define a
larger area, encompassing several towns, by picking a
regional market center to delimit the system. And in
western Guatemala, one would find that a regional
system (one larger than a province), included both
highlands and lowlands. For the major central places
of western Guatemala (one rural and one urban), exist
to articulate trade between highlands and lowlands, the
two parts of western Guatemala most distinct with
respect to division of labor--above the level or rural-
urban differences. In other words, it is immediately
apparent when looking at the spatial distribution of
towns of various sizes, examining trade flows, or
discussing supplies and trade routes with traders
(basic elements of central-place methodology), that
Quezaltenango (the largest urban center of the area)
and San Francisco el Alto (the largest rural center of
the area) articulate highland and lowland market
exchange.   The market interdependence of highlands and
lowlands in western Guatemala is thus revealed by
analysis of the range of its major market centers.

     As noted above, central-place theory is based on the
notion that market centers are hierarchically
organized. This notion is based on the following
assumptions. Economic considerations (as well as
common sense) dictate that if demand for a commodity is
heavy and frequent, many centers will carry it.
Conversely, if demand for a commodity is light and
infrequent, few centers will carry it. Thus, the maize
eaters of Guatemala would be expected to support many
market centers supplying their staple food; and being
primarily poor Indian peasants, they would be expected
to support very few centers offering televisions, or
even radios. On the supply side, if consumers are
widely distributed, as they are in agrarian societies,
suppliers of items such as radios, for which demand is

low (termed high-order goods), must tap demand from larger areas than suppliers of such items as maize, for which demand is high (low-order goods). Suppliers of high-order goods can stay in business only if they can be the exclusive suppliers for wide areas--that is, if they meet all of the infrequent demand from a large number of dispersed rural consumers. Thus, suppliers of high-order goods should be not only fewer but more widely spaced than suppliers of low-order goods, and centers with only suppliers of low-order goods should have small hinterlands that fall within the hinterlands of centers with suppliers of high-order goods. There is little controversial about these assumptions. And if met, these assumptions dictate a hierarchical ordering to market centers.

The fundamental measurement for a central-place study, therefore, is that which allows one to classify a market center by position within a market hierarchy. How does one do that? Basically, one does it by counting onions and other commodities. Marshall (1969) describes this procedure in detail: one must first develop a way to count commodities (or commmodity bundles) sold in particular market centers by dividing them into functional types (more easily said than done in marketplace studies); one must then devise measures for assessing the range of commodities (or functions) in different market centers, usually with a centrality index that measures the importance of a place by the diversity (not just the number) of its functions; and one must finally work out a grouping procedure which allows one to ignore small-scale variability in size and concentrate on functional similarity in position. (To see how one modifies Marshall's methods to deal with marketplace functions rather than town functions, see Smith 1972a.) At the end, one has grouped different market centers into different levels, based on what one assumes is their position in a hierarchy of market exchange. One then examines the pyramidal sequence (numbers of centers in each level of the hierarchy) to see what kind of marketing system one has.

What does a pyramidal sequence tell you? It normally tells you the depth and range of a marketing system--which are measures of its diversity, integration, and efficiency. If there are many levels in the system (i.e., the system is deep), one can assume that considerable specialization exists within it. Conversely, if there are few levels, one can assume that the division of labor in the market economy

52

is limited. The range of each center tells one about the functional integration of the system. If there are many lower-level centers dependent on each high-level center, one can assume that the system is relatively poorly integrated, whereas the opposite is true if there are few lower-level centers per high-level center. Beyond these basic points, central-place theory predicts particular kinds of sequences of market levels if constraints of space economy or efficiency played the most important role in market development. And Christaller (1966) worked out several different kinds of sequences that suggest the dominance of different economic principles in the development of a central-place system: administrative convenience, traffic convenience, or marketing convenience. But whether or not one finds the predicted sequences, one can say a great deal about the market economy on the basis of the sequence one finds. The only pattern that is completely unexpected is that which is non-pyramidal--i.e., a pattern that has about the same number of centers at a lower level than those found at a higher level. Such a pattern indicates that the system in question is not hierarchically organized. And any commodity economy that lacks hierarchy is most peculiar indeed. Yet that is precisely what I found in the pyramidal sequence for market centers in western Guatemala.

My procedures for measuring market levels, and my findings on the market hierarchy of western Guatemala (up to this point), were the following. First, I carried out various controlled counts and censuses of western Guatemala's town centers and marketplaces to obtain data on market commodities, trader types, and types of trade transactions. Then to describe the hierarchy of marketplaces in western Guatemala, I followed Marshall's methods for measuring urban central-place levels with considerable care, modifying them where necessary to deal with the special attributes of rural centers or periodic marketplaces (see Smith 1972a for a detailed discussion of my modifications). And, at the end, I could classify most of western Guatemala's marketplaces into five different levels. Because of the care with which I had gathered my data and organized it, I had a great deal of confidence that my measures of each marketplace were appropriate by the normal conventions of central-place measurement. Yet when I finished this part of the analysis, I had a very unusual ordering of market levels. There was one center at Level 1 (San Francisco el Alto), 13 at Level 2, 21 at Level 3, 30 at Level 4, and 144 at Level 5. (I had sufficient data to delimit levels on 209 of western Guatemala's marketplaces, all but a handful of very minor centers.) This particular pyramidal sequence has far too many high-level centers for any normal marketing hierarchy. Moreover, the major centers identified by my procedures were closer to each other than to minor centers, violating every principle of central-place theory. [2]

Why did this happen? Why did western Guatemala's market hierarchy have so many market centers at the "middle" levels? Did it mean that suppliers of certain kinds of middle and high-level goods located in different kinds of centers? Did it mean that Guatemala divided into different kinds of producing or consuming populations? Did it mean that central-place theory was inapplicable to rural marketing systems? The novel methodology I had to develop to answer these questions told me much more about Guatemalan marketplaces than did the methodology strictly borrowed from central-place theory. The rest of this essay describes that methodology.

II. DIFFERENTIATING MARKETPLACE FUNCTIONS FROM MARKETPLACE LEVELS

Field experience told me that Guatemalan marketplaces are not only retail centers but also wholesale centers, providing outlets to western Guatemala's specialized producers, who are located in the central part of the region. In addition, the different populations of western Guatemala, Indians and Ladinos [3], have different relationships to the market. Indians, who produce most of the goods sold in marketplaces, use markets to sell in as much as to buy in, whereas Ladinos, who depend on markets for food much more than do Indians, buy in markets but only rarely sell in them. (In fact, less than 2 percent of all marketplace sellers are Ladinos.) Thus, where there are large Indian concentrations, one finds large wholesale marketplaces, and where there are instead large Ladino concentrations, one finds large retail marketplaces. Finally, market characteristics differ depending upon whether they are located in large towns or in rural areas. Such functional variation, typical of marketplaces used by peasants, suggests that in agrarian societies one must differentiate market centers by more than level. One must also differentiate them by market function.

In the first part of my analysis I had assumed that

Guatemalan marketplaces could be analyzed strictly in
terms of their supply characteristics--that two centers
supplying the same variety and quantity of goods were
exactly equivalent to each other. In most urban
central-place studies, whose measurement procedures I
had followed fairly closely up to this point, this is a
reasonable assumption. One usually finds a direct
relationship between the quantity of goods present in a
center and the area supplied by that center. To the
degree that one center has a large supply of retail
goods, it supplies smaller centers with some of those
goods on a wholesale basis for later retail
redistribution. Since most of the goods supplied to a
local region are produced far away, they flow down
rather than up the local market hierarchy. Those few
goods locally produced (such as wheat in an
agricultural region) flow through market channels
distinct from the retail market channels. Under these
circumstances, the student of urban central-place
systems can reasonably ignore wholesale market channels
altogether (Marshall 1969).

In simple agrarian economies, however, goods flow in
both directions through the same market channels. Thus
one finds and counts both retail and wholesale goods in
local marketplaces, since marketplaces provide the only
means by which locally produced goods can be
redistributed. In Guatemala, for example, some market
centers supply only consumers, while others supply
traders or middlemen who in turn supply yet other
centers. Centrality indices based on the variety and
quantity of goods found in agrarian marketplaces,
therefore, do not measure the reach of those centers to
consumers alone, they measure the importance of those
centers to traders as well as to consumers. And if
locally produced goods are sold in local marketplaces
(to be moved by mobile traders who sell in other local
marketplaces) rather than sold through distinct market
channels (such as trucks moving directly from the
production site), one needs to discriminate between the
retail goods and the wholesale goods supplied in each
marketplace. Otherwise, one risks lumping into a
single type centers with high retail functions but no
wholesale functions and centers with low retail
functions but high wholesale functions. And there is
reason to believe that these two types of market
center, which may appear equivalent through measures of
goods but which are not equivalent because they perform
different functions in the marketing system, may have a
special locational relationship in an agrarian economy.
In Guatemala, for example, I found that large wholesale

55

marketplaces rather than small retail marketplaces locate between large retail marketplaces. This special locational relationship may be common to agrarian societies where mobile traders buying in local marketplaces distribute locally produced goods.

III. MEASURES OF MARKETPLACE FUNCTION

If the marketing system under study has some of the characteristics described above, how should one determine the various possible redistributive functions of a local market center and assess its centrality for both consumers and traders? I found that the proportions of different kinds of traders in a marketplace gives the best indication of specialized market activity. In the case of Guatemala, three different kinds of trader, each handling different kinds of goods in different ways, exists. First, there are producer-sellers who sell local goods (usually, but not invariably his or her own) in the local marketplace, without procuring the goods in other markets or other marketing systems. (Such sellers handle most food items produced in the region.) Second, there are middlemen who sell goods produced (and usually purchased for resale) elsewhere, the goods having moved through the hands of local dealers at both ends of the marketing chain. (Such sellers handle most goods imported to the region, including some foodstuffs.) Finally, there are long-distance traders from a few specialist townships who sell either the products or supplies of local craftsmen mostly at the retail level. (Such sellers handle most of the clothing worn by rural peasants or urban workers as well as pottery, rope, baskets, and the like.) Middlemen and long-distance traders are fulltime specialists, but the middleman typically sells in a single marketplace, whereas the long-distance trader usually sells in many.

Since each type of seller in the marketplace moves goods in a different way (through a different redistributive pattern), one can discriminate among marketplaces with respect to their role in redistribution by the proportion of these three seller types in the marketplace.[4] The presence of many producer-sellers indicates that the center is basically an arena for local exchange or for bulking goods for upward redistribution to other marketplaces; in any event, producers bring local goods to market which potentially flow up the marketing chain. Where local middlemen predominate, we can be relatively sure that

56

they are selling goods for either local consumption or for downward redistribution, since by definition retailing middlemen sell imported goods which flow down the marketing chain. Finally, if there are very large numbers of long-distance trade specialists, the center is most likely a place for wholesale exchanges among these trade specialists. Where the proportions are balanced, possibly all of these functions are being performed.

If the normal assumptions of central-place theory are met, major differences in redistributive functions should relate only to the level or importance of the center in question. We would expect, for example, a higher proportion of middlemen in higher-level or major centers, because middlemen in such centers should be the sources of supply for smaller centers. And we would expect a higher proportion of producer-sellers in lower-level or small centers because such centers would not need market specialists for wholesaling goods to other marketplaces. But for reasons given above, I had reason to expect that functional variation in Guatemalan marketplaces (as measured by proportion of different seller types) did not parallel the size or importance of Guatemalan marketplaces. Thus it was important to test the degree of association between function and level for this case.

To do so I categorized all marketplaces into the five levels already distinguished by quantity and variety of goods. Then I categorized all marketplaces into four types as measured by proportions of particular seller types: (1) those whose sellers were predominantly (more than 50 percent) long-distance traders; (2) those whose sellers were predominantly (more than 50 percent) producer-sellers; (3) those whose sellers were predominantly (more than 50 percent) local middlemen; and (4) those whose sellers were of all sorts (no particular type predominating). Table 1 compares all 152 market centers in western Guatemala on which I had full information on these two dimensions, level and proportion of seller types. (I did not have complete data on 47 very small market centers, located in hamlets, since I did not personally census them.)

The cell entries in Table 1 are not random, in that the redistributive function of centers, as measured by proportions of seller types, shows a general correlation with central-place level. The single Level 1 (and Type 1) marketplace (San Francisco

57

TABLE 1:   DISTRIBUTION OF MARKETPLACE LEVELS BY
           MARKETPLACE TYPES

Types	Type 1 50% or more long-distance traders	Type 2 50% or more producer-sellers	Type 3 50% or more middlemen	Type 4 Less than 50% any seller type	Total
LEVELS					
1	1	0	0	0	1
2	0	6	2	7	15
3	0	12	5	9	26
4	0	21	6	5	32
5	0	42	30	6	78
Totals	1	81	43	27	152

---

el Alto) is clearly distinguished from all others by
its high proportion of long-distance traders. Markets
with balanced proportions of seller types (Type 4) tend
to be higher-level markets. And markets with either
producer-sellers (Type 2) or local middlemen (Type 3)
in greatest number tend to be lower-level markets
(Levels 4 or 5).

Yet no particular type of marketplace predominates
at Levels 2 through 4. There are more markets with high
proportions of producer-sellers in them at the lower
levels, but this is only because there are more markets
of this type than any other. (Several high-level
markets are also dominated by producer-sellers.)
Clearly, we cannot assume that only redistributive
functions determine (or are determined by)
central-place levels in Guatemala. Can we, then, still
assume that the array of goods in a center describes
the extent of its demand hinterland? Does the
centrality index retain any meaningfulness in this
context, or should a new index that measures only
retail functions of centers be constructed, an index
that disregards wholesale sellers?

Given that central-place theory is designed to
explain the distribution of retail, not wholesale
centers my initial impulse was to scrap my first
centrality index and develop a new one measuring only
retail sellers. Eventually, though, I decided that
such a procedure would lead to an artificial depiction
of Guatemalan marketplaces. After all, some Guatemalan
marketplaces do have important wholesale functions and
this feature of their organization should affect their
locations and regional patterning. Moreover, the goods
in each marketplace, whether wholesale or retail, still
represent goods that will be consumed or purchased by
some demand population; therefore, all the goods in a
particular marketplace represent the actual demand-
range of that particular center. If the goods are
mainly wholesale rather than retail goods, that
center might draw mobile traders rather than
consumers. Hence, marketplace organization in Guatemala
might well be affected by supplier distance-
minimization rather than (or as well as) consumer
distance-minimization. The next problem, then, is to
reassess the demand hinterlands of marketplaces--to
develop measures that will discriminate trade or
wholesale centers from retail centers--and then to see
what locational relationship these different kinds of
centers have to each other.

This involves handling two sets of problems, actually. The first set concerns marketplace specialization. We must look for a way to distinguish marketplace types nonarbitrarily; then we must discover what determines different marketplace types. In other words, we must ultimately come up with a theory explaining and accounting for marketplace specialization. The second set of problems concerns the location of specialized market centers. We must find out if there is any regularity in the spatial patterning of different marketplace types and see what this relationship has, if any, to marketplace level. Then, we must use whatever model we come up with that accounts for marketplace specialization in Guatemala to modify central-place theory (which has no concept of central-place specialization) when and where necessary. The next two sections of this paper deal with these problems.

IV. DESCRIBING MARKETPLACE TYPES

In grouping marketplaces by function or specialization, I continued using the very simple approach of creating four types--three in which one of the three seller-types was in the majority, and one in which no single seller-type predominated. The question now before me was to single out those features of the region that created variation in marketplace type. The regional marketing system of western Guatemala can be subdivided into twelve local subsystems, most of which have distinctive ecological or population characteristics (see Smith 1977). By looking for the local conditions within these subsystems that seemed to produce the different market types it was possible to develop hypotheses about the social and economic conditions that led to market differentiation in the region. It was also important to determine the degree to which marketplace type variation was regionally imbalanced, which subsystem analysis allowed me to assess.

Table 2 shows the distribution of the four market types by ten of the twelve marketing subsystems in the region. (Since my information on the lowland subsystems was incomplete I grouped all three lowland subsystems into one category.) We find only one major wholesale center (Type 1), San Francisco el Alto, centrally located in the marketing subsystem of Totonicapan. There are 81 Type 2 or producer-seller centers (more than half of the total), some in each subsystem, though fewest in the lowland area. More

60

TABLE 2:   DISTRIBUTION OF MARKETPLACE TYPES BY MARKET
           SUBSYSTEMS

Market Subsystems

Market-place Types	Chimaltenango 1	Solola 2	Totonicapan 3	Quezaltenango 4	Suchitepequez 5	San Marcos 6	S. Huehuetenango 7	N. Huehuetenango 8	N. Quiche 9	S. Quiche 10	ALL
Type 1 (long-distance traders)	0	0	1	0	0	0	0	0	0	0	1
Type 2 (producer-sellers)	4	10	6	7	2	10	10	8	13	11	81
Type 3 (middle-men)	4	1	1	3	17	5	6	3	2	1	43
Type 4 (balanced)	3	3	2	3	4	3	1	3	3	2	27
Totals	11	14	10	13	23	18	17	14	18	14	152

----

a For the definition of marketplace types, see Table 1.

than one third of the 43 middlemen centers (Type 3) are found in the single lowland grouping, but each subsystem has one or more more of them. And there are 17 balanced centers (Type 4) distributed relatively evenly across the ten marketing subsystems. Thus, with the exception of the middlemen centers, we find most types of marketplaces distributed fairly evenly across the region. But we must still account for that distribution, especially for the distribution of middlemen market centers.

Middlemen centers dominate the lowland subsystems, comprising 85 percent of their marketplaces. This is not entirely unexpected because most of the coastal lowlands is devoted to plantation agriculture, whose export market channels bypass local marketplaces. This gives little room for the existence of producer-sellers who might sell in the local marketplaces. And middlemen centers are marked, essentially, by the relative absence of producer-sellers. But we must still explain why the remaining 26 middlemen centers, located in highland subsystems, do not support appreciable numbers of producer-sellers. Eleven of these 26 centers were located in the lowland portions (below the 1200 meter line) of what I had classified as highland marketing subsystems; the users of these particular centers, moreover, produced mostly for export rather than for domestic consumption. Production variables thus account for most middlemen marketplaces. The 15 middlemen centers that are not located in lowland areas are tiny (Level 5) marketplaces founded so recently that they have not yet taken on "normal" characteristics.[5]

We can also account for middlemen market centers by the ethnic composition of the township in which the marketplace is located. Ninety percent of middlemen centers (located in a township center) are found in townships where more than 50 percent of the population is Ladino; conversely, 88 percent of the producer-seller marketplaces are found in townships that are predominantly Indian. The reason that the ethnic composition of a township correlates so well with the producing characteristics of a market's hinterland is that very few Ladinos produce goods for local marketplace distribution, whereas most Indians do.

If there were no clear locational pattern to western Guatemala's different forms of production or to the distribution of its different ethnic populations, we would have to expect a great deal of irregularity in the locational pattern of marketplace types. Fortunately, this is not a problem. Most Ladinos and most middlemen marketplaces can be found in the coastal lowlands. The 11 middlemen centers located in the highlands are distributed fairly evenly in the highlands. Since these particular centers are all very small, and thus without redistributive functions, they should not interfere with the regional pattern of major central places.

What accounts for the difference between middlemen and balanced markets (Types 3 and 4 in Table 2)? I noted a possible variable distinguishing them when plotting the distribution of the two types on a map. Most balanced marketplaces were located in highland urban centers. Middlemen marketplaces, in contrast, were located either in rural areas (when in the highlands) or in the lowlands (when urban). I tested the strength of this association in two different ways. First, I checked to see if urban population size created balanced markets, using the population of 1,000 as a starting point. The correlation was statistically significant, but there were too many deviant cases for it to constitute a satisfactory explanation: 32 cases did not fit the prediction out of a test population of 123 centers (I had excluded San Francisco el Alto and hamlet marketplaces, for which I had no urban population figures, from the sample).

In Guatemala, however, the population size of a town does not predict its commercial centrality very well. Thus it was possible that specific urban functions rather than urban population produced balanced marketplaces. Accordingly, I tried correlating marketplace type with town functions, using a town centrality index similar to the index I constructed for marketplaces. I was able to construct such a measure for 128 towns with marketplaces. Correlating urban functions with balanced marketplaces gave a much better level of association: 18 of the 21 towns with balanced marketplaces had high centrality scores (13 or more different town functions) and 100 of the 107 towns with other types of marketplaces had low centrality scores (fewer than 13 different town functions). Not only did 87 percent of the balanced marketplaces have the right kind of setting--a major commercial town--but the largest commercial towns in the highlands all had the predicted type of marketplace--a balanced one. Deviations occurred largely in the southern lowlands: most cases of

63

balanced marketplaces located in minor towns were located there, and all of the large towns with the "wrong" kind of marketplace (always middlemen-dominated rather than balanced) were located there.

Only about half of the large marketplaces (those of Level 3 or higher in Table 1) are located in major towns, however. The others are located in small, rural settlements and tend to be dominated by producer-sellers--as do most of the small highland markets. Marketplaces dominated by producer-sellers also have Indian rather than Ladino hinterlands. The major distinguishing feature of all producer-seller markets, in fact, is a very low absolute number of Ladinos around them. Why should this be true? It seems to follow from the fact that Indian consumers, unlike Ladino consumers, do not buy large quantities of imported goods and therefore do not support large numbers of local market middlemen. Rather, they tend to buy from local producers, always other Indians and usually of the same local group, or from the ubiquitous long-distance traders (who are also always Indians), who sell domestic goods at cheaper prices than do sendentary middlemen. Middlemen functions--bulking, selecting, grading items by quality--are simply not appreciated by Indian consumers, who perceive these functions as merely adding to retail price.

Given Indian consuming patterns, what accounts for the very large (Levels 2 and 3) producer-seller (Type 2) marketplaces? I found that all of them, as opposed to all minor marketplaces, have large numbers of vendors in them (50 percent or more of all vendors) selling specialized goods in wholesale quantities to long-distance traders. (The long-distance traders in this case are the buyers rather than the sellers.) Minor marketplaces (Levels 4 and 5) of all types, by contrast, have few wholesalers in them of any kind. Wholesaling, in fact, is the main feature distinguishing major and minor marketplaces, regardless of type. The level of wholesaling in major producer-seller marketplaces, however, is much higher than that in major centers of other types. (San Francisco el Alto provides the only exception, as it does on most dimensions, more than 75 percent of its vendors selling in wholesale quantities.) In major markets of Types 3 and 4 (middlemen-dominated and balanced, respectively), the proportion of sellers who sell wholesale varies from 25 to 50 percent. In all minor marketplaces, fewer than 25 percent sell wholesale; in fact, one usually finds no wholesaling

64

taking place in small markets.

The large rural market centers of Type 2 tend to be concentrated in the central part of western Guatemala, in the area between San Francisco el Alto and the six provincial (administrative) towns surrounding it. The population of this area is dense (and mostly Indian), supports large townships (in both area and population), and specializes in producing artisanal products for market sale (see Smith 1975a). In various publications, I have termed this the core area of western Guatemala. In the remaining highland area, surrounding the core (which I have termed the periphery), populations are sparser, townships are smaller, and fewer peasants specialize in producing market commodities. Rural marketplaces in the periphery are mostly small. The production and population factors cannot be considered independent causes of the market patterns, since the market patterns also influence production and population distribution. I have attempted to explain the complex of factors creating a core-periphery division of labor and division of market types in other publications (Smith 1975b, 1977, 1978). Here I merely note that patterns of peasant production and population distribution strongly influence size and type of local marketplace.

We now have the economic and ethnographic elements to construct a theory that will account for marketplace specialization in western Guatemala. First, where there are many peasants around a market center, that center will be dominated by producer-sellers. Whether it is large or small will depend on the economic characteristics of the township holding the marketplace. If the peasants of the township produce mostly subsistence goods, gain most of their income from wages, or the township is very small, the market will usually be small; but if many peasants in the township specialize in producing market commodities, the market will usually be large. Second, where there are large numbers of plantations or export-producers in the producing hinterland of a center, that center will be dominated by middlemen. It the market is large, it will be in a large plantation town; if it is small, it will be in a small plantation town (or else it will be very recently established). Third, where there are substantial numbers of both peasants and nonpeasants near a center, that center will have both producer-sellers and middlemen; that is, it will be balanced. One usually finds substantial numbers of

65

peasants associated with nonpeasants in Guatemala only around large highland towns.[6]

What these elements tell us is that Guatemalan marketplaces mirror the supply and demand characteristics of their immediate hinterlands quite precisely. If many people in a market hinterland produce goods that require distribution through a marketplace, their marketplace will have many people selling their own products. If, on the other hand, people in a market hinterland do not produce for the marketplace, their markets will have mostly sellers of goods that come from other places, and these sellers will naturally be middlemen. And if there are both many producers and many nonproducers near a market, the market must accomodate both groups.

The pattern of supply and demand is closely related to the ethnic identity of Guatemalans because of basic differences in their economic lives. Indians tend to be rural producers, while Ladinos tend to be urban consumers--unless they are rural producers for the export market. Even where Ladinos live in small, highland communities, their relationship to the market differs substantially from that of Indians who live in similar communities. Because such Ladinos rarely sell their goods in marketplaces, their communities support very small marketplaces that carry imported goods, if they support marketplaces at all. I found no highland Ladino community with a "normal" highland marketplace. In fact, most Ladinos in the highlands do not live in small rural communities. They are the "town-building" element, as many Guatemalan specialists have noted, and as such they form the commercial core of all major highland towns. Because towns have to be fed, yet few Ladinos are food producers, one never finds a major highland town that does not have a large Indian hinterland that produces its food. The only area where major towns do not have large Indian hinterlands is the southern lowland area. The towns in this area are fed by large numbers of long-distance traders from the Indian highlands.

V. CORRELATING MARKETPLACE FUNCTIONS AND LEVELS

Making sense of a regional marketing system with five levels of centers (by size or centrality) and four types of marketplaces (by seller composition) would be quite difficult. Fortunately, I was able to reduce these distinctions to more manageable dimensions (three market levels and two market types) for my regional analysis of market relations by thinking through the functional aspects of the market variation I had found. The four marketplace types, it should be noted, had been produced by an essentially arbitrary cut along a continuum of seller-type proportions. I had no reason to consider this to be the only or even the most relevant way to group varied marketplaces, when I turned to consideration of market performance. It was just a simple way to look for the associations which could ultimately explain how Guatemalan marketplaces functioned. No elaborate explanation is needed for dropping the two lower levels in the market hierarchy (Levels 4 and 5) from the regional analysis of the system. Only the top three levels of centers played a role in the regional redistribution of goods; smaller centers had only local significance.

Other simplifying assumptions needed to carry out the regional analysis were equally straight forward. I could safely set aside the distinctive seller composition of San Francisco el Alto (the single Type 1 center) on the grounds that it was also the single Level 1 market in the system and thus could be expected to have distinctive trade characteristics (cf., Table 1, Level 1 and Table 2, Type 1). With respect to functional characteristics, moreover, it was easy to see why San Francisco had emerged as a distinct marketplaces "type." As the major rural marketplace in the region, it was also the center for wholesale exchanges between long-distance traders, the most prominent sellers in that center. Insofar as location was concerned, the single Level 1 marketplace presented no problems of analysis: it was unquestionably the market center of the region; and it was located centrally in the region.

There was no such easy correspondence between Levels 2 and 3 centers and Types 2, 3, and 4 marketplaces. But considerations of functional similarity did allow me to group Type 3 (middlemen-dominated) and Type 4 (balanced) market centers into a single category. My rationale was that the wholesaling operations taking place in Type 3 (middlemen) and Type 4 (balanced) centers--as opposed to those taking place in type 2 (producer-seller) centers--was very similar. The only thing distinguishing Type 4 from Type 3 centers was that the former had many producer-sellers who sold retail, while the latter lacked such sellers, which they made up for with larger numbers of long-distance traders.

The explanation for the variation between Types 3 and 4 centers was simple. Large Type 4 centers were urban marketplaces located in the highlands; they had plenty of producer-sellers in their hinterlands who could supply them with basic foods. Large Type 3 centers, in contrast, were urban marketplaces located in the plantation lowlands, where few producer-sellers lived. They relied on a larger proportion of long-distance traders for much of their their basic food provisioning. With respect to redistributive functions, however, Type 3 and Type 4 centers in the region were virtually identical. In both types of centers, local, sedentary middlemen with large stocks of imported goods were the major wholesalers who supplied the smaller marketplaces in their hinterlands with goods. Thus both Type 3 and Type 4 centers were important in the downward distribution of imports.

Major producer-dominated marketplaces (Type 2 in Table 2) had very different wholesaling characteristics.[7] The wholesalers in these centers were buyers rather than sellers--long-distance traders who bought up large quantities of local goods for resale in other major marketplaces. Thus, the goods wholesaled in major producer-seller markets were destined to flow up the market hierarchy to the major redistribution centers dominated by local middlemen, or simply outward--to any market center, regardless of level, directly served by long-distance traders. San Francisco el Alto was a special variant of this type. The sellers in San Francisco were primarily (75 percent) long-distance traders, who had bought goods in other major producer-seller markets and resold them in San Francisco to other long-distance traders who would take them to different areas of the country.

From this perspective, then, major marketplaces fall into two broad categories: bulking centers (Types 1 and 2), always located in rural areas, through which goods enter market channels for distribution to other high-level centers; and bulk-breaking or dispersing centers (Types 3 and 4), which receive goods from the bulking centers and disperse them to low-level centers. In other words, rural bulking centers channel goods up and out to high-level marketplaces, while urban bulk-breaking centers channel goods down and out to low-level marketplaces. The bulk-breaking centers subdivide into highland and lowland variants, the former having many retailers who are local producer-sellers, and the latter having many retailers who are long-distance traders. This differentiation

68

(and that which distinguishes Type 3 and 4 markets) stems from hinterland characteristics and does not affect redistributive functions.

I should note once again that rural, bulking marketplaces provide arenas for much more wholesaling than do urban, bulk-breaking marketplaces, evidence that the rural centers are oriented primarily to buyers who are traders rather than to final consumers. Those with high centrality values derive those high values mainly from the goods bulked in them for later redistribution. Had I counted only those goods sold to local consumers in my centrality indices, I would have found little difference between major and minor Type 2 (producer-seller) marketplaces. Like minor marketplaces, major producer-seller marketplaces carry small quantities of goods for local consumption. Also like minor marketplaces, virtually all major producer-seller marketplaces meet only one day per week.

The major urban marketplaces in both lowland and highland areas (Types 3 and 4) are dominated by local middlemen. These vendors normally operate daily in permanent market stalls, similar to little shops, and provision both local urban consumers and small-scale middlemen who sell in the minor marketplaces nearby. They are themselves provisioned by long-distance traders who come to them from rural bulking markets, by their own buying trips to rural bulking centers, and by trucks from the largest urban centers of the country (Guatemala City, Quezaltenango, and several large towns in the lowlands). Unlike sellers in rural bulking centers, urban middlemen carry a wide variety of goods imported from all parts of Guatemala. Because many of these imports are too specialized to support traders in lower-level centers, urban middlemen sell the largest portion of these goods retail rather than wholesale. Consequently, the urban bulk-breaking centers draw final consumers from wide hinterlands, while the rural bulking centers draw only traders from long distances.

So far I have distinguished two kinds of marketplaces by their economic settings and functions. One kind of marketplace (Types 1 and 2) is rural, is supplied by producer-sellers or by long-distance traders carrying locally produced goods, and functions to provision major urban centers as well as the local rural populace. The rural populace that both supplies and is supplied by this kind of market is almost entirely Indian. Given the functional characteristics

69

of these major marketplaces, I have termed them Rural
Bulking Centers (RBCs). The other kind of marketplace
(Types 3 and 4) is urban, is supplied from a wide
variety of sources and thus holds a great variety of
consumer goods, and functions to provision minor market
centers in its hinterland as well as the local urban
populace. (In fact, the nine Level 2 marketplaces of
this kind are located in the nine largest towns of
western Guatemala, whose location at the nodes of
warehousing and transport clearly facilitates local and
regional redistribution.) The urban populace in most
of these centers is almost entirely Ladino, though the
market middlemen are mostly Indians. To distinguish
these major marketplaces from the others, I have termed
them Ladino Market Towns (LMTs).

Normally, we expect to find that all high-level
centers redistribute goods to nearby low-level centers
and that they have equally important retail and
wholesale functions. In western Guatemala, however,
these expectations hold only for LMTs. Obversely, we
normally do not expect to find high-level marketplaces
bulking local goods for distribution to other
high-level marketplaces, nor do we expect these centers
to have weakly developed local retail functions.
Nevertheless, that describes western Guatemala's RBCs.
Let us now consider what these findings tell us about
the marketing economy of western Guatemala.

Essentially, western Guatemala has not only two
very different kinds of producing and consuming
economies, related to the ethnic/class divisions of the
region, but it also has two very different kinds of
market economies, also related to the ethnic/class
divisions of the region (and to the different producing
and consuming economies). This fact, together with the
finding that western Guatemala has nearly twice as many
high-level marketplaces (Levels 2 and 3) as one finds
in "normal" central-place hierarchies, suggest that
there are two basic central-place systems in the
region, related to each other in a non-hierarchical
pattern. One system, consisting of the RBCs (including
San Francisco el Alto) is associated with rural market
production, long-distance traders, and the upward (or
outward) redistribution of goods. The other system,
consisting of the LMTs (including Quezaltenango) is
associated with urban market provisioning, trucking,
and the downward redistribution of goods.

In other publications I have described how these
two systems relate to each other spatially and

70

hierarchically (see Smith 1972b, 1975a). Essentially I found one central-place model describing the spatial pattern of LMTs (the K=4 pattern) and another model describing the relationship of RBCs to LMTs (the K=3 pattern).[8] The RBCs or major producer-seller centers "act" as low-level centers in this pattern, inasmuch as they are oriented to three "higher-level" LMTs. In some respects, then, all major LMTs (Levels 2 or 3) can be considered the Level 2 centers of the region, while all major RBCs (Levels 2 and 3) can be considered the Level 3 centers of the region. I should point out, however, that there is no independent spatial patterning of RBCs--they form a network rather than a hierarchy when considered independently of LMTs. This finding should not surprise us, since it is the movement of long-distance traders who ultimately integrate the two systems and they operate in non-hierarchical patterns. The hierarchy of the system is given only by the LMTs--the urban centers of the region.

Let me now review the procedures I used to differentiate market types, which allowed me to explain the spatial patterning of marketplaces in western Guatemala. The measures I used for discriminating among marketplaces were simple ones, each of which reduced a great deal of information to a few crucial elements. The first and most basic measure was that of size or level in the marketing hierarchy. But the information contained in this measure, while important and necessary for all aspects of the analysis, was not sufficient to account for either the layout or the functioning of Guatemala's market economy. To achieve the latter result, I also had to consider the seller composition of marketplaces. This measure involved only a simple trichotomization of sellers by their functions, which could be used to categorize market centers by dominant seller type (leading to four basic marketplace types), on the first step and an even simpler dichotomization of commodity movement, which could be used to categorize market centers by wholesale function (leading to two wholesale marketplace types), on the second step. But while simple, this procedure divided market centers into two groups that made sense in terms of Guatemala's production characteristics, ethnic characteristics, rural-urban characteristics, and trading (wholesaling versus retailing) characteristics. This particular method is flexible in application, in that it can take into account any special features of a given market economy to group marketplaces with similar functional characteristics, regardless of what those functional characteristics

71

might be. It also helps illuminate certain economic features of a market economy that account for its functioning.

To my knowledge, this procedure has not heretofore been used to group central places. I developed it simply on the logic of market function and location in the Guatemalan context. Being quite frankly surprised at how well this procedure explained the unusual centrality characteristics (and locational patterns) of Guatemalan marketplaces, my initial reaction was merely relief that it worked. Now, however, I see it as a basic procedure that should be necessary for making sense of markets in most agrarian societies. Agrarian markets are rarely simple retail supply centers, they are also centers for wholesale redistribution through mobile traders. As such, they should have characteristics that differ from urban central places, whose suppliers are not so mobile.

VI. CONCLUDING REMARKS

Central-place theory is a theory of retail distribution centers, not a theory of wholesale distribution centers. So it is not surprising that it could not, in the strict sense, predict the locational relationship of retail/wholesale markets in western Guatemala. Once wholesale functions were taken into account and the economic relationship between wholesale and retail centers deduced, however, a particular locational pattern could be found. One might generalize beyond western Guatemala to suggest the following modifications of central-place theory. If some market centers are primarily wholesale and others are primarily retail in nature, service relations rather than centrality values will determine their locational relationships. And if wholesale centers exist for bulking rural goods to feed the towns of a system, which themselves produce little for redistribution, one would expect the rural bulking centers to be located in a regular pattern in relation to the towns in order to service them. Finally, if these wholesale centers not only bulk foodstuffs for the town but also specialized goods for a whole region, to be distributed by mobile retail traders, their centrality values (even of just bulked goods) will not be strictly determined by location.

It is also important to note that the measurement procedures utilized here made use of the information that the two major ethnic groups of Guatemala, Indians

72

and Ladinos, play significantly different roles in the economy. Ladinos are concentrated in urban centers, and their centers reflect the fact that Ladinos control certain aspects of the economy--transportation, storage, import-export wholesaling, and the like--as well as the political structure. Indians, on the other hand, almost by definition, live in rural areas and produce goods to feed the urban Ladino population. The distribution of their major centers (the RBCs) clearly reflects the economic roles of Indian producers and Indian long-distance traders in the Guatemalan economy. Had the basic economic differences of Indians and Ladinos in Guatemala been ignored, even a successful application of a "regular" central-place model would have been seriously misleading about the nature and the degree of economic integration in the region.

The main point to be made from this study, however, is that marketplaces in agrarian societies must be distinguished analytically from one another not merely by size but also by function. Wherever a dense network of rural marketplaces exists, it is almost always found in association with urban or elite centers--places that more often consume than produce domestic market goods. Urban centers usually also hold marketplaces, sometimes periodic ones, but these marketplaces are not simply larger or more complex versions of rural marketplaces. Their main functions are to feed large urban populations and, secondarily, to service small rural marketplaces with urban or imported goods. Rural marketplaces, by contrast, exist primarily as centers for peasants to sell their goods, a good part of which are destined for urban consumers. Only secondarily do they exist to provision peasant consumers, who usually strive to provision themselves in basic commodities.

Retailing and wholesaling goes on in both rural and urban centers, but these functions are different in each: goods retailed in rural marketplaces are usually both local goods and urban imports; goods retailed in urban marketplaces are usually only rural products, because other distribution channels (shops and other permanent establishments) handle goods imported into the region. The goods wholesaled in rural marketplaces are destined to be carried to consumers everywhere in the region, and each major rural center bulks only local specialties for redistribution. But the wholesaling that takes place in urban marketplaces is much less specialized; these marketplaces bulk goods

73

from everywhere in the region but then redistribute them only to the small, dependent marketplaces in their local hinterlands. Given these rather significant functional differences, we cannot understand the systemic patterning of rural and urban marketplaces in a regional economy without giving close attention to wholesaling as well as retailing, the special demands of different consuming populations, and the variety of market channels that exist outside the periodic marketplace system.

The claims that I make here are hardly controversial, but few students of regional marketing systems build these basic distinctions into their analyses. I hope that my procedures, developed by trial and error after I did fieldwork--because I, too, assumed that a marketplace is a marketplace and gave little thought to different types of marketplaces--will spare others the time that I invested in figuring out the basic (and now obvious) dynamics of a regional marketing system integrating rural producing areas and urban consuming centers.

ACKNOWLEDGMENTS

The framework for this study was first developed to answer anthropological questions by G. William Skinner (1964, 1965). My study followed Skinner's theoretical lead, but was novel with respect to methodology. I had the good fortune of working with both G. William Skinner and William O. Jones when analyzing my data. I thank both of them for their tolerance of my unorthodox approach to economic and central-place measurement, as well as for their insistence that I make all my assumptions and reasoning explicit. A full description of the measurement procedures used in analyzing the Guatemalan market data can be found in my dissertation (Smith 1972a).

NOTES

1. This paper is an abridged version of a paper that will appear in RESEARCH IN ECONOMIC ANTHROPOLOGY, 1985. An early version of this paper was delivered at a conference on Methods and Measurements in Anthropology in 1975. The present version was prepared for delivery at the annual meeting of the Society for Economic Anthropology, Davis, California,

April 1984.

2.   Characteristic of all regular central-place
      patterns are at least two hierarchical levels of
      market centers, an even distribution of all
      centers in each level of the hierarchy, and a
      regular orientation of smaller centers to one or
      more large centers such that small centers
      nest within the hinterlands of
      progressively larger centers. Around each
      center is a hexagonal tributary area or
      hinterland to which the center provides
      services (see Berry 1967, Marshall 1969).

3.   Guatemala's population is more than 50 percent
      Mayan Indian (socially recognized as such).
      The remaining people in Guatemala have
      assimilated Guatemalan national culture,
      whether as European immigrants, as
      products of European and Indian biological
      mixture, or as Indians wishing to change their
      social identity. All of the latter are
      considered "Ladinos" in Guatemala.

4.   In order to take wholesaling into account, I
      began with six seller-type categories, rather
      than three, distinguishing each of the three
      types described here into retail and wholesale
      vendors. Because I used the marketing chain
      data (based on three seller types) in this part
      of the analysis, and the wholesale/retail data
      (based on two seller types) later, I do not
      elaborate here on how I actually described each
      seller type along two dimensions. Anyone wishing
      to use these methods, however, should consider
      two dimensions of each vendor: place in the
      marketing chain, and retail versus wholesale
      selling orientation (see Smith 1972a).

5.   It is noteworthy that new marketplaces in
      western Guatemala are always founded by
      middlemen and only after it is clear that such
      centers will thrive do producer-sellers begin
      attending them with regularity. There are no
      marketplaces oriented strictly to local
      exchanges.

6.   Major towns are usually found in townships that
      are predominantly Ladino in the center but
      largely Indian in the rural area. Thus, one is
      unlikely to find a major town in an all-

Ladino or an all-Ladino township. No major
highland towns have only Ladinos in their rural
hinterland. One suspects that a major town
outside the plantation area needs a large rural
Indian population to support it.

7. In fact, I have more elaborate data on
wholesaling than reported here, since I
categorized all seller types not only by
their location in the marketing chain of the
commodities they sold, but also by whether or
not they sold in wholesale or retail quantities
(see Smith 1972a).

8. The basic difference between $K=3$ and $K=4$
resides in the way low-level centers nest
within the hinterlands of high-level centers.
In a $K=3$ system, sometimes called the
"marketing" pattern, each lower-level çenter
is partially dependent on three higher-level
centers, whereas in a $K=4$ system, called the
"traffic" pattern, each lower-level center
is partially dependent on two higher-level
centers. There is a different pyramidal
sequence of market centers at each level in these
different patterns (see Christaller [1966] and
Marshall [1969]).

REFERENCES CITED

Berry, Brian J.L.
    1967   Geography of Market Centers and Retail
            Distribution. Englewood Cliffs, N.J.:
            Prentice-Hall.

Christaller, Walter
    1966   Central Places in Southern Germany.
            Translated by C.W. Baskin. Englewood
            Cliffs, N.J.: Prentice-Hall

Marshall, John U.
    1969   The Location of Service Towns: An Approach
            to the Analysis of Central Place Systems.
            Toronto: University of Toronto, Department
            of Geography.

Skinner, G. William
    1964   "Marketing and Social Structure in Rural
            China, Part I." Journal of Asian Studies
            24:3-43.

1965   "Marketing and Social Structure in Rural China, Part II." Journal of Asian Studies 24:195-228.

Smith, Carol A.
1972a   The Domestic Marketing System in Western Guatemala: An Economic, Locational, and Cultural Analysis. Ph.D. dissertation, Stanford University.

1972b   "Market Articulation and Economic Stratification in Western Guatemala." Food Research Institute Studies 11:203-233.

1975a   "Examining Stratification Systems Through Peasant Marketing Arrangements: An Application of Some Models from Economic Geography." Man, N.S. 10:95-122.

1975b   "Production in Western Guatemala: A Test of von Thunen and Boserup." In Stuart Plattner (ed.) Formal Methods in Economic Anthropology. Special Publications, American Anthropologist, No. 4. Pages 5-37.

1976   "Causes and Consequences of Central-place Types in Western Guatemala." in Carol A. Smith (ed.) Regional Analysis, Volume I: Economic Systems. New York: Academic Press. Pages 255-300.

1977   "How Marketing Systems Affect Economic Opportunity in Agrarian Societies." In Rhoda Halperin and James Dow (eds.) Peasant Livelihood: Studies in Economic Anthropology and Cultural Ecology. New York: St. Martin's Press. Pages 117-146.

1978   "Beyond Dependency Theory: National and Regional Patterns of Underdevelopment in Guatemala." American Ethnologist 5:574-617.

MARKETPLACE DEVELOPMENT IN THE GAMBIA RIVER BASIN

Gordon Appleby, Planning Division O.M.V.G.

Marketplaces are strategic institutions. Here, for a few hours a day, while people come together to trade and to transact other businesses, one can see at a glance what crops people grow, what crafts they make, what goods they buy, and what services they require. One can also inquire into which goods come from the countryside, which from town, and from which towns. Over the course of a week or two, one can visit enough markets in an area to be able to piece together a picture of the rural economy and the relationship between town and country. In short, markets are strategic in that here one can quickly appraise the regional economy.

Marketplaces are also bewildering phenomenon. Most last only a few hours. People are constantly coming and going. An extraordinary number of items is available in any market, and individual sellers often seem to have put any jumble of goods together into an array. Even the distinction between buyer and seller blurs. It just seems impossible to sort out all this activity in the few hours any market is functionning.

Fortunately, both the theory and the methods necessary to make sense out of this seeming chaos are available. Professor Skinner has elucidated the bases of marketing development in his pioneering application of Christallerian central-place theory to the Chinese marketing system (1964-65) and, subsequently, in his extended reanalyses of those systems (1977). Professor Smith (1972, 1976) has operationalized these concepts for fieldworkers. Together, their work not only indicates what marketing systems 'should' look like, it also provides the means of finding out what they do look like and how they operate. Further, where the findings do not accord with the expectations, their work provides valuable leads for understanding the divergences.

This paper looks at the markets in two areas of the Gambia River Basin in West Africa. After a brief review of some central-place hypotheses and a quick overview of the region, the paper focusses on three concerns: the evolution of marketplaces, the composition of marketplaces, the operation of the marketing system. The comparison of two related, but different areas is intended to highlight similarities and differences in terms of central-place expectations. The aim is to assess the markets in each area in order to describe the regional economies there, and along the way, to reorient usual understandings of marketplace development.

I.   CENTRAL-PLACE THEORY

Central-place theory provides some very clear expectations about the evolution and organization of retail trade.   The theory posits that trade intensifies in direct relationship with demand density, which is a complex function of population density, commercialization and transport.   In the short run, increasing demand density means that centers will supply more specialized goods--in central-place jargon, goods of a higher threshhold--and increase their periodicity.   Thus, in the longer run, demand density underlies a succession to more permanent commercial institutions.   Periodic markets appear on the landscape, these evolve into daily markets, and finally markets give way to shops and stores. At the same time the competition among centers for consumer patronage leads to a regular spatial patterning among centers in the region (Christaller 1966).

Classic central-place theory allows for a great deal of variation and complexity in actual patterns. Inasmuch as consideration is limited to retail trade, all centers perform the same function: retail distribution.   But the goods available in the markets of any two regions may be completely different. Indeed, even within a region, markets at the same level may not offer all the same goods if, for example, all things--population, commercialization, transport--are not equal.   In this instance, however, there are reasonable expectations for an orderly addition of goods to centers inventories.   As demand density increases, higher-order goods appear, which is to say that markets in areas with greater demand density will offer all goods available in less well endowed areas as well as an additional assortment of more specialized goods.   It is this regularity that underlies central-place methods based on vendor counts (Smith 1972).

Anthropological studies of regional marketing systems have confirmed several central-place expectations and refined others.   The very existence of marketplaces does imply a particular demand density, standard of living, or level of economic development.

80

And, differences in the goods available in the markets of neighboring areas do reflect differences in demand density. Nonetheless, it must be added that wholesaling is a usual rural market function, and that urban and rural markets constitute parts of the same system, despite differences in periodicity. Finally, goods at wholesale move through that hierarchy in specific ways, but the individual patterns must be discovered. It is these expectations that will be examined in two areas of the Gambia River Basin.

II. BACKGROUND

The Gambia River Basin is a natural hydrographic region defined by the drainage area of the Gambia River (Map 1). The River flows 1,200 kilometers from its source 15 kilometers north of Labé, in the Fouta Djallon, to its embouchement at Banjul, on the Atlantic Ocean. Along its way, the river drains nearly 78,000 square kilometers of territory: 7,000 square kilometers in Guinea, 60,000 square kilometers in Senegal, and 11,000 square kilometers in the Gambia. The river is so flat throughout the Gambia and the western part of Senegal Oriental that tidal influences are felt half-way up its course, to Goloumbou, 536 kilometers upstream of Banjul. The terrain becomes hillier in southern Senegal Oriental, near Kedougou, and truly mountainous in the Fouta Djallon of Guinea, where peaks rise to 1,150 meters above sea level.

Climate changes as one moves north from the Fouta Djallon. The entire region is marked by a short, erratic rainy season from June until September. However, rainfall levels are appreciably higher in the south than in the north. On average, the Fouta Djallon receives 1,750 mm of rainfall each year, southern Senegal-Oriental about 1,300 mm, and central Senegal Oriental about 900 mm. Temperatures are warm year-round, peaking just before and after the rains at 30 C, with a minima of 14 C in December, January, and February. Temperatures are lower during the cool months in the Fouta Djallon, and higher during the hot months in Senegal Oriental.

Population densities vary widely throughout the basin. In the Fouta Djallon, densities are heaviest around Labé, where there are more than 50 people per square kilometer, and thinnest in the northern frontier with Senegal, where there are less than 10 people per square kilometer (Suret-Canale 1970: 148). Senegal Oriental is the least densely populated area in the

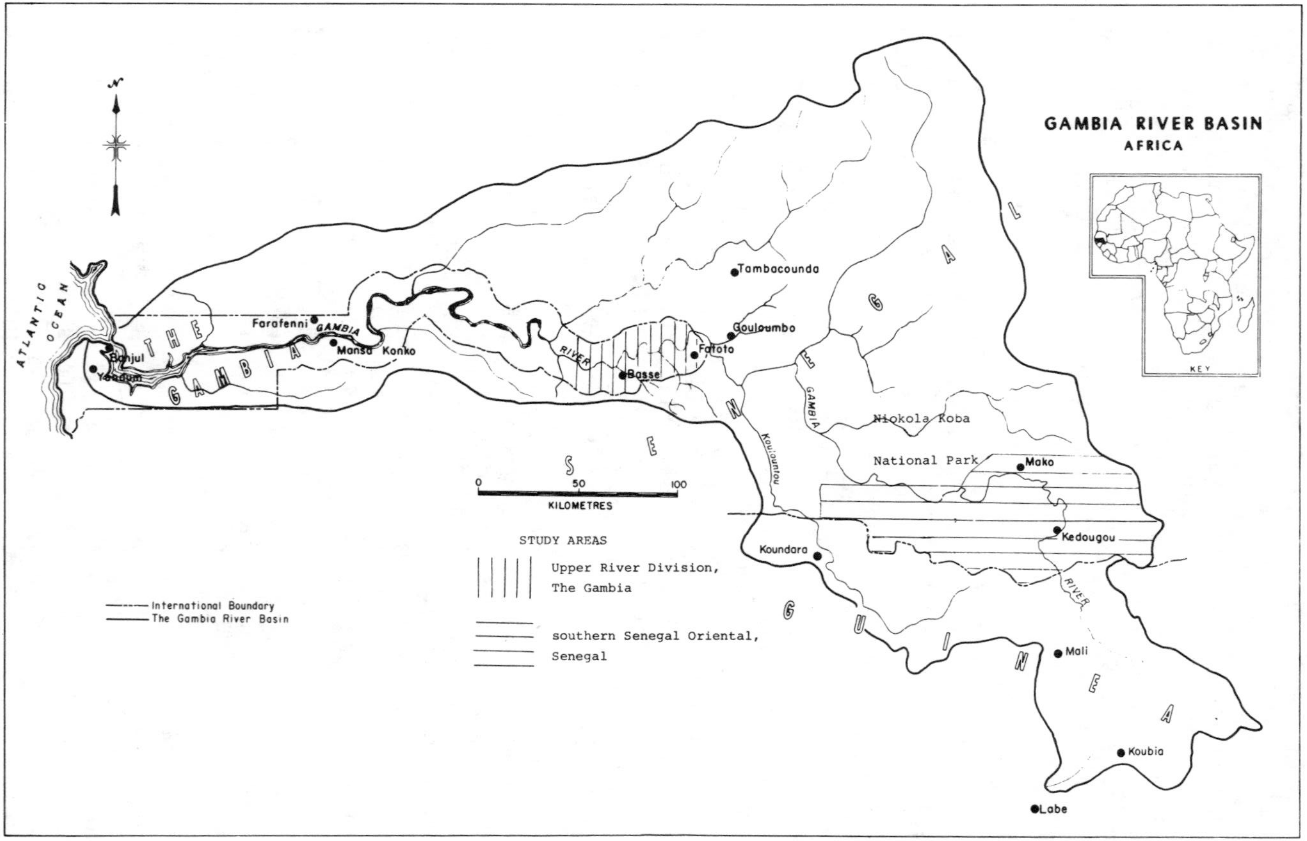

GAMBIA RIVER BASIN

AFRICA

STUDY AREAS

Upper River Division, The Gambia

southern Senegal Oriental, Senegal

KILOMETRES

0   50   100

------ International Boundary

——— The Gambia River Basin

Map 1. Gambia River Basin, Africa

82

basin, with less than 5 people per square kilomater. In eastern Gambia, the density averages 44 people per square kilometer. But here, too, there are large variations between local areas: densities on the south bank of Upper River Division average 52 people per square kilometer, while those on the northern bank average only 32.

The same ethnic groups are found throughout the basin, although their distribution is notable. The Fouta Djallon is largely Peul, with some Jahanke and Dialanke populations in the east. Southern Senegal Oriental is Peul and Mandink (or Malinke), with significant pockets of smaller groups such as the Bassari, Bedik, Jahanke, and Dialanke. Central Senegal Oriental is largely Mandink and Peul, with a fair number of Serahuli and Wolof villages. This same distribution characterizes the neighboring Gambia.

The same crops are also found throughout the basin. People depend upon fonio, millet, sourghum, or maize for their consumption, though swamp rice is an important cultivar along the lower course of the river. Livestock is everywhere important. A major difference is that Gambia and central Senegal Oriental compose part of the peanut basin, the area which has produced groundnuts for export since the Nineteenth Century.

The transport system developed in accord with the needs of this export trade. In the Gambia, peanuts were early on evacuated to Banjul through a chain of riverine ports. The road system remained poor until recently: the main south bank road was paved to Mansa Konko only in the 1960's, reaching Basse in 1968. The north bank is served to this day by a good all-weather dirt road. There are no bridges across the Gambia River; transit across the river is by ferry. In Senegal, a single-line railroad between Dakar and Bamako, Mali, carried most of the peanut trade since early in this century. A network of paved primary roads was built in the western portion of the peanut basin only after Independance. Indeed, the link from Kaolack to Tambacounda, the regional capital of Senegal Oriental, and thence south to Velingara, in Casamance, was not completed until the 1980's. The road from Tambacounda to Kedougou is still paved only half way, and there are no paved roads in southern Senegal Oriental, apart from two streets in Kedougou itself.

This comparison of marketplace development and operation focuses on two areas within the basin:

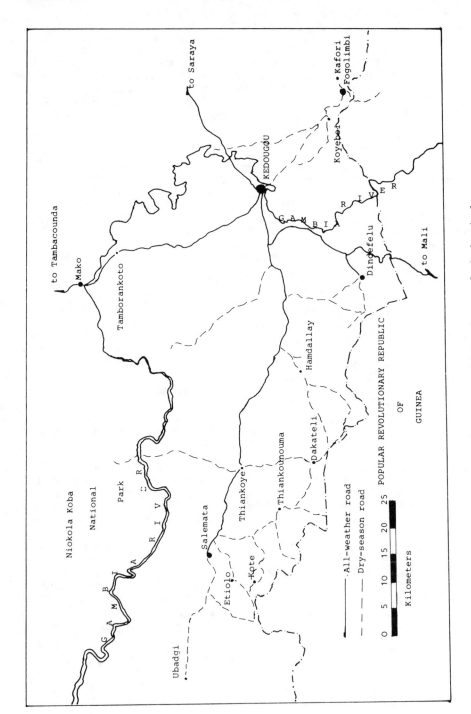

Map 2. Marketplaces in Southern Senegal Oriental.

southern Senegal Oriental, which depends on the town of Kegoudou (Map 2), and Upper River Division in the Gambia, which is provisioned from Basse (Map 3). Both areas have markets, and they are close enough to share many characteristics. At the same time, they contrast in population density, commercialization, and transport, so that they constitute a natural experiment on the forces underlying marketing development today.

III. THE DEVELOPMENT OF MARKETPLACES

The factors underlying marketplace development-- population density, commercialization, transport efficiency--pattern quite neatly in these two areas. Upper River Division with 41 people per square km is more heavily populated than southern Senegal Oriental, with only 5 people per square kilometer. The people in both areas farm and raise cattle. But only the Gambian farmers produce their own subsistence foods and grow peanuts for export, thereby earning significant amounts of cash. There is no cash crop in southern Senegal Oriental, where transport is also far less readily available. In fact, there are more owners of bush taxis in the hamlets around Fatoto in Upper River Division than there are in all of southern Senegal Oriental. Clearly, the central-place expectation is that markets would develop earlier and more fully in Upper River Division than southern Senegal Oriental.

In fact, just the reverse is true (Table 1). The first markets were established in Senegal Oriental in the late 1940's, and most markets now there were founded before 1970. By contrast, there were no rural marketplaces in Upper River Division until 1979, and almost half the markets there were founded in the past year or two. In short, contrary to expectations, the area least favored for marketplace development actually established markets well before the better endowed area.

The development of markets in southern Senegal Oriental has a unexceptional story line. Peul from the Fouta Djallon have been colonizing this zone since at least the turn of this century. Both the authochones and the immigrants became seasonal labor migrants to the peanut basin. The number of people involved in this movement are nearly unbelievable: in 1912, there were an estimated 5,000 labor migrants, that is, between a sixth to a seventh of the entire population of the area (David 1980:162), which may be unduly high because of the difficulty of distinguishing Guineans

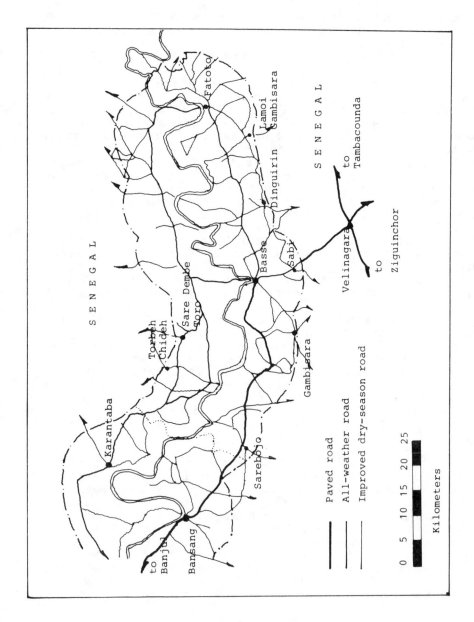

Map 3. Marketplaces in Upper River Division, The Gambia.

TABLE 1: Marketplaces in Upper River Division and Southern Senegal Oriental.

Area	Date founded	Market day	Ethnicity	Remarks
Upper River Division				
Basse Santa Su	Colonial period	Everyday	All	
Fatoto	Colonial period	Everyday	All	
Sabi	1979	Sunday	Serehuli	
Dinguiri	1979	Thursday	Serehuli/Fular	
Gambi Sara	1981	Monday	Serehuli	
Sarengai	1982	Monday	Fular (Peul)	
Sare Bojo	1983	Tuesday	Fular	
Gambissari Lamoi	1983	Saturday	Serehuli	
Sari Demba Toro	1983	Tuesday	Fular	Inactive in rainy season
Senegal Oriental				
Kédougou	Colonial period	Everyday	Mixed	
Fogolimbi	1946	Thursday	Fular/Diallonke	
Dindefelo	1947	Sunday	Fular/Bassari	
Salemata	1953	Tuesday	Fular/Bassari	Thursday schedule until 70s
Hamdallay	1956	Tuesday	Fular/Serehuli	
Kote	1956	Monday	Fular/Bassari	Thursday schedule until 70s
Mako	1957	Saturday	Fular/Malinké	
Lande	1958	Thursday	Fular/Bedik	Failed in 1979
Udagi	1961	Saturday	Bassari	
Tuba Nyeneniki	1965	Saturday	Fular	Failed in 1966
Thiankounouma	1970	Thursday	Fular/Jakanke	
Dakateli	1979	Wednesday	Fular/Diallonke	
Koyeboi	1983	Sunday	Fular/Diallonke	
Kafori	1983	Monday	Fular/Diallonke	
Thiankoye	1984	Thursday	Fular	Earlier attempts in 70s failed
Tamborankoto	1984	Thursday	Fular	Earlier attempts in 70s failed
Etiolo	1984	Sunday	Bassari	Former site of Salemata market

Table 1. Marketplaces in Upper River Division and Southern Senegal Oriental.

from Senegalese. Even so, the estimate of 750 men in 1926 still represents 3 percent of the entire population.[1] Not only were population density and level of commercialization increasing, but by mid-century there was a revolution in transport as well. Albenque (1970:571,573) appreciated the importance of trucking for the major markets of the area in the mid-1960's. In Fogolimbi, one resident trucker-merchant supplies all imported goods available in that market.[2] The markets at Salemata and Dindefelo were even more dependent on truckers: it was the truckers who come from Kedougou with vendors and their wares that gave these markets their special importance. The smaller markets, which were established later, attracted no outside traders and remained strictly local affairs.

Thus marketing development in southern Senegal Oriental appears to be a natural consequence of increasing demand density. As Albenque (1970) notes, this area was provisioned by itinerant peddlers from Kedougou and Younkounkoun (Guinea) through the 1940's. At that point, village chiefs began petitioning colonial authorities for the permission to establish markets. The Peul, in particular, already had a model for such local action: markets had been established in parts of the Fouta Djallon earlier in this century. But it is the coalescence of greater population, greater commercialization, and better transport for traders that sustained this new institution in Senegal Oriental.

The seemingly natural development of markets in the peripheral area of Southern Senegal Oriental only makes their absence until recently in the core area of the peanut basin--Sine-Saloum, central Senegal Oriental, and the Gambia--even more puzzling. Everything that can be said about the economic history of the Kedougou area is even more true in these areas. What, then, prevented the rise of markets in the core area?

The answer lies in the organization of the peanut trade. This trade is quite old. It dates in the Gambia to the second quarter of the Nineteenth Century, when groundnuts were first shipped to Sierra Leone (Haswell 1975:55). By the mid-Nineteenth Century, the trade was well-established, for the river made possible the evacuation of the crop. In Senegal, by contrast, the expansion of peanut production awaited the imposition of colonial rule and subsequent construction of the railroad. In the last quarter of the Nineteenth Century, peanut production was centered in the north of the country, expanding south into the Sine-Saloum by the turn of the century, and then east into central Senegal Oriental only in the last forty years. Peanuts dominate throughout this zone to this day.

Until the 1960's the peanut trade was in private hands and the same firms dominated this trade in both Senegal and the Gambia. This trade was organized straightforwardly: the firms maintained offices and agents in the interior in order to buy peanuts and sell merchandise. There were in the Gambia, for example, "two kinds of intermediaries: traders and dealers. The trader..dealt in the name and on behalf of company. The dealer was a wholesale customer who took merchandise on credit and sold it on his own account; in most cases he operated in buildings which belonged to the company" (Haswell 1975:75). The companies financed the peanut trade by sending money to traders and dealers just before the season opened, by issuing goods on credit to dealers, and by providing the companies' own traders with goods (pp. 76-77). The dealers and traders, in turn, sold the goods directly to the farmers against their future harvest or to farmers who acted locally as petty traders. In this way, the firms captured all trade: farmers grew peanuts to sell to the merchants for the cash to buy a variety of basic goods imported by those same firms.

The goods involved in this trade constitute an inventory of basic rural purchases. To take but one example, in 1953 the United African Company, Ltd. imported rice, cigarettes, sugar, flour, and tobacco; print cloth, bleached shirtings, woven checks and striped material, and headkerchiefs; hessian bags, cement, sewing machines, enamelware, iron and steel sheets, singlets, footware, shirts, packed medicines, perfumery, and soap (Haswell 1975:78). With the exception of sewing machines and construction materials, this list of imports is not greatly different from what can be found in the markets of the area today.

Despite ups and downs in the international market, the peanut trade ran along these basic lines until Independence. At that point, however, the leaders of the two newly independent countries intervened in the trade. In Senegal, in 1960, the government reorganized farmer cooperatives and set up national marketing agencies. This new marketing system soon became

89

dominant. Government participation grew from 22 percent of the peanut crop in the 1960/61 season to 63 percent by the 1966/67 season (Nelson et al. 1974:274). In the Gambia, similarly, the government invested the Gambia Produce Marketing Board with the sole right to purchase and process peanuts.

With a government monopoly on the peanut trade, the colonial firms lost their export role and with it, the raison d'etre for their network of agencies in the interior. In response, they closed their shops, which left many areas short of basic goods. Nguyen (1978:656) notes that many goods, including burial cloth, were absolutely unavailable once the European firms closed their branch stores in the interior. Thus while rural demand for foodstuffs and merchandise remained strong, government intervention in the wholesale peanut trade inadvertantly disrupted the organization of retail trade, leaving country demand relatively unsatisfied.

The rural response was not long in coming. Periodic rural marketplaces were being established by local people by the mid-1960's. Importantly, the spread of marketplaces across the landscape accords well with central-place expectations. Markets appeared first in the northern peanut basin, which is more densely populated, is more highly commercialized, and has better transport. Subsequently, in the 1970's, markets were established in northern Senegal Oriental and eastern Gambia. Today the countryside is dotted with large, viable rural markets. The only surprise is that most sprang up in just the last five years.

The paradox of marketplace development is thus explained. The peripheral areas, such as southern Senegal Oriental, were very much affected by the peanut trade in that they provided much of the labor. But these areas lie outside the domain of the colonial import-export firms. Thus, they developed markets in natural response to greater demand density. Meanwhile, in the core area, the colonial firms captured all trade through their network of agencies in the interior. However, at Independence, the new governments took over the wholesale peanut trade, and these firms retrenched into the capital cities as importers, leaving the countryside relatively unprovisioned. Soon thereafter, the local populace began founding rural markets in order to fill this need, so that today there exists a reasonably thick system of markets in the core area also.

IV. MARKETPLACE GOODS AND FUNCTIONS

The different historical forces giving rise to markets in the core and the periphery lead to the question of whether or not markets in the two areas are similar in the goods they supply and in the functions they perform.

Unsurprisingly for two regions that are but 150 kilometers apart, the basic inventory of goods in the markets of each region is similar. Allowing for ecological and production differences, the same foodstuffs are available in both areas. Some countrywomen offer products foraged from forests, such as baobab leaves and monkey fruit. Others bring in garden crops, such as dried okra, onions, and tomatoes. And still others bring small quantities of regional staples from their larders--fonio, rice, millet, corn. It is the same for craft goods and merchandise. There are sellers of bamboo mats, straw bowls and covers, rope, and pottery in both areas, as well as vendors of cloth, plastic thongs, enamelware, cosmetics, and used clothes.

At the same time, however, vendor counts reveal important diagnostic differences (Table 2). The amount and range of merchandise available in the markets of Upper River Division is far greater than that in Senegal Oriental. Whereas half of all sellers in the Gambian markets proffer merchandise, barely 20 percent of the Senegalese traders carry such goods. Stated otherwise, foodstuffs dominate in the markets of Senegal Oriental, where on average two-thirds of all sellers proffer local produce, compared to about a quarter of all vendors in Upper River Division.

These differences clearly reflect different standards of living. A significant proportion of the food vendors in the Senegalese markets around Kedougou offer foraged products--boabab leaves, bush yams, monkey fruit--or household products--home-made soap and chalk for spinning, as well as foodstuffs. These goods, though available in the Gambian markets, are not common there. Instead one finds a remarkable assortment of merchandise. There are sellers of used clothes, cosmetics, cloth, hardware, bicycle parts, and enamelware. But only here are there also traders with specialized arrays of pre-recorded casettes, agricultural implements, and Koranic supplies. That more specialized arrays and higher-order goods appear in the markets of Upper River Division but not in those

Figure 2: Marketplace Composition by Functional Category, Upper River
Division and Southern Senegal Oriental

AREA	Number (and percent) of Sellers of Commodities, by Functional Category					
	Food	Goods	Services	Whole-saling	Animals	Total
Senegal Oriental						
Fogolimbi	233 (73%)	31 (10%)	26 (8%)	13 (4%)	16 (5%)	319 (100%)
Dindefelu	79 (56%)	28 (20%)	17 (12%)	9 (6%)	9 (6%)	142 (100%)
Mako	43 (48%)	21 (24%)	13 (15%)	9 (10%)	2 (2%)	88 (99%)
Hamdallay	53 (55%)	23 (24%)	7 (7%)	13 (14%)	Wholesale	96 (100%)
Rural Subtotal	(63%)	(16%)	(10%)	(7%)	(4%)	(100%)
Kédougou town	297 (66%)	96 (21%)	60 (13%)	0	0	453 (100%)
Upper River Division						
Dingiring	109 (29%)	161 (44%)	76 (21%)	0	21 (6%)	367 (100%)
Lamoi	44 (21%)	112 (52%)	52 (24%)	0	6 (3%)	214 (100%)
Sabi	78 (33%)	112 (46%)	37 (16%)	0	11 (5%)	238 (100%)
Gambisara	72 (27%)	127 (48%)	47 (18%)	0	17 (7%)	263 (100%)
Sarabojo	74 (26%)	144 (50%)	47 (16%)	0	23 (8%)	288 (100%)
Rural Subtotal	(27%)	(48%)	(19%)	0	(6%)	(100%)
Basse town	118 (28%)	236 (57%)	63 (15%)	0	0	417 (100%)

Table 2. Marketplace Composition by Functional Category,
Upper River Division and Southern Senegal Oriental.

92

of Senegal Oriental accords well with the central-place expectations for demand density.

It should also be noted that the urban markets resemble the rural markets in their areas more they do each other. To be sure, there are differences between urban and rural markets. Urban markets meet daily, attract more vendors, offer more specialized goods, and lack any wholesaling function. But even so, the urban markets are not distinctively different from the rural markets. In southern Senegal Oriental, Kedougou attracts more vendors than any rural market and offers more merchandise. But the proportion of vendors by commodity type is similar to that in the rural markets: about two-thirds sell food, one-fifth sell merchandise, and a tenth offer different services. The same urban-rural comparability obtains in Upper River Division, though the proportions are different. A quarter of all sellers offer foodstuffs, about half sell merchandise, and a seventh (15%) provide services in both the urban (Basse) and the rural markets. At least for these two regions, the common distinction between urban and rural markets appears to be overdrawn and misleading.[3]

A second major difference concerns wholesaling. There are two types of wholesale trade in Senegal Oriental. The regional wholesale trade involves female urban traders who go out to the larger rural markets with condiments and other cooking supplies that they sell or exchange with farm women for regional staples that will later be retailed in town. This inconspicuous trade helps provision the towns. Meanwhile, an interregional wholesale trade involves local traders and townsmen who bulk commodities in kilo lots for shipment out of the area. In this region, farmers collect forest products for sale to the wholesale buyers--tamarind, honey, and fruit, depending upon the season. In effect, here in the periphery there are cash collectibles rather than cash crops. Together, these two forms of wholesaler trade help families meet their subsistence and consumption needs.

Neither wholesale function appears in the markets of Upper River Division. Peanuts, of course, are monopolized by the government, which forbids this trade in rural marketplaces. But the domestic or regional wholesale trade among women is also absent. There are no urban ladies bulking small amounts of regional staples for retail distribution in town. In other words, these markets are strictly periodic retail centers. They perform no role in the provisioning of regional towns.

The presence or absence of wholesaling, particularly domestic wholesaling, reveals a fundamental difference in regional integration, which relates to the historical context of marketing development. In Senegal Oriental, markets sprang up in response to increasing rural demand density, better transport, and, one may add, growing urban demand for food. The markets therefore not only offered commodities for the country people, they also bulked foodstuffs and other commodities for consumption in town. In Upper River Division, however, markets grew up in the response to unmet rural retail demand after the reorganization of the colonial peanut trade. Contrary to Hodder's expectation that rural markets lose their wholesaling function as they develop (1971:353), the markets in Upper River Division never had such a function. Whether they will develop one remains to be seen.

Finally, it should be noted that despite the differences in market composition and function, the movement of goods through the two systems is strikingly similar and corresponds to that found elsewhere. Generally, farm products and crafts come from the local area only. Imported condiments and foodstuffs may be purveyed by urban traders, usually women, who obtain their stocks in the regional or a higher-level center (Banjul inthe Gambia; Tambacounda or even Dakar in Senegal) or by local residents who usually buy in the regional center of Basse or Kedougou. Merchandise follows the same pattern. Urban based traders obtain supplies in higher-level centers, whereas local traders may replenish their inventories there or in the regional center. Commodity flows, thus, do not appear to be affected by differences in historical, or economical development.

V.   CONCLUSION

In conclusion, markets exist today throughout most of the Gambia River Basin, and there are strong similarities among markets in different parts of the basin. Most notably, the inventory of goods is similar, commodities flow in the same patterns, and the daily urban markets are essentially no different from their periodic rural counterparts. Nonetheless, there are important differences. The markets of Upper River Division offer much more merchandise and artesanry than those of southern Senegal Oriental because of greater

94

demand density. More surprisingly, the Upper River Division markets lack the wholesaling functions that are so important in southern Senegal Oriental, which is due to their recent development in response to unsatisfied rural demand after government intervention in the peanut trade. In fact, that is the biggest surprise: that government intervention inadvertantly sparked thedevolution in retail trade that resulted almost overnight in the proliferation of rural markets.

None of these basic observations of these two areas took very long to discover or to document because the theory and methods necessary for regional analysis are already available. Vendor counts in the markets of each area made manifest the similarities and the anomolies. While accounting for these differences requires some familiarity with the economic and political history of the areas, it was the conceptual and methodological tool kit developed for marketplace study by anthropologists that provided the hypotheses and the means for honing in on the answers. It was, in other words, central-place theory and methods that made possible the study of marketplaces as strategic institutions for rapid rural appraisal. Equally important, this approach has helped clarify the curious relationship between contemporary peasant marketing systems and the earlier export economies that seem to have spawned them.

NOTES

1. Nguyen (1978:655) emphasizes the importance of Guinean navatanes passing through this area on their way to and from the peanut basin. Local labor migrants would, however, seem more important. All navetanes sold their crop in the basin and bought merchandise there. Those transiting would not spend much time or money in southern Senegal Oriental, where prices would necessarily be higher. By contrast, those resident there would return with new desires and the cash to obtain them.

2. This shopkeeper brought in rice, salt, kola, soap, cloth, shoes, basins, sugar, candy, cigarettes, matches, batteries, flashlights, locks, bike parts, razor blades, blueing, perfumes.

3. Hodder (1971:347) remarks that "Perhaps the simplest yet at the same time most significant classification of markets in West Africa is one which distinguishes between periodic and non-periodic (daily or

continuous) markets" because the distinction helps "in the analysis of market types, distribution, processes, and economic functions". In the Gambia River basin, however, this distinction would rend the fabric of local marketing systems.

REFERENCES CITED

Albenque, Alexandra
1970   Les marchés hebdomadaires de la région de Kédougou (Sénégal Oriental). Bulletin de l'Institut Fondamental de l'Afrique Noire, No. 30 (Series B), pp. 558-587.

Christaller, Walter
1966   Central Places in Southern Germany. (Translated by C.W. Baskin.) Englewood Cliffs, N.J.: Prentice-Hall.

David, Philippe
1980   Les Navetanes: Histoire des migrants saisonniers de l'arachide en Senegambie des origines à nos jours. Dakar: Nouvelles Éditions Africains.

Haswell, Margaret
1975   The Nature of Poverty. London: MacMillan.

Hodder, B.W.
1971   Periodic and Daily Markets in West Africa. In The Development of Indigenous Trade and Markets in West Africa. Claude Meillassoux, ed. London: Oxford University Press, pp. 347-358.

Nelson, Harold D. et al.
1974   Area Handbook for Senegal. Washington, D.C.: U.S. Government Printing Office.

Nguyen-van-Chi-Bonnardel, Régine
1978   Vie de Relations au Sénégal: La circulation des biens. Momoire de l'Institute Fondamental d'Afrique Noire, (Dakar), No. 90.

Skinner, G. William
1964   Marketing and Social Structure in Rural China, Part I. Journal of Asian Studies 24:3-43.

1965   Marketing and Social Structure in Rural

China, Part II. _Journal of Asian Studies_ 24:195-228.

1977 _The City in Late Imperial China._ Stanford: Stanford University Press

Smith, Carol A.
1972 _The Domestic Marketing System in Western Guatemala: An Economic, Locational, and Cultural Analysis._ Ph.D. dissertation, Anthropology Department, Stanford University.

1976 _Regional Analysis (Vol. I)._ New York: Academic Press.

Suret-Canale, Jean
1970 _La Republique de Guinée._ Paris: Editions Sociales.

PART TWO

ECONOMIC BEHAVIOR
IN MARKET CONTEXTS

PART TWO

ECONOMIC BEHAVIOR IN MARKET CONTEXTS
Stuart Plattner

The regional, systemic spatial concerns of the central-place theorists in the previous section grew out of a long tradition in economic anthropology. The early culture area theorists also wanted to explain the spatial distribution of social and economic forms on this macro-level of analysis (e.g., Kroeber, 1939). The more micro-level of analysis, consisting of the attempt to make sense of the behaviors of individuals as reasonable decision-makers and problem-solvers in specific social and economic systems, also has a long history. For example Malinowski's diatribe against his straw figure, the "primitive Economic Man", was an attempt to show the native rationality behind exotic economic behavior (1922).

This point of view is represented by the papers in this section, which try to understand the reasons individuals make economic decisions in market contexts. Much of the history of this tradition in economic anthropology can be read as the fieldworkers'defense of the "natives' rationality", against the critique (explicit or implicit) of the natives by Western market rationality. Certainly some of the defense was vacuous, since the picture used of Western economic theory was misinformed or simplistic (the famous example of Herskovits and Knight talking past each other comes to mind)(1952, 1941). On the other hand, much of the defense of the natives' reasons for behaving as they did was a strong attack on the unreality of the basic microeconomic model of individual behavior (e.g., Cancian 1972). Note that "the natives" of the papers included here "are us", meaning the exotic behavior to be explained, or interpreted as reasonable problem-solving, happens to be observed in the United States. The papers in this section draw from some recent theory in economics and in business, and point to an exciting direction for new research.

Acheson tries to explain an apparent paradox of interpersonal behavior in the Maine lobster market. He notes "a good deal of suspicion and tension" in relationships between lobster and the dealers to whom they sell. Like primary producers everywhere, they resent and mistrust the middlemen with whom they must

101

deal. Acheson shows how the distrust is based on the
pervasive ignorance of the fishermen about the causes
of price changes. The fishermen know a good deal about
the market they spend their lives in, but they do
tend to overestimate the price-setting ability of
independent dealers. Acheson quotes one fisherman as
complaining "Them misarble fuckin bahstids have the
whole thing rigged. When we got lobsters, they bring
the price down. When lobster is scarce, they put
the price up higher than hell. Either way, they don't
pay nothing and we don't earn nothin." Acheson
shows how the seasonality and perishability of
the product causes the market price to fluctuate, and
he gives the economic reasons why individuals develop
long-term bilateral relationships with such mistrusted
partners.

Economic anthropologists have been interested in
long-term personalistic economic relationships since
the first studies of primitive trade. Primitive or
tribal trade was usually conducted under the cover of
formalized political partnerships between eminent
individuals, such as in the Kula ring. When people
described similar personal relationships between
traders in agrarian market-dominated societies, this
seemed understandable in vaguely similar terms. Mintz
(1961) and Geertz (1963) made important contributions
when they gave economic and systemic explanations for
market personalism, which they attributed
fundamentally to risk-sharing. Plattner's paper defines
these long-term relationships as one of two contrasting
ways to shop in a market, the other being to search for
the best deal available at that moment with no concern
for past or future. He discusses the attributes of
goods, transactions, and actors which make personalized
trading relationships preferable, and points out the
key importance of information. Plattner goes on to
analyze the infrastructural causes for these
attributes. The result is an explicit theoretical
statement that can be tested with empirical studies.

Byrne asks a similar question: do firms in a
marketplace for fresh produce stock a constant,
identifiable assortment in the face of the variability
of opportunity presented by the seasonal, perishable
nature of fresh produce? Using a set of data gathered
in a year-long study of a public marketplace, he uses
multi-dimensional scaling and cluster analysis
techniques to demonstrate the existence of such market
niches. He shows that the firms cluster into
categories of large-scale fruit and vegetable

102

merchants, and small-scale fruit merchants. The
assortments on the firms' stands are determined by the
functional correspondance of items of produce in the
dining room (i.e., lettuce goes with tomatoes, which go
with green peppers, cucumbers, and other salad items).
Of course, casual observation shows such
correspondances. The value of this quantitative
analysis is the demonstration that the pattern is there
in reality over time, in distinction to the other
intuitively expectable patterns such as short-term
profit seeking.

REFERENCES

Cancian, Frank
    1972   Economic Man and Economic Change, pp. 189-
                199 in Change and Uncertainty in a Peasant
                Economy, Stanford: Stanford University
                Press.

Geertz, Clifford
    1963   Peddlers and Princes: Social Change and
                Economic Modernization in Two Indonesian
                Towns, Chicago: University of Chicago
                Press.

Herskovits, Melville
    1952   Economic Anthropology, New York:Knopf.

    1941   Economics and Anthropology: A Rejoinder.
                Journal of Political Economy, 49:269-278.
                also reprinted in Herskovits 1952,
                Appendix.

Knight, Frank
    1941   Anthropology and Economics, Journal of
                Political Economy, 49:247-268. also
                reprinted in Herskovits 1952, Appendix.

Kroeber, Alfred
    1939   Cultural and Natural Areas of Native North
                America, University of California
                Publications in American Archaeology and
                Ethnology, vol. 38.

Malinowski, Bronislaw
    1922   Argonauts of the Western Pacific, London:
                Routledge, Kegan Paul.

Mintz, Sidney
    1961   Pratik: Haitian Personal Economic
             Relationships. <u>Proceedings of the 1961</u>
             <u>Annual Spring Meeting of the American</u>
             <u>Ethnological Society</u>, pp. 54-63. Seattle:
             University of Washington Press.

THE SOCIAL ORGANIZATION OF THE MAINE LOBSTER MARKET

James M. Acheson, University of Maine

I. INTRODUCTION

The marketing system for lobsters in Maine is dominated by a large number of small specialized firms, which have developed long term bilateral relationships with each other. A fisherman ordinarily sells to only one lobster dealer with whom he has developed a special relationship; and that dealer normally sells his lobsters to only a few wholesale outfits. No vertically integrated firms have been developed whose employees do everything from catching the lobster to distributing them in distant markets. Fishermen, dealers, truckers, and wholesalers all own their own small firms and buy and sell lobsters to each other. Yet none of the men in these various types of firms in the marketing chain operates like a textbook entrepreneur in the neo-classical model of economics, buying and selling to the highest bidder with only economic optimization in mind. Rather, they buy and sell at the established market price to the same finite number of firms with whom they have developed ties. In this respect, the situation in Maine closely resembles the "praktik" relationship described by Mintz (1964), and a number of other marketing situations in the world summarized by Plattner (1985). However, there are differences as well. The relationship between fishermen, lobster dealers and wholesalers is very ambivalent. On the one hand a good deal of suspicion and tension pervades the relationships between those who buy and sell lobsters. This is particularly true between lobster fishermen and the dealers to whom they sell. Often, it takes very little for open hostility or conflict to erupt.

From the point of view of the fisherman, the whole marketing process is shrouded in fog, mystery and rumor. He has very little idea where his lobsters actually go, or how many hands they pass through on their way to the consumer. He has even less idea about the way prices are set, although he knows that they vary widely over the course of a year, and can jump suddenly from one day to another. He suspects the worst. From the point of view of the fisherman, anyone connected with the marketing of lobsters is at least slightly tainted, if not an outright crook. Yet ironically, the fisherman's response traditionally has

been to form very close ties with one particular
dealer--a man who he often suspects is part of a
conspiracy to defraud him at every opportunity. The
relationship between dealers, wholesalers and
distribution firms who regularly do business with each
other is usually more businesslike and neutral, but
even here suspicion abounds.

In recent years, some seventeen cooperatives have
been formed. However, in this paper, we shall
concentrate on relationships between fishermen,
individual dealers and wholesalers, because most
fishermen are still engaged in such relationships and
the vast majority of lobsters are sold through private
dealerships.

II. GENERAL FEATURES OF THE MAINE LOBSTER INDUSTRY

The American lobster (Homarus Americanus) is found
in North American waters from Newfoundland to Virginia.
However, Maine consistently produces far more lobsters
than any other state. There are approximately 2800
full time lobster fishermen and another 7000 part time
fishermen. The convoluted coastline has over 200
harbors of various sizes and each one has at least ten
lobster boats.

Lobsters are caught in wooden or wire traps
constructed to allow free circulation of seawater while
retaining the large, legal-sized lobsters. The traps
are fitted with a funnel-shaped nylon net or "head"
which lets the lobsters climb in easily, but makes it
difficult for them to climb out. Traps are attached to
a small styrofoam buoy by a "warp line" made of hemp
rope or polyethylene. The buoys of each fisherman are
marked with a distinctive set of colors which are
registered with the state. These traps are baited with
fish remnants obtained from fish processing plants.
Most lobstermen fish alone from gas or diesel powered
boats from 30 to 38 feet long, which are ordinarily
equipped with a hydraulic trap "hauler," a radio, and a
depth sounder. A typical lobster fisherman might have
between 300 and 600 traps.

According to Maine law, anyone who has a license is
allowed to go lobster fishing. In reality, there are
social requirements as well. To go lobster fishing at
all, one must be accepted by the group of men fishing
out of a particular harbor, and once one has been
accepted by such a "harbor gang," one is only permitted
to go fishing in the established territory of that

"gang" (Acheson 1972, 1975, 1979). These territories are usually under 100 square miles, which means that fishermen spend most of their time within ten miles of their home harbor. Interlopers in these areas are strongly sanctioned, occasionally by verbal threats, but more usually through the surreptitious destruction of their lobstering gear.

A. The Marketing Chain

Lobsters from Maine docks are distributed throughout the United States, Canada, Europe and Japan through a complicated network of dealerships, pounds, wholesale firms, shippers, and retail distributors. Some of these firms buy and sell lobsters only in Maine or New England; others air freight them literally all over the world.

There are, however, only a very limited number of kinds of firms and marketing channels in the whole chain. At one end are the cooperatives and lobster dealers in Maine who handle most of the Maine catch. At the other end is the consumer, who is very apt to be a hotel or restaurant. Most seafood sold in the United States goes to the "institutional trade," and lobster is no exception. It is estimated that at least 70 percent of all lobsters are eaten in restaurants, hotels, clubs or other institutions, although an increasing amount is being sold to supermarket chains.

Between the fisherman and the ultimate consumer are six other kinds of firms. There are, first, dozens of small wholesale and retail firms. These firms buy lobsters from dealers and cooperatives, sell them retail in their own local area, or sell them wholesale to hotels, restaurants, or other wholesalers in distant cities. The number of such firms needs to be stressed. an estimated 22 firms in Boston wholesale lobsters; another 33 are in Portland, and still another 65 are located in the smaller cities and towns of Maine.

There are approximately 34 lobster pounds in Maine, which have an estimated capacity of 2.5 million pounds. Pounds are enclosed ocean areas where lobsters are stored live. Many are made by fencing off a small bay or inlet. The largest are several acres in size, and store up to 250,000 pounds of lobsters at one time. Pound operators buy lobsters from both Maine and Canadian dealers, cooperatives, wholesalers, and fishermen,and sell them in mid-winter to other wholesale firms, distributors, or truckers. Lobsters

107

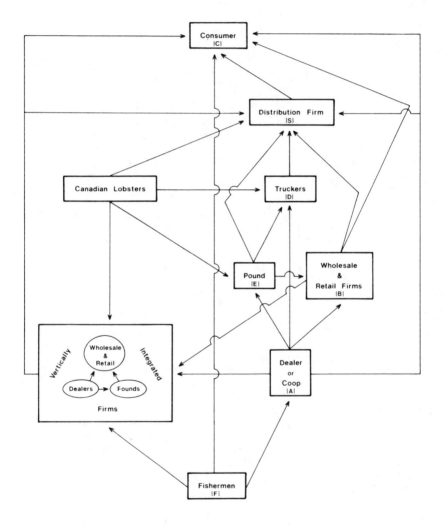

Figure 1.   The Marketing Chain for Maine Lobster

108

which are pounded are sold through the same channels as
any other lobsters; they are simply held off the market
for a few months to take advantage of the substantial
rise in price which occurs in the late fall and winter.
Some pounds are run and managed by their owners; others
are leased to wholesale firms and other kinds of
dealers.

There are innumerable small trucking operations.
Many have little more than one or two trucks and
perhaps one or two employees. They buy lobsters from
dealers and cooperatives and sell them in the larger
cities along the east coast. Many are small, fly-by-
night operations which come and go every few months.
Some are run by fishermen, who take a few loads of
lobsters to market over the course of the year.

There are only a few vertically integrated firms in
the lobster marketing business, but they are some of
the largest and most important in the industry. Such
firms ordinarily have several buying stations or
dealerships, and pounds, as well as wholesale and
retail operations located in some of the larger cities.
The largest, without question, is Bay State Lobster
Company which has about 25 dealers in Maine attached to
it by various means; at least two pounds; a fleet of
trucks; and a large wholesale and retail operation.
This firm and two others like it have their
headquarters and wholesale operations in Boston. They
ship lobsters air freight all over the U.S. and the
world.

Last are the distribution firms, which are scattered
all over the nation, Europe and Japan. In this
category are the seafood wholesale firms. Large
amounts of lobsters are handled by these firms, located
in major cities, which sell lobsters to fish stores,
restaurants, and other outlets in their own local
areas, and to food chain stores, which sell mainly to
individual customers.

In addition, millions of pounds of lobsters enter
the marketing channels in the U.S. from Canada. These
lobsters are sold in Maine to the large vertically
integrated firms, or pound operators, or to wholesale
firms. The largest proportion of Canadian lobsters is
sold to the Fulton Fish Market in New York and to
distribution firms throughout the U.S.

Approximately 65 percent of all Maine lobsters are
bought by the cooperatives and small private dealers;

an estimated 25 percent is handled by the three largest vertically integrated firms. Only an estimated ten percent of the total Maine catch is sold by fishermen directly--although it is perfectly legal to do so.

While these generalizations about firms and marketing channels are accurate, there is enormous variation in each individual firm's operations. Many firms have an almost unique niche. They combine different types of businesses, they buy lobsters in distinct places, they sell them in places where no one else does, and the amounts of lobsters they sell via various channels differ substantially.

For example, in one town there are two dealers. One runs a very large lobster pound in addition to dealing with local fishermen. He obtains lobsters to pound not only from his own fishermen, but also from Canadian sources. The other dealer has two other buying stations as well as one in this town. He sells to wholesalers on the west coast.

The same kind of variation can be seen in the various wholesale houses. One Portland firm buys a very high proportion of its lobsters from Canada, and only a small percentage from local Portland fishermen; it air freights much of its lobsters to distant cities in the U.S. and Canada. Another nearby wholesale firm buys all its lobsters in Maine, and trucks them to markets in the Mid Atlantic states and Canada; it also does a sizeable business with restaurants and other outlets in a two hour radius of Portland.

B. Prices and Catches: The Annual Round

Over the long run, the lobster catch in the state of Maine has remained relatively constant; between 1947 and 1981 it has run between 16 million and 24 million pounds. During that time, the average annual price has generally increased. The average price paid in 1947 was $.37 per pound, while in 1981 it was $2.09 (Townsend and Briggs, 1981:10).

Over the course of the annual round, however, catch volumes and prices change radically, sometimes with dramatic suddenness. On the whole, though, there is a general pattern in price and catch changes, which varies little from one year to another. These cyclical swings not only are connected to changes in the fishermen's behavior over the annual round, but also influence the strategies of buyers, pound operators and

110

others in the marketing chain. The general pattern of changes in price and supply can be seen clearly in Figure 2 which records the average catches of one fisherman, along with the average prices he received for his catch and the number of days he fished. This man is a "highline" (very successful) fisherman who fishes in one of the more productive island areas and is able to negotiate a premium price for his catch. Although his catches are higher than the average fisherman's and the price he receives is a few cents per pound higher as well, the general pattern of changes over the annual round is very typical.

During the winter months, lobster catches are very low. Lobsters are very inactive at this time of year and fishermen are reluctant to go out in cold and stormy seas for small catches. The fisherman in Figure 2 kept some traps in the water all winter, although he only pulled them two to four times a month. Many men do not fish at all during these months, and devote their time to constructing new traps and repairing equipment. The exvessel price, however, is very high during these months; normally, the annual high is reached between February and mid-April.

Towards the middle and end of April, lobsters become more active, as the water temperature warms, and begin to migrate in towards shore. Fishermen begin to pull their traps more often as the weather improves, and the number of lobsters caught increases. The end of April and first part of May usually see a rapid increase in both number of days fished and catches. During May, however, prices usually fall dramatically. Demand for lobsters is relatively weak since there are few tourists around, and the increase in catches tends to cause a short term glut on the market.

During the latter part of June and the first part of July, catches again fall as lobsters begin to molt in large numbers and become very difficult to catch. At this time, fishermen do not pull their traps often, and devote a good deal of time to repairing equipment and painting their boats. During July, the price picks up again as tourists by the hundreds of thousands pour into the coastal regions and strengthen demand for lobster.

From the middle of August to the first part of November, catches increase as a new year class of lobsters that have recently molted into legal size become available to fishermen and begin to migrate off

111

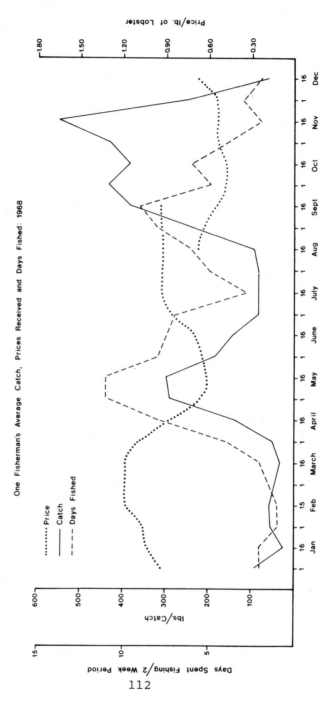

One Fisherman's Average Catch, Prices Received and Days Fished: 1968

Figure 2. One Fisherman's Average Catch, Prices Received and Days Fished: 1968.

shore. For most fishermen, the three month period from the middle of August to the middle of November is a period of intense activity. Most try to get out as much as possible during this season, when catches are typically at their annual high. In this respect the fisherman in Figure 2 is a little unusual because, in 1968 at least, his fishing effort began to decline after the first of October.

Late in the summer, dealers offer different prices for hard shell and soft shell lobsters. The hard shell lobsters, which have not yet shed, bring a higher price since they are packed with meat. As summer turns to fall, few hard shell lobsters are being caught because the vast majority have shed by that time. Consequently, only one price is offered--the lower price for soft shell lobsters. This single price structure is then maintained thoughout the rest of the year.

Several aspects of this general seasonal cycle in catch and prices deserve emphasis.

First, and foremost, catch and price are inversely related. When the catch is lowest, the price is highest; when the catch is highest, the price is low. The price comes to its annual peak during February and March when catches are at their annual low. The late summer and fall see the lowest prices of the year. Not only are lobsters plentiful, but, with the exodus of tourists, demand is relatively weak. There is nothing odd about this situation. It is called the law of supply and demand.

Second, fishermen are responding far more to availability of lobsters than to price. They intensify their fishing efforts at the times when large numbers of lobsters are available. They plan to have a maximum number of traps in the water and devote all their efforts to fishing between August and November and again in the late spring. This is reflected in the number of days spent fishing shown in the example in Figure 2. Fishing activity slows down considerably in February and March and again during shedding season because fishermen know that few lobsters will be caught regardless of how much effort they exert. They do not put forth maximum effort when prices are highest. If they were responding primarily to price, maximum fishing effort would occur in March and July--the times when fishing effort is actually at its lowest ebb.

Responding to the availability of lobsters, not price, is a conscious and perfectly rational strategy given the economics of the business. In the words of one fisherman, "You make more money fishing when there are a lot of lobsters and the price is low than you do when the price is $3.50 a pound and there aren't any lobsters to catch."

The fisherman who contributed the data in Figure 2 earned far more per day of fishing when the price of lobster was at its annual low than when it was at its annual high. From February 26 to April 2 when the price was $1.18 per pound this man pulled his traps four times and caught a total of 155 pounds, giving a gross income of $182.90 for the period, or $45.72 for each day he spent fishing. In contrast, between October 9th and October 28th, when the price had dropped to the annual low of $.48 per pound, this fisherman pulled his traps ten times and caught a total of 4088 pounds, giving a gross income of $1962.24 for the period or $196.22 per day. In short, this man grossed over four times as much money per day fishing when the price was at the annual low than when it was at the annual high. Regardless of how angry fishermen might be over "low prices," they still keep fishing. It is irrational for them to do anything else.

Third, although the general pattern of cyclical changes in prices and catches is well known to everyone connected with the industry, it is impossible to predict price levels or price changes at any given time. It is virtually impossible to predict at the start of the year what prices or catches will be in any given month or when highs or lows will occur. Every year sees substantial differences in prices and amounts caught at various times of year. For example, in 1978 the highest price of the year was $3.90 and was paid at the end of February; two years later it was $3.65 and occured during the fourth week of March. Between March and May, the price of lobster can drop anywhere from 70 to 150 percent. In some years, lobsters can be caught in some quantity up until December; in other years there is a marked drop off in abundance early in November. In 1968, spring lobster fishing was very good; in the early 1980's spring fishing was very bad. In some years there are a lot more lobsters to catch than in others. Moreover, fishermen stress that sharp changes in price occur often and without warning. One can go out in the morning and be promised a price and return in the evening to find out that the morrow will bring a price $.20 or even $.30 less per pound. Price

114

jumps of up to $.50 per pound have been recorded in a
single day. In 1968, the fisherman in Figure 2
received $1.23 per pound on April 7; on April 11, he
got $.98 per pound, and by April 20 the price had
fallen to $.78 per pound. This is a 37 percent drop in
price in under two weeks. Such rapid and generally
unpredictable changes are the rule--not the exception.
They introduce a large element of uncertainty into the
business of marketing lobsters.

What produces this price instability? Part can be
traced to the great variation in supply over the
seasonal round. Perhaps more important is the nature
of the demand curve involved, and the reactions of
dealers and wholesalers to it. The demand curve for
lobsters is unquestionably highly inelastic--especially
in the high price ranges. In this respect lobster is
similar to most other luxury goods, meaning that a
change in price will result in a less than proportional
change in the quantity of lobsters purchased. This
inelasticity is traceable, in the main, to the fact
that a very large proportion of the catch is consumed
in restaurants and institutions, which tend to purchase
a constant supply and charge the same amount for it
regardless of changes or seasonal variations. As a
result, when there are large supplies the storage
facilities fill up. At such times, dealers and
wholesalers are offered far more lobsters than they can
sell and the price is bid down, sometimes drastically,
by those holding unsold lobsters in an effort to find a
market. Many of these excess lobsters are bought up by
pound operators when the price drops low enough. In
times of scarcity, dealers and distributors will bid
the price of lobster up in order to get an adequate
supply to keep their customers happy. If they are
desperate for lobsters and face the prospect of loosing
a customer, they will sometimes offer fishermen or
dealers a sharply higher price to increase supply. It
is at such times that pounded lobsters are apt to be
put on the market. In any case, changing the price
does not have a proportional effect on the amount sold.
Lobsters are a luxury good, and the restaurants in New
York and San Francisco are going to sell about the same
amount of them regardless of whether the price drops a
dollar a pound or increases two dollars.

C. Reactions to Uncertainty

Everyone in the marketing chain, from dealers to
distributors, are caught in a situation where they have
to supply a steady flow of lobsters to their customers

with a highly variable supply. Their problem is how to get enough lobsters in times of scarcity (such as the mid summer and winter) and how to find markets for a vast overabundance in the fall months.

In a very real sense, dealers and wholesalers are caught between the expectations of fishermen and those of consumers of lobsters. The fisherman demands to be paid for his catch on the day he catches it, regardless of how many or how few lobsters he brings in. Restaurants, hotels and other institutions ordinarily want a steady supply of lobsters, and they want to charge a steady amount for it--in some part because of a reluctance to reprint menus. This means that dealers and wholesalers are under a great deal of pressure to supply their customers with a given amount of lobsters. If they fail, that customer--whether it is a distribution firm, a retail store or a restaurant--will buy lobsters elsewhere and may never come back again.

A major problem for all firms in the marketing chain is predicting the price. Like the fisherman, dealers, wholesalers, and other purchasers know the general seasonal changes that will occur over the annual round, but they do not know exactly what the price will be on any given day or week, particularly since prices can change sharply with little warning. A dealer can buy a load of lobsters at one price expecting a certain profit, only to find that the price of lobster has changed overnight so that he makes far less than expected. His problems are exacerbated by the secrecy that reigns in the industry. Information is the stock in trade for the firms in the marketing chain. One is very reluctant to talk about deals, prices and markets because loose talk can result in unwanted competition and a loss of trade secrets.

How do people in the marketing chains operate in this kind of uncertain, unstable environment, in which the prices are apt to change suddenly and the information is difficult to come by and costly? The answer is that they establish a set of ties with others in the marketing chain to reduce risk and uncertainty. They have one set of established relationships with the people and firms they buy lobsters from and sell to. They have still another set of relationships with other firms at the same level of the market. Each set of social ties has different uses. We will discuss the ties between dealers and wholesalers first and those involving fishermen later.

D.   Dealers and Wholesalers: Negotiations and
     Agreements

     For all firms in the marketing chain the most
critical ties are those between firms that buy and sell
lobsters to each other. These firms usually have an
informal understanding that they will do business with
each other over the long run. They do not ordinarily
set up fixed obligations regarding the price to be
paid. The price is the "going price" for that time of
year. Exactly what that "going price" is is left to
negotiations.

     The most important part of such agreements is the
understanding that the partners will continue to do
business with each other at all times of year
regardless of supply. In the words of one wholesaler,
"If a man keeps you in lobsters in the summer [when the
demand is very high] you always buy some of his
lobsters in the fall--even when you have so many
lobsters you don't know what to do with them all."
Even though such agreements are informal, most of those
in the marketing chain, from the person in the lobster
buying station to the distributing firms around the
country, are loathe to violate these agreements with
their "steady suppliers" and customers. These
arrangements are highly valued because they go a long
way toward stabilizing the supply of lobsters.

     Such bilateral agreements also give a certain amount
of financial security. This is important in a business
where sharp business practices are rife. There are
many stories in the industry about firms that have sent
shipments of lobsters to distant parts of the country
and then have had great difficulties collecting their
money. Other firms have sold lobsters to out-of-state
trucking firms for a good price only to find that the
check was no good.

     At the same time, there is a good deal of suspicion
and not very latent hostility between those in firms up
and down the marketing chain. Most agreements, once
made, are carried out faithfully, but in the
negotiations to establish an agreement one is always
looking out for one's own interest. It is very common
for individuals to withhold information from those with
whom they do business in an effort to strengthen their
hand in the negotiations concerning price. Bluffing
and deception, not to say outright lying, are not
uncommon. Sellers will tell tales about the high
prices they have had to pay for lobsters; buyers will

117

complain about poor markets, prospects of falling prices, and so on. Dealers with no markets will hide that fact in conversations; and buyers who are desperate for lobsters will rarely admit that fact. To admit such information is to weaken your hand. There is probably a good deal of truth in the statement of the dealer who said, "They will take you if they can. Your only protection is to know who you are dealing with. Even then you have to look out."

The number of firms with which a wholesaler or dealer has steady ties varies depending on size to a large degree. It is not unusual for some small dealers to sell most of their lobsters to one wholesaling firm; and small wholesale houses may sell most of their lobsters to three to five customers. The larger wholesale and retail firms buy and sell to more firms, but still the number with which they regularly do business is relatively small.

Firms in the same locality, at the same level of the marketing chain have a very different, but no less essential relationship with each other. Even they are competitors for the same customers and sources of supply, they are often very cooperative and depend on each other for certain essential things. The most essential thing they exchange is information, and this is of critical importance in an industry where fast changes in price and supplies are the rule. Lobster dealers and coop managers in any local area know each other and are part of a dense network. They are constantly on the phone concerning prices, sources of bait, fuel, and so on. In a similar fashion, the wholesale and retail firms in any city all know each other and exchange information about business regularly. The Portland and Boston dealers, as one man phrased it, "all have their heads together;" and the same could be said about the people in the Fulton Fish Market in New York.

Men at any given level of the chain can give each other very useful information since they face many of the same problems and operate in the same environment. The information they can get from each other is often far more accurate than they can get from the people they buy and sell to, who, after all, have an ulterior motive for being very deceptive.

Much of the information exchanged concerns prices, and is primarily useful in negotiating price with dealers and wholesalers. Often dealers and wholesalers will try to raise or lower the price simultaneously in the hopes that they can do together what no one of them can do alone. In the words of one dealer, "Once or twice a year, four or five of us [other dealers] will hold out for a certain price." Sometimes these ploys work; other times they do not.

Often, more tangible assets are exchanged. Dealers and managers of cooperatives in a local area frequently sell each other bait when one of them is short and the other has an adequate supply. They also lend each other equipment.

This is not to suggest that all is sweetness and light between nearby dealers, cooperative managers and wholesalers. Sometimes bitter enmity exists between some of them, which usually finds its roots in faulty information or taking over markets or sources of supply belonging to another. Usually the relationship between nearby dealers and wholesalers, etc. is some mixture of cooperation and competition. Sometimes the double edged nature of the relationship between nearby firms at the same market level is revealed in phone calls in which friendly jokes and accurate information are mixed with deceptive data and barbed commentary--sometimes within a five minute period.

The way that these horizontal and vertical ties are used in negotiating prices is complicated and beyond the scope of this paper. Several factors need to be emphasized, however.

On any given day, dealers and cooperative managers set the boat prices (the price paid to fishermen) by contacting other local dealers and cooperative managers to find out what they are going to pay their fishermen. During these calls they exchange information and speculation on impending price changes, supplies of lobsters, and the way the market is going. They might also call one or more wholesalers with whom they do business, but information from them often is taken with a grain or two of salt.

The price that the dealer or cooperative manager sells lobsters for is calculated in terms of the "boat price." A normal markup in 1984 was about $.30 to $.35 over the boat price, and this is what most dealers and managers try to get from their wholesalers.

Wholesalers will again set their selling prices in terms of a fixed increase over their buying price.

Exactly what the selling price is depends in great part on the distance of the customer and the type of services the wholesaler is providing.

There is extreme pressure on any dealer or wholesaler to pay the same price others are paying for lobster in his local area at his level of the market. If he is paying a lower price than other dealers and coop managers in the local area, he will face some very unhappy fishermen who will likely make their discontent known by selling some or all of their catches to other dealers or by switching dealers entirely. On the other hand, if he pays his fishermen more than other dealers, he often cannot pass on his increased costs to the firms to which he sells. Why should a wholesaler pay $.15 per pound more for lobster from this dealer when he can get it for less from others in the same area? As a result, dealerships in the same local area usually have essentially the same boat price on any given day.

Negotiating a new price, dealers and wholesalers insist, is an uncertain business and one that takes a great deal of skill. One Portland dealer said "I just go by the seat of my pants. I try to get what I think the market will bear. Sometimes I get the price I ask; sometimes I don't." Successful negotiating depends on information to a large degree. The best way to get the price up or down is to be able to demonstrate that someone else is already buying lobsters at the desired price, or is willing to sell them at that price. This puts pressure on the person with whom one is negotiating because everyone in the industry knows how important it is to be in accord with the market.

Obtaining information is a costly,time-consuming business. Marketing lobsters is a full time occupation. It is not a game for amateurs. One can usually get accurate information from a few nearby firms at the same level in the marketing chain. Much of the information about prices comes through the process of dickering itself and observing the negotiations of other firms.

Large firms have much better information, which in turns appears to give them an edge in the negotiating process. A small dealer who is dickering with only one or two wholesalers who regularly buy his lobsters might only know that he cannot get the price he asked for lobsters from those two firms. A buyer from a large wholesale house who is on the phone to literally dozens of dealers, pound operators, firms in Canada and distributing firms in Florida and California during a day has a much better idea of what the market will bear. The smaller firms are fully aware of this,and watch the largest firms closely to get a sense of what is happening in the market.

Sometimes when an individual wholesaler or dealer jumps the price he pays for lobster, the price change will go reverberating up and down the coast and a new price will be "established."

Without question, the most important factor involved in price jumps is the supply of lobsters. In the words of one wholesaler, "The reason the price jumps up is someone got short of lobster and hiked the price to get more." Others in need of lobsters follow suit. The obverse is also true. When prices go down, people had an unsold inventory of lobsters. Someone lowered the price and a number of firms followed suit.

E. Fishermen and Dealers: Negotiations and Agreements

The entire process by which prices are negotiated and changed is deliberately hidden from fishermen. The primary reason for this is that no one wants to admit to lowering the price, which can anger a lot of fishermen. A dealer who got the reputation as being a prime mover of lower prices could very well lose some of "his" fishermen to other dealers or cooperatives.

There is a strong, and understandable, reluctance on the part of dealers, wholesalers, and other buyers to talk about the whole negotiating process. They tend to talk about the price moving up and down as if magical forces were responsible, rather than human decisions. Dealers often hint or tell fishermen they merely take the prices that wholesalers set for them or just go by the established price. It is very common for price change to be blamed on the largest companies. Bay State Lobster Corporation often is cast in the role of villain. However, all of this tends to obscure exactly how prices are set and the role of one's own dealer in the process.

Fishermen are not completely unaware of the game. Gene Witham from Owls Head points out that when dealers raise prices, they are always quick to take credit. "When the price gets lowered, it's always someone else far to the westward who did it and they [dealers in his area] are forced to go along. Somehow you can never find out who the first one was that cut the price."

Dealers--especially in the past--have used their differential knowledge to good advantage in negotiations with fishermen. A great deal of opportunistic behavior, if not downright cheating and lying, was standard. In the past decades, fishermen have formed 17 cooperatives in various harbors along the coast in order to get what they considered a "fair price" for their catches.

Cooperatives have helped all the fishermen along the coast. Cooperative managers are hired by the fishermen and try to get as high a price as possible for their member fishermen. The price the cooperatives are paying for lobsters has become the standard by which all fishermen judge the prices they are receiving. Since the advent of cooperatives, fishermen all along the coast have been getting better prices for their catches. If cooperatives were to disappear, there can be little question that ex-vessel prices would generally be lower again.

Given the opportunistic behavior of dealers--especially in the past--and the degree to which the price negotiating process is hidden from fishermen, it is scarce wonder that fishermen's statements about the lobster market are both hostile and inaccurate.

The subject of marketing can bring out vituperation from the mildest of fishermen. Many fishermen would agree with the older man who said: "Them miserable fuckin bahstids have the whole thing rigged. When we got lobsters, they bring the price down. When lobster is scarce, they put the price up higher than hell. Either way, they don't pay nothing and we don't earn nothin. .... Them Canadians ain't helping either. At times, they bring in lobsters by the truck load. That don't help our price any you know."

While this quotation is short and pungent, it reflects two of the most important assertions fishermen make about the marketing system: first that the Canadians' import policy does a maximum amount of damage to Maine lobster fishermen and their incomes; second, that the price of lobster is controlled by a conspiracy of people in the marketing chain, who further their own interests at the expense of the fishermen. Many fishermen believe that the largest two or three vertically integrated firms set the price.

There is little evidence to support either of these assertions. One recent study points out that the

122

Canadian policy of setting seasons so that a large percentage of their catch occurs in the winter (when catches are low in the U.S.) smoothes out price fluctuations and adds many millions of dollars to the income of lobster fishermen in the U.S. and Canada (Contas and Wilson, 1982).

More important, the best evidence suggests that the large Boston wholesale firms do not have the ability to dictate the price of lobsters, although they might possibly have a limited ability to influence price under certain circumstances. Jim Wilson, an economist who has served as expert witness in antitrust cases points out (1984), "It would be impossible for a single firm to continually fix price. There are too many other outlets for lobsters." It is true that dealers have taken advantage of fishermen, but that is a far cry from being able to dictate the price regardless of gluts and scarcity in the market.

All this underlines the fact that fishermen as a whole do not fully understand the lobster marketing system. Their strong negative assertions do not reflect a balanced, informed appraisal of the marketing system, as much as their hostility towards people in the marketing system who always have more information and always seem to have the upper hand in any negotiations.

Given the ambivalence and suspicion many fishermen feel for those in the marketing chain, why do most fishermen sell their lobsters to only one dealer with whom they have developed a long-term bilateral agreement?

Such arrangements involve an intricate set of exchanges. The dealer for his part allows "his" fishermen to use his dock at no cost. Many even provide "their" fishermen space for gear storage or a workshop. This is worth a great deal. Not only are docks very expensive to build, but access to the water has become a problem for many fishermen since every inch of coastal land has been bought up at very high prices by summer people. The dealer also supplies "his" fishermen with gasoline, diesel fuel, gloves, paint, buoys, and bait at cost or with only a small markup. Supplying bait causes dealers the most problems because it is such a critical item and supplies are irregular. Perhaps most important, a dealer gives "his" fishermen a steady, secure market for their catches. Dealers always buy all of the

123

lobsters their fishermen offer for sale regardless of how glutted the market might be.

In addition, dealers often loan "their" fishermen very large amounts of money for boats, equipment, and traps. In many cases the dealer sets fishermen up in business. These loans, it needs to be stressed, are ordinarily interest free. Usually, they are given only with the provision that the fisherman will continue to do business with the dealer, and some provision for repayment is ordinarily agreed on. It is not uncommon for loans to be paid off by dealers taking a certain percentage of each day's catch.

Sometimes, fishermen are able to negotiate special prices with dealers as well. For example, one family in the Penobscot Bay area was able to get $.05 per pound more for their lobsters when they all agreed to sell to one dealer. The same is true for the fishermen on one island.

The exact arrangement between a dealer and one of his fishermen is normally individually negotiated. Dealers are very careful to whom they lend money, for example; and only certain people can negotiate a special price. It is not at all uncommon for some fishermen to get preference on bait when it is scarce, while others may get special consideration concerning dock space. Ordinarily such "special" deals are kept as secret as possible, and are likely to occur when the fisherman and dealer have been doing business for some time and have built up a relationship of trust. This is not always the case, however. At times dealers will offer fishermen special consideration as a means of enticing them away from another dealer.

The problem for dealers is to get a large, steady supply of lobsters. They need a steady supply to be able to satisfy their customers, who will go elsewhere if their needs are not met. The supply needs to be as large as possible to maximize profits. (As a result of the fixed markup on lobsters, the dealer who handles the most lobsters obtains the highest gross revenue.) Given the fact that there is little price competition, the only way to obtain a large and steady supply of lobsters is to attach as many fishermen to a dealer as possible. Thus, from the perspective of the dealer, low cost gas and bait, dock space and interest free loans are being exchanged for a large, reliable supply.

From the point of view of the fishermen, the

exchange involves different considerations. Fishermen are exchanging lobsters at the going price for loans, bait, gas, dock space and a certain market.

By agreeing to sell their catches for the going rate, they are largely giving up the right to bargain about prices. That is more and less of a sacrifice than it might at first seem. Fishermen as a group have few optional markets for their catches. There are only a few dealers or cooperatives in any given area; and all are offering approximately the same price. In addition, fishermen are at a distinct disadvantage in negotiating with dealers, who have superior information. Last, fishermen are price takers. They maximize their incomes if they concentrate their fishing effort when lobsters are available in large numbers regardless of how low the price might be. Lobster fishermen, in short, are not in a good position to bargain on price; and it makes little sense for them to schedule their fishing activities when the price is highest. The exchange they are making is one in which they are agreeing to sell their catches at the "going price" to one dealer in exchange for other valuables.

It is very difficult to determine whether fishermen or dealers get the better of the bargain. Fishermen as a group resent their inability to bargain much about price. They feel, with some justification, that dealers are in position to take advantage of them economically. However, a dealer's ability to cheat them is limited. If blatant cheating occurs too frequently, fishermen will sell their catches elsewhere. The dealer's ability to take advantage of fishermen has been especially constrained since the advent of cooperatives in the 1940's. In reality, the advantages of these long term bilateral agreements in the Maine lobster industry accrue to both parties. Dealers and fishermen enter into them because they lower risk and uncertainty for both.

III.LONG TERM BILATERAL AGREEMENTS BETWEEN FISHERMEN
    AND DEALERS: NEITHER MARKET NOR HIERARCHY

The organization of the firms in the Maine lobster industry is enigmatic at least. The industry is characterized by many small scale fishing enterprises, dealers, and wholesalers who have long-term ties to each other.

There is no large vertically integrated firm that does all steps in the production and marketing of

125

lobsters from operating boats to final retailing to consumers. Nor do these small firms act like economic optimizers and buy and sell to the highest bidder. Under what conditions do such arrangements arise? In the past few years, Coase, Williamson, and other economists concerned with the nature of elementary transactions have developed a body of theory that appears to be relevant to understanding these questions.

Coase points out that an entrepreneur can obtain goods and services either by expanding his own firm (i.e., hiring employees, etc.) or by purchasing the same goods and services from other firms. Most entrepreneurs do both. This means that an entrepreneur is involved in two kinds of transactions: exchanges within the firm (i.e., between departments or between employees) and exchanges outside the firm. The kind of firms that evolve depends on the costs of internal transactions as opposed to costs of transactions between firms. When the costs of internal transactions are lower than those of external transactions, then entrepreneurs expand the size of their firms to obtain needed labor and goods from their own employees. If internal costs of transactions are higher, then the entrepreneur does not rely on his own employees to produce the goods and services he requires, but rather obtains them from other firms in the open market.

Williamson points out that if external transaction costs are relatively efficient, the industry will be organized into many small firms each doing one specialized task in the production of a final product. In such an industry, the market regulates the flow of goods and services between firms, and prices serve as the best source of information. If external transactions are relatively inefficient, then it makes sense to organize firms into a hierarchy, in which several different productive processes are done by different departments of a single firm under the directorship of a single owner. According to Williamson, these external transaction inefficiencies which result in hierarchies are primarily due to two causes: opportunism (i.e., cheating or taking advantage of other parties) and asymmetrically distributed information between parties to an exchange (Williamson 1975: 29-31). This is, of course, exactly the situation that exists in the lobster industry. Dealers have much more information about markets and prices than fishermen; and they have not been reluctant to use this information to their own benefit. Under these conditions, Williamson would predict that hierarchically organized firms should result.

Why haven't vertically integrated firms (hierarchies) come about in the lobster industry? Why haven't dealers purchased boats and hired fishermen to run them and bought up pounds and wholesaling and retailing outlets so that both the production of lobsters and the marketing functions would be combined in one firm? Such firms should be more efficient in that they would automatically abolish all the transaction costs currently incurred in the elaborate, unfriendly dance between fishermen, dealers, and wholesalers.

There are three reasons why no firm buys boats and hires its own fishermen. First, it is very difficult for an owner to supervise a fisherman at sea. A man who hired a fisherman to operate his boat would almost certainly sustain higher than average costs of bait, fuel, maintenance and trap losses. Second, the value placed on "independence" and the economic gains to be had make it unlikely that a highly skilled lobster fisherman would want to work for someone else. Third, and most important, lobster fishermen are highly territorial and the primary object in owning territories is to control the numbers of fishermen who are allowed to fish there. Any would-be-entrepreneur who attempted to set himself up as a dealer and hire a number of fishermen would meet with very stiff and certain resistance.

A few vertically integrated firms are organized in Maine by people who own entire islands and all the fishing area off them. These island owners have been able to buy a small fleet of boats and hire fishermen to work for them. Arrangements vary considerably, but typically in such vertically integrated firms the "owner" provides "his" fishermen with a boat and traps. The fisherman provides his own fuel and bait. They split the catch evenly. But such vertically integrated firms are rare and occur only where a single man or family owns an island.

Another set of constraints inhibits firms or coops from acquiring a number of dealerships, wholesale houses and retail outlets in distant cities. Distance combined with managerial problems are apparently the primary factors. Managing a dealership, pound or wholesale operation takes a lot of skill, experience and long hours. Good managers are very difficult to

127

hire since the type of man who can successfully manage a dealership for a big firm would prefer to own his own business. The managerial problem might be eased if the various dealerships, etc., were in the same location where they might be supervised from a central office. But they are not: dealerships are in Maine, but wholesale and retail outlets are in distant cities. There are three vertically integrated firms, but an official of one company admitted, "Conditions in every locality are different. We have a difficult time making a go of our operations in Canada. There is no way we would open a retail outlet in Florida." These firms attempt to solve these problems by becoming silent partners of owners of dealerships and pounds. The cooperatives experienced other problems when they attempted to integrate vertically. In the late 1970's the Maine Association of Cooperatives, "Big Mac," was formed to market the catches of all member cooperatives jointly in the hopes of being able to negotiate very favorable prices. "Big Mac" joint marketing efforts failed after a few months due to severe internal conflict among member cooperatives. Managing a single cooperative is a formidable task (Fox and Lessa 1983). Managing a number of cooperatives proved to be impossible.

Despite the fact that there are structural blocks to forming integrated lobster fishing and marketing firms, the advantages of a hierarchy remain. As a result, fishermen and dealers form long lasting bilateral relationships in which dealers give a steady market, interest free loans, and supplies at cost in return for a steady supply of lobsters at the so called "established price." Such arrangements maintain fishing firms and marketing firms as distinct entities, but still give many of the benefits of a hierarchy. These arrangements reduce the problems of obtaining information which fishermen would incur if they attempted to sell their catches to the highest bidder. They also give the dealers an incentive to curb their opportunistic behavior. From the point of view of the dealers, these "arrangements" reduce uncertainty and risk by helping to ensure them a more certain supply of lobsters. In similar fashion, dealers, wholesale firms and retail firms maintain longstanding ties to ensure steady supplies and customers for their lobsters, while avoiding the managerial costs accompanying vertical integration.

In summary, fishermen, dealers and wholesalers in the Maine lobster industry do not rely on either markets or hierarchies, but on long-term, dyadic ties, which are an intermediate solution. Our data suggest that these long-term bilateral ties are found in situations in which differential access to information and opportunism make hierarchies highly desirable, but cultural and social factors produce such high internal transaction costs that they are impossible to generate. The long term dyadic ties are a kind of intermediate solution. This conclusion would come as no surprise to Williamson (1984). Markets and hierarchies, he believes, are best considered as two extreme organizational types on a continuum. Many other organizational modes fall in between. The kinds of long term dyadic ties seen in the Maine lobster industry is one such intermediary organizational form.

ACKNOWLEDGMENT

The data in this paper were collected during a project entitled "University of Rhode Island-- University of Maine Study of Social and Cultural Aspects of Fisheries Management in New England Under Extended Jurisdiction," supported by the National Science Foundation, Grant AER-77-06018. Much of the analysis was done during 1983 when the author was Visiting Fellow at the Center for International Studies at M.I.T.

REFERENCES CITED

Acheson, James M.
    1972   Territories of the Lobstermen. Natural History 81 (4). April 1972.

    1975   The Lobster Fiefs: Economic and Ecological Effects of Territoriality in the Maine Lobster Industry. Human Ecology 3 (3): 183-207.

    1979   Variations in Traditional Inshore Fishing Rights in Maine Lobstering Communities. In North Atlantic Maritime Cultures. Ed. Raoul Andersen. pp. 253-276. The Hague: Mouton.

Coase, R.H.
    1952   The Nature of the Firm. In Readings in Price Theory. George Stigler and Kenneth Boulding, eds. pp. 337-50. Chicago: Richard D. Irwin, Inc.

Contas, John, and J. Wilson
    1982   "The Effects of Canadian Lobster Regulations
            on the Price of Lobster". Unpublished
            Manuscript, Department of Economics,
            University of Maine, Orono, Maine.

Fox, Catherine, and William Lessa
    1983   Fish Marketing Cooperatives in Northern New
            England. New York Sea Grant Extension
            Publication, Cornell University, Ithaca, New
            York. 27 pp.

Mintz, Sidney
    1964   The Employment of Capital by Market Women in
            Haiti. In Capital, Savings and Credit in
            Peasant Societies. Eds. Raymond Firth and
            B.S. Yamey. pp. 256-86. Aldine: Chicago.

Plattner, Stuart
    1985   Equilibrating Market Relationships. Markets
            and Marketing. 1984 Proceedings of the
            Society for Economic Anthropology. (This
            volume)

Townsend, Ralph, and Hugh Briggs, III
    1982   Maine's Marine Fisheries: Annual Data 1947-
            1981. Maine - New Hampshire Sea Grant
            Program. University of Maine, Orono, Maine.

Williamson, Oliver E.
    1975   Markets and Hierarchies: Analysis and
            Antitrust Implications. New York: The Free
            Press.

Wilson, James A.
    1980   Adaptation to Uncertainty and Small Numbers
            Exchange: The New England Fresh Fish Market.
            Bell Journal of Economics and Management
            Science 11 (2): 491-504.

    1984   Lecture at the University of Maine Law
            School.May19,1984.Personal Communication

EQUILIBRATING MARKET RELATIONSHIPS

Stuart Plattner, Department of Anthropology, University of Missouri-St. Louis

I. INTRODUCTION

There are two contrasting ways to buy or sell in a market: you can search for the best deal available at that time, or you can establish a relationship with a customer with whom you expect to deal on a reciprocal basis. This paper will show how reciprocal economic relationships are instrumental responses to social constraints. They reduce risk in transactions which would otherwise be too uncertain or expensive to undertake.

A. Reciprocity

Economic anthropologists have studied reciprocity as a mode of exchange for many years. The term usually means a personalized dyadic relationship, with socially integrative effects, focused on the exchange of valuables over the long run. Mauss' classic work analyzed the basic principles of economic exchange in "primitive" society as the obligation to give, receive, and repay gifts (1967 [1923]). His description of economic evolution from a primitive state of "total prestation" to the modern condition of "pure individual contract" allowed him to interpret the market reciprocity he saw in his own society as anachronism. In this paper I will show how uncertain information makes such relationships economically functional in any society.

Polanyi's influential work of economic history defined reciprocity and redistribution as the fundamental principles of exchange in bands, tribes and primitive chiefdoms, opposed to the administered trade and market principles of state economies (1957). A generation later Sahlins focused upon generalized, balanced and negative reciprocity in tribal society (1972). He insightfully showed how the mode of exchange was affected by distance in kinship, rank and wealth in addition to the nature of the goods exchanged. His approach hinted at this paper's attention to the nature of the exchange situation and its context.

Until recently economists ignored the transactional

133

and personal attributes of exchange relationships. Boulding's economic theory of the "grants economy" distinguished economic exchange (i.e., market purchase) from grants, defined as "one-way transfers" or gifts (1973). He discussed reciprocity as "mutual grants". His work foreshadowed this analysis by situating reciprocity in between the extremes of market exchange and grants, and by examining how reciprocity and grants fostered the integration of the social group.

Williamson asked when an efficient firm should buy all its inputs on a "spot" market and when it should internalize the production of inputs (for example, a restaurant may buy bread, cakes and pies from a local marketplace or may set up a bakery in-house). He showed that this is one of a family of strategic choice problems between discrete, short-run versus relational, long-run transactions. In his analysis, the more uncertain, frequent, and transaction-specific the exchange, the more efficient an integration will be (1981).

This paper draws upon recent work in anthropology and economics to make a theory of reciprocal economic relationships in market societies. I will begin by defining a continuum ranging from a focus on the qualities of the things exchanged to a concern with the qualities of the personal relationship between the exchangers. Next I will show how imperfect information about goods, transactions, and traders can make personalized modes of exchange economically preferable to impersonal market exchange.[1] I then analyze the causes of imperfect information, focusing upon local problems created by the economic, social and political infrastructure.

II. MODES OF EXCHANGE: IMPERSONAL VS. PERSONAL

The concept "mode of exchange" is used here to denote the behavioral norms appropriate to exchange in different contexts. The impersonal market mode refers to short-run, closed-ended exchanges, where each transaction has few implications for the future. The relationship between the buyer and seller of a car or a home are good examples. The transactions usually have no meaning aside from the specific things exchanged, and are openly instrumental, in the sense that the dominant goal for each actor is to protect and maximize self interest. The relationship exists to support and facilitate the exchange (cf. Cancian's 1966 discussion of "maximization as norm").

Impersonal market mode transactions are decomposable into separate elements, each of which is negotiable. The monetary unit of account, the standard of measurement, the store of value, the terms of trade, and the conditions of exchange are in principle independently negotiable and often written in contract form. For example buyers often are willing to pay more for a home if it can be occupied sooner. Sellers in spot markets will often lower the price for cash payment. The norm is to balance accounts in full, with a quid pro quo clearly specified. If norms are violated an appeal to outside authority is expected and is often specified in a contract. The transaction is defined in terms of independent individuals, at the fundamental cultural values which govern the norms are ideally "faceless". A market allocation based on personality rather than on profit would be defined as improper in this mode.

The opposite extreme is represented by economic exchanges within families, and can be called a personal market exchange. The hiring of dependent children by family firms is a good example. Here the relationships are long-term, open-ended and generalized with a strong affective, non-instrumental component. Values from different realms or domains of existence are often exchanged for each other in an ad hoc, processual way. Thus money can be exchanged for goods, services, affection or loyalty.

The continuance of the relationship is the dominant goal governing any specific transaction, and it is impolite to attempt to decompose transactions and negotiate each element separately. The units of account are correspondingly generalized, accounts are ideally never fully balanced, and contract enforcement is expected to occur within the group. If an extra-familial authority is called in, it is usually a sign that the family structure has lost its integrity.

The group is the basic actor whose interest governs those of each individual, and many values are totally unique to personalities. Thus it is

135

expectable that economic decisions are made with long-term family goals in mind. For example a father who did not give preference to his children in business matters would be criticized for immorality in this mode.

In reality impersonal and personal market modes are not so neatly separated. Corporations often want their employees to feel a "family" loyalty towards the firm. This normally means they should place the corporation's interests above their own in the short run, in return for the expectation of sharing the firm's long run success. Family farmers often exchange services and goods in the name of "neighboring" and friendship, while they secretly record a count of the economic values exchanged "to keep things straight" (Bennett 1968).

Long term trading partnerships, in which elements of impersonal and of personal modes intermingle, are often found in peasant marketplaces. The goal of each actor is his or her economic self-interest, yet the maintainance of the relationship is valued over an immediate short run profit. Transactions are contracted in specific commercial terms but a parallel relationship of generalized reciprocity seems to support the strictly commercial relationship. The key element is that exchanges do not have to be balanced in the short run, since past or future short-falls are adjusted in the continuing stream of exchanges.

I name this latter class of economic relationships "equilibrating" to call attention to these key features: the predominance of long- over short-run goals and the flexible, continuing process of reciprocating value in a relationship that is explicitly instrumental. Several ethnographic examples will be given before an analysis of the importance of information in exchanges.

III. ETHNOGRAPHIC CASES OF EQUILIBRATING RELATIONSHIPS

In some circumstances equilibrating relationships become so strong and regular (i.e., formalized) that they are described as "trading partnerships". One of the most significant contributions of the economic anthropology of markets has been to analyze such relationships in the markets of underdeveloped societies. Mintz

136

provided the seminal description of these partnerships in Haiti, where they are known as pratik:

> A buying pratik who knows her selling pratik is coming will wait at the proper place and time, refusing to buy stock from others that she is sure her pratik is carrying ... to the extent that her stock is committed in such arrangements a selling pratik will refuse to sell to others until she has met her pratik buyer. (Mintz 1964:61).

Likewise in Jamaica:

> All country higglers have regular "customers" among growers and town higglers and weekend town higglers ... if she comes to the market regularly, there will always be some who will buy plentiful, because they want to keep scarcity ... Established stall holders (town higglers) have built up a clientele among country people who come directly to them each time they come to the market, rather than search among town higglers whom they do not know for the highest price obtainable. (Katzin 1960:300).

Trager characterizes Nigerian Onibara relationships as:

> ...long-lasting dyadic ties formed between individuals operating in the market place. At a minimum, they imply the existence of regular transactions between the individuals. They may also involve extension of credit, concessions in quantity, reduction in price, and multiplex social ties (1981:133).

Geertz discusses "clients" in a Moroccan bazaar:

> ...by partitioning the bazaar crowd into those who are genuine candidates for his attention and those who are merely theoretically such, clientelization reduces search to manageable proportions and transform a diffuse mob into a stable collection of familiar antagonists. The use of repetitive exchange between acquainted partners to limit the costs of search is a practical consequence of the overall institutional structure of the bazaar and an element within that structure (1978:30).

Szanton describes Suki relationships in the

137

Philippines:
> Filippino vendors and buyers direct most of their attention to establishing personal contacts as the basis for exchange, rather than focusing on the quality and price of the goods themselves (1972:100).

Davis elaborates upon these Suki relations:
> [they] are important mechanisms for the reduction of trading risks, and as such they are advantageous to both parties. On his side, the seller obtains a greater measure of control over some important economic variables in the marketplace sector. Most important, the seller is able to achieve secure market outlets for his stock through suki relations, and these give him more complete information regarding the minimal size of the market to which he should orient his operation. He is able, by these means, to commit only a minimum amount of his capital to inventory and to use his reserves in other investments which might be more profitable. When demand is high and business is brisk, sellers complain privately that conditions oblige them to pursue a strategy which leads the slow turnover of their capital. But at the same time they realize that for the better part of the year their suki customers are their salvation (1973:225).

And Swetnam summarizes the feelings of Guatemalan marketers about cliente relations:
> Rural cultivators of fruits, vegetables, and flowers feel that they must sell their goods in a single day for their goods will decline in quality before the next selling opportunity. Middlemen with whom a producer does not have personal relationships sense this advantage and bargain vigorously to drive the price as low as possible. A cliente, in contrast, will pay the prevailing price with no bargaining, and will accept delivery of the goods unless he has absolutely no use for the product. In return, the agricultural producer is expected to deliver his best produce to the middleman (1978:147).

Traders report many reasons for these

138

relationships. The sellers' desire to stabilize and regularize their incomes, and the buyers' wish to do the same for their value over the long run are fundamental. Mintz's summary can serve for all:

> Those middlemen who make pratik state that they trade some part of their gain in return for long-range security, and some protection from the vagaries of the market (1964:262).

IV.   ELEMENTS OF EXCHANGES: GOODS, TRANSACTIONS, ACTORS

In order to understand why a trader concentrates on security before income, the concept of an exchange will be analyzed into three major components: goods, meaning the things exchanged (including services in the same term for simplicity); transactions, referring to the rules, understandings and procedures which pertain; and actors, meaning the persons engaging in the exchange. The classic model of perfect competition is predicated on full information about goods, transactions, and actors. In the real world the information necessary for safe and sensible decisions is always imperfect and incomplete.

A. Goods

Goods possess multiple attributes, or qualities, which a buyer must learn about. Nelson (1970) has distinguished two aspects of goods: "search" and "experience" quality. The former denotes obvious attributes - the style, size, or color in clothing, for example. The consumer's problem is to locate the preferred bundle of attributes in the market. "Experience" quality refers to those attributes revealed only through use, such as durability in clothing. The buyer's information problem is to find out any particular good's "experience" quality before purchase, when that quality is not apparent.

For example a new car is high in "search" quality, since it is standardized. A buyer may assume that any given car of a particular make and model is the same as any other, and devote his or her time to searching out the best deal. But a used car is an "experience" good. It may be a normal specimen or it may be a "lemon". How is an average buyer to know?

139

Consider the plight of the seller of a used car in perfect condition: a "cream puff". The seller knows that his car is worth more than most similar cars, but how does the buyer? Unless the seller can give accurate information about his unique automobile to the buyer, the latter will normally only offer an average price (since used cars are not standardized like new cars, the original equivalence of model and price no longer holds).

Akerloff's influential work shows how the situation becomes worse as the used car market is flooded with "lemons", or below-average cars (1970). Since buyers cannot evaluate the cars as well as sellers, lemons can be sold as averagecars for profit. The reasonable buyer who becomes familiar with the market will not offer more than the value of a "lemon" if he cannot evaluate each car. A seller of an average or superior car will be faced with accepting less than fair value, or of not selling his car at all.

The problem is that the buyer and the vendor do not have the same information about the value of the good. Since the buyer cannot rely upon a standardized rule to assess value (as he can with new cars), he and the vendor must somehow agree upon a fair, accurate measure of the value of unique and variable goods.[2] Equilibrating relationships resolve this problem by extending the payment schedule of each transaction, the quid pro quo, in time so that problems can be adjusted. Others must rely on the seller's reputation in the community, spend the resources to evaluate the car on their own, take the risk of buying a "lemon", or stay out of the market.

In more general terms, market performance is impaired, in fact a market may cease to function without government intervention, in conditions of "asymmetrical imperfect information" (Spence 1976).[3] This issue is relevant to the developing world, since most goods traded in traditional market systems are unstandardized and highly variable. Hence the problem of establishing value is crucial. Akerloff's contribution is to show that unequal information about variable goods is at the heart of the market problem. The solution chosen in most situations of cheap labor is to personalize the trade relationship, so that equilibration can reduce the risks created by imperfect information.

B. Transactions

The information most relevant to a transaction is the price, the conditions of payment, and the probability that the transaction will be successfully completed. Knowledge of the price alone is not enough, since one must also know the context. Exchanges which occur under short-run profiteering conditions are obviously different from those where the terms of the transaction are in line with a long-run pattern. For example the unreliable distribution of commodities to an area allows local monopolization. When the sugar (or cooking oil, etc.) delivery fails to arrive to a hinterland town, the storeowners may withdraw old stock from their shelves in order to mark it up or sell it "under the counter". Consumers with long term relationships may buy at the "normal" price, or may be assured of a supply in this circumstance. Automobile drivers in the U.S. learned this lesson in the gasoline shortages of the mid 1970's, when some drivers found it convenient to make off-hours appointments with their gasoline dealer to buy a tank of gas.

The rules which define payment include the specification of what things may be exchanged (cash, other valuables, services) and the time frame (immediate or deferred payment, credit charges, etc.). If the transaction mode allows value to generalize to other domains, then an imbalance in the quid pro quo means less than otherwise. For example long-distance itinerant traders I studied in Chiapas, Mexico would sell their goods cheaply to hinterland Indian customers from whom they would buy food and lodging. In the traders' minds the lower income received for goods was worth the assurance of hospitality; for the Indians the sowing of hospitality reaped cheaper manufactured goods and cultural brokerage (Plattner 1975).

People in rich economies tend to assume that transactions will probably be completed as specified. Communities in the U.S. have small claims courts, Better Business Bureaus, and consumer protection agencies as support systems. Businessmen have all the legal protection they can buy. People in most poor countries have little faith in transactions with distant partners. Liberal laws may exist, but social resources to protect economic transactions are usually not available.

141

Even with the social protection available in wealthy countries, the nature of some goods prohibits a full inspection of quality before sale. Wilson shows how fishermen and packers create equilibrating relationships to overcome the uncertainties of transactions in fresh fish (1980). It is simply impossible to unload a shipload of fish before a sale to verify the precise value of such a perishable and variable commodity. In addition to that uncertainty, the resale price obtainable by the packers is not knowable at the time of purchase. Acheson (this volume) shows how the lack of market information in the Maine lobster industry stimulates long term dyadic ties.

Buyers of fresh produce on wholesale spot markets face the same problem. The conditions under which they transact their business make it impossible to examine the entire lot. They buy produce in the middle of the night, with strong social pressures to buy large quantities of boxed produce, that cannot be inspected until it is unpacked at the point of retail sale. The best buyers are those who have efficient personal relationships with wholesalers (Plattner 1982, 1983).

In summary, problematic information about prices, payments and probabilities increases risk in transactions. Williamson interprets this risk as a heavy cost to producers, and assumes that it is the major variable explaining why firms choose to incorporate the production of intermediate goods rather than purchase them on a spot market (1981). Ouchi extends Williamson's transaction cost analysis to hypothesize that "clan" industrial organization - where productive efficiency is obtained through high levels of goal congruence and ambiguous measures of individual performance - can solve problems of market failure too severe for bureaucratic firms (1980) (Ouchi uses the term "clan" loosely, and gives for example the Japanese industrial practice of lifetime employment). In fact, this is not an all-or-nothing proposition, and the ethnographic literature shows that traders use equilibrating modes of relationships to decrease their risk of loss in a market.

C. Actors

Economists from Adam Smith to Milton Friedman

142

have dreamed of a market where the smooth workings of competition insures economic efficiency between faceless traders. But problems of information create incentives for people to know more than the nature of the goods and the transaction.

A well-known example of troublesome personal information concerns "adverse selection" in an insurance market. A vendor of dental insurance, for example, can set his rates by calculating the cost of fixing an average person's teeth. People with bad teeth will have incentives to sign up, since they expect heavy dental bills. The insurance, being predicated on the average need, will cost less than they expect to spend. People with good teeth may or may not sign up, depending upon their preference for insurance. But if the people with dental problems are over-represented in the insurance company's clientele, then the insurer must raise the rates to cover the higher-than-average costs. The higher the rates, the less likely the healthy folks are to join, and the higher the proportion of expensive clients, bringing about even higher costs, and so on.

This is a problem of information, as Akerloff points out (1970:493). The vendor of insurance does not know the likelihood that his insured population will claim benefits as well as the buyers do. Without accurate information about the personal characteristics of each client - a look in each horse's mouth - or some institutional support like group rates or Medicare, the market will fail. This will leave eople who want to buy insurance unable to deal with people who want to sell.

In circumstances of pervasive market ignorance the most significant piece of information to know about a trader is what social category he or she belongs to. In the extreme this may be a caste identity, otherwise it may be a class, kinship or social network affiliation.[4] Knowing who a trader is may sometimes be the best way to know what he is buying or selling. Ben-Porath argues that specialization in identity can also create savings (1980). He generalizes Adam Smith's argument that specialization lowers costs because of returns to scale in production. The scale benefits exist when a significant part of the costs are "set-up" as opposed to production flow costs (the difference between a license to trade and a tax on sales). The larger the fraction of total costs

143

that are one-time expenses, the cheaper the unit cost can be with expanded production. The same fixed cost is divided into ever smaller parts.

If a significant part of costs are transaction costs, and if a large part of these can be fixed through repeated exchanges with the same traders, then traders gain real cost savings by dealing with known partners (cf. Coase 1937). These may include the costs of defining the rules of the exchange or of establishing the liklihood that trade will be effective and fair. In situations where these costs are likely to be significant, identity becomes an important factor. Traders invest in resources specific to trusted partners to create a "specialization by identity". This specialization creates the long run relationship which allows equilibration of value in the short run. Acheson (this volume) gives several excellent examples of how this process works in the Maine lobster fishery.

To summarize the argument so far, I have characterized economic exchanges on a continuum whose polar extremes are impersonal and personal modes of behavior. When information about important elements of exchanges is lacking, the impersonal mode of behavior (implying faceless traders and transactions without past or future), involves excessive risk and cost. It may be inadequate to sustain economic exchange if traders deal in goods which are high in experience quality, which can create a restricted "lemons" market; or if prices are variable and transactions are risky; or if traders are ignorant about important attributes of trading partners, so that adverse selection is a problem. In such conditions traders choose to invest their resources in establishing long term relations with partners whose identity becomes a factor of economic value (if the government does not interve to support the market). The more significant the transaction costs, and the larger the share of set-up over production flow costs, the more likely are traders to seek equilibrating relationships. In the next section I discuss how infrastructural poverty increases risks and costs.

V. MARKET INFRASTRUCTURE: COMMUNICATIONS, POLITICAL INTEGRATION, TRANSPORTATION AND STORAGE

Institutional poverty in communications,

political control, transportation and storage creates problems for buyers and sellers:

A. Communications

If there is no efficient communication network for news of the availability of goods to flow between producing, distributing, and consuming areas, then buyers and sellers must seek out those who have the relevant information and judge for themselves whether their sources are truthful or not. This process is obviously more risky the further one gets from a personal network.

B. Political Integration

If society is poorly integrated under one legal authority, so that contracts made between strangers in one area are not easily enforceable elsewhere, then anyone attempting to trade with someone outside his personal network will face some risk of loss.

For example, in 1968 I studied rural Ladino (non-Indian) traders in the Mayan Indian town of Bachajon, Chiapas, Mexico. They obtained their dry goods from the stores in the regional center of San Cristobal de Las Casas, a three-day walk distant. The rural retailers were born in San Cristobal and the personal contacts that they had were the only reason they were provisioned from San Cristobal rather than from other sources in the region. They knew that prices were lower in the state capital. But they had no credit with wholesalers in the capital since they didn't live there, and could not afford to buy merchandise with cash (Plattner 1975). Retailers also knew that factories in Mexico City sold merchandise more cheaply, but they could not afford the trip (by mule to the regional center and by bus to the capital, a one-way total of four travel days) and did not have the contacts needed to place their orders.[5]

C. Transportation and Storage

If the state of roads, railways, and other avenues of transportation makes costs extraordinarily high, then poorer people will be priced out of the market. Likewise if processing or storage facilities are not available to prolong the life of perishable items, then the variability of goods

145

will be increased, as will the problems discussed above with respect to experience goods. The factors mentioned here heighten seasonal variation in agricultural goods and cause sporadic fluctuations in the supply of all goods not produced in a local area. Mintz describes the effects of this in Haiti, where

> ...distribution is likely to have a markedly irregular character. This unevenness is magnified when seasonal variation in the supply of various goods, and income, is often sharp, ... Under such circumstances, pratik relationships stabilize sequences of dyadic economic transactions. Taken together, they afford greater order to the distributing system as a whole (1961:55).

D. Factors of Production: Cheap Labor and Scarce Capital

In markets where capital is expensive and labor cheap, the "style" of economic relationships requires a heavy input of time. Barbara Ward's seminal work has shown how the credit market in traditional societies is instituted on the need for personal relationships between creditors and debtors (1960). Ward shows that asymmetrical information about credit causes adverse selection, which is avoided by knowledge from personal relationships. Her work is important because she showed that a non-Western style of relationships was based upon familiar economic constraints.

Equilibrating relationships ordinarily require much personal service and time. Geertz, for example, explains the intensive personal effort that marketing in a Moroccan Suq requires:

> Indeed, the enormous multiplication, not only of marketplaces and cycles of marketplaces, but of units within marketplaces, and the fractionization of exchange, the elongation of transaction chains, and the intensification of specialization that go with that multiplication...are related features of a system in which exchange is mediated across a thousand webs of informal personal contract. (1979:220)

146

In summary, the infrastructural problems that give rise to the need for equilibrating relationships also maintain a low value of labor, and facilitate the process of specialization by identity. The "old-fashioned" style of business in many "traditional" countries, where personal conversation and sociability circumscribe business relationships, has a clear basis in economic structure (cf. Dannhaeuser 1979).

VI. CONCLUSION

In socioeconomic environments rich in information, impersonal market relationships are suitable for goods high in "search" quality. The poorer the information, the higher the "experience" quality of the goods, and the higher the transaction costs, then the riskier the exchange and the more valuable an investment in personalized relationships.

This discussion has dealt with market societies, but the principles generalize to any economic exchange. A New Guinea tribesman seeking to barter feather plumes for shells must also be concerned with the risk that his transaction will fail (Healey 1984). Exchanges that are consummated immediately usually take place between unrelated persons. Most transactions where the payback is delayed are between kinsmen. The additional support of a kinship tie is relied upon to reduce the risk of default.

In many cases tribesmen seeking to exchange goods call unrelated persons by kinterms. This extension of kinship expectations to non-kin is built on relationships such as natal residential ties between the traders' mothers. Healey notes that "the search for kinship ties between erstwhile strangers introduces moral principles that should obtain between the parties" (1984:55). In other words, the lack of political integration between local communities increases the risk that traders will default, so individuals personalize their exchange relationships. Embedding such relationships in a kinship matrix lowers the risk because of the added moral sanction.

In later papers I will add to this analysis by examining how status as a buyer or seller, the market order or scale of the goods, and the buyer's expertise affects the relationship. For example vendors of produce, of clothing, and of machinery in marketplaces will have different needs for equilibration based on the different supply and demand characteristics of the goods they deal in. These concerns will not simply be mirrored on the demand side, since buyers will be influenced by their own budgetary situations. Buyers of new and complex goods such as computers need to establish service relationships with knowledgeable sellers. These sorts of factors make people sensitive to the importance of long-term relationships versus short-term economic gain.

In this paper I have shown how individuals struggle to get around problems of inefficiency and disequilibrium by creating and using the personal networks available to them. The approach taken here is to analyze the difference in economic behavior between societies as due to economic constraint and rational choice, rather than to differences of cultural or economic values and goals. This is not meant to deny the importance of such differences, but to put them into perspective.

ACKNOWLEDGMENTS

I owe thanks to John Bennett and Steve Sellers for helpful critical discussions. An early version of this paper was written by Matthew Hall, Suzanne Monastra, and the author in spring 1982. The analytical sections have been substantially revised since then, but the significant, creative contributions of Hall and Monastra are gratefully acknowledged.

NOTES

1. I use the term equilibrating rather than reciprocal for these intermediary modes in order to point to the balancing procedure that the back-and-forth transactions are aimed at. The term does not imply equilibrium in the conventional economic sense.

2. Note that the individual's problem of not having enough information to make a sensible decision translates into society's problem of the useless market which brings sellers and buyers together who cannot agree upon a price.

3. Akerloff's model is perfectly general, its application to the used car market being merely convenient for exposition. However note Bond's (1982) study of a real-world market for used pick-up trucks which was not saturated with "lemons". The repair rate of trucks bought used and trucks bought new was not different once age and use had been controlled for. Bond suggests that used truck buyers have lower effective repair costs than new truck buyers.

4. Akerloff describes a model of economic discrimination by the identity of actors, in an analysis of market problems caused by inaccurate measures of individual production. He discusses exchanges in a caste system where "any transaction that breaks the caste taboos changes the subsequent behavior of uninvolved parties toward the caste-breakers (1976:609). He also shows how a racially discriminated group may fall into a "lower-level equilibrium trap" where predictions of inferior performance are self-fulfilled. These can be seen as problems of information, in that some proxy measure such as race or caste membership is used instead of an accurate measure of a person's performance.

5. By 1982 the economic development of the region had advanced so that goods were available by telegraph order from central Mexico, or from large warehouses in the state capital. Plattner 1982a describes the impact of economic development on a community of traders.

REFERENCES CITED

Akerloff, George
    1970   The Market for "Lemons": Quality Uncertainty and the Market Mechanism. Quarterly Journal of Economics 84:488-500.

    1976   The Economics of Caste and of the Rat Race and Other Woeful Tales. Quarterly Journal of Economics 90:599-617.

Bennett, John
    1968   Reciprocal Economic Exchanges Among North American Agricultural Operators. Southwestern Journal of Anthropology 24:276-309.

Ben-Porath, Yoram
1980   The F-Connection: Families, Friends, and
        Firms and the Organization of Exchange.
        Population and Development Review 6:1-30.

Bond, Eric
1982   A Direct Test of the "Lemons" Model": The
        Market for Used Pickup Trucks. American
        Economic Review 72:836-840.

Boulding, Kenneth
1973   The Economy of Love and Fear. Belmont, Ca:
        Wadsworth.

Cancian, Frank
1966   Maximization as Norm, Strategy and Theory.
        American Anthropologist 68:465-470.

Coase, Ronald
1937   The Nature of the Firm. Economica 4:386-405.

Dannhaeuser, Norbert
1979   Development of a Distribution Channel in the
        Philippines: From Channel Integration to
        Channel Fragmentation. Human Organization
        38:74-78.

Davis, William
1973   Social Relations in a Philippine Market.
        Berkeley: University of California Press.

Geertz, Clifford
1978   The Bazaar Economy: Information and Search in
        Peasant Marketing. American Economic Review
        68:28-32.

1979   Suq: The Bazaar Economy in Sefrou.   in
        Meaning and Order in Moroccan Society, C.
        Geertz, H. Geertz, & L. Rosen, pp. 123-314.
        New York: Cambridge University Press.

Healey, Christopher
1984   Trade and Sociability: Balanced Reciprocity
        as Generosity in the New Guinea Highlands.
        American Ethnologist 11:42-60.

Katzin, Margret
1960   Business of Higglering in Jamaica. Social
        and Economic Studies 9:297-331.

Mauss, Marcel
  1967   The Gift. N.Y.:Norton. (Translated from the
          French "Essai sur le don", L'Annee
          Sociologique Paris, 1923.)

Mintz, Sidney
  1961   Pratik: Haitian Personal Economic
          Relationships. Proceedings of the 1961 Annual
          Spring Meeting of the American Ethnological
          Society, pp. 54-63.

  1964   The Employment of Capital by Market Women in
          Haiti. in Capital, Saving and Credit, R.
          Firth & B. Yamey eds, Chicago: Aldine. pp.
          256-286.

Nelson, Paul
  1970   Information and Consumer Behavior. Journal
          of Political Economy 78:311-329.

Ouchi, William
  1980   Markets, Bureaucracies and Clans.
          Administrative Science Quarterly 25:129-142.

Plattner, Stuart
  1975   The Economics of Peddling. in Formal Methods
          in Economic Anthropology, S. Plattner,
          editor, Washington D.C.: American
          Anthropological Association. pp. 55-76.

  1982   Economic Custom in a Public Marketplace.
          American Ethnologist 9:399-420.

  1982a   Fifteen Years of Economic Development in
          Chiapas Through the Viewpoint of Barrio
          Cuxtitali. English translation of ms.
          prepared for conference "Forty Years of
          Anthropological Studies in Chiapas", July 19-
          23 1982, San Cristobal de Las Casas,
          Chiapas, Mexico.

  1983   Economic Custom in a Competitive Market
          Place. American Anthropologist 85:848-858.

Polanyi, Karl
  1957   The Economy as Instituted Process. in Trade
          and Market in the Early Empires. K. Polanyi,
          C. Arensberg & H. Pearson, eds. Glencoe,
          Il:Free Press. pp. 243-270.

Sahlins, Marshall
  1972   On the Sociology of Primitive Exchange. in
          Stone Age Economics. Chicago: Aldine.   pp.
          185-275.

Spence, Michael
  1976   Informational Aspects of Market Structure: An
          Introduction. Quarterly Journal of Economics
          90:591-597.

Swetnam, John
  1978   Interaction Between Urban and Rural Residents
          in a Guatemalan Marketplace.   Urban
          Anthropology 7:137-153.

Szanton, Maria
  1972   Right to Survive.   University Park: Penn.
          State U. Press.

Trager, Lillian
  1981   Customers and Creditors: Variations in
          Economic Personalism in a Nigerian Marketing
          System. Ethnology 20:133-146.

Ward, Barbara
  1960   Cash or Credit Crops? Economic Development
          and Cultural Change 8:148-163.

Williamson, Oliver
  1981   The Economics of Organization: The
          Transaction Cost Approach. American Journal
          of Sociology 87:548-577.

Wilson, James
  1980   Adaptation to Uncertainty and Small Numbers
          Exchange: The New England Fresh Fish Market.
          Bell Journal of Economics 11:491-504.

ECONOMIC RATIONALITY IN A COMPETITIVE MARKETPLACE: WHEN TO MIX APPLES AND ORANGES

Daniel Byrne, School of Social Sciences, University of California, Irvine.

I. INTRODUCTION

The assumption that firms seek to maximize profits, and act in a rational manner to achieve this goal, underlies microeconomic theory. While economists admit that most firms in fact do not and often cannot calculate marginal costs and revenues, and hence do not strictly maximize profits, nonetheless the profit maximization hypothesis persists; many economists operate on the working assumption that firms which survive competition must be profit maximizers since competition enforces profit maximization as a norm (Nicholson, 1983:293). If firms are surviving but are not profit maximizers, then what are they doing? I argue here tha many firms survive by trading off short-run profits for long-term security. They do this by specializing in a particular market niche and establishing regular customers.

Specialization is not a profit maximizing strategy to the extent that the set of products which define a firm's niche may not be the "most profitable"[1] set of products at any given time. A profit maximizing firm would search for the most profitable set of products; this set would certainly vary over time, thus the firm would not occupy any narrowly-defined market niche.

Specialization favors long-term security to the extent that firms develop expertise, avoid risk involved in handling unfamiliar products and attract regular customers. This risk-averse strategy is consistent with what economic anthropologists have found in other contexts (Cancian, 1979; Johnson, 1977). Specialization also simplifies a firm's decision making by relegating potential decisions to habit or custom (Plattner, 1982).

The main problem addressed here concerns the demonstration of specialization in a public marketplace. While it may seem obvious upon inspection that certain firms regularly stock certain products, an empirical demonstration of the presence of consistent market niches and corresponding product clusters provides rigorous support for the argument that specialization is an important component of the economic rationality underlying the behavior of many firms in a public marketplace.

Plattner (1982:416) argues that fresh produce merchants in a competitive public marketplace "rely on custom and habit, as well as on market information, in order to solve their weekly decision problem." This contention is based primarily on the positive contributionto a firm's gross sales (ceteris paribus) statistically attributable to the constancy of its produce inventory from week to week. Plattner used 'constancy of produce assortment' as a proxy measure of the degree to which firms participated in regular vendor-customer relationships. The statistical relationship between 'constancy' and gross sales was interpreted as an indication of the importance of economic custom or habit at the marketplace studied. He hypothesized that firms would avoid making major decisions each week about their produce inventory, rather they would tend to remain in the same 'market niche' (e.g., small-scale fruit merchant), despite the fact that a profit-oriented economic rationality should predispose them to select the most profitable produce portfolio each week. The logic underlying his argument is simply that vendors are familiar with a particular niche (often inherited from their parents), and that they are catering to customers who regularly buy the same products from the same stands each week (Plattner, 1984).

Plattner used a variable called 'Similar' to measure the degree of 'niche constancy' (and economic custom by implication) for each firm each week. This similarity coefficient measured the degree of correspondence between a firm's produce assortments at each pair of adjacent weeks.[2] Unfortunately this similarity coefficient is a potentially ambiguous indicator of niche constancy in the long run, or even over a five week period, because it does not distinguish between a change of niches (produce assortments) or simply the temporary unavailability of some key produce items. Consider the following hypothetical scenario: a firm exhibits a high similarity coefficient for the first pair of adjacent weeks, then a low similarity for the next two pairs of weeks, and then a high similarity for the last pair of adjacent weeks. This could mean that most of the firm's 'regular' produce items were not avialable at the wholesale market during the third week; or it could mean that the firm changed niches and

154

adopted a fundamentally different set of items!

What is needed to resolve this indeterminacy is a demonstration of the presence of consistent, identifiable niches on the market during the sixty week period of data collection. Such a demonstration is presented in the following pages. I will show that two dominant clusters of firms (i.e., niches) are identifiable by virtue of distinctive produce inventories, thus providing empirical support for the hypothesis that economic specialization is an important part of the rationality or logic underlying the behavior of merchants. Firms form clusters by virtue of their common tendency to stock the same products (and thus niches are defined). From the opposite perspective, corroborative support will be derived from a demonstration of the presence of clusters of products, which are similar by virtue of their tendency to appear together on the stands of many different merchants.

II. SOULARD MARKET

The data for this analysis come from Plattner's study of economic decision making at Soulard Market, Saint Louis, Missouri from 1978 through 1979.[3] Soulard Market is a bustling public marketplace located just south of downtown St. Louis. The market consists of an 'H' shaped structure composed of a central building housing a Market Master's office and several enclosed shops, and four wings of stalls extending from the central building on an east/west axis. Parts of the southeast and southwest wings are enclosed by walls while the rest of the wings are open-air roofed sheds. There are 272 numbered stalls, most of which are rented yearly by farmers (33%) and produce merchants (40% in 1977), many of whom rent multiple, contiguous stalls. Most merchants are open on Friday and Saturday throughout the summer, with a few remaining year round. Most farmers conduct business on Saturdays from spring through fall. Vendors sell a wide range of fresh produce items to consumers drawn from nearby neighborhoods and suburban St. Louis.

The nature and history of ethnicity and occupations at Soulard Market, and its economic functions within a nationwide wholesale produce distribution system dominated by supermarkets have been discussed elsewhere (Byrne & Plattner, 1980; Eckstein & Plattner, 1978; Plattner, 1978). An interesting aspect of ethnicity and occupations at Soulard worth mentioning here is

155

that most (69%) of the produce merchants are of Italian descent while most (79% in 1977) of the farmers are German. Moreover, many tenants are related to each other and/or to past market tenants through affinal and consanguinal ties, for which reason this pattern of ethnic specialization has persisted for several generations.

Produce merchants shop the wholesale market ("Produce Row") each week early in the morning (2-5am) on Thursday, Friday and occasionally Saturday. Decisions about which produce items to stock and in what quantities are made in this all-male atmosphere. This is also the place where "special deals" are made between enterprising vendors and brokers or jobbers who are stuck with odd lots or shipments that have been damaged in transit or rejected by buyers from supermarket chains. While these "special deals" are a potentially important source of a produce merchant's profits each week, it is my contention that they are peripheral to the normal, customary produce selection process which results in the merchant's specialization in a particular market niche.

III. DATA ANALYSIS

The original dataset consists of observations of products (and prices) on the stands of 69 firms on 60 consecutive Saturdays from the last weekend of June, 1978 to the second weekend of August, 1979. The present analysis is concerned with produce merchants only, thus data pertaining to 27 farmers and 11 `combinations' (farmers who buy some of their produce for resale) have been omitted. During the period of data collection 119 different products were observed at Soulard Market. The 45 fresh produce items to be analyzed here are those which remained after:

1)   products that never appeared on the stands of merchants were omitted (e.g., kohlrabi, salsify, etc.);

2)   products that were marginal were omitted (i.e., those which had fewer than 120 observations); and;

3)   products that are minor varieties of a major item were omitted (e.g., endive lettuce, concord grapes, green apples, etc.). [4]

156

A. Methods

Data for 31 merchants (restricted to the set of 45 products) provided the input for the computation of a merchant/merchant similarity matrix. Likewise data for 45 products (restricted to the set of 31 merchants) were used to compute a product/product similarity matrix.[5] These two matrices in turn became input (separately) for an additive tree fitting (hierarchical cluster analysis) program (ADDTREE) and a multidimensional scaling (MDS) program (KYST). [6]

Both of these methods produce a visual representation of how a set of objects are interrelated. In the case of cluster analysis this takes the form of a tree diagram where objects (or previously formed clusters thereof) are progressively paired with their 'nearest neighbors' to form a series of nodes which ultimately converge at a common root. The tree thus portrays a family of nested partitions of the set of objects.

In the case of MDS the 'picture' depends on the number of dimensions in which the inter-object relationships are to be represented. MDS takes a matrix of proximities between each pair of objects and determines a configuration of points in a space of N (user-specified) dimensions whose coordinates are chosen so as to minimize the amount of 'stress'; stress is a measure of the 'badness of fit' between the matrix of distances among the generated points and the matrix of distances among the objects. [7]

In this analysis MDS has been performed in 1, 2, and 3 dimensions in order to determine whether a substantial decrease in stress resulted as dimensions were added. With both similarity matrices the reduction in stress between 1 and 2 dimensions was substantial, while the differences between 2 and 3 dimensions were not.[8] Thus the results reported here are derived from MDS representations of inter-object similarities in a two-dimensional (Euclidean) space.

The analyses of merchant/merchant and product/product similarities represent direct and indirect assessments of the presence of niches at Soulard Market. In all cases the objective was simply to determine the nature and extent of structure in the representations of each set of objects. Structure is visible to the extent that most firms (and most products) are amalgamated at a high level of similarity

157

(i.e., most objects would be placed close to the root of the tree while clusters of objects would occur far from the root of the tree); and MDS plots of firms (and products) would exhibit distinctive or interpretable patterns. The presence of structure supports the presence of market niches to the extent that it suggests that firms are making customary decisions when they select their produce assortments each week. However it is conceivable that a specific cluster of firms may represent a niche of 'profit-maximizers' who sell whatever the most profitable set of produce is each week at the wholesale market; while this is unlikely it remains a weakness of the present analysis.

B. Cluster Analysis of Merchants

Figure 1 presents the tree diagram produced by the ADDTREE cluster analysis of the merchant/merchant similarity matrix. The simple principle underlying this representation is that similar firms are placed near each other; the distance between any pair of firms is a linear function of the length of the horizontal lines (arcs) separating them. Three major market niches may be deduced from this diagram; these are labelled and identified in Table 1. The first cluster represents a niche of large-scale fruit and vegetable merchants; the second niche consists of small-scale fruit merchants. The third niche is slightly anomalous; firm #17 should be classified as a large-scale fruit and vegetable merchant but he was only on the market for 12 weeks (due to illness), and firm #22 is a small-scale vegetable merchant and the only black vendor on the market. The remaining five firms concentrate almost exclusively on one or two items (e.g., potatoes; watermelons; lettuce and tomatoes). Ethnographic evidence supports this classification scheme with minor exceptions, notably that several fruit merchants also carry a few common vegetables (e.g., lettuce, tomatoes, green peppers and corn). The measure of stress for this analysis is 0.0667 which suggests a fairly good fit between the original similarity matrix and the ADDTREE model.

C. MDS Analysis of Merchants

Figure 2 presents the final configuration of points (representing firms) in two dimensions produced by the KYST (MDS) computer program. Lines have been drawn around the two groups of firms classified as large-scale fruit and vegetable and small-scale fruit merchants by the ADDTREE cluster analysis; that these

FIGURE 1. ADDTREE CLUSTER ANALYSIS OF 31 PRODUCE MERCHANTS [STRESS=.0667]

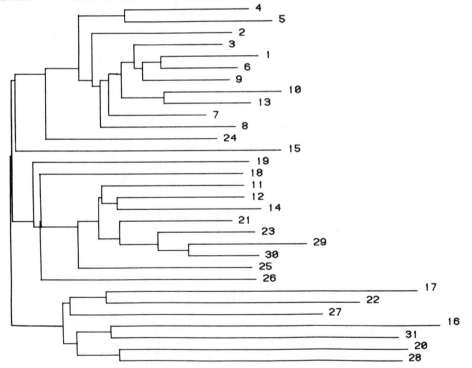

Figure 1.   ADDTREE Cluster Analysis of 31 Produce
Merchants.

159

TABLE 1

Market niches derived from ADDTREE analysis of 31
merchants.

NICHE	FIRM #	Average number of items (s.d.)
LARGE-SCALE FRUIT	1	38.9 (4)
AND VEGETABLE	2	22.8 (4)
MERCHANTS	3	27.8 (7)
	4	19.2 (6)
	5	12.7 (9)
	6	27.6 (8)
	7	24.8 (6)
	8	19.4 (7)
	9	22.3 (5)
	10	19.0 (3)
	13	16.5 (2)
	24	10.7 (4)

Average = 21.8 (7.2)

SMALL-SCALE FRUIT	11	14.4 (4)
MERCHANTS	12	9.7 (4)
	14	8.4 (3)
	18	10.6 (4)
	19	8.8 (5)
	21	9.5 (3)
	23	10.3 (3)
	25	8.2 (3)
	26	8.7 (4)
	29	7.4 (2)
	30	8.3 (2)

Average = 9.48 (1.8)

UNIQUE AND	16	1.7 (2)
ANOMALOUS	17	18.8 (6)
MERCHANTS	20	3.3 (4)
	22	10.1 (4)
	27	6.0 (3)
	28	3.2 (2)
	31	3.7 (2)

Average = 6.69 (5.6)

| UNCLASSIFIED | 15 | 7.9 (5) |

----

two groups do not overlap in space corroborates the
ADDTREE classification, and further supports the
contention that niches are present on the market. The
horizontal dimension of the MDS plot may be loosely
interpreted as corresponding to a fruits-vegetables
continuum. The measure of stress for this analysis is
0.141 which indicates a poor fit relative to the
ADDTREE model, but a moderately good fit for MDS
considering the number of firms in the analysis.

D. Cluster Analysis of Products

Figure 3 presents the tree diagram resulting from an
ADDTREE analysis of the product/product similarity
matrix based on data for 31 produce merchants. Several
clusters of products are apparent. Reading from the
top of the page, apples and oranges are a natural
combination (despite the cliche), and bananas and
tomatoes are the two most frequently observed fruits on
the market; these two pairs of fruits form the
characteristic core fruit inventory of all produce
merchants. This set of four fruits is combined with
lemons, medium and small oranges, pink grape-fruit,
black grapes and pears to form a set of basic fruits;
grapes and pears are somewhat unexpected here since
both are more seasonal than the other fruits in this
set. Green grapes, cherries, red and black plums and
nectarines are highly seasonal while cantaloupe and
peaches are less seasonal and are available from local
farmers during summer. Pineapples are quite exotic and
were only carried by one merchant regularly; yellow
corn here is anomalous.

With the exception of corn and pineapples, the above
fruits constitute the 'core and periphery' of the
typical fruit merchant inventory and the characteristic
fruit section of the inventory of a typical large-scale
fruit and vegetable merchant. However, as noted
earlier, it is the case ethnographically that several
fruit merchants carry lettuce (to go with the tomatoes)
and use green peppers, cucumbers, celery and carrots as
"shelf items" (i.e., items placed in small quantities
on a shelf that extends from the main body of the
stand; this is substantiated by the proximity of these
five items to the root of the tree. These five
vegetables constitute the characteristic soup and salad
vegetable section of the inventory of a typical fruit
and vegetable merchant, while green onions and radishes
are slightly less common salad vegetables. These soup
and salad items are combined with broccoli, cauliflower
and cabbage to form a cluster of common vegetables.

161

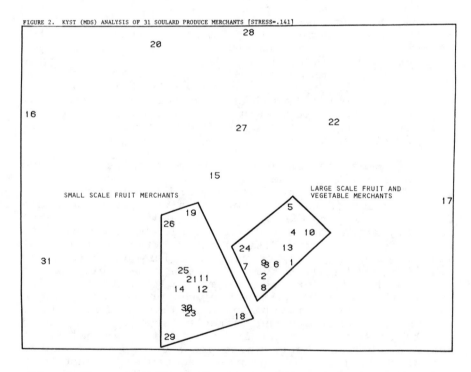

FIGURE 2.   KYST (MDS) ANALYSIS OF 31 SOULARD PRODUCE MERCHANTS [STRESS=.141]

Figure 2.   KYST (MDS) Analysis of 31 Soulard Produce
            Merchants.

162

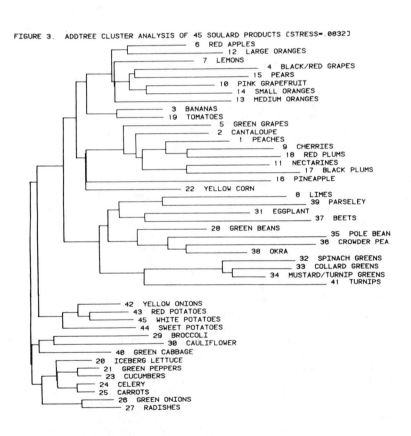

FIGURE 3. ADDTREE CLUSTER ANALYSIS OF 45 SOULARD PRODUCTS [STRESS=.0832]

6   RED APPLES
12   LARGE ORANGES
7   LEMONS
4   BLACK/RED GRAPES
15   PEARS
10   PINK GRAPEFRUIT
14   SMALL ORANGES
13   MEDIUM ORANGES
3   BANANAS
19   TOMATOES
5   GREEN GRAPES
2   CANTALOUPE
1   PEACHES
9   CHERRIES
18   RED PLUMS
11   NECTARINES
17   BLACK PLUMS
16   PINEAPPLE
22   YELLOW CORN
8   LIMES
39   PARSELEY
31   EGGPLANT
37   BEETS
28   GREEN BEANS
35   POLE BEAN
36   CROWDER PEA
38   OKRA
32   SPINACH GREENS
33   COLLARD GREENS
34   MUSTARD/TURNIP GREENS
41   TURNIPS
42   YELLOW ONIONS
43   RED POTATOES
45   WHITE POTATOES
44   SWEET POTATOES
29   BROCCOLI
30   CAULIFLOWER
40   GREEN CABBAGE
20   ICEBERG LETTUCE
21   GREEN PEPPERS
23   CUCUMBERS
24   CELERY
25   CARROTS
26   GREEN ONIONS
27   RADISHES

Figure 3.   ADDTREE Cluster of 45 Soulard Products.

163

Limes and parsley, like pineapples are exotic and are only carried by a few large fruit and vegetable merchants who can afford such peripheral items.

The remaining vegetables constitute a set of less common items appreciated by many of the lower-income people who reside in neighborhoods (or housing projects) near the market and make up a substantial proportion of the regular shoppers. Within this set, the subset of spinach, collard, mustard and turnip greens constitutes the core of a major market niche dominated by a few farmers (and combinations), and accessible to a few large-scale produce merchants only during winter. A final notable cluster here is that of yellow onions, red and white potatoes and sweet potatoes, which constitute a natural set of less perishable staples. The measure of stress for the tree in Figure 3 is 0.0832 which indicates a fairly good fit between the ADDTREE model and the original product/product similarity matrix.

E. MDS Analysis of Products

Figure 4 presents the result of a two dimensional MDS analysis of the product/product similarity matrix derived from data for 31 merchants. As with the MDS analysis of firm/firm similarities, the horizontal dimension seems to represent a fruits-vegetables continuum. The measure of stress for this configuration is 0.157, which indicates a poor fit relative to the ADDTREE model, but a good fit for MDS given the number of items. The position of tomatoes on the border between fruits (bananas) and vegetables (lettuce) reflects its double role as a key item in the inventories of both large-scale fruit and vegetable merchants and small-scale fruit merchants.

IV. CONCLUSIONS

The preceding analyses have demonstrated that two dominant niches are consistently 'inhabited' by produce merchants at Soulard Market: large-scale fruit and vegetable merchants and small-scale fruit merchants. A third 'residual' niche composed of unique or anomalous merchants has also been noted. In order for a set of firms to be clustered at a high degree of similarity they must consistently stock the same produce. As noted above this could occur if all of the firms in a niche had the same items each week, but if the set of products that were the "same" changed from week to week as firms collectively (yet independently) made the same

164

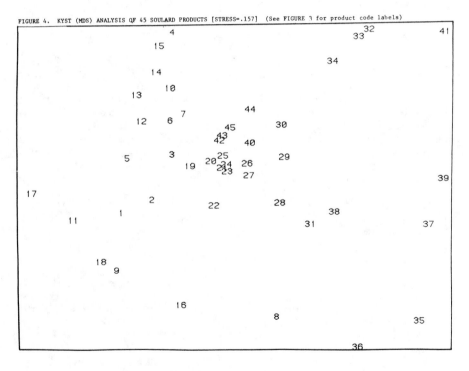

Figure 4.   KYST (MDS) Analysis of 45 Soulard Products.
(See Figure 3 for Product Code Labels)

decisions to buy a relatively different set of items each week; for instance, they may all decide to buy the 'most profitable' set of items, which certainly changes from week to week.

The analysis of firms alone cannot resolve this theoretical indeterminacy about whether niches are defined by products or profits, but an analysis of products can address this issue directly. The analyses of product/product similarities have indicated that certain items consistently appear together on the stands of many firms. This could only occur if many firms were consciously electing to buy clusters or sets of products rather than just one which might happen to be the most profitable while the others (taken alone) may not generate sufficient profits to cover costs. If there is an 'economic rationality' underlying the behavior of merchants in this marketplace, it is one which recognizes the importance of the inherently complementary relationships which obtain within particular sets of produce items. This complementarity is culturally defined: for example, if you're going to buy lettuce you will need tomatoes too, and why not spruce up that nascent salad with some green peppers and cucumbers.

The large-scale fruit and vegetable and small-scale fruit niches are thus defined by 'rational' combinations of complementary products. This has been demonstrated by analyses of both merchant/merchant and product/product similarities using different techniques. These results are not suprising since qualitative ethnographic evidence suggested the above conclusions. The value of this analysis is that it provides rigorous, quantitative evidence and validation of what seems apparent, though not so clearly structured, in the eyes of the participant-observer walking down the aisles of the market on a busy Saturday morning.

NOTES

1. Profitability in this context refers to the difference between the retail price per unit and the wholesale cost per unit. This ignores scale and quantity constraints which are specific to individual firms and would confound aggregate level analyses.

2. For any given firm the similarity coefficient for a pair of adjacent weeks is defined as follows. X and

Y are vectors of 119 zeros and ones, where a 1 indicates that the firm had the product corresponding to that position in the list; X is the inventory vector for the first week and Y is the inventory vector for the second week. Then the similarity S(X,Y) between two weeks' inventories is S(X,Y) = (2(ΣXY))/(ΣX = ΣY); 0 ≤ S(X,Y)≤ 1 and S(X,Y) = S(Y,X). S(X,Y) is generally less than Pearson's r(X,Y) since items that are absent both weeks do not have any effect. The computer program to compute these similarity coefficients, and similarity matrices for firms and products was written by the author.

3. The author worked as a research assistant with Plattner on this project and was responsible for gathering the majority of the inventory data, and for writing several computer programs used to manage and analyze the data. The research was supported by the National Science Foundation and the Offices of Graduate Studies and Research, and International Studies at the University of Missouri, Saint Louis.

4. There were 1436 product/merchant/week observations, where an observation consists of recording the presence of one of the 45 products on the stands of one of the 31 merchants on one of the 60 consecutive Saturdays of data collection.

5. Merchant/merchant and product/product similarities were computed using the same method as described in Note 1: for firms, X and Y are a pair of firms' inventory vectors and are summed across all 60 weeks; and for products, X and Y are vectors of 31 zeros and ones marking which firms had product X and which had product Y each week, then summed across all 60 weeks.

6. The cluster analysis program is named ADDTREE/P (Version 1.2) and was written by James Corter (1982); it is a modification of an original program and algorithm developed by Sattath and Tversky (1977). It represents an improvement on other hierarchical clustering programs (e.g., the MDS(X) series program HICLUS) by removing the "ultrametric inequality" assumption. The effect of this assumption is to put all objects an equal distance from the root of the tree, which implies that the similarity between any object and all other objects is a constant. For information on the KYST (MDS) program see Kruskal and Wish (1978).

7. Kruskal and Wish (1978) aptly summarize the MDS problem as being the opposite of being given a map and asked to produce a distance matrix; MDS starts with a distance matrix and attempts to `draw' the corresponding map, unfortunately in most cases the true dimensionality is not known and the dimensions produced may have no empirical interpretation.

8. The Stress (Formula 1) values for KYST analyses of merchants and products in 1, 2 and 3 dimensions are reported below.

Dimensions	Merchants	Products
1	0.2954	0.3031
2	0.1410	0.1570
3	0.0925	0.1051

REFERENCES CITED

Byrne, Daniel and Plattner, Stuart
    1980   Ethnicity at Soulard Farmers Market since 1930. Bulletin, Missouri Historical Society 36:174-181.

Cancian, Frank
    1979   The Innovator's Situation. Stanford: Stanford University Press.

Corter, James
    1982   DDTREE/P: A PASCAL program for fitting additive trees based on Sattath and Tversky's ADDTREE program. Behavior Research Methods and Instrumentation 14:353-354.

Eckstein, Lorraine and Plattner, Stuart
    1978   Ethnicity and Occupations in Soulard Market, St. Louis, Missouri. Urban Anthropology 7:361-371.

Johnson, Allen
    1977   Security and Risk-Taking among Poor Peasants. In Studies in Economic Anthropology. American Anthropological Association Monograph 7. G. Dalton, ed., pp. 143-150. Washington, DC.

Kruskal, Joseph and Wish, Myron
    1978   Multidimensional Scaling. Beverly Hills: Sage Publications.

Nicholson, Walter
    1983   Intermediate Microeconomics and Its
              Applications. New York: The Dryden Press.

Plattner, Stuart
    1978   Public Markets: Functional Anachronisms or
              Functional Necessities. Ekistics 273:444-
              446.

    1982   Economic Decision Making in a Public
              Marketplace. American Ethnologist 9(2):399-
              420.

    1984   Economic Decision Making of Marketplace
              Merchants: An Ethnographic Model. Human
              Organization 43(3):252-264.

Sattath, Shmuel and Tversky, Amos
    1977   Additive Similarity Trees. Psychometrica
              42(3):319-345.

PART THREE

MARKET STUDIES IN
ECONOMIC DEVELOPMENT

PART THREE

URBAN MARKETS, THE INFORMAL SECTOR, AND DEVELOPMENT
Lillian Trager and Norbert Dannhaeuser

The papers in this section focus on a set of interrelated issues concerning urban markets, the informal sector, and development. The concept of an urban informal sector was originally introduced as part of a critique of earlier dualistic models of development, which tended to distinguish between the "modern" sector of the economy and the "traditional" sector. Hart (1973) and many others since have shown how those economic activities labelled as "traditional" include a vast array of employment opportunities, most of which are not at all traditional but rather are generated in the context of modern third world economic processes. Despite the utility of the concept in identifying a highly significant range of economic activity, and in helping to explore the characteristics of that activity, the concept has also generated considerable controversy and criticism. The papers here accept some of those criticisms and try to move beyond them. Three of the papers focus explicitly on informal sector trade and commerce, while the others use somewhat different approaches to examine relationships between urban markets and development.

These papers differ in two respects from many of the other studies of the informal sector and its role in the urban economy. First, much of the recent research on the informal sector has focused on informal sector production. Such studies tend to stress the ways in which modern industry has displaced small-scale productive units. In contrast, with the exception of Cook, the papers here are primarily concerned with trade and commerce rather than production. Secondly, all the papers, with the exception of McGee's, examine economic activities in the context of provincial and regional urban centers rather than capital cities. While Lessinger studies the large regional center of Madras, Babb, Trager, Dannhaeuser and Cook examine provincial cities ranging in size from 45,000 (Huaraz, Peru) to approximately 200,000 (Ilesha, Nigeria). Relatively little research has been done on economic processes in secondary cities of this sort (cf. Rondinelli, 1983).

The papers in this section examine the following issues: 1) processes of change in urban markets and the informal sector; 2) conceptual issues concerning the informal sector model; 3) implications that studies of

173

change in urban economies have for understanding development.

Babb's study of Huaraz, Peru and Trager's of Ilesha, Nigeria both examine dimensions of informal sector commerce. Building on earlier criticisms of the dualism implicit in the informal sector concept, both are concerned with linkages between change in the formal sector of the economy and informal sector activities. Trager suggests that the construction of a modern industry--a brewery--has led to new commercial opportunities for those in positions to take advantage of them, while Babb argues that, in general, the autonomy of traders has been eroded as formal sector industry has moved further into distributive activities. In addition, both are concerned with noting the internal differentiation and heterogeneity among informal sector traders, and how that diversity affects changing situations of traders in the urban economy.

Lessinger also notes the internal differentiation, but argues that involvement in political movements helps to overcome internal divisions as the traders become united in their efforts to seek political benefits as a group. However, she is concerned only with market place traders--especially those in illegal, squatter markets. The question remains whether there is much likelihood of political organizing among larger sets of traders, whose interests may be quite diverse. In addition, as Lessinger points out, the larger political culture plays an important part in the viability of political movements.

All three of these papers--Babb, Trager, Lessinger-- are concerned with small-scale retail trade, either in the market place or outside. In contrast, Dannhaeuser moves away from the informal sector focus to examine distribution channels, ranging from small to large scale. He argues that, in a situation where there is a mass market for industrial consumer goods, the informal sector approach leads to a focus on only one end of a larger process. The study of distribution channels, in contrast, enables linking the large-scale formal sector supply side with retail marketing. Dannhaeuser uses his research in two cities--one in India and one in the Philippines--to argue that strategies of metropolitan- based formal sector manufacturers and distributors affect the retail structure of intermediate towns. In some situations, companies seek to control distribution by hiring their own dealers; in others, they use lower- level channels--i.e., small-scale, informal sector retail traders. In both cases, marketing strategies, including the use of advertising, affect the overall retail structure.

McGee's paper looks at the other end of the distribution process--the role of consumption in the development of mass markets. Like Dannhaeuser, he is primarily interested in the industrially-produced consumer goods; unlike Dannhaeuser, he stresses the ways in which consumption influences the development of mass markets. Both emphasize the role of advertising as a means by which, on the one hand, consumer needs are created, and on the other hand, retailing strategies are pursued.

Cook's paper takes a still different approach. Less concerned with markets and distribution as such, he emphasizes the role played by merchant capital in production in Oaxaca, Mexico. His focus is on businesses engaged in selling locally-produced craft products; he shows that the largest of these tend to be those which engage in their own production. Interestingly, he is studying a situation where local craft goods are produced for tourist trade and export, in contrast to all the other papers which are concerned with distribution of industrial and other products for the local market.

The authors raise a number of conceptual issues. Most of these revolve around the informal/formal sector model. Trager, McGee, Dannhaeuser, Babb and Lessinger review the criticisms of this model and try to improve its utility from either a structural economic or Marxist perspective. Though offering different solutions, they agree that the dynamic properties of the relations between the sectors need more study.

Trager considers much of the debate surrounding the informal sector arid and believes that the concept is here to stay. But she does not accept it uncritically. She finds the concept of an informal sector useful as long as it is seen in dynamic interaction with the formal sector of the economy and as long as it is realized that members of this sector are not homogeneous in their characteristics. Her paper illustrates the inter-sectoral relations by tracing the impact of new productive facilities upon informal sector traders.

After noting advances in the study of the world political economy, rural-urban migration, and the persistence of poverty in the Third World, McGee turns

175

to the informal sector. He prefers the notion of circuits to stress the interpenetration of the various parts of the urban economy. He argues that in a situation in which a mass market is spreading in the urban and rural population, the different circuits should be regarded as one circuit, in effect discarding the dual sector approach. He believes that this will help us build models describing the capitalist penetration of Third World economies.

Dannhaeuser introduces the channel concept into the debate. He shows that organized market channels constitute institutions of major importance that bridge the formal and informal commercial sectors as the industrial consumer market grows. To understand the character of urban traders in both sectors, one has to understand the channels they are locked into.

The dynamic character of the informal sector is approached differently by Lessinger. She argues that members of this sector frequently change occupations and class positions during their lives. She enriches the concept by adding a political dimension which, among other things, illustrates the effect of capitalist development upon the informal market sector.

Babb's approach also sheds light on the linkage between the formal and informal sectors. She uses the concept of petty commodity production to emphasize the distinct characteristics of small producers and traders and their subordinate position in the capitalist society. Classifying small traders as petty commodity producers also uncovers the productive role of marketing, which makes it possible to analyze how surplus value is transferred from small traders to the capitalist sector.

The productive role of traders is also the subject of Cook, the only author in this section who does not directly enter the informal/formal sector debate. But he does so indirectly. He analyzes the extraction of surplus value by merchant manufacturers, in particular the exploitation occurring in the piece wage work prevalent in the Oaxaca craft business. After noting the super- and hyper-exploitation involved, he discusses the degree to which the urban merchant manufacturers (some of them large, many small) invest the surplus into simple industry and services, rather than into integrated capital industry. Here, craft business and merchant traders are seen as potential, even if not as actual, generators of economic activities in more capital intensive and formally organized productive sectors.

All of the papers suggest implications for development. Using the informal sector approach, Trager and Babb stress rather different types of process. Whereas Babb sees increasing dependence and subordination of informal sector traders, Trager emphasizes the ability of some to respond successfully to changes in the larger economy. In part, the differences are due to differences in the political economy and role of the informal sector in the countries studied. However, both also note instances of opposing trends. For example, Babb says that some traders are able to expand and hire others, thus increasing the differentiation in the informal sector. Trager, whose study took place following a boom period in the Nigerian economy, notes that, in the present poor economic situation, the informal sector is expanding at the lower levels, a process that will no doubt intensify as the economic situation worsens.

Lessinger stresses the important potential for political action by informal sector traders, who may in that way protect and advance their own interests. Further study is needed of possibilities for political movement in other contexts; however, given that many countries do not have a legitimate role for protest, as India does, this may not be a route open in other situations.

McGee argues that the increasing importance of mass consumption in third world cities has important implications for development, with larger amounts of household income going to private consumption stimulated by mass advertising. Further, he argues that the growth of mass markets may lead to the destruction of the "little markets" generally studied by anthropologists. This, however, does not mean the elimination of the informal retail sector, given the evidence in some of the other papers. In particular, Dannhaeuser shows how mass marketing of consumer products can lead, with some marketing strategies, to proliferation of small-scale retail outlets. Further, Trager's data on beer distribution provide an example of a situtation where the same individuals previously engaged in marketing of agricultural products are now distributing an industrially-produced consumer product.

Finally, Cook argues in his study of merchant capital involvement in production of craft products that

177

industry of this sort cannot lead to development. Instead, he proposes that large formal sector industry, even if using external capital, is necessary for development. He does not, however, discuss affects on marketing activity likely to result from such industrial development.

With the possible exception of Madras, none of the cities in which the studies are based have extensive industrial development of the sort advocated by Cook. They are predominantly commercial centers in which the distribution of industrial goods produced elsewhere is a key activity, while distribution of agricultural products also continues to be important. The diffusion of consumer goods on such a massive scale causes the connections between the informal and formal sectors in intermediate cities to become increasingly pronounced. As a number of authors in this section point out, such a condition requires that greater attention be given to these connections in future studies of urban commerce.

REFERENCES

Hart, Keith
    1973   Informal Income Opportunities and Urban Employment in Ghana. Journal of Modern African Studies 11:61-89.

Rondinelli, Dennis A.
    1983   Secondary Cities in Developing Countries. Beverly Hills: Sage Publications.

178

URBAN MARKET CHANNELS UNDER CONDITIONS OF DEVELOPMENT: THE CASE OF INDIA AND THE PHILIPPINES

Norbert Dannhaeuser, Texas A&M University

I. THE COMPARTMENTAL PARADIGM

For two decades it has been standard to consider Third World urban economies as internally compartmentalized. In the most popular version of this paradigm these economies are divided into two sectors, a formal and an informal one. [1] Although this dualistic model has been useful--in a rough way it reflects reality, and it has encouraged the study of the heretofore neglected small-scale economy--it has also lead to difficulties.

For one, there is the matter of the number of sectors. Instead of proposing a dual structure, some prefer to regard Third World city economies as composed of three parts (Friedmann and Sullivan 1974); others stress the complexity of conditions in these settings and apply the concept of fragmentation to describe it (Breman 1976). For another, there is the link between the sectors. Only few argue that the sectors are essentially closed systems with little communication and material flow between them (Tidalgo and Jurado 1978). More commonly, links are admitted to exist, though opinions vary about the nature of the connection. Some see it in terms of super-and subordination in which the informal sector is subsidiary to, yet a necessary complement of, the formal one "in the same way that day requires night in order to be so" (Davies 1979:97; cf. Santos 1979). Here the informal sector serves as a labor cheapening device for the capitalistic expansion of the economy. Others see the relation in terms of the complementary flow of services between the sectors which may be beneficial (or harmful) to all participants (Barth 1984; Hackenberg 1980; House 1984). Finally, regardless of how the link is perceived, more effort has been put into studying each sector than the relation between them.

The compartmental paradigm has prevailed and dualism has been the most popular model also in studies of Third World city commerce. One of the reasons for this is that commerce in Third World cities seems not only to be characterized by labor, but also by product and supply segmentation. Under such condition informal sector traders deal mainly in goods derived from the informal production sector, serve mainly informal sector consumers, and have only limited contact with the formal component of urban commerce (Tokman 1978:197; see also Friedmann and Sullivan 1974:394; Geertz 1963; Slater, et al. 1969). In other words, Third World city trade appears to be divided into two parts. One is composed of labor intensive, small, and familistically organized trade units handling mostly domestic and non-industrial commodities; the other contains capital intensive and bureaucratic enterprises that deal mainly in non-domestic industrial goods. Given this perspective, it is hardly surprising that also in this case each sector has received more attention than the connection between them. [2]

A few years back McGee asked "why the dominant mode of capitalist production [the formal sector] is not acting to dissolve the non-capitalist [informal] modes." One of his answers was, because the petty production sector is unprofitable for the capitalist mode of production since that mode is mainly export oriented and oriented to provision the better off strata of the society (1979:51). This may be true with respect to production, but what about those involved in product distribution?

Since the fifties even in such Third World countries as India and the Philippines (which are hardly in the forefront of development) many large-scale producers and merchant houses have undergone a fundamental reorientation. The domestic consumer market has become important to them. This includes not only provisioning the better off strata of society, but also the poorer levels, though the urban consumer is more exposed to this than the rural. A mass market of industrial consumer goods has come into being which has existed now for quite some time in such low cost items as cigarettes, soft drinks and mill derived textiles, and which is currently spreading into such decidedly modern areas as household electronics and similar durables (Andrade 1976:178; Asia Pacific Center 1982:49-60; Business International 1982; Euromonitor 1983).

Industrial consumer goods first entered the informal retail sector of the urban Third World via traditional store merchants, and they now have also become part of the inventory of neighborhood stores, market place vendors, and other small traders. Moreover, these goods have spread on a massive scale from Third World metropolitan centers into intermediate towns and beyond (Kano 1978; Kapoor 1977). As a result, for many formal sector producers and distributors, domestic retail institutions, whether small or large, are not to be ignored anymore; they are to be used and, if possible, to be manipulated (Glade, et al. 1970:144-155; Thomas 1981).

What are the implications of this to the dual model of Third World urban trade? First, whatever autonomy has existed between the formal and informal sectors, it is becoming a thing of the past. Second, the principal contact between the sectors runs along the path taken by domestic and imported industrial products as they are distributed to poor and not so poor consumers. Third, to understand urban commerce it becomes imperative to study in detail the distribution channels traversed by industrial consumer products all the way from the large-scale metropolitan concern to the small upcountry retailer and consumer. Fourth, in addition to trade sectors, the basic analytical unit in the study of Third World urban commerce should be market channels.

In the next few pages I will, to begin with, review the channel concept. Much work has been done on the process of mass consumer goods distribution in the urban context of developed economies. This work has shown that distributive channels take on peculiar characteristics in such contexts, characteristics which are now appearing in developing societies (Goldman 1974, Gultinan 1974, McCammon and Bates 1967; Mehta 1980). If these insights are combined with those derived from the study of peasant market networks and product exchange in the informal urban sector, we gain a powerful tool to illuminate Third World city commerce. I will then show how the large-scale supply side has affected, in some instances determined, the retail structure of two intermediate towns: Nasik (260,000 inhabitants (1980) and 160 km from Bombay, India), and Dagupan (98,000 inhabitants (1980) and 200 km from Manila, Philippines). I will do so by describing the retail communities in both cities and showing that a number of differences between them can at least partly be accounted for by variations in the supply channels. The paper will end with the argument that the study of market channels leads us beyond perceiving Third World city commerce in dualistic, tripartite, fragmented or any other compartmental terms, models which under current conditions are

181

becoming outmoded.

II. CHANNELS

In Third World cities a range of distributive channels have evolved which can be grouped according to three dimensions: structure, dominance, and marketing behavior. The structure of channels is given by the number of levels and firms they contain, and by the size and types of firms each level is composed of. In underdeveloped complex societies the number of channel levels tends to be large and each level is likely to contain of a multiplicity of small firms (Moyer 1965).

Channel domination refers to the degree to which one or a small number of channel members control the rest. It is here that the most important characteristic of channels under conditions of capitalistic development is illustrated. There are two possibilities.

In conventional channels vertical fragmentation between levels is the norm and power is diffused throughout the system. No channel member influences others except in terms of products and prices offered. Firms on the various levels relate to one another as legally and actually independent entities. Conventional channels are not integrated, structurally they are complex, and although they contain reciprocal relations between vertically arranged middlemen, these members have little regard for the overall performance of the channel.

In coordinated channels control is held by few members, be they manufactures, traders, agents, or consumers. Manufacturers and large distributors usually dominate coordinated distributive channels in the urban Third World, while in developed economies, especially the U.S., power has shifted downward, and wholesalers or retailers (occasionally even consumer groups) shape much of the channels (Craverns and Finn 1983:141-2). The initial phase of development of many Third World countries has resulted in the rapid growth of assembly facilities and domestic merchant houses behind the protective walls of import control (Murdoch 1980:237-9). This has brought about a power concentration on upper channel levels which the fragmented sub-wholesale and retail levels have had difficulty to resist (Anderson 1970; Grub and Miele 1969). This period is also characterized by economic uncertainty, and it has been shown that growth oriented concerns under such circumstances often seek to extend their control over the distribution of their products down the trade channel (Blair and Kaserman 1978; Dickson 1983:4). True, conventional channels continue to be important in Third World cities; in fact, coordinated ones can devolve into conventional ones (Dannhaeuser 1981). But generally speaking, channel coordination has spread in the urban Third World together with the mass distribution of industrial consumer products.

Next to channel structure and dominance, there is the marketing behavior of channel members. Several possibilities exist (see Dannhaeuser [1983] for a more detailed discussion). Channel members may wait in their premises for customers, enticing them only with the product range they handle and prices. This passive strategy is typical in conventional channels. In a variant form of this--I have called it semi-passive--traders try to gain customers through offering informal, often covert, favors which go beyond price and product type. Favors usually are based on friendship, kin links, and ethnic identity, and the personalized goodwill offered may range from special credit facilities to unpublished discounts and products reserved for particular customers. Otherwise no effort is made to push products down the channel or to create a demand among consumers. Conventional channels tend to co-occur with the semi-passive strategy, and this strategy is especially important in traditional multi-ethnic urban markets and continues to be significant in Third World cities today.

In addition to these passive strategies, there are overtly active ones. They are encountered in conventional channels, but are particularly prevalent in channels in which power is concentrated in few hands and in those Third World societies into which the ideology of U.S. derived modern marketing has diffused. Active marketing entails either pull or push tactics. Consumers are either pulled to the product by means of mass advertising, retail display, and promotions. Or products are pushed down the channels by encouraging middlemen to handle them. This is done by sending fieldmen to cater to them (sales penetration), by establishing downstream franchises or branches (contractual or corporate penetration), or by launching promotionals among wholesalers or retailers.

For quite some time active marketing has been an important tool used by concerns handling mass consumer goods to survive in developed societies. What I want to point out in this paper is that nowadays this strategy, and the channels it is associated with, are having considerable repercussions on the retail trade level of intermediate towns in some of Asia's developing societies.

Before turning to the case of Nasik and Dagupan, however, one more point remains to be made. It refers to channel congruence.

The notion of channel congruence is occasionally used in the literature to denote whether or not the goals of firms on different trade levels mesh. If they do, if they are congruent, reciprocal exchange is said to exist and the internal dynamics of the channel will tend toward stability. If not, if they are non-congruent, conflict will result and the channel, or a part thereof, will likely be transformed (Mentzer, Samli, and Lederhaus 1980:252; Michman and Sibley 1980:421). For instance, when growth oriented suppliers face subsistence oriented retailers the suppliers may decide to shift to other outlets.

Here I would like to add organizational congruence to the dichotomy because it is sensitive to the formal/informal divide. Market channels can be classified on the basis of whether or not firms on different levels are organized according to the same principles. Are they all family concerns, or are some corporate units? Is their business organization constructed and maintained according to modern management techniques, or is it for some the result of ad hoc adjustments to daily needs? On the broadest level, organizational non-congruence is indicated if the channel runs across the formal/informal divide. However, intra-channel conflict and pressure for change does not automatically result from this. Formal sector suppliers may prefer the services of small, informal sector outlets, whereas others may want to modify, replace, or by-pass them. In other words, organizational non-congruence along a channel can be contradictory or complementary. The former condition is likely to result in change, the latter not.

III. NASIK AND DAGUPAN: DIFFERENCES

In some respects Nasik's and Dagupan's retail communities are similar. Both are fragmented into a large number of small trade units, and both communities contain five categories of retailers which roughly overlap with geographical zones: 1) itinerant market and street vendors selling in the vicinity of the market places (some of them periodically fan out to serve suburban areas); 2) marketplace stall vendors; 3) neighborhood stores scattered throughout urban and suburban areas 4) traditional stores located mostly along narrow business streets; 5) modern retail establishments concentrated along broad commercial boulevards readily accessible by motor vehicle. For convenience I will call trade categories one and two, marketplace traders; categories four and five I will refer to as street stores.

Marketplace traders and neighborhood stores are part of the informal trade sector, but what about the street stores? The great majority are family based units, and the religio-ethnic identity of the operators--Chinese and Filipino in Dagupan; Sardarji, Parsee, Jain, Marwari, Bohra Muslim, etc. in Nasik--partly determine their position in trade. Does this mean that in both communities these stores belong to the informal sector? Only if their business operations are not formalized.

Street stores are differentiated by whether or not their product display, floor layout, and store facilities can be considered as 'modern' (glass windows, cash register, display cases, promotional material, contemporary advertisements, etc.; both categories carry mainly industrial consumer goods). Though classed here as modern, category five establishments do not all belong to the formal sector. They may be modern on the surface, but only if their business operation is formalized are they part of the formal sector; that is, if they exhibit features such as functional division of labor, fixed prices, inventory control, receipts, bookkeeping, steady supply points, and margins according to turnover speed. In Nasik and Dagupan only a minority of street stores are formal in this sense.

Given these similarities between the retail communities of Dagupan and Nasik, what are the differences? I will concentrate on three: the importance of modern street stores, the prevalence of neighborhood stores, and the extent of active retailing and innovative trade organizations in both communities.

Along Dagupan's commercial streets modern retail stores have made greater inroads than in Nasik. They constitute numerically 35 percent of all street stores (categories four and five) and 49 percent of trade realized by street stores flows through them. In

185

Nasik, where the proportions are nine and 30 percent respectively, this category is less important (see Table I). [3]

What about neighborhood stores? They are known as sari-sari stores in Dagupan and stock a wide variety of products neighbors may need at a moments notice (Dannhaeuser 1980). An average three-fourths of their turnover is derived from industrial sources, mainly soft drinks, soaps, and cigarettes. Even though only 13 percent of the non-marketplace retail turnover is channeled through neighborhood stores, 68 percent of all categories three to five stores belong to this type. In Nasik the equivalent of sari-sari stores are the kirana stores. They handle nearly everything found in sari-sari stores, although non-industrial goods, most notably edible oils and grains, make up a greater proportion of the turnover. Neighborhood stores have a more subdued role in Nasik's commercial community: they are responsible for 8 percent of the non-marketplace turnover and numerically they constitute only 30 percent of all stores. These low figures are only partially offset if we stretch the notion of neighborhood stores to include a traditional specialty outlet of long standing in India, and that is the pan shop. These shops are small affairs, and specialize in the trade of betel nut preparations, native cigarettes (bidi), and, increasingly so, in modern cigarettes. If these outlets are added to the genuine neighborhood stores, then 11 percent of turnover passes through this category (similar to Dagupan) and 38 percent of all stores belong to it (still considerably less than in Dagupan) (Table I).

There are other differences. In Dagupan aggressive retailing and promotions are more readily used especially by traders handling high cost items, than in Nasik. Below Dagupeno dealers of motor vehicles, electrical appliances, phono equipment and similar goods, there exists a pyramid of petty traders in constant search of urban and rural customers. Many of the dealers employ itinerant salesmen, and there are scores of part-time non-exclusive tipsters who try to bring customers to dealers in return for a commission. Dagupeno merchants have even reached beyond the town and established franchises and branches in neighboring communities. Finally, there are long term installment plans which nearly all dealers offer either through finance companies or on their own. Only little of this is practiced in Nasik.

TABLE 1. Distribution of Street and Neighborhood
Stores in Nasik and Dagupan

Retail Categories 4 and 5*

	Nasik	Dagupan
Number of Stores:**	1,540	500
(Percent of them Category 5):	(9%)	(35%)
Total Daily Turnover:+	Rs.1,036,000	P1,415,000
(Percent of it by Category5):	(30%)	(49%)

Retail Categories 3, 4, and 5*

	Nasik	Dagupan
Number of Stores:**	2,490	1,550
(Percent of them Category 3):	(38%)	(68%)
Total Daily Turnover:+ Rs.	1,160,000	P1,625,000
(Percent of it by Category 3):	(11%)	(13%)

----

* Category 3: neighborhood stores (including pan stores)
  Category 4: traditional street stores
  Category 5: modern street stores

** Establishments combining retail with wholesale trade are included in these figures.

+ The rupee and peso exchange rates in 1982 were Rs. 11 to $1 and P9 to $1.

Finally, certain innovative retail organizations which have recently been introduced into Dagupan are absent in Nasik. While self-service has not yet appeared in Nasik in any form, grocery superettes have existed in Dagupan since the sixties, and in 1978 a full-line supermarket opened its door. Recently two small department stores have started up business, a mall is being constructed near the town center, and on a less grandiose scale, a number of pharmacies have adopted a decidedly clinical look and use an electric numbering system to announce that prescriptions are ready.

Nasik, though, boasts its own innovative outlets that cannot be found in Dagupan. While the shoe trade in Nasik, like in Dagupan, is mostly carried out by traditional stores and market place traders, there are several large and formally organized establishments in the town which specialize on national brands and use facilities standard in the West. Furthermore, over a dozen textile stores in Nasik engage in heavy advertising and promotions, display cloth behind glass cabinets, push particular brands, and even do away with flexible prices. In Dagupan the textile trade remains traditional, and even in those shops which boast modern layout, flexible prices remain the norm, brand identity is rare, and promotions are seldom undertaken.

A.   Nasik and Dagupan: Differences Explained

In this section I will show that these differences in Nasik's and Dagupan's retail systems can be explained to a large extent by the manner in which metro-suppliers channel products into both communities. But first a word about the larger context.

Market strategies do not exist in isolation, but are an expression of the economic, social, and political environment that obtains. In the Philippines these environmental factors have encouraged metro-suppliers to develop active sales strategies and channel coordination into intermediate towns. Conditions in India have done so to a lesser degree. What are these conditions?

Briefly, there is first the scale and complexity of both societies; the larger size of India than the Philippines and the fragmented nature of its society, makes it more difficult for metro-suppliers there to control sales into upcountry cities. Second, the colonial experience of India and the Philippines is important; American colonial rule of the Philippines has led to an earlier introduction of the U.S. derived notion of aggressive mass marketing than into India. The third factor, the higher literacy rate and per capita income in the Philippines compared to India has had a similar effect by attracting metro-sources earlier into upcountry markets of the Philippines. [4] Fourth, and finally, there are the taxes and government regulations; municipal border taxes in much of India protect conservative middlemen, and government restrictions on the production of 'luxury' consumer goods discourage active marketing by modern suppliers-- both of these factors are less important in the Philippines.

How, then, does the market penetration of Nasik and Dagupan differ in detail and what are the repercussions locally?

Low cost mass consumer durables (packaged foods and bottled drinks, cigarettes, soaps, batteries; but not textiles) find their way into both communities by metro-companies engaging in sales penetration. This strategy, however, reaches deeper down the channel in the case of Dagupan than Nasik. Dominant Manila based companies (e.g. Procter and Gamble, Colgate-Palmolive, San Miguel) either maintain their own branch warehouses in Dagupan, or they use local wholesale dealers, mostly Chinese, as warehouses by selling products to them and later rebuying some (or all) of these goods for further distribution among retailers. In either case, many retailers, including neighborhood stores, are regularly contacted by company salesmen who take orders, deliver, collect, and implement promotions. Wholesale dealers in Dagupan, to compete, are forced to do the same. Less frequently, company supervisors visit important retail customers to hear complaints and offer general advice about display, operations, and store layout. A number of superettes and display innovations have been the result.

Metro-companies are represented in Nasik by stockists. These are equivalent to Dagupan's wholesale dealers, except that they are expected to sell all of their principal's products to the next channel level by means of their own marketing effort. Only occasionally do company salesmen visit retailers and pass orders on to their stockists, and, with the exception of those representing very large and aggressive companies (e.g., Hindustan Lever, Parle), the sales effort of stockists consists of waiting for retail customers to place

189

orders. The result? Nasik's retailers are hardly ever approached by the sales personnel of metro-sources; retail promotions are filtered through stockists and are thereby diluted; and stockists act more like conservative general-line wholesalers who hold a monopoly over the sub-wholesale level than representatives of large companies out to guide their customers.

These differences, and their repercussions among retailers, are epitomized in the case of neighborhood stores. In Dagupan sari-sari operators have many complaints, but only seldom does one hear from them that access to suppliers is difficult. Over the years large mass consumer goods companies have gone out of their way to make the traditional sari-sari store in Dagupan (and elsewhere) a major point of final distribution. Through extensive advertising and deep sales penetration they have seen to it that their product brands--be they Tide, Coke, Champion cigarettes--are important items carried by these traders. The widespread availability of company delivery and promotional services (together with credit links with local wholesale dealers), has been one ingredient not only leading neighborhood store operators to stock formal sector products--true also for Dagupan's market vendors--but also for individuals to enter the business in the first place. [5]

Much of this attraction, to be sure, involves Dagupenos choosing among various opportunities offered by suppliers; but some of it is the result of more active manipulation by metro-companies and their local representatives. To give a few examples: large concerns repeatedly organize contests or raffles the winners of which receive a fully stocked sari-sari store; soft drinks companies lease refrigerators at nominal cost to neighborhood store operators in return for a commitment by these traders to stock only their brand of products; local wholesale dealers, not to be outdone, offer initial store inventory on consignment to (trusted) newcomers into the trade. In other words, suppliers not only encourage neighborhood store operators to handle their products, they also manipulate their store facilities and consciously entice individuals into the trade.

In Nasik such incentives are far less common. Lacking easy access to suppliers, including local stockists, is a recurrent theme in the complaints of kirana store operators in Nasik. This is an especially serious handicap when individuals want to initiate such a business. A person opening a substantial sari-sari store in Dagupan soon attracts visits and offers from potential suppliers. In Nasik it usually takes a person several months to find all relevant stockists after establishing a kirana store. During the interim he has to buy from general line wholesalers, and these do not offer the initial inventory on consignment. Individuals in Nasik have to rely on resources other than those of their suppliers to open and operate a kirana store.

One exception to this is the cigarette trade. Cigarette companies have identified some time ago the pan shop as an important gateway to consumers. Companies, such as I.T.C. and Golden Tobacco, press their stockists to curry favors with pan vendors by asking them to send order takers to these vendors, to offer special promotions, credit, free billboards, and similar services. No wonder that during recent years pan shops in Nasik have multiplied especially fast. [6]

The effect of deeper sales penetration and more aggressive marketing by formal sector suppliers into Dagupan than Nasik, therefore, has been two-fold. It has encouraged, especially in Dagupan, small informal sector neighborhood outlets, and a classic case of organizational non-congruence of the complementary type has come into being. Second, deep sales penetration has enabled metro-suppliers to be more instrumental in transforming traditional store outlets in Dagupan into, in appearance at least, modern ones. As a result, the modern store category plays a more important role in that town than in Nasik. There is another reason for this, however, and that is channel coordination.

Compared to Nasik, metro-suppliers entered Dagupan through contractual and corporate penetration at an earlier date and, in relation to its smaller size, on a larger scale. Retail branches and franchises (or metro-dependent outlets) began to multiply there in the fifties, while in Nasik they did so only a decade later. Today there are 80 of these metro-dependent establishments in Dagupan, in Nasik there are 75. Moreover, their average size is larger in the former community than in the latter. [7]

What does it mean when retail outlets in Dagupan or Nasik become metro-dependent, or when new ones are established? There are two implications. It implies, first, that these establishments are likely to be formal in the sense discussed above, not only modern. This is because metro-companies usually regulate, either through contract or ownership, the operating procedures of their retail outlets. Should these outlets eventually become independent, as, for example, many appliance stores in Dagupan have become, they are likely to retain their formal character.

The second implication of the appearance of metro-dependent outlets concerns emulation by others. Independent merchants who compete with retail franchises and branches of large companies often find that they have to copy aspects of their operations to survive. Even if they do so only superficially by modernizing display, it means that they become part of the modern retail trade category. In other words, the proliferation of metro-dependent retailers has been an important force modernizing the retail communities in both towns, although in Dagupan, into which coordinated channels have entered proportionately on a more massive scale, this process has gone further.

I have noted that store retailers in Nasik engage in less active and innovative retailing than in Dagupan. This turns out to be particularly true with respect to metro-dependent outlets. Once again, the difference is due to the supply side. After expanding fast during the sixties, franchising and branching into Nasik have stagnated. Legislation has been partly to blame, but more fundamental has been chronic shortages of goods in certain key lines (motor vehicles, appliances, gasoline) which created a seller's market. [8] Although coordinated channels between metro-suppliers and Nasik outlets continue to exist, these circumstances have removed much of the incentives for companies and retail branches/franchises alike to push products among consumers. As a result, vertical integration in the metro-Nasik trade axis is combined with passive marketing strategies followed even by dominant suppliers.

In the Philippines oversupply of household durables has led to a different situation: channel coordination combined with continuing active distributive strategies on all trade levels. [9] Metro-suppliers urge their franchise/branch outlets in Dagupan to extend their sales efforts via tipsters, itinerant salesmen, sub-dealers, promotions, credit, and by other means beyond their own premises. Competitive pressure has also led a number of companies to form radically new retail ventures in Dagupan. Although encouraged by suppliers,

192

superettes are a local phenomenon. It needed a Manila concern, however, to open the first supermarket in the town, and another one is scheduled for the new mall. The recent innovations in drug retailing were introduced by franchises of a metro-company, and one of the more successful department store is operated by a Manila based company and is now emulated by local merchants.

I have indicated that retail innovations, especially in the textile and shoe trade, are not absent in Nasik. These are connected with the supply side as well. The Philippine textile trade has remained quite conservative owing to the fact that large Chinese wholesalers, by financing mill operations, have kept producers from establishing retail outlets of their own. These wholesalers, in turn, maintain long term personal relations with Chinese sub-wholesalers and retailers in Dagupan, and the semi-passive strategy within a fragmented channel characterizes the trade.

The power distribution along the channel from Indian textile mills to upcountry retailers is different. Wholesalers and semi-wholesalers in Bombay and other production centers also play an important role in the channel, but they do not control the producers. This has enabled a number of mills (Raymond, Tata, Mafatlal, Bombay-Dyeing among them) to appoint retail franchises (known as authorized dealers) in upcountry towns during the past decades. There are now 15 of these in Nasik, and due to their contracts with the mills, which cover such things as display, prices, quotas, and training, these dealers are an important component of the modern retail category in the town. So far, however, the mills have not been strong enough to create a totally exclusive channel and retail dealers are permitted to carry competing brands. Two companies in the shoe trade have taken this additional step.

With the exception of the recently established department stores, the distribution of shoes into Dagupan remains conservative. India has the Bata and Carona Sahu shoe companies, large operations which have been famous for their innovative marketing effort over the years. Both maintain several retail branches in Nasik which handle only company products aimed at the lower middle to upper class. These operations are totally in the hands of the metro-companies and are considered among the most sophisticated in town. This is not all. Both companies pursue a dual channel strategy. Next to the exclusive channel which handles

193

prestigious Bata and Carona brand shoes, the concerns also serve the informal sector retailers and consumers by using the more traditional stockist system. Exclusive agencies are given to local stockists who handle lower priced B.S.C. and C.S.C. brand shoes-- stockists may not handle competing lines--who then resell them to sub-wholesalers, store retailers, vendors, and hawkers. Organizational non-congruence, therefore, is handled in two ways by these concerns: by eliminating it through branching, and by accomodating themselves to it through deep sales penetration. In this way they take advantage of the competitive strength of both channel organizations and are able to cover the entire range of consumers in Nasik.

IV.   SUMMING UP AND IMPLICATIONS

Dagupan and Nasik show that even in intermediate towns of the Philippines and India--and by extension, in those of many other Third World societies--the distribution of industrial consumer products occupies much attention of retailers. They also show that suppliers of these products play a far from passive role in their relations with retailers. Large firms actively try to push products down the channels, and while doing so, they affect the nature of the retail structure. As development proceeds this is likely to intensify.

The foregoing does not deny the importance of wider socio-economic and cultural factors, or the buying habits and credit needs of consumers in shaping the retail organization. Nor does it deny that innovations among retailers can be initiated locally. It does show, however, that the large-scale supply side is one important, and I would add here, often not fully appreciated, force affecting the retail organizations of medium-range Third World cities. This role is likely to expand because at the early stages of development manufacturing and distribution firms tend to grow at a more rapid pace and take on a more concentrated form than retail institutions. Power becomes focused in the upper channel levels, and once these supply firms turn toward mass marketing, many of them are led, insofar that resources permit, into active distribution and a desire to control product flow into intermediate towns.

Metro-companies seeking such control encounter, to begin with, non-congruent conditions between channel levels: they, as suppliers, are large and formally organized; upcountry retailers are small and informal in their organization. At this point suppliers have a choice of two strategies, both found in the metro-Nasik and metro-Dagupan trade axes. Either they create channel congruence by appointing retail dealerships and building up branches. Or they adapt themselves to a situation of non-congruence and create complementary relations between themselves and lower channel levels. This they do by employing an itinerant sales force, which, together with appointed wholesale dealers or stockists, advertising and other incentives, encourage upcountry outlets to carry their products.

In both cases suppliers influence the retail level. This is most noticeable when metro-dependent retail establishments are created. These take on an organizational form set by their mother company, and it is through them that trading innovations are introduced into peripheral markets. Some of these innovations are adopted and at times even improved upon by local independent traders. Although the influence from the supply side may be less visible in the case of traditional upcountry retailers, it need not be any less real. Dagupan's sari-sari store operators and Nasik's pan vendors illustrate how formal sector suppliers can be in close contact with small and traditional outlets and not only use them, but also help them to increase in numbers. [10]

This brings us back to the compartmental paradigm of Third World city commerce.

If, while analyzing the commercial community of Third World cities, one focuses on such matters as capital intensity of traders, the products they handle, their internal organization, or their social mobility, one is easily lead to view such communities as divided into two or more sectors. If, instead, Third World city traders are perceived as forming nexuses along a network of product exchange, then the channel becomes the significant unit and the duality concept loses some of its force. Under conditions in which industrial consumer products are widely diffused among all but the poorest consumer class, a large proportion of small traders in Third World cities share with large and formally organized ones the same set of channels. To these traders, the channels they share and compete in are at least as, if not more important than the respective sector, formal or informal, they themselves represent.

195

The channel concept encourages us to perceive Third World urban commerce as a fluid and open system. It also encourages us to adopt a holistic viewpoint incorporating the full range of commercial institutions. This can be done without losing sight of details in the organization and choices of individual enterprises. I believe that such an approach will bring us further in understanding the trade community in Third World cities than to argue that the dualistic character of this community can only be understood as an expression of capitalistic development in peripheral regions in the context of international capitalism (Davies 1979). Though this may be true on a gross level, such observation will help us little to explain differences in commercial organization of Third World cities, such as exist between Nasik and Dagupan. Ultimately the structure of retail trade is a reflection of broad socio-cultural and worldwide economic conditions. But most of these conditions have an impact on traders only after they are filtered through the channel of which they are members.

From asking what the properties of various trade sectors in Third World cities are, we should now ask what the proporties of those institutions are which, under conditions of development, transverse these sectors and change them. Third World urban market channels need more of our attention.

ACKNOWLEDGMENTS

The Indo-American Fellowship Program supported research in Nasik during 1981/82. I was affiliated with the IPC, Ateneo de Manila University, as Research Associate while conducting research in Dagupan in 1983. Financial support was provided by a Texas A&M summer grant. Unless otherwise indicated, the material on Nasik is for 1982 and that on Dagupan, 1983.

NOTES

1. One of the more useful definitions of the informal sector is provided by Sethuraman: "it is a sector to which entry by new enterprises is comparatively easy; enterprises in this sector rely on indigenous resources and are family owned; they operate on a small scale, in unregulated and competitive markets, and use labour-intensive and adapted technology; their workers have skills acquired outside the formal school system" (1976:71). I would also stress that firms in this

196

sector are not organized according to bureaucratic and formal management principles (cf. Hackenberg 1980: 398).

2. Even the notion of upper and lower circuits, introduced to pay "greater attention to the linkages between these two sectors" (McGee 1979:49), has illustrated these links only to a limited degree because it has been mainly used to study the informal commercial sector (McGee 1973; McGee and Yeung 1977). The originator of the circuit concept, Santos (1979), does make the connection between the upper and lower circuits his main concern. But his treatment covers Third World city commerce only incidentally.

3. The turnover figures are estimates based on census material, lincense lists, and field checks conducted by the author in both communities.

4. The per capita income in India is less than one-half, and the literacy rate about two-thirds of that found in the Philippines (Far Eastern Economic Review 1983:6-7). Concerning income, however, the difference between Nasik and Dagupan is less pronounced. Owing to a new industrial zone nearby, Nasik's earnings are high for urban India. I estimate that per capita income there is between one-half and two-thirds of that in Dagupan.

5. The number of neighborhood store operators entering the trade because of the supply side is difficult to judge because usually a mixture of motives exist for initiating a business. The following merely suggests the difference between Nasik and Dagupan. While only three percent of 96 surveyed kirana/pan store operators in Nasik indicated that assistance from the supply side was a factor inducing them into trade (1982), in Dagupan 14 percent of 252 neighborhood store operators expressed this motive (1974).

6. Between 1962 and 1978 pan stores multiplied in average two percent annually. Between 1979 and 1982 the annual growth rate was 10 percent.

7. In Dagupan the average metro-dependent retail and wholesale/retail establishment employs ten individuals and has a turnover of P4,000 per day; in Nasik it is six individuals and Rs. 2,200 per

day. Included here are trade units which once were metro-dependent and now are independent.

8. The Monopolies Restrictive Trade Act of 1969 in India has discouraged large firms from vertically integrating during the past decade. Large suppliers, however, have not failed to find loopholes. For instance, they reclassify exclusive stockists of theirs as "independent wholesalers" with the confidential understanding that these wholesalers will not handle competing lines (cf. Varma 1981).

9. This situation, true for the past twenty years, may be changing. Economic difficulties the Philippines has experienced during the past years have lead since August 1983 to drastic cuts in imports and a reduction of domestic industrial production. The Indian government, by contrast, is in the process of easing import restrictions and raising the ceiling on the domestic production of consumer luxuries (Far Eastern Economic Review 1983: 174-175; 250-251).

10. One could even argue that these retailers in effect have been formalized when they became an integral part of channels dominated by large supply firms, even though they retain their small scale, organization based on familism, and, in many cases, a subsistence orientation (cf. Armstrong and McGee 1968:370-372).

REFERENCES

Anderson, D.
    1970   Marketing and Development: The Thai Experience. East Lansing: Institute for International Business and Economic Development Studies, Michigan State University. Pp: 172-179.

Andrade, R.P.
1976   "Mass retailing among low-income consumers in Guatemala city." In D. Izraeli, D.N. Izraeli and F. Meissner (eds.), Marketing Systems for Developing Countries, Vol. I. Toronto: John Wiley. Pp. 172-179.

Armstrong, W.R. and T.G. McGee
    1968   "Revolutionary change and the Third World

city: A theory of urban involution."
<u>Civilization</u> 18:353-378.

Asia Pacific Center
1982   <u>Marketing Trends in the Asia Pacific
Region. Economic Forecasts and Consumer
Development</u>. Aldershot, England: Gower
Publ. Co.

Barth, G.
1984   "Employment and earnings in food marketing
in a Philippine regional center." <u>Human
Organization</u> 43: 38-43.

Blair, R.D. and D. L. Kaserman
1978   "Uncertainty and the incentive for
vertical integration." <u>Southern Economic
Journal</u> 45:266-72.

Breman, J.
1976   "Dualistic labor system? A critique of the
'informal sector' concept." <u>Economic and
Political Weekly</u> XI:1870-1944.

Business International
1982   <u>Distribution in Asia/Pacific's Developing
Markets</u>. Hong Kong: Business
International Asia/Pacific Ltd.

Cravens, D.W. and D.W. Finn
1983   "Supplier selection by retailers: research
progress and needs." In W.R. Darden and
R.F. Lusch (eds.), <u>Patronage Behavior and
Retail Management</u>. New York: North-
Holland. Pp: 225-244.

Dannhaeuser, N.
1983   <u>Contemporary Trade Strategies in the
Philippines. A Study in Marketing
Anthropology</u>. New Brunswick: Rutgers
University Press.

1981   "Evolution and devolution of downward
channel integration in the Philippines."
<u>Economic Development and Cultural Change</u>
29:577-95.

1980   "The role of the neighborhood store in
developing economies: the case of Dagupan
City, Philippines." <u>The Journal of
Developing Areas</u> 14:157-174.

199

Davies, R.
1979   "Informal sector or subordinate mode of production? A model." In R. Bromley and C. Gerry (eds.), Casual Work and Poverty in Third World Cities. New York: John Wiley and Sons. Pp: 87-104.

Dickson, P.R.
1983   "Distributor portfolio analysis and the channel dependency matrix: new techniques for understanding and managing the channel." Journal of Marketing 47:35-44.

Euromonitor
1983   Retail Trade International. London: Euromonitor Public.

Far Eastern Economic Review
1983   Asia Yearbook 1984. Hong Kong.

Friedmann, J. and F. Sullivan
1974   "The absorption of labor and the urban economy: the case of developing countries." Economic Development and Cultural Change 22:385-414.

Geertz, C.
1963   Peddlers and Princes. Social Development and Economic Change in Two Indonesian Towns. Chicago: University of Chicago.

Glade, W.P., et al.
1970   Marketing in a Developing Nation. Lexington: D.C. Heath and Co.

Goldman, A.
1974   "Outreach of consumers and the modernization of food retailing in developing countries." Journal of Marketing 38:8-16.

Grub, P.D. and A.R. Miele
1969   "The changing marketing structure in the industrial development of Venezuela: Part II." Journal of Developing Areas 4:69-80.

Gultinan, J.P.
1974   "Planned and evolutionary changes in distribution channels." Journal of Retailing 50:79-91, 103.

200

Hackenberg, R.A.
   1980   "New patterns of urbanization in Southeast
               Asia: an   assessment."   Population
               Development Review 6:391-421.

House, W.J.
   1984   "Nairobi's   informal   sector;   dynamic
               entrepreneurs or surplus labor?" Economic
               Development and Cultural Change 32:277-
               302.

Kano, H.
   1978   "City development and occupational change
               in Iran: a case study of Hamadan."
               Developing Economies 6:298-328.

Kapoor, M.S.
   1977   "Rural retail marketing: A pilot study."
               Indian Management 16:21-28.

McCammon, B.C., Jr., and A.D. Bates
   1967   "The emergence and growth of contractually
               integrated channels in the American
               economy."   In B. Mallen (ed.), The
               Marketing   Channel.   A Conceptual
               Viewpoint. New York: John Wiley and
               Sons. Pp: 287-298.

McGee, T.G.
   1979   "The poverty syndrom: making out in the
               Southeast Asian City," In R. Bromley and
               C. Gerry (eds.), Casual Work and Poverty
               in Third World Cities. New York: John
               Wiley and Sons Pp: 45-68.

   1973   Hawkers of Hong Kong: A Study of Planning
               and Policy in a Third World City. Hong
               Kong: University of Hong Kong.

McGee, T.G. and Y.M. Yeung
   1977   Hawkers in Southeast Asian Cities.
               Planning for the Bazaar Economy. Ottawa:
               International Development Research Center.

Mehta, G.C.
   1980   Marketing. Environment, Concepts and
               Cases. New Delhi: Tata McGraw-Hill.
               Publ.

Mentzer, J.T., A.C. Samli, and M.A. Ledershaus
   1980   "Stability and efficiency in marketing

channels: the theory of double exhcange."
In C.W. Lamb, Jr. and P.M. Donne (eds.),
Theoretical Developments in Marketing.
American Marketing Association Proceedings
Series. Pp: 251-254.

Michman, R.D. and S.D. Sibley
    1980   Marketing Channels and Strategies.
                Columbus: Grid.

Moyer, R.
    1965   Marketing and Economic Development. East
                Lansing: Institute for International
                Business Management Studies, Michigan
                State University.

Murdoch, W.W.
    1980   The Poverty of Nations. The Political
                Economy of Hunger and Population. London:
                John Hopkins University Press.

Santos, M.
    1979   The Shared Space. The Two Circuits of the
                Urban Economy. London: Methuen.

Sethuraman, S.
    1976   "The urban informal sector: concepts,
                measurement and policy." International
                Labor Review 114:69-81.

Slater, C.C. et al.
    1969   Market Process in the Recife Area of
                Northeast Brazile. East Lansing:
                Michigan State University, Latin American
                Studies Center.

Tidalgo, R.L.P. and G.M. Jurado
    1978   "The informal services sector in the
                Greater Manila Area, 1976." The
                Philippine Review of Business and
                Economics XV:17-54.

Thomas, T.
    1981   Managing a Business in India. Bombay:
                Allied Publishers.

Tokman, V.
    1978   "Competition between the informal and
                formal sectors in retailing: the case of
                Santiago." World Development 6:1187-1198.

202

Varma, D.P.S.
1981   "MRTP Act and the sewing machine industry." _Capital_ (July 20).

MASS MARKETS: LITTLE MARKETS, SOME PRELIMINARY THOUGHTS ON THE GROWTH OF CONSUMPTION AND ITS RELATIONSHIP TO URBANIZATION: A CASE STUDY OF MALAYSIA.

Professor T.G. McGee, University of British Columbia

I. INTRODUCTION

The study of contemporary urbanization in developing countries in the seventies has been characterized by four new approaches that have greatly enhanced our theoretical understandings of the urbanization process.

First is the emergence of the "world political economy" approach to the study of urbanization as represented by the work of Frank (1967), Amin, (1974), Wallerstein (1974), Walton (1976a, 1976b), Portes and Walton (1981), Cohen (1981), Friedmann and Wolff (1982), Soja et al. (1983), and many others, which raises questions about the manner in which urban systems and urban centers in Third World countries are a reflection of the role that the national states play in the international economic system. Although some of the major writers from this perspective have shared an ideological distaste for capitalism, a sharp difference of opinion has emerged between such writers as the late Bill Warren, and Frank and Amin. Frank and Amin focus upon the role of Third World cities as the institutional structures that permit the accumulation of capital in the Third World countries and its siphoning off to the metropolitan centers of the developed countries. According to this perception, Third World cities play a crucial role in the underdevelopment of the Third World. Warren (1973, 1978), on the other hand, argues that this integration of Third World countries has created the conditions for rapid independent capitalist development and has set in motion a definite process of industrialization that focuses on the major urban places. His arguments have been further advanced in the work of Roberts (1978) on Latin America. The significance of this debate is that it indicates how developments in the international economic system have ramifications on the urban system of Third World countries, and suggests they be taken into account in research proposals.

One further aspect of this political economy approach is to focus upon the role of international urban hierarchies in the process of developing regional systems or groupings of Third World states. Thus, in considering questions of urban development in the Association of Southeast Asian Nations (ASEAN) region, it is useful to evaluate the role of Singapore as a regional center. The internationalization of the world economy has increased the importance of such regional centers.

A second major theoretical and empirical contribution to an understanding of the urbanization process in Southeast Asia has been made by demographers, geographers, and anthropologists who have begun to look critically at the processes of population movement between rural and urban areas. Research by Hugo (1975), Goldstein (1978), and Pryor (1979) utilizing censuses and survey data have contributed to a much more sophisticated picture of the process of population mobility to and from urban centers. This research has drawn needed attention to the persistence of circulatory migration. It has also provided a careful analysis of urban residence, revealing the weakness of distinctions between rural and urban residence. These important contributions should enable a much more sophisticated analysis of the 1980-81 round of census data than would otherwise be possible, which will be of great assistance to policy makers concerned with rates of urban growth and the characteristics of rural-urban migration.

A third theoretical development, which has emerged from a broad body of development theory but has important implications for policy aimed at smaller urban centers, has been the growing concern about the persistent poverty of sizable proportions of the Third World populations (most of them located in rural areas) and the need from some program of imcome redistribution that can deliver basic needs to these deprived populations. Although there has been economic growth (summarized by Ajit Singh, 1979), it is widely accepted that an efficient urban system plays a major role in delivering these basic needs. At least one writer, Michael Lipton (1977), has argued that most national policies in developing countries are biased in favor of the larger urban areas despite a rhetoric that emphasizes the role of smaller urban centers and rural development. Other writers, notably Lo et al. (1978), have grappled with this problem of urban bias by advocating policies that would combine certain elements of selective regional closure with rural development. These policies would enable small towns to provide more services, and, it is hoped, employment, which would lead to the wider provision of basic needs. The policies' major contributions are the emphasis on integrated development and a clear understanding of the function of the urban system in a nation's economy.

The final theoretical development relates to the concept of the informal sector (see McGee, 1971, 1973, 1974, 1976; McGee and Yeung, 1977). The idea of the informal sector has emerged from the tradition of dualistic models of the structure of Third World economies put forward by such writers as Boeke (1953) and Lewis (1954). The specific circumstance that gave rise to the growing interest in the informal sector was the concern over the inability of many Third World countries to generate sufficient wage-earning opportunities during the 1960's and the realization that many people were employed in what were essentially family or small-scale activities. These activities involved production (agriculture and manufacturing), distribution (e.g. vending), and construction (squatter housing). Conventional economic attitudes toward these activities had been unfavorable. It was argued that low incomes and low productivity of the informal sector were a drag upon economic development. But a series of studies during the 1970's notable by the International Labour Office (1972) and Hart (1973), have questioned this pejorative view. Increased concern with income distribution and meeting basic needs has buttressed arguments that policy makers should adopt policies that would encourage entrepreneurial activity and capital accumulation in the informal sector. Supporters of policies favourable to the informal sector are attempting to persuade policy makers that the persistence of the informal sector is a consequence of a rapidly growing labor force and the wage sector's inability to create sufficient jobs. Some writers (e.g. Squire, 1979, and Roberts, 1978) have argued that many Third World countries have done much better at creating jobs in the wage sector than had been thought possible earlier. For instance, Squire has calculated that between 1960 and 1970 industrial employment in the less developed countries grew at twice the rate experienced by developed countries between 1900 and 1920. But fact growth of the population and the labor force has retarded the transformation of the industrial structure of the less developed countries' labor force (Squire, 1979: table 6).

In the last few years several researchers have criticized the concept of the informal sector. They have argued that for theoretical purposes the concept

207

is too descriptive and leads to a tendency to ignore the relationships between the formal sector and the informal sector. They also argue that it is profitable for the formal sector and the state to allow the persistence of the informal sector. (See Gerry, 1974; Bromley and Gerry, 1979; and McGee, 1978a, 1978b, 1979, 1982a, for a summary of these arguments.) This may seem to be a contradictory position, for they have also argued that the state has adopted policies designed to eliminate activities of the informal sector. In fact, the wide variety and complexity of activities in the informal sector often cause the state to adopt contradictory policies. For instance, the state may carry out clearance operations against cooked-food vendors while enacting price subsidy policies on rice that enable vendors to purchase rice and sell it at low prices.

Other critics have drawn attention to the difficulty of applying the concept of the informal sector to the Third World, arguing that there is persistent confusion over whether it is the unit of economic organization or the form of employment that is being used to define the informal and wage sectors (Mosley, 1977). Yet other critics (e.g., Santos, 1979) have drawn attention to the lack of dynamism in the dualistic model, suggesting that it would be more accurate to conceptualize the economic structure of Third World cities as different circuits of economic activity that are in a constant flux and interaction. While Santos conceptualizes these circuits as a lower and upper circuit, it is not difficult to perceive them as one circuit of activity as, for instance, with transport and retailing. [1] Finally, the informal-formal sector dualism has been criticized particularly as it applies to the labor markets by writers such as Breman (1976), who argue that it oversimplifies the "fragmented" labor markets that characterize many of the Third World countries.

These conceptual advances of the 1970's have enhanced our understanding of urbanization processes and as a consequence have implications for both research programs and policy options. To reiterate, these advances have, first of all, placed increased emphasis on the understanding of national urban systems as being, in part, a reflection of the manner and incorporation of developing countries into the international economic system. This process of incorporation has important effects on the urban hierarchy such as primacy, the functional characteristics of the urban system, and the labor force structure and distribution. Second, the conceptual advances have placed increased emphasis upon the mobility of populations both within rural and urban areas and between them. This new understanding of the mobility of population enables more accurate analysis of the pace of urban transformation, the relative importance of different-size centers in the urban hierarchy, and the relative importance of rural and urban linkages. Third, the revised concepts of the 1970's have placed increased emphasis upon the study of the processes that create both spatial and structural inequalities in countries, and have led to a consideration of the manner in which the states may intervene in these processes so as to reduce such inequalities. Finally, they have led to increased emphasis upon a critical evaluation of the models that are used to conceptualize the economic structure of Third World cities, and in particular upon the need for more detailed studies (e.g., micro-level) of economic activity in order to build more sophisticated models.

II.   NEGLECTED ASPECT OF RECENT URBANIZATION STUDIES: A THEORETICAL FRAMEWORK FOR INVESTIGATING THE MASS MARKET.

Despite these considerable advances in research on the urbanization process in developing countries, there has been surprisingly little focus upon the growth of the mass market in these countries, particularly as it applies to the increasing ownership of consumer durables, such as automobiles and the influence that this has upon the urbanization process.

While many studies deal with some aspect of the role of "consumption" there have been few comprehensive attempts to look at this sphere of economic growth as an integral component of the development process. This paper presents a theoretical framework for this investigation and a preliminary analysis of the growth of the mass market in Malaysia.

In general my argument for the theoretical framework is quite simple. Existing studies of economic development whether stemming from conventional or more radical approaches have tended to concentrate upon the production aspects of the development process and ignored the spheres of circulation and consumption. What I believe we see occuring in the development process of the Third World countries is a tendency for increased divergence between countries in the sphere of production (most clearly shown in the case of the African countries of the Sahal as compared to Singapore) while there is an increasing <u>convergence</u> in the spheres of circulation and consumption in the larger urban centers of the Third World Countries.

The considerable technological improvements at the circulation level (transport), which facilitate the movement of commodities and labor, together with the growth of information flows (television, education, improvements in literacy, etc.), have greatly facilitated the ability of the international and national capitalist sectors to create felt needs for people of Third World countries [3]. It is well known that there is also a class dimension to this process. The styles and patterns of consumption of the national bourgeoisie which imitate those of the advanced capitalist countries are held up as the models of life-style which Third World populations wish to emulate. To quote a journalistic commentary on Malaysian urban life:

> "Status appears to be the name of the game in the rise of fast food popularity. In Malaysia, where a car sticker bearing the name of an overseas university can open doors, and where office workers plunk down a month's wages to buy a belt with a designer buckle, chomping American burgers and guzzling root beer helps promote the wished for 'man about town image'", Robinson, 1982.

My own view is that the essential qualities of consumption and circulation are becoming similar throughout the Third World, a similarity most obvious in the built environments, transport and life styles of the cities, but also increasingly a feature of the countryside. It is important to note that the changes in circulation characterized by greater speed of goods and information are crucial to the changes occurring in the consumption sphere.

Historically, four crucial components have been necessary to bring about the increase in demand which allows the creation of these mass markets. Hamish Fraser (1981) has shown how these components operated in Britain between 1850 and 1914. First, between 1850 and 1914 there was a growing Market in terms of number of customers. Secondly there was a growing amout of disposable income. Thirdly, there was a growing rate of literacy and education on the part of customers. This, together with organizational changes in the

210

structure of retailing, credit, distribution and production facilitated the mass production of commodities for this growing population. Finally, the growing differences between the bourgeoisie and the working classes created an ideological environment in which advertising would utilize status as an important promotion style in creating demand for the mass products.

This latter component of the creation of the mass market (mass advertising), was to become much more important in the twentieth century, and was most fully developed in the United States after 1910. This process now reaching its peak in the world advertising campaigns of the transnationals is brilliantly described in Stuart Ewen's book, Captains of Consciousness.

Underlying this growth of the mass market were two major processive changes that not only facilitated it but were crucial to its emergence. The first was the large increase in wage workers concentrated in urban centers. The second change was the creation of a new family form separated from the production process. The emergence of industrial capitalism led to a restructuring of the family as a consumption unit within which new needs began to take shape. The reconstitution of the family did not take place quickly or evenly, but by the twentieth century the family in countries such as the United States and Britain became the major market for mass produced goods. As Zaretsky points out:

"Mass production forced the capitalist class to cultivate and extend that market, just as it forced it to look abroad for other new markets...Working people now see consumption as an end in itself, rather than as an adjunct to production, and as a primary source of both personal and social (i.e. 'status') identity". Zaretsky, 1976.

Now while I would not wish to arguethat a these processes are identical in Asia to those in England and the United States, but it is surely no coincidence that the countries which have been the major locations for the emergency of the most rapid proletarianization (Republic of Korea, Taiwan, Hong King, Singapore, and Malaysia) have also been the countries in which these processes and conditions outlined in the preceding section have been most developed.

211

This assertion is particularly true of Malaysia. In the decade of the nineteen sixties the rate of growth of the Gross Domestic Product adveraged 5.7 percent per annum and in the seventies 7.2 percent. As a result the Gross National Product has increased from 12 billion dollars in 1970 to 49 billion by 1980 lifting per capita income from $M1.404 in 1973 to $M2.066 by 1980. This growth has been associated with a very rapid growth in both private and public consumption. Thus private consumption at constant prices rose from 8,918 million Malaysian dollars in 1973 to 15,022 million by 1980: an increase of 68 percent while public consumption increased by 2,591 million to 5,131 million (102 percent). "This period also showed a shift to the purchase of consumer goods with higher import content with the import of consumer durables rising at the annual rate of 30.2 percent between 1976 and 1980 compared to the rate of 14.79 percent in 1971-75, (Tan, 1984, p. 331). This economic growth has been associated with highly significant changes in the social patterns of Malaysia with a growing movement of rural people to the towns, rapid urbanization (estimated 37 percent by 1980) an increase in the ownership of consumer durables, increased education and other facets of the quality of life which are generally assumed to be part of the development. These changes have also been part of the process of significant change in the sectoral contribution with agriculture declining and industry and services contributing a larger proportion to the Gross Domestic Product [4].

III.   THE CREATION OF THE MASS MARKET IN MALAYSIA - SOME PRELIMINARY DATA

The implications of the theoretical framework to the creation of the mass market in Malaysia are obvious. With the growth of income and population there is a growing increase in the proportion of household income spent on non-food items which can be supplied by both foreign imports and national "import substitution" industrial production. However in order to prise this expenditure loose from households (where it may be held in the form of savings or used for social expenditure) it is necessary to create a "need for these products". This is where the third component of the creation of the mass-market comes into play, namely advertising, through the medium of various visual and auditory media. This process is greatly aided by value change in which products can be represented as giving "status" to the person who possesses them and is most obvious in the area of the "style" of clothing, and consumer

212

durables. Finally the considerable increase in education and literacy helps this aspect of the growth of the mass market. The most obvious statistical sources to provide information on this process are Household Surveys that indicate changes in household expenditure through time. In the case of Peninsular Malaysia two peninsular - wide household surveys were carried out in 1957/58 and 1973 and another is due to be administered in 1984. Table 1 presents data for the changes between 1957/58 and 1973 - a period of sixteen years.

Table 1 suggests that in the period of sixteen years during which average household expenditure increased by 60.8 percent, the proportion devoted to food and housing (1 & 9) has declined from 63.9 percent to 51 percent with a consequent increase in non-food items of almost 13.5 percent in which transport, household goods and services are of major importance. In his analysis of this data Ishak Shaari suggests three important factors that may have contributed to these changes in household expenditure. First, that much of the increase in household incomes occurred in the middle and upper income groups. Secondly that the change in relative prices may have effected the pattern. Thus the food price retail index increased by 12.4 percent while that for transport grew by 26.4 percent. Finally that the level of urbanization was also significant for it increased rapidly during the period. This urban-rural distinction is important as Table 2 clearly indicates with the urban household spending rather less on food although a much higher proportion is consumed outside the home. The other major difference is in the amount spent on gross rent, fuel and power which reflects the more expensive urban demands. Surprisingly differences in expenditures in the durable foods patterns are not obvious at this time. This is a pattern which is to change radically by the early nineteen eighties.

Table 2 also reflects the fact that the majority of middle and high income consumers are concentrated in urban areas. Thus the 1973 Household Survey shows that the percentage on food decreased from 50 percent of household expenditures in the households with below $199 Malaysian per month, to 33 percent in the $500-799 bracket and to 20 percent from those households with income above $800 per month.

Since 1973 there has been no comprehensive survey of household expenditure and one must rely upon micro

213

TABLE 1:   PERCENT HOUSEHOLD EXPENDITURE FOR MALAYSIAN
           HOUSEHOLDS.   PENINSULA MALAYSIA 1958/59 &
           1973

Expenditure Group	1957/58	1973
1) Food	57.9	46.4
2) Drinks and Tobacco	6.3	7.1
3) Clothing	5.0	6.3
4) Household Goods	1.8	3.0
5) Fuel and Power	3.2	2.8
6) Transport	3.7	12.3
7) Services	7.0	10.7
8) Sundry Items	10.1	6.8
9) Rent	5.0	4.6
10) Average Household Expenditure ($M)	190.83	306.93

Source: Ishak Shaari (1978) "Expenditure Determination
        and the Determination of the Poverty Line in
        Peninsular Malaysia" in Kamal Salih (ed.),
        1979, p. 56.

TABLE 2: PERCENT HOUSEHOLD EXPENDITURE FOR MALAYSIAN HOUSEHOLDS ,PENINSULAR MALAYSIA, RURAL PENINSULAR MALAYISA, URBAN PENINSULAR MALAYSIA 1973.

	Peninsular Malaysia	Rural Peninsular Malaysia	Urban Peninsular Malaysia
Food	36.2	41.3	30.1
Food Out of Home	6.3	4.6	8.1
Beverages & Tobacco	3.8	4.2	3.5
Clothing & Footwear	5.6	6.1	4.9
Gross Rent, Fuel & Power	11.9	12.7	17.5
Furniture Furnishings, Household Equipment	4.1	4.0	4.3
Medical Care	1.7	1.5	1.9
Transport-Communications	12.2	11.9	12.7
Recreation, Entertainment Education & Cultural Services	6.7	5.5	8.1
Miscellaneous Goods & Services	8.5	8.2	8.9

Source: Ishak Shaari (1978), p. 59.

surveys carried out on the level of the village or household, or less direct data available from industrial production data, trade statistics and surveys of Wholesale and Retail Trades. However the Mid Term Review of the Fourth Malaysia Man 1981-85 does provide some information on per capita monthly household income by state and urban-rural strata based upon the Household Well Being Survey conducted by the Socio-Economic Research Unit in 1981 and 1982. The results are shown in Table 3.

Generally they indicate the dominance of the urban areas particularly the Federal Territory, Selangor, and Negeri Sembilan, which have incomes almost two thirds above the remaining areas. This pattern should be recalled when we discuss the growth of urban markets in the next section of the paper.

Table 4 attempts to set out some of the macro-statistics of Peninsular Malaysia which underly the growth of the mass-market in Malaysia. As it clearly indicates Peninsular Malaysia appears to have experienced virtually all the requirements for the creation of the mass market. The population has almost doubled in the decade of the seventies, per capita income has increased almost threefold, urbanization has grown dramatically; education levels have improved; communication has greatly improved with an increase in roads and telephone usage; electricity has been extended to almost 69 percent of the occupied residential units and the number of telephones has grown by three times. There has also been a sharp increase in the number of motor vehicles which has become the leading edge of the growth of consumption of consumer durables. Much of this latter development has been aided by a massive increase in advertising through television, newspapers and radio concentrating on the increase of purchase of products such as automobiles, houses, furniture, electronic products, clothing, cosmetics and food products such as "fast foods" often franchised by multinational companies.

From the point of view of conventional economists this growth in the consumer market in the decade of nineteen seventies can only be seen as beneficial,for it has been the basis of the continuing growth in the "import substitution" industry and the linkages that are a consequence of the growth (motor vehicle, electronics, house repair, etc.) have considerable employment and income growth generating effects. But as Khor Kok Peng has poinged out the growth of the

216

TABLE 3:   PENINSULAR MALAYSIA: PER CAPITA MONTHLY
HOUSEHOLD INCOME BY STATE AND URBAN-RURAL
STRATA, 1982

$ IN CURRENT PRICES

State	Total	Urban	Rural
Johor	116	181	89
Kedah	78	143	70
Kelantan	92	114	84
Meraka	109	154	95
Negeri Sembilan	130	207	98
Pahang	102	180	109
Perak	91	130	74
Perlis	76	–	76
Pulau Pinang	120	140	101
Selangor	171	268	120
Trengganu	90	113	74
Federal Territory	308	308	–
PENINSULAR MALAYSIA	128	204	89

Source: Interim Review of the Fourth Malaysia Plan
1981-85, p. 156.

TABLE 4:   PENINSULAR MALAYSIA,   SELECTED STATISTICS
           1970-80

	1970	1980
Population (000's)	6,278	11,426
Density (psk)	31.6	41.4
Level of Urbanization (%)	29.0	37.0
Ethnic Proportion (Urban) (%)		
Malays	27.0	33.0
Chinese	59.0	54.0
Indian	13.0	12.0
Others	1.0	1.0
% Enrollment in Primary & Lower Secondary Schools as % of Total Enrollment		
% of Total Enrollment	94.3	89.4
Hard Surface Roads (kms)	16,686.4	22,647.4
Motor Vehicles per KM or		
Hard Surface Road (ratio)	40.0	104.0
Telephones (per 1000)	16.0	45.0
TV/Radio (licences % of		
Household's)	5.9	10.7
Per Capita Income (M$)	180.1	449.0
Electric Lighting (% of occupied units)		
Penang	74.9	88.2
Selangor	61.2	77.3
Kedah	22.3	51.4
Peninsular Malaysia	43.7	68.4
Total Contributions to Employees		
Provident Fund ($millions)	4,465.0	9,047.8

Source: Department of Statistics (1982), Social
        Statistics Bulletin, 1980, Federation of
        Malaysia, Kuala Lumpur.

"mass market" has not been without cost for it has led to a "bias" in the market towards what he labels "non-essential consumer items". Using a variety of data Khor shows that in 1981 Malaysians spent "...about $1,200 to $1,400 million on cigarette and tobacco products, about $700 million in alcoholic beverages, around $250-280 million on soft drinks and syrups, above $100 million in powdered infant milk, and around $2,500 million in motorcars" (Khor, 1984, p. 77). He goes on to suggest that this consumer expenditure is greatly in excess of government expenditures for development. For instance, federal development expenditures for health in the six years 1977 to 1982 was only $485 million, or about a third of what Malaysians spend on cigarettes in a single year (Ibid, p. 78). Finally he suggests that there should be a re-channelling of expenditure away from these "non-essentials" to "basic needs" as a more rational form of consumption.

From the point of view of the state such suggestions, while they may be morally acceptable, have to be balanced against the significant fact that the sales tax and import duties revenue earned from the sale of these "non-essentials" are a major source of government revenue. In addition they are the source of significant corporate revenues which again provide corporate taxes to the state. The state is thus faced with a "bottom line" dilemma. How can it dampen the enthusiasm for the "consumer revolution" in "non-essential" items without decreasing state revenue, causing unemployment and perhaps most significantly vastly increasing its unpopularity with the middle and upper class consumers who have been manipulated by "advertising" into a belief that the possession of consumer items is not only their right but also is basic to their fulfillment of "life". In this respect Zaretsky's argument concerning the reconstitution of the household as a consumption unit is crucial. This is further compounded in situations of slow growth of other major revenue sectors (of exports of primary products) such as began to emerge in Malaysia in the early nineteen eighties when consumer demand slackens. Thus any research project on the growth of the mass market has to analyse State Policy towards these developments.

This growth of the mass market is even more complicated by the fact that the expansion of the market is highly uneven between income groups and spatially within any given market. While it is

219

difficult to document these developments because of the lack of household expenditure surveys the next section attempts to document some of these developments in Peninsular Malaysia utilizing data available from the Surveys of Wholesale and Retail Establishments utilizing value of output for retail trades. For the purposes of these surveys "Retail trade is defined as the resale (sale without transformation) of new and used goods to the general public for personal or household consumption or utilization by shops, department stores, etc." (Federation of Malaysia, 1976, p. 22). The survey covered all establishments with value of output about $5000 that kept accounts which excluded many small scale establishments in the informal sector. Value of output was defined as Turnover value plus Fixed assets produced for own use (i.e. own construction). The surveys thus concentrate primarily on formal sector retailing. I have been unable to ascertain what proportion this sector would make up of total retailing but it is possible to suggest that it is almost a 100 percent of higher order goods (automobiles) and much less for food and lower order commodities.

Table 5 sets forth the basic information on value of output divided between urban and rural Malaysia for 1976 and 1980. While the analysis of this data is subject to the same limitations as the analysis of household data, particularly with respect to controlling for price increases, it clearly shows that value of retail output was highly concentrated in urban areas which increased their proportion by 11 percent in 4 years between 1976 and 1980. When it is recalled that the proportion of population resident in urban areas made up only 33 percent and 37 percent of the population in 1976 and 1980 respectively it can be seen that the growth of the mass market was highly concentrated in urban areas (see Table 6).

Table 6 also shows that the value of output per retail establishment was almost ten times that of the rural areas. Thus it is clear that the mass market is highly concentrated in urban areas, where disposal income is much greater particularly among middle and upper income consumers. This emphasis on urban consumption is undoubtedly biased because rural dwellers utilize urban centres for more expensive consumer durable purchases. But this data base does not permit us to control for this feature.

What is more, this pattern is further spatially

TABLE 5:   VALUE OF OUTPUT ($M000'S) FOR RETAIL
ESTABLISHMENT, URBAN AND RURAL PENINSULAR
MALAYSIA 1976 AND 1980

	1976	TOTAL %	INC. %	1980	TOTAL %
Urban	3,620,011	55	118	7,925,478	66
Rural	2,943,877	45	38	4,091,745	34
Total	6,563,888	100	84	12,107,223	100

Source: Sample Survey of Wholesale and Retail Trades in
Peninsular Malaysia 1976 and 1980.

TABLE 6:   PROPORTION OF URBAN/RURAL AND NUMBER OF
           RETAIL ESTABLISHMENTS, PENINSULAR MALAYSIA,
           1976 & 1980

URBAN	1976		1980
Prop. Urban (PM) %	33	[1]	37
No. of Retail Est's	8,318		13,324
No. of Employees	50,900		73,204
Ratio Empl/Retail est.	6.1		5.4
RURAL			
Prop. Rural (PM) %	67		63
No. of Retail Est's	71,857		76,703
No. of Employees	146,746		183,603
Ratio Empl/Retail est.	2.0		2.0

[1]
    Estimated proportion

Source: See Table 5

222

concentrated by value of output when it is analysed for the largest urban areas shown on Table 7. Thus the two largest metropolitan areas of Kuala Lumpur and Penang with approximately 35 percent of tne urban population in 1980 had 48 percent of the value of output although other urban areas also had substantial proportions. Even more important is the fact that the Kuala Lumpur Metropolitan area/value of output grew by 161 percent in 4 years, and at a rate almost double that of Peninsular Malaysia and well in excess of other Malaysian urban areas.

In the light of these developments it is scarcely surprising that a third Television channel has been approved for the Kuala Lumpur Metropolitan area which will be highly oriented to commercial advertising.

The final facet of this growth of the mass market relates to the sale of particular commodities. Table 8 presents data on selected commodities for rural and urban areas focussing on higher order consumer goods which have been the leading edge of the growth of the mass market. No attempt has been made to present a comprehensive picture of these sales because of the underestimation of good retailing establishments in the census which means that the proportion of value of output of higher order consumer goods would be unduly inflated. Thus the goods selected in this table are chosen because they were the first 7 commodity groups in value of output in 1980. Together they account for 80 percent of value of output in 1980 for Peninsular Malaysia as recorded in the Sample Survey of Retail Trades.

Table 8 shows a clear division between urban and rural Peninsular Malaysia with respect to the value of output. First, motor vehicles and petrol make up more than 42% of the value of output in urban areas compared to only 6.8 percent in the rural areas. It is of course possible that rural dwellers are buying both automobiles and patrol in urban areas but the extent of these differences cannot be totally explained by such an inference. The same pattern is true of electronics where urban areas grew by 173 percent. The most rapid growth is exhibited by general merchandise stores which indicates the growth of department stores in urban areas. On the other hand the rural areas exhibit greater rates of growth for clothing and jewellery which possibly reflects the use of smaller amounts of disposable income in a more traditional manner.

223

TABLE 7:   VALUE OF OUTPUT (M$000'S) FOR RETAIL
ESTABLISHMENTS IN KUALA LUMPUR METROPOLITAN
AREA, PENANG METROPOLITAN, OTHER URBAN
MALAYSIA 1976 AND 1980.

	1976	Total Urban v.o.	Inc.%	1980	Total % Urban v.o.
KL Met.	1,141,963	31.0	161.0	2,988,330	38.0
Penang Met.	390,065	11.0	109.0	816,665	10.0
Other Urban	2,087,983	58.0	97.0	4,120,483	52.0
Total Urban	3,620,011	100.0	118.0	7,925,478	100.0

Note: KL Met. and Penang Metropolitan include
adjacent urban areas such as Kelang and
Butterworth.

v.o. = Value of Output

Source: See Table 5.

TABLE 8: SELECTED COMMODITIES VALUE OF OUTPUT
(M$000'S) 1976 AND 1980, URBAN/RURAL
PENINSULAR MALAYSIA

A. URBAN MALAYSIA

	1976	% Inc.	1980
General Provisions (Rice)	535,402	77.0	949,936
Motor Vehicles	890,765	151.0	2,236,333
Petrol	541,316	102.0	1,096,612
Electrical Goods	308,621	173.0	842,684
Clothing	353,520	50.0	533,391
General Merchandise	140,777	242.0	481,497
Jewellery	207,411	86.0	386,876
Total Urban	3,620,011	118.0	7,925,478

B. RURAL MALAYSIA

	1976	% Inc.	1980
General Provisions (Rice)	1,590,041	42.0	2,264,022
Motor Vehicles	58,648	76.0	13,900
Petrol	147,480	81.0	267,408
Electrical Goods	136,966	39.0	177,096
Clothing	147,909	68.0	248,995
General Merchandise	48,726	6.0	51,604
Jewellery	36,415	143.0	88,664
Total Rural	2,943,877	38.0	4,091,745

Source: See Table 5.

A final facet of this growth of the mass market concentrated upon the urban areas relates to the physical setting of the household - namely the house in which they live. Throughout the urban areas of Peninsular Malaysia a "suburban revolution" has occurred as Malaysians have increasingly occupied low density housing spreading outwards from the city cores. Thus in the period between 1970 and 1980 the number of private living quarters in Peninsular Malaysia increased from 1.6 million to 2.21 million (37.5 percent) while the number of households per occupied dwelling fell from 1.23 to 1.077 indicating a tendency towards single family households. Of the 744,000 units built during the decade, the public sector accounted for 207,590 units and the private sector the remaining 536,410. Much of the private sector development was carried out by private developers who developed and sold 313,820 housing units in the decade of which almost 74 percent were built in the period 1976 to 1980. Most of the houses were in the medium and high price category and about 70 percent of those approved in the last 5 years of the decade were single and double story terrace houses. An estimated 29 percent of the houses were in the Federal Territory, 23 percent in Johore, 11 percent in Selangor, 11 percent in Perak and 7 percent in Pulau Pinang. Thus almost 71 percent were located in the five largest urban areas and their surrounding areas which we have indicated earlier accounted for a major part of the increase in value of retailing output [6]. Returning to the theoretical framework presented in Part 2 the preceding analysis would suggest the capitalist expansion in Malaysia has been advancing in all spheres of the economy. In particular it has been in the sphere of private consumption that private capital, both multinational and national, (aided by the state provision of the necessary infrastructure for collective consumption, energy, roads, etc.), has been moving with great speed. This has fuelled the growth of a Malaysian urban middle and upper class in which the household is the central unit of consumption.

IV.   CONCLUSION

I would be the first to admit that the ideas in this paper are speculative and the data analysis is preliminary, but they do suggest that there is a considerable need for more detailed analysis of the growth of the mass market in developing countries. In the capitalist economies of the Third World the Mass Markets are invading and destroying the "little

226

markets",for so long the focus of research of the economic anthropologist. It may well be the time to shift the focus on this research from "little" to "mass markets".

NOTES

1. My former colleagues at the Department of Human Geography at Australian National University and I have attempted to do this in a study of food distribution and retailing in the urban areas of the New Hebrides. Although we make no claims for the thoroughness of our research methods, we managed to arrive at some estimates of the value of sales for various commodities through different types of outlets. This enabled us to arrive at some policy prescriptions designed to encourage the marketing and sale of indigenous foodstuffs. (See McGee et al., 1980).

2. Cited in Kamal Salih (1981). Quotation taken from Muzaffar, 1979.

3. See Lagbao and Rogella (1981).

4. These changes are documented in a series of Malaysia 5 Year Plans and Mid Term Reviews published by the Malaysian Government between 1971 and 1984. For recent reviews of the Malaysian economy see Khor (1983) and (1984) and Lim and Chee (1984).

5. Peninsular Malaysia refers to that part of Malaysia located between Thailand and Singapore. The states of Sabah and Sarawak which form part of the Malaysian nation are not included in this analysis.

6. Figures presented in the Federation of Malaysia Fourth Malaysia Plan 1981-85, pp. 359-64.

REFERENCES

Amin, S.
    1974   Accumulation on a World Scale: A Critique of the Theory of Underdevelopment. 2 vols. New York: Monthly Review Press.

Boeke, J.H.
    1953   Economics and Economic policy of Dual Societies as Exemplified by Indonesia. New York: Institute of Pacific Relations.

Breman, J.
    1976   "A Dualistic Labour System? A Critique of
            the Informal Sector Concept", Economic and
            Political Weekly 11 (48), 1870-75; 11 (49),
            1905-8; 11 (50), 1939-44.

Bromley, R.J. and Gerry, C., eds.
    1979   Casual Work and Poverty in Third World
            Cities. London: Methuen.

Cohen, R.B.
    1981   "The New International Division of Labour,
            Multinational Corporations and Urban
            Hierarchy", in Michael Dear and Allen J.
            Scott, Urbanization and Urban Planning in
            Capitalist Society. New York and London:
            Methuen, pp. 287-315.

Ewen, Stuart
    1976   Captains of Consciousness: Advertising and
            the Social Roots of the Consumer Culture.
            McGraw Hill Book Co., New York.

Frank, A.G.
    1967   Capitalism and Underdevelopment in Latin
            America. New York: Monthly Review Press.

Fraser, W. Hamish
    1981   The Coming of the Mass Market, 1850-1914.
            Archon Books, Hamden, Conn.

Friedmann, John and Wolff Geotz
    1982   Future of the World City, paper presented at
            a Conference on Urbanization and National
            Development, East-West Center, Honolulu,
            January 25-29.

Gerry, C.
    1974   Petty Producers and the Urban Economy: A
            Case Study of Dakar. Research Working Paper
            No. 8, World Employment Programme, Geneva:
            International Labor Office.

Goldstein, Sydney
    1978   Circulation in the Context of Total Mobility
            in South-East Asia. Paper prepared for
            International Seminar on the Cross-Cultural
            Study of Circulation, East-West Center,
            Honolulu, Hawaii.

Hart, K.
   1973   Informal Income Opportunities and Urban
             Employment in Ghana. Journal of Modern
             African Studies, 11 (1):61-89.

Hugo, Graeme
   1975   Population Mobility in West Java.
             Unpublished Ph.D. thesis in demography,
             Australian National University, Canberra.

International Labor Office
   1972   Employment, Incomes and Equality: A
             Strategy for Increasing Productive
             Employment in Kenya. Geneva.

Kamal Salih et al
   1975   Industrialization Strategy, Regional
             Development and the Growth Centre Approach.
             A Case Study of West Malaysia. UNCRD,
             Nagoya.

Kamal Salih
   1981   "Malaysia and the World System: A
             Perspective Essay on Incorporation, Social
             Groups and the State". Unpublished paper
             presented to the Development Centre OECD,
             Paris.

Khor Kok Peng
   1983   The Malaysian Economy Structures and
             Dependence. Institut Maskarakat/Marican &
             Sons Ltd., Kuala Lumpur.

   1984   Recession and the Malaysian Economy.
             Institut Maskarakat. Penang.

Lagbao, Floredeliza Y and Rogella E. Pa
   1981   Transnationals and Consumerism. Impact on
             Filipino Tastes and Values. State and
             Society , Vol. 2, No. 1, pp. 91-99.

Lewis, W.A.
   1954   Economic Development with Unlimited Supplies
             of Labour. Manchester School of Economics
             and Social Studies 20:139-92.

Lo, F.C. and Salih K. (eds.)
   1978   Growth Role Strategy and Regional
             Development Policy. Asian Experience and
             Aalternative Approaches. Pergamon Press,
             Oxford.

229

Lipton, Michael
   1977   Why Poor People Stay Poor: Urban Bias in
             World Development. Canberra: Australian
             National University Press.

Lim Lean Lin and Chee Peng Lim (eds.)
   1984   The Malaysian Economy at the Crossroads,
             Malaysian Economic Association, Kuala
             Lumpur.

McGee, T.G.
   1971   The Urbanization Process in the Third World:
             Explorations in Search of a Theory. London:
             G. Bell & Sons, Ltd.

   1973   "Peasants in Cities: A Paradox, A Paradox,
             a Most Ingenious Paradox", Human
             Organization, 32 (2):135-42.

   1974   Hawkers in Hong Kong: A Study of Policy and
             Planning in the Third World City. Hong
             Kong: Centre of Asian Studies, University
             of Hong Kong.

   1976   "The Persistence of the Proto-Proletariat:
             Occupational Structures and Planning of the
             Future of Third World Cities", Progress in
             Geography 9:1-38.

   1978a   "An Invitation to the Ball: Dress Formal or
             Informal?" in P.J. Rimmer, D.W. Drakakis-
             Smith, and T.G. McGee, eds., Food, Shelter
             and Transport in Southeast Asia and the
             Pacific. Publication HG/12, Department of
             Human Geography, Canberra: Australian
             National University.,

   1978b   "Rural-Urban Mobility in South and Southeast
             Asia: Different Formulations, Different
             Answers". In William H. McNeil and Ruth S.
             Adams, eds., Human Migration: Patterns and
             Policies. Bloomington: Indiana University
             Press.

   1979   "Conservation and Dissolution in the Third
             World City: the Shanty Town as an Element
             of Conservation". Development and Change 10
             (1):1-22.

   1982a   "Labour Mobility in Fragmented Labour
             Markets: The Role of Circulatory Migration

in Rural-Urban Relations in Asia", In Helen
Safa, ed. Towards a Political Economy of
Urbanization in Third World Countries
Delhi: Oxford University Press, pp. 47-66.

1982b   "Proletarianization, Industrialization and
Urbanization in Asia: A Case Study of
Malaysia. Flinders Asian Studies Lecture
No. 13. Adelaide: Flinders University.

McGee, T.G., R. Gerrard Ward, and D. Drakakis-Smith
1980   Food Distribution in the New Hebrides.
Monograph No. 25. Development Studies
Centre. Canberra: Australian National
University.

McGee, T.G. and Yue-man Yeung
1977   Hawkers in Southeast Asian Cities: Planning
for the Bazaar Economy. Ottawa:
International Development Research Centre.

Mosley, P.
1977   Implicit Models and Policy Recommendations:
Reflections on the Employment Policy in
Kenya. Paper prepared for Institute of
British Geographers Symposium on the urban
Informal Sector in the Third World, School
of Oriental and African Studies, University
of London, London.

Portes, Alejandro and Walton, John
1981   Labor, Class and the International System.
Academic Press, New York.

Pryor, Robin J. ed.
1979   Migration and Development in Southeast Asia:
A Demographic Perspective. Kuala Lumpur:
Oxford University press.

Roberts, Bryan
1978   Cities of Peasants: The Political Economy
of Urbanization in the Third World. London:
Edward Arnold.

Robinson, Susan
1982   "A Change from Nasi Lemak", Business Times,
Saturday, June 26, Singapore.

Santos, Milton
1979   The Shared Space: The Two Circuits of the
Urban Economy in Underdeveloped Countries.

London: Methuen.

Singh, Ajit
  1979   "The Basic Needs Approach to Development vs.
          the New International Economic Order: The
          Significance of Third World
          Industrialization", World Development 7:535-
          606.

Soja, Edward, R. Morales, and G. Wolff
  1983   "Urban Restructuring: An Analysis of Social
          and Spatial Change in Los Angeles", Economic
          Geography, Vol. 59, No. 2, April, pp. 195-
          230.

Squire, Lyn
  1979   Labor Force, Employment and Labor Markets in
          the Course of Economic Development. World
          Bank Staff Working Paper No. 336.
          Washington, D.C.: International Bank of
          Reconstruction and Development.

Tan Tat Wai
  1984   "Trends in Malaysian Economic Development"
          in Lim Lin Lean and Chee Peng Lim (eds.),
          The Malaysian Economy at the Crossroads.
          Malaysian Economic Association, Kuala
          Lumpur, pp. 319-366.

Wallerstein, I.
  1974   The Modern World System: Capitalist
          Agriculture and the Origins of the European
          World Economy in the Sixteenth Century. New
          York: Academic Press.

Walton, J.
  1976a   "Political Economy of World Urban Systems:
          Directions for Comparative Research", In J.
          Walton and L.H. Massoti, eds., The City in
          Comparative Perspective: Cross-National
          Research and New Directions in Theory. Los
          Angeles: Sage Publications.

  1976b   "Urban Hierarchies and Patterns of
          Dependence in Latin America: Theoretical
          Biases for a New Research Agenda". In A.
          Portes and H.L. Browning, eds., Current
          Perspectives in Latin America Urban
          Research. Austin: University of Texas.

232

Warren, Bill
   1973   "Imperialism and Capitalist
           Industrialization", New Left Review, 1981
           (September-October)

   1978   "The Postwar Economic Experience of the
           Third World". Unpublished paper, University
           of Sydney.

Zaretsky, E.
   1976   Capitalism, the Family and Personal Life.
           Pluto Press, London, p. 68.

CRAFT BUSINESSES, PIECE WORK, AND VALUE DISTRIBUTION IN THE OAXACA VALLEY, MEXICO

Scott Cook, The University of Connecticut

This paper reports on a recent study of rural and urban businesses engaged in the production and/or marketing of craft products in Oaxaca, Mexico. Various types of businesses are identified and several aspects of their social and economic status, as well as their performance, are described and analyzed. Special attention is devoted to businesses which combine intermediary and manufacturing operations, and to their relationships with labor through the piece wage system. Finally, some implications of these data for our understanding of the piece wage system and of capitalist development and underdevelopment in Oaxaca will be discussed.[1]

I. THE CRAFT BUSINESS POPULATION: A GENERAL PROFILE

The population of business operators studied can be classfied into four groups according to the location of their businesses, as follows: (1) operators of separate extra-marketplace establishments in Oaxaca City - 38 cases (this is a very heterogeneous group ranging from large stores/manufactories to small family shops); (2) sellers in an open air street market for craft products in Oaxaca City - 10 cases; (3) operators (caseteros or locatarios) of permanent stalls in two large Oaxaca City marketplaces (20 de Noviembre and the Central de Abastos) - 21 cases; and, (4) merchant-embroiderers in the district of Ocotlán (town and village-based) - 30 cases. Survey coverage was essentially complete for the Oaxaca City extra-marketplace retail and wholesale businesses which deal exclusively in craft commodities. It also approached completeness for the stall-operators in the two major Oaxaca City marketplaces who deal in "ropa típica" (e.g. embroidered blouses and huipiles). Although the survey was not complete for the Ocotlán district embroidery merchants, it did cover most of the principal "putters-out" residing in five different communities in the district.

The average age of these business operators, who are equally divided between the sexes, is 45 years (which is identical with that of the heads of rural direct producing household enterprises surveyed separately). However, the combined average age of the

235

two most important groups of Oaxaca City business operators (the extra-marketplace business proprietors and the marketplace stall operators) is 50 years, and they have operated their businesses for an average of 20 years (compared with an average of only 10 years for the other operator groups). Predictably, the business operators who reside in Oaxaca City average 8 years of formal schooling vs. only 3.6 years for the town and village-residing operators; 47% of the former had at least 3 years of post-elementary schooling whereas only one town or village operators had this much schooling. Even more telling is the fact that 28% of the extra-marketplace business proprietors in Oaxaca City had more than 12 years of schooling (i.e., university study), whereas none of the marketplace business proprietors had any "higher education". Incidentally, the years of schooling of Oaxaca City business proprietors turns out to be an accurate indicator of the larger scale, the higher performance and the greater managerial sophistication, and professionalism of their businesses. Thus, more than one-third of them employ professional bookkeepers or accountants as compared to only one of the 40 town- or village-dwelling merchants. [2]

Of the 99 business operators surveyed, only 16% inherited their businesses, whereas 84% either started these themselves or purchased them. The start-up or initial capital for the business derived from the following sources in order of priority: savings from prior work (32%), inheritance (20%), and saved earnings from other businesses (13%). Family loans were relevant in only 8% of the cases, whereas bank loans were obtained in 7% of the cases (significantly all of the latter were Oaxaca city-residing merchants). The embroidery merchants stand out from all the others because 60% of them initiated their careers as "putters-out" with capital accumulated from work as embroiderers. Indeed, the embroidery industry provides the best example from my research of a rapid growth labor-intensive industry in which the proliferation of a class of dependent direct producers has also been associated with the emergence from the latter of independent employer units which become competitive in scale and volume of operations with the largest established units.

II. ANALYSIS OF THE OPERATORS BY BUSINESS TYPE

Given their closer ties with the rural economy it is not surprising that the embroidery merchants and the

open-air craft marketplace sellers are more likely to
pursue other occupations than are the members of the
two other business groups. Of the 21 marketplace-stall
operators 40% indicated that they were also working
artisans or part-time agriculturists in addition to
being intermediaries, whereas 30% of the embroidery
merchants worked part-time at occupations ranging from
peasant cultivator, livestock breeder, tailor, and
baker to grocer, agricultural products trader, and
mason. To a large extent, this dual occupational
involvement is associated with the relatively low
income generated from their craft businesses and is
found only among the male segment of the embroidery
merchants. [3]

By contrast, 45% (17) of the extra-marketplace
business proprietors in Oaxaca City were artisans (most
of them continuing parental occupations); 18% had other
occupations or businesses, with the rest indicating
involvement in the professions or other commercial
enterprises. Only one of the marketplace-stall
operators indicated involvement in a second occupation.

Of the four merchant groups the marketplace-stall
operators have the least direct involvement in
production: most of them purchase finished products
from either direct producers or village-to-marketplace
intermediaries and do not operate production facilities
of any sort. Three of them do have putting-out
operations in embroidery and employ family labor in
pattern-design and finishing activities. As it turns
out, the median monthly value of products produced by
these three units is three times larger than the median
for products purchased by the non-producing units
($1000 dollars vs. $311 dollars). All marketplace-stall
business transactions are on a cash basis, with cash
advances sometimes being made to the direct producers;
finished products are not taken on consignment by the
marketplace stall-operators as they sometimes are by
village-to-marketplace intermediaries (Beals 1975:147-
148) -- a pattern that probably reflects seller
preference and the general lack of relationships of
confidence between villagers and their urban clients.

Both the extra-marketplace business operators and
the Ocotlán embroidery merchants are heavily involved
in production -- 86% of the estimated average monthly
value of all products handled for the first group vs.
99% for the second was produced directly by them or
under their direction. The extra-marketplace businesses
are engaged in production primarily through workshops

237

(42%) and secondarily through own-family or outworker units (32%); the embroidery merchants are engaged both as members of family production units and as operators of extensive putting-out networks (90%).

Nevertheless, the extra-marketplace businesses, as a rule, also purchase large quantities of finished commodities from direct producers, whereas the Ocotlán embroiderers occasionally purchase only small quantities of embroidered products from independent producers. Five of the Ocotlán embroidery merchants employ between 150 and 400 outworkers each; but the majority of them (19 of 24) employ between one and 12 outworkers (median = 4). By comparison, of the eight extra-marketplace businesses which employ outworkers, seven employ between 1 and 9 (median = 4) and one employs 38 outworkers. This latter case is an American expatriate who exports high quality hand-spun yarn and hand-woven textile products to the United States. With regard to the craft-marketplace sellers, 30% exclusively sold products produced by family or hired labor in workshops, another 30% exclusively sold products purchased in a finished state from direct producers or from village-to-marketplace intermediaries, and the remaining 40% sold products from a combination of sources (including three merchants who employ from one to three outworkers).

III.   CAPITAL ACCUMULATION AND DIFFERENTIATION IN THE
       CRAFT BUSINESS SECTOR

It is apparent from what has been said above that the craft businesses are differentiated in terms of objective measures of size and performance between and within the four groups. In this section the sources and nature of this differentiation will be examined in greater detail.

Two categories of variables can be constructed which have a direct bearing on differentiation: one includes variables that measure the value of material means of production (e.g. tools, equipment, facilities, motor vehicles, raw materials on hand); another includes variables that measure the value of finished products (e.g., value of products produced or purchased for resale, finished product inventories, sales estimates). An examination of frequency distributions for the variables in these two categories discloses, with some exceptions, a similar inter-group rank order of median values per business unit as follows (from highest to lowest): (1) extra-marketplace proprietors

238

in Oaxaca City; (2) marketplace-stall operators in Oaxaca City; (3) embroidery merchants in the district of Ocotlán; and (4) sellers in the open air craft market in Oaxaca City. [See Tables 1 and 2]

Although the median values for the variables in Tables 1 & 2 essentially support the order which ranks the extra-marketplace businesses as the most prosperous and the open-air sellers as the least prosperous, it should be emphasized that the range of values is wide for most of these variables. For example, the values indicated for one or more embroidery units may exceed those indicated for several Oaxaca City extra-marketplace or marketplace-stall units. Thus, two embroidery enterprises reported gross annual sales exceeding one million pesos which is higher than reported sales of 80% of the extra-marketplace and of all of the marketplace-stall enterprises. Likewise, three of the open-air market sellers reported gross annual sales ranging from 104,000 to 245,000 pesos which are higher than figures reported by 23% of the extra-marketplace businesses and by 77% of the embroidery units. In short, inter-group ranking does exist as a central tendency, but individual units within each group may deviate significantly from the central tendencies for one or more variables and, consequently, be statistically unrepresentative of their group. [4]

When these businesses are disaggregated and placed in a rank order according to reported values for selected variables measuring scale and business performance, the extent to which patterns derived from aggregate analysis are violated becomes clear. For example, in a rank order of 25 businesses for two separate estimates of the value of total annual sales, 72% of the businesses on both lists are extra-marketplace businesses in Oaxaca City, underlining their predominance in the craft sector. The Ocotlán embroidery businesses come out a distant second: 24% of the top 25 cases in aggregate yearly sales and 20% in gross yearly sales. Nevertheless, on the basis of the aggregate data presented in Tables 1 and 2 -- where the Ocotlán embroiderers are next to last in terms of median measures of material assets and business performance -- one would not predict their presence among a select group of top performing businesses. It is noteworthy that two of the eight businesses which appear in the top ten in both rank orders are operated by rural embroidery merchants.

TABLE 1.   Selected Variables for Material Means of Production for Four Groups of Oaxaca Valley Merchants*

	Tools	Facilities Sales and/or production)	Equipment (sales)	Assets
Business Proprietors (extra-market place) (n = 38)	25,000 200,457 344,375 (n = 14)	625,000 211,125 410,882 (n = 8)	125,000 61,833 183,971 (n = 22)	60,000 371,156 828,891 (n=32)
Stall operators	20,000 (n = 1)	0	1,000 1,384 865 (n = 13)	10,500 22,100 22,583 (n=20)
Embroidery merchants (n = 30)	3,100 5,382 (n = 27)	75,000	0	3,000 27,257 (n = 9)
Open-air sellers	1,050 662 544 (n = 6)	0	0	300 (n = 3)

*Values are listed in the following order: medians, means, and standard deviations. Single value listings are medians. All values are given in pesos. The peso-to-dollar exchange rate in 1979 was approximately 22.50 to 1.

TABLE 2.   Selected Variables for Value of Products
            Bought, Produced and Sold by Oaxaca Valley
            Merchants*

	Value/Mo. of Products bought	Value/Mo. of Products produced	Total Value/Mo. of all Products (sun of cols. 1,2 medians only)
Business proprietors (extra marketplace)	10,150 17,068 25,693 (n = 16)	30,000 97,173 252,160 (n = 15)	40,150 (n = 31)
Stall Operators	7,000 6,216 3,066 (n = 6)	22,500 (n = 2)	29,500 (n = 8)
Embroidery merchants	2,050 (n = 2)	3,100 10,073 18,737 (n = 6)	5,150 (n = 31)
Open-air sellers	1,600 (n = 3)	3,150 2,612 3,064 (n = 6)	4,750 (n = 9)

*Values are listed in the following order: medians,
means, standard deviations. Single value listings are
medians. All values are given in pesos.

Six Oaxaca City extra-marketplace businesses appear in the top ten in two separate rank orders of businesses by total annual sales. Four of these businesses were directly engaged in production: one is a cotton products manufactory (manteleria), one is a pottery manufactory, one is owned by a treadle-loom weaver who operates a weaving manufactory in his village (Teotitlán del Valle), and the fourth has an extensive putting-out and buying-up operation in basketry. In addition, one of the remaining two businesses operated a cutlery workshop which was closed down shortly before our survey was conducted. This demonstrates once again the importance direct involvement in production has as a capital-generating activity in these businesses. The median for products produced annually by the fifty businesses which are directly engaged in production is $3,466 dollars.

To summarize the data presented and analyzed in this section, it can be said that craft products businesses in the Oaxaca valley are quite heterogeneous with respect to the location, size, organization and conduct of their operations. It appears that, with some exceptions, the most successful businesses are those in which capital directly engages labor power in either dispersed or congregated manufacturing -- but does so in conjunction with, rather than as an alternative to, intermediary operations. Whereas, rank orderings for selected variables measuring size and performance of these businesses demonstrate the overall predominance of city-based over village-based capital there are several important exceptions -- especially in the embroidery industry.

IV. CAPITAL, LABOR, AND PIECE WORK

In the craft sector of the Oaxaca valley economy value is created by the labor-power of village-dwelling peasant-artisans and artisans, as well as by the labor-power of a town- and city-dwelling artisan proletariat or petty bourgeoisie. While it is beyond the scope of this paper to attempt to precisely quantify the distribution of value between capital and labor -- and recognizing that the search for general patterns or regularities is bedeviled at every step by empirical complexities -- it does not distort the empirical record to observe that the pattern of distribution is unequal and skewed in the direction of capital. This is not to say that capital is necessarily parasitical, or that its profits are uniformly gratuitous or unmatched by the contribution of productive services. The degree

242

to which profits to capital are unearned or excessive requires empirical determination at the level of specific enterprises; and, in any case, the results of such a determination would be subject to political-economic debate. [5]

However, it is unreasonable to deny that the relationship between labor and capital in the Oaxaca valley, as it is everywhere, is characterized by exploitation. This simply means that the capitalist gets more work out of his workers daily than[6] he pays them in wages. In formal marxist terms this is expressed by saying that the economic forces of capitalist society assure that there is "a difference between the exchange value of labor power and the exchange value of what is produced by its employment (that is, the exchange value of the product); and this difference is the source of the capitalist's profit"[7] (Howard and King 1975:42).

If we examine more carefully the nature of the wage relationship through which capital engages labor in the craft sector of the Oaxaca valley economy, we find that the piece-rate (destajo) form prevails. Of the 52 businesses surveyed which engaged in production, three-quarters (40) employ wage laborers; but only five do so on a time basis with the piece-wage prevailing in the rest. Three of the five businesses which pay their workers a time-wage are pottery manufactories. However, another pottery manufactory does pay piece-wages to its workers. This means that the piece-wage payment form cross-cuts lines of production: from needlework and textile manufacture to tinwork, basketry, leather working, jewelry making, and pottery manufacture. Incidentally, it also prevails in the brick industry where I have conducted a detailed analysis of it (Cook 1984). Consequently, one key to understanding capital-labor relations in Oaxaca valley craft industry surely lies in understanding the piece wage form.

Marx (1967:552-53) argued that the piece wage was merely a version of the time wage but recognized that either of these two payment forms might, under appropriate historical circumstances, contribute more to the development of capitalist production than the other. It was before the rise of "machinofacture" in England, during the period of "manufacture" -- the "stormy youth of Modern Industry" at the end of the 18th and the beginning of the 19th centuries -- that Marx saw the piece-wage form operating as "a lever for the lengthening of the working day, and the lowering of

243

wages" (1967:556). His discussion of the topic is supported by documentary material extracted mostly from factory inspection reports on industries such as spinning and weaving, tailoring, and pottery. The source of the leverage for lengthening the working day, according to Marx, resided in the piece-wage form's enhancement of the individual worker's material incentive, making it in his "personal interest ... to lengthen the working-day, since with it his daily or weekly wages rise" (1967:554). Under the piece-wage regime, the value of the piece is not measured by the working time incorporated in it; rather, the working time expended by the laborer is measured by the number of pieces he has produced (1967:552-553).

In essence, under the piece-wage regime, labor is structurally propelled toward self-exploitation -- though ideologically this is represented as enhanced "liberty, independence, and self-control" (Marx 1967:555). The individual worker is encouraged to believe that he is master of his own economic destiny -- that he will earn in direct proportion to his product. A Oaxaca City shop proprietor put it this way: "Although we have a schedule I give the workers liberty. The artisanal system isn't compatible with schedules. There can be no fixed average salary because salary depends upon the will of the workers." According to Marx (ibid.), this form of remuneration promotes competitiveness among individual workers in a given branch of production; but it has the material effect of raising individual wages above the average as it tends to lower the average itself (i.e., cheapening the cost of labor-power to capitalists). [8]

How, specifically, is this outcome accomplished? In his analysis Marx anticipated the arrival of Taylorism or "scientific management" to capitalist industry. The practice of "scientific management" by capitalist employers does not prevent workers from temporarily increasing their pay through piecework incentives but it does assure that production times of the faster workers will be used by employers to cut rates, thus lowering the wage for all workers (Lamphere 1979:261; cf. Braverman 1974:98-99). For example, the determination of piece-rates by Taylorian methods in the contemporary costume jewelry industry in Providence, Rhode Island has been described as follows: "Through analysis of the time and study data and other inputs ... management determines that 200 rings...can be produced per hour. By lining up this hourly production rate with the hourly rate of pay, i.e., 200

rings for $2.70, management determines a piece rate:
$1.35 per 100. Through this method management has
effectively predetermined that the company will have to
"pay out" little extra piecework money" (Shapiro-Perl
1979:289-290). However, when a few fast workers master
a job and begin "making money", management has the job
re-timed and the piece rate lowered -- a practice
commonly known as "rate busting" (Shapiro-Perl
1979:292).

As far as I can determine "scientific management"
of this formalized sort is mostly absent from the
Oaxaca city manufactories. Piece rates in particular
industries like weaving are set by practical knowledge
of what the average product of a day's work is (e.g.,
the average number of meters of cloth woven per
weaver). This production rate is then roughly "lined-
up" with the going minimum wage rate (per diem rather
than per hour)-- which is periodically issued by the
federal government. However, Oaxaca City manufactory
operators do not engage in "rate busting" and are not
concerned if their pieceworkers earn more than the
official minimum wage which, in any case, is widely
recognized to be well below the value of labor (i.e.,
less than its cost of reproduction in terms of
conventional life necessities) or below a level of
income required to clothe, feed, and house a wage
earner's family without some degree of nutritional
stress (Murphy and Selby 1981:250-251). Indeed, Oaxaca
City is among the poorest cities of its size in Mexico;
65% of its households have been estimated to have a
"less than adequate income" (Murphy and Selby
1981:251). Under such conditions the price of labor is
so low that not even the most rapacious capitalists
need be concerned with strategies for intensifying the
rate of exploitation.

Given this situation, it is my impression that the
city craft shop employers use the piece rate more as a
means to recruit labor and to cope with an apparently
dwindling and erratic supply of labor -- especially in
jobs like treadle loom weaving which apparently are
unattractive to laborers who migrate to the city. It is
a pay form imposed upon employers by the conditions of
artisan labor rather than a scientifically applied
instrument to exploit artisan labor. This is what we
should expect when we are dealing with representatives
of an archaic form of merchant capital rather than of a
modern form of industrial capital (Marx 1967,III:327-
328).

245

In an interesting application of Marx's ideas about piece wages to contemporary Tunisian tailors, Hopkins (1978) notes a parallel between the "sweating system" in 19th-century England -- established through the "interposition of middlemen between the capitalist and the laborers" -- and the role patrons play between Tunis coat dealers and tailoring industry workers in a provincial town (1978:478). This appears to be similar to the situation existing within the Oaxaca valley embroidery industry where putting-out merchants often employ a series of commission agents who operate at the village level to recruit, supply, and pay outworkers. Also, in the basket industry the Oaxaca City buyers-up make contracts for so much per basket of a particular type with one village master basketmaker who is then responsible for recruiting and paying other basketmakers in his village. As Marx said about this type of arrangement: "The exploitation of the laborer by capital is here effected through the exploitation of the laborer by the laborer" (1967:554). Finally, in the Oaxaca valley manufactories where the patron is also a worker the situation parallels that in the Tunisian tailoring workshops where patrons push themselves to work just as hard as their piece-workers because their income also depends on output (Hopkins 1978:478).

Given the widespread use of the piece-rate system, differential wages among individual workers are typical in Oaxaca manufactories. For example, the proprietor of a tin products manufactory with 45 workers responded as follows to our question as to how much he paid his tinworkers per day: "Well, this varies a great deal. The head of my tinworkers earns 12,000 pesos monthly. Then I have three who earn 4,000 pesos monthly. The great majority earn between 2,000 and 2,500 pesos monthly." He was then asked what the basis was for this differentiation and he responded: "Their output, because we base our salary on a commission per piece." When asked if there was a basic salary for all of his tinworkers, he replied: "No. There are some workers who can earn a month's salary in a day. There's one worker, for example, who can make 350 tin boxes in one day -- a product that we sell in large quantities. On the other hand, there is another worker who has a hard time making 24 boxes daily. It depends on their skill." The next follow-up question was whether, in fact, this employer paid workers per day or per piece, to which he responded as follows: "Almost by the piece. We pay them the minimum salary required by law [which was 70 pesos or 3 dollars daily in 1979] and above that a commission by the piece so that they produce all that they can."

246

Unfortunately, the data to support a more complete analysis of the economic consequences of the piece-wage in this case are lacking. What is clear from the available data, however, is that in this shop the time-wage, apparently without being "lined-up" with a fixed "average" rate of worker output, was used to cover the minimum wage; and the piece-wage was introduced to provide a material incentive for the intensification of production. It is the latter which seems to be of primary importance to this and other Oaxaca city workshop operators, rather than an overriding concern with the rate of exploitation as is the case, for example, in the Rhode Island costume jewelry shop.

One final point about the piece-wage form: it is incorrect to view it as linked to a unidirectional evolution from independent handicraft to capitalist manufacture, and to view the "freedom" of the direct producer under it as absolute. Marx observed that time-and piece-wages often coexisted in the same branches of industry and in the same shops (1967:551), and was scathing in his criticism of the following statement made by Watts in 1865 [quoted in Marx ibid.]: "The system of piece-work illustrates an epoch in the history of the working-man; it is halfway between the position of the mere day-laborer depending upon the will of the capitalist and the cooperative artisan, who in the not too distant future promises to combine the artisan and the capitalist in his own person. Piece-workers are in fact their own masters, even whilst working upon the capital of the employer." In short, under the piece-wage system the equality between employer and worker is illusory (Hopkins 1978:477). Yet, as I have argued above, in Oaxaca it may be equally illusory to consider the piece-wage system as an systematic instrument for the maintenance of designated rates of exploitation of labor by capital in labor-intensive industries. Rather it is the form of remuneration most suited to the general conditions of labor which confront its employers --especially those in rural areas but those in urban areas as well.

V. CRAFT BUSINESSES AND THE DISTRIBUTION OF VALUE

What can be gleaned from the statistical data regarding the distribution of total product between capital and labor in these manufactories? Aggregate statistics comparing fifteen city manufactories with thirty rural embroidery units serve as a basis for estimating the volume and distribution of value in these two groups of businesses. Aggregate gross monthly profits for the fifteen Oaxaca city manufactories are just under $20,000 dollars (28% of the value of aggregate monthly product), which averages out to $1,217 dollars monthly per manufactory. This compares with aggregate gross monthly profits for the thirty Ocotlán embroiderery merchants of $2,700 dollars (20% of the value of the aggregate monthly product), which averages out to only $88 dollars monthly per merchant. Given the higher organic composition of capital (i.e., cost of means of production/wage bill or C/V) in the Oaxaca city manufactories (.48 vs. .01) it follows that the aggregate wage bill in embroidery represents a much higher proportion of total product (42%) than it does in the city manufactories (11%). However, the per capita monthly wage is three times higher for the city manufactory pieceworker ($32 dollars) than it is for the embroidery outworker ($10 dollars) -- yet the fact remains that it is substantially below the monthly official minimum wage for Oaxaca City of the peso equivalent for 80 dollars - Murphy and Selby 1981:251. In sum, the city manufactory does much better relative to the Ocotlán embroidery unit in appropriating the total social product than does the city pieceworker relative to the village outworker.

The mean wage for the city manufactory pieceworker must be interpreted in the context of an urban economy in which the median monthly household income in 1979 was 2,518 pesos or $112 dollars (1,966 pesos or $87 dollars for "poor" households) [Murphy and Selby 1981:253]; and in which the median monthly household per-adult-equivalent income was 667 pesos (400 pesos for the "marginally poor" [Higgins 1983:173]. Although the mean pieceworker wage is in line with these other figures, my impression is that it is nonthelesss skewed to the low side because an undetermined percentage of the total workforce is casual or part-time. In the words of one weaving workshop proprietor: "When they want to work, they work all day; and when they don't want to work they don't come. We are short of workers but we have to manage. We lack human material. All of them want to be professionals. There are no longer many who want to be artisans." Among other things this pattern of irregular work is associated with an urban situation in which "the majority of households have as many teenage and adult members working as possible" and where "there is a lack of unemployment because the majority of people are underemployed" (Higgins 1983:7). It is also possible that low-wage jobs in the service sector are more attractive to members of these households than are

248

piecework jobs in archaic manufactories.

By contrast, the low mean per capita wage for rural embroidery outworkers is a reflection of the sex and age composition of that population: a significant proportion of embroidery outwork is done by young, dependent, unmarried, and childless females (38%), although a majority (51.5%) of the embroidery outworkers are married and have dependent children. Regardless of who performs it, embroidery work is tedious and poorly remunerated. Out of fifteen outworker households for which detailed budget data is available, the highest hourly return was just under six pesos (25 cents U.S.) and the lowest a paltry sixty centavos (3 cents U.S.)! As I have argued elsewhere, from the perspective of the female embroidery outworkers the critical issue is not so much low remuneration as it is no remuneration. They have relatively few cash-earning alternatives which are so easily adaptable to daily household routines (Cook 1982:64). In other words, the Oaxaca valley countryside provides a fertile recruiting ground for outworkers -- a fact which is borneout by the remarkable proliferation of the embroidery industry in the district of Ocotlán and elsewhere in the valley over the last decade.

The aggregate cost, output and sales data also make it possible to calculate two favorite Marxist ratios for these groups of businesses, the rate of surplus value or exploitation (S/V) and the rate of profit (S/[C + V]). In accordance with the patterns already described, the rate of exploitation of labor in the city manufactories is substantially higher (256%) than it is in the Ocotlán putting-out units (47%). The same is true regarding the profit rate: 173% for the city manufactories vs. 46% for the putting-out units. For reasons which are not entirely clear, estimates of rates of surplus-value realized by merchant-manufacturers in the Oaxaca valley are substantially higher than an independent estimate of 74% for Oaxaca City buyers of reed basket products (Bailon Corres 1980:108); and are much higher than estimates of rates realized by Yucatan hammock industry merchants studied by Littlefield (1978) where the rate for rural intermediaries was just over 15% and for city merchants about 54%.

Like the Yucatan case, however, this rate soars for intermediaries in Mexico City and beyond, who regularly resell Oaxaca craft products at mark-ups of

249

200 to 300%. Moreover, the rate is bifurcated between the male and female labor force in both cases so that one of Littlefield's (1978:504) concluding arguments is as valid for the Oaxaca valley as it is for Yucatan: "This differential in the average wages of men and of women...allows labor in weaving [and embroidery - my insert] to be paid less than its value in terms of the conventional necessities of life." This conclusion takes on added significance in light of the fact that the average price of male labor-power in Oaxaca, as indicated above, is itself undervalued. So, if men in Oaxaca can be said to suffer super exploitation, women such as embroiderers and thread-spinners suffer hyper exploitation.

VI. SOME IMPLICATIONS FOR PROVINCIAL CAPITALIST DEVELOPMENT

While the preceding analysis requires further substantiation through longer-term and more detailed case studies, I think that it partially closes a gap in our knowledge about craft businesses in the Oaxaca valley and provides a sound basis for future research. In this concluding section I will make some additional observations on the subject and draw out some of the implications of the above analysis for development/underdevelopment discourse.

The more I read about and investigate the history of Oaxaca valley economy and society, the more convinced I am that the city-based merchant-manufactory in handicrafts is only a pale shadow today of what it was in the past. There is no manufacturing operation in Oaxaca city today -- and probably has not been one in this century -- which can match in scale the colonial gremios or obrajes (Semo 1973:161-187); and the social, political, and economic importance of today's merchant class cannot compare with that of 17th and 18th (and, perhaps, 19th and early 20th) century merchant classes (Hamnet 1971; Chance 1978). Those classes -- and the artisan-proletariats which they exploited -- were dominant forces in the regional development of mercantile capitalism, whereas today's counterparts are subsumed players in a "provincial capitalism" (Cook 1984)which is even more statized and bureaucratized than it was under the Spanish or, for that matter, in the post-colonial dictatorship of Porfirio Díaz. With few exceptions, all of the businesses I have dealt with above are adjuncts of the tourist sector of the Oaxaca economy which has experienced an accelerated development since 1940. They produce and/or traffick in

250

essentially luxury commodities, the social demand for which originates among affluent urbanites outside Oaxaca and, in a majority of cases, outside Mexico. These businesses process raw materials which are, for the most part, not produced locally or regionally and injecttheir finished commodities into marketing channels which do not have local or regional destinations.

Whereas this merchant manufacturing sector has historically diminished in overall importance in the regional economy, it will not soon disappear. However, there are many signs that its direct involvement in material production is either undergoing a relocation to the countryside (e.g., the treadle-loom weaving manufactories) or is surrendering this sphere to complete worker control (e.g., the tinworking shop was sold to the workers in 1980) -- primarily because of its inability to adapt in any other way to the changing structure of the wider state capitalist economy with its proliferating corruption, bureaucracy, and corporatist legalism. Also, the locus of merchant-manufacturing is shifting to the countryside as a concomitant of capital accumulation and social differentiation occurring there (e.g., the case of embroidery). This retreat from production by urban merchants is matched by an expansion of their intermediary operations in handicrafts (or, paradoxically, by their abandonment of the craft sector altogether), or by a diversification of business interests primarily in the burgeoning service sector (e.g., tourist agencies, restaurants, real estate agencies, insurance agencies). So, in contemporary Oaxaca City the "union of a sale shop with the workshop" (Bucher 1901:206) is not so much reflective of an evolutionary trend as it is of conjunctural expediency.

I do not intend to create a scenario here which precludes a role for labor-intensive industrialization in the future of capitalist development in Oaxaca. What I am suggesting is that this role -- in the tourist crafts line of production, at least -- will be increasingly played-out in the countryside. However, there may be a significant role in the city, as well as in the countryside, for a new type of labor-intensive feeder industry -- either of the assembly-shop (maquiladora) variety, or of rejuvenated or newly established manufactories or factories producing or assembling new lines of commodities for absentee mass-merchandising and/orproduction enterprises(cf. Cook

251

1981:61-66).

Authentic industrial capitalist development is nascent in the Oaxaca valley; it is developing from within simple commodity forms in the countryside in industries like weaving, mezcal distilling, and brickmaking. It has been successfully introduced in modern capital-intensive forms in a handful of industries like plywood production, hydrated lime quarrying and processing, and tractor-trailer assembly; but unsuccessfully introduced in milk pasteurizing, brick making and, it appears, in mezcal distilling. So, the well-documented "underdevelopment" of the Oaxaca valley political economy is associated with a relative absence, not with a significant presence, of authentic, modern industrial capitalist enterprise.

This statement puts me in the company of Marx and Lenin -- and in opposition to most contemporary Marxists -- regarding the potential of industrial capitalism for generating economic development in poor nations and regions. I believe, along with some political economists (Mandle 1980; Warren 1980), that a "reluctance to acknowledge the growth-promoting nature of capitalism has unnecessarily handicapped" Marxist analysis (Mandle 1980:871). Indeed, before Marxists can make an effective case against the inequities and irrationalities endemic to capitalism, I agree with Mandle that "acknowledgement is first required that capitalism is capable of promoting a significant revolution in productive capacity" (1980:872).

Even though regional capitalist development in today's Third World usually means dependency upon big national and/or transnational capital, it seems to me that there is a correlation between the relative presence of industrial capital and the material well-being of the general population in various regions of Mexico: namely, that the areas of highest concentration of capitalist industry are those with the highest percentages of households with greater than minimum adequate income. Such a correlation has at least been made in one recent study comparing Oaxaca City, with three northern Mexican cities (Murphy and Selby 1981).

Whether or not this correlation is suggestive rather than definitive, one thing is certain: underdevelopment in Oaxaca cannot be eliminated by the triumvirate of simple commodity production, merchant capital, and commercial capital. The significant out-

252

migration of population from the Oaxaca valley and its
hinterland over the years -- and the flow of migrants
to more highly capitalized regions -- are diagnostic of
the failures of this triumvirate to generate the
quantity and quality of employment opportunities
required and expected by the migrating masses. Without
the simultaneously "destructive" and "regenerating"
forces of industrial capital -- not in its labor-
intensive simple or its capital-intensive enclave forms
but in its capital-intensive integrated form -- the
Oaxaca economy will remain underdeveloped for a long
time to come. Without further crystallization and
organization of modern social classes and
intensification of class struggle, which industrial
capital excels in generating, the possibility for
Oaxaca's working people to achieve a more equitable
share of the social product created by their
participation in the Mexican political-economy will be
remoter still.

NOTES

1. I wish to thank Leigh Binford for his contribution
   to the computer processing and statistical analysis
   of the quantitative data, as well as for his
   critical reading of an earlier version of this
   manuscript. Also, I wish to acknowledge the
   contribution of Alice Littlefield and Ana Emma
   Jaillet for their roles in the collection of the
   craft business data. The overall project, of which
   the business study was one component, was funded by
   the National Science Foundation.

2. Given the well-documented importance of women in
   craft industries in Oaxaca and elsewhere, it will
   come as no surprise that half of these craft
   business proprietors are women, nor that the
   embroidery group has the highest proportion of
   females (83%). With one notable exception (i.e.,San
   Isidro Zegache in Ocotlán district -- where men
   regularly embroider), embroidering is a task
   performed mostly by females in the Oaxaca valley
   division of labor. The overrepresentation of females
   as proprietors of embroidery businesses is countered
   by their underrepresentation as proprietors of the
   extra-marketplace businesses in Oaxaca City.
   However, it is noteworthy that women are proprietors
   of three of the eight businesses in this group which
   rank in the top ten businesses (covering all groups)

253

with the highest annual gross sales.

3. Only 29% of the business operators indicated that they currently had agricultural land. Relatively few of the permanent Oaxaca City dwellers had any agricultural land holdings: 11% of the extra-marketplace merchants reported that they held such land but only 5% of the marketplace-stall operators did. By contrast, 60% of the open-air craft market sellers and of the embroidery merchants -- all of whom are rural-dwelling -- reported having agricultural land. The average landholding is non-irrigated and measures 2.8 hectares.

4. The great disparity between the means and the medians in these tables, as well as the exceptionally large standard deviations, derive from distributions skewed by the presence of a few cases with abnormally high values. Because the data nowhere fit the normal curve, the best measure of central tendency is the median. The variations in "n" throughout the tables result from the fact that for many of the units surveyed in all groups, the relevant data were incomplete or not reported.

5. The controversial matter of capital's right to a share of the produce of labor, or whether its income is earned or unearned, was the subject of a comprehensive and seminal study by Menger (1899). For example, with regard to intermediaries like the Oaxaca valley craft products dealers it can be argued that they render specific services for which they merit remuneration. Mintz expressed this argument as follows: "The services are not imposed on customers; they are salable because buyers and sellers require them. Intermediaries transport, process, accumulate stock, break stock, grant credit to agricultural producers and to urban consumers, pay taxes, keep truckers employed, and contribute much else to the ready functioning of the economy" (1964:4). One clear implication of such an argument seems to be that direct producers in a commodity economy are not entitled to the whole product of their labor simply because the "commoditization" of those products requires the provision of intermediary services; and that the providers of such services (which may or may not add value to commodities already produced) are entitled to a share of the value created by direct producers. See Cook 1984: Chapter 4 for a discussion of these issues in the brick industry.

6. In Marxist terms this is explained by saying that
    the capitalist does not buy the worker's labor, but
    his labor power. That is, he does not buy the
    "worker's productive activity, or what the worker
    creates in a specified period of time" but, rather,
    he "buys his labor power, the worker's capacity for
    labor, or control over the worker's creative
    capacity for a specified time period" (Howard and
    King 1975:42).

7. Marx elaborated this theory in volume 1 of Capital
    by arguing that the worker's day is bifurcated into
    "necessary labor time" (that period during which the
    magnitude of the value that he creates is equal to
    the value of the commodities he indirectly receives
    from the wage paid to him by the capitalist -- i.e.,
    wage goods); and "surplus labor time" (that period
    during which the worker creates value in excess of
    that received in his wages). Thus, the rate of
    exploitation is the ratio of surplus to necessary
    labor time or S/V (Howard and King 1975:42).

8. An important difference between the piece- and the
    time-wage was emphasized in a comprehensive study by
    the International Labor Office as follows: "The
    chief characteristic of systems of payment by
    results under which the worker's reward varies in
    the same proportion as his output is that any gains
    or losses resulting directly from changes in his
    output accrue to him (leaving to the employer any
    gains or losses in overhead costs per unit of
    output). In contrast, when the worker is paid by the
    hour or by the day all gains or losses resulting
    from changes in his output accrue to the employer"
    (1951:7). It is significant that three of the
    principal advantages of piece wage systems listed in
    the ILO study (1951:178) are quite compatible with
    Marx's analysis, namely: (1) "They can make a
    substantial contribution to the raising of
    productivity, to lower costs of production and to
    increased earnings for the workers" [here Marx would
    say "temporarily by some workers"]; (2) "In general,
    less direct supervision is required to maintain
    reasonable levels of output than under payment by
    time..."; and (3) "Workers are encouraged to pay
    more attention to reducing lost time and to make
    more effective use of their equipment...". The same
    study also notes that one of the principal
    disadvantages of piece work is that "wide
    differences in the ability or capacity of workers
    working in close proximity may lead to large

255

differences in earnings and to ill-feeling between workers" (1951:178-9).

My study of the brick industry (Cook 1984) indicates that differences in worker ability or capacity is less an issue than differences in piece rates between brickyards; and that these differences may lead to conflict between brickyard operators and their pieceworkers. The ILO study acknowledges that, "One of the greatest difficulties with systems of payment by results is in the setting of piece ... rates" (1951:152).

REFERENCES CITED

Bailón Corres, M.
  1980   "Artesanías y capital comercial en los valles centrales de Oaxaca," in Benitez Zenteno, R. (ed.), Sociedad y Política en Oaxaca 1980. Oaxaca: Instituto de Investigaciones Sociales, UABJO.

Beals, R.
  1975   The Peasant Marketing System of Oaxaca, Mexico. Berkeley and Los Angeles: University of California Press.

Blanton, R. et.al.
  1981   "The valley of Oaxaca," in R.E. Blanton et.al.,(eds.), Ancient Mesoamerica, A Comparison of Three Regions. Cambridge University Press.

Braverman, H.
  1974   Labor and Monopoly Capital. New York: Monthly Review Press.

Bucher, C.
  1901   Industrial Evolution. New York: Henry Holt.

Chance, J.
  1978   Race and Class in Colonial Oaxaca. Stanford University Press.

Cook, S.
  1981   "Crafts, capitalist development, and cultural property in Oaxaca, Mexico," Inter-American Economic Affairs 35, (3):53-68.

  1982   Zapotec Stoneworkers. Lanham, Md.: University Press of America.

1984   Peasant Capitalist Industry. Lanham, Md.:
        University Press of America.

Cook, S. and M. Diskin, (eds.)
    1976   Markets in Oaxaca. Austin: University of
            Texas Press.

Hamnett, B.
    1971   Politics and Trade in Southern Mexico.
            Cambridge University Press.

Higgins, M.
    1983   Somos Tocayos. Lanham, Md.: University Press
            of   America.

Hopkins, N.
    1978   "The articulation of the modes of production:
            tailoring   in Tunisia," American Ethnologist
            5,3:468-483.

Howard, M. and J. King
    1975   The Political Economy of Marx. London:
            Longman.

International Labor Office
    1951   Payment By Results. Geneva:International
            Labor Office.

Kowalewski, S. and L. Finsten
    1983   "The economic systems of ancient Oaxaca: a
            regional perspective," Current Anthropology
            24,4:413-442.

Lamphere, L.
    1979   "Fighting the piece-rate system: new
            dimensions of an   old struggle in the
            apparel industry," in A. Zimbalist   (ed.),
            Case Studies on the Labor Process. New York:
            Monthly   Review Press.

Littlefield, A.
    1978   "Exploitation and the expansion of
            capitalism: the case   of the hammock
            industry of Yucatan," American Ethnologist
            5:495-508.

Malinowski, B. and J. de la Fuente
    1982   The Economics of a Mexican Market System.
            London: Routledge and Kegan Paul.

257

Mandle, J.
  1980   "Marxist analyses and capitalist development
          in the   third world", Theory and Society
          9:865-876.

Marx, K.
  1967   Capital. New York: International Publishers.

Menger, A.
  1899   The Right to the Whole Produce of Labour.
          London: Macmillan.

Mintz, S.
  1964   "Peasant   marketplaces   and   economic
          development in Latin America." The Graduate
          Center for Latin American Studies, Occasional
          Paper No. 4.

Murphy, A. and H. Selby
  1981   "A comparison of household income and
          budgetary patterns   in four Mexican cities,"
          Urban Anthropology 10,3:247-267.

Semo, E.
  1973   Historia del Capitalismo en México: Los
          Origenes, 1521- 1763. México, D.F.:
          Ediciones Era.

Shapiro-Perl, N.
  1979   "The piece rate: class struggle on the shop
          floor.   Evidence from the costume jewelry
          industry in Providence,   Rhode Island," in
          A. Zimbalist (ed.), Case Studies on the
          Labor Process. New York: Monthly Review
          Press.

Warren, B.
  1980   Imperialism: Pioneer of Capitalism. London:
          New Left   Books.

FROM YAMS TO BEER IN A NIGERIAN CITY: EXPANSION AND CHANGE IN INFORMAL SECTOR TRADE ACTIVITY

Lillian Trager, University of Wisconsin-Parkside

On my return to Nigeria in the summer of 1983, for the first time in more than five years, I found many changes in the city of Ilesha,[1] where I had done research in 1973-74. Some of these were expected: I knew that the oil economy of the 1970's had generated an influx of money into many communities and was not surprised to find evidence of that in Ilesha, along with evidence of the more recent period of economic austerity (Trager, in press). I knew as well that a brewery had been constructed and opened in the city in late 1978 but did not know what impact it had had on the local economy. However, I was unprepared for other changes. When I went to the market place to look for people who had been part of my 1973-74 research and who I had visited in 1977, I was unable to find certain key individuals. Particularly noticeable was the absence of two women who had been yam traders; one was the head of the yam traders' association, the other, an important figure in long-distance yam trade. Upon inquiry, I was told that I would find one in a shop outside the market place, where she was selling beer and soft drinks, and that the other was "at home." Numerous visits to the latter's house turned up many cases of beer stacked in front of the house, but I found the woman herself only when I visited on a Sunday afternoon, as she was busy the rest of the week buying and distributing beer.

I was surprised by these changes, perhaps because I had assumed that as yam traders in the urban market place, these women were settled in a more or less "traditional" occupation at which they were very successful, and that they would be unlikely to change until old age or some other problem led them to give up some of their activities. While I had viewed urban market place trade as part of a broad set of informal sector commercial activities in the city, I had not considered the implications of that view, in terms of the dynamics and complexity of the informal sector.

This paper considers the changes in these women's activities, as well as more general patterns of change in informal sector commercial activities in the city, in terms of two key issues: 1) diversity and differentiation within the informal sector and 2) linkages between the informal and other economic sectors, particularly the ways in which changes in formal sector activities help to shape changes in the informal sector. I argue that the informal sector is fully part of the modern urban economy, constantly being shaped and reshaped by changing conditions. In Ilesha, the opening of a new formal sector industry, the brewery, has played an important role in affecting patterns of informal sector activity. At the same time, the responses of individuals to new opportunities has further shaped the overall pattern of informal sector activity. These individuals are operating in a cultural and economic context in which distributive activities have long been carried out by small-scale independent business people, and where it is believed that entrepreneurial activities represent an important avenue for success.

The first part of the paper briefly reviews conceptual and theoretical issues concerning the informal sector. The second part presents data which allow us to examine the diversity and dynamics of informal sector commercial activities in the city of Ilesha over the past ten years. Since essentially all retail trade in the city falls within the broad category of the informal sector, it is necessary to consider the diversity of the sector, as well as the ways in which it is changing. Finally, this data is analyzed in terms of the theoretical issues raised.

I. THE URBAN INFORMAL SECTOR-CONCEPTUAL AND THEORETICAL ISSUES

The term "urban informal sector" was first used by Keith Hart in the early 1970's to identify a set of income-earning opportunities in which urban migrants in Ghana were engaged (Hart 1973), and was subsequently employed by the I.L.O. and other development organizations as they recognized that much of the data on urban employment simply did not include the vast array of income-earning activities in which people in third world cities were engaged. Each use of the concept tended to generate its own definition. Hart's emphasized the distinction between wage-earning (formal sector) activities and self-employment (informal sector) (1973:68), while the I.L.O. distinguished formal from informal by presenting a list of seven contrasting characteristics such as easy vs. difficult entry, small vs. large scale, family vs. corporate ownership, and unregulated vs. protected (I.L.O. 1972:6; see also I.L.O. 1974 and Moser 1978 for other

I.L.O. studies). The World Bank, on the other hand, focused on a dichotomy within the urban labor market, describing the informal sector as "unprotected" in contrast to the formal "protected" sector (Mazumdar 1976).

Each of these definitions generated criticism. For example, a number of studies have shown that there is not necessarily "ease of entry" to informal sector activities (e.g., Peattie 1980; Sinclair 1977). Others have proposed different terminology: the "proto-proletariat" (McGee 1976); "casual labor" (Bromley and Gerry 1979); lower and upper "circuits" of the economy (Santos 1979), and most simply and descriptively, "small-scale" vs. "large-scale sectors" (Roberts 1978:114), with some adding an "intermediate sector" (Steel 1976; O'Connor 1983:154-155).

Other more fundamental criticism has argued that the 'informal sector is not a theoretical category (Smith 1981) and that a better approach to understanding urban economic activities is to use an alternative framework--that of petty commodity production (Moser 1978:1055; Smith 1981). This last approach has in turn been criticized as not encompassing the totality of informal sector activities (Portes and Walton 1981:86).

The terminological debate seems to me a fairly arid one, particularly since, from a pragmatic standpoint, the concept of informal sector seems to have entered the literature to stay. It continues to be widely used, both in empirical studies (e.g., Onokerahoye 1977) and in policy-oriented work, such as the recent I.L.O. studies of the informal sector in eight countries (Sethuraman 1981; see also West Africa 1983:2469-70).

On the other hand, the critical literature has raised three issues of considerable importance for an understanding of informal sector activities in third world cities: 1) the dualism of a division of the urban economy into two sectors, frequently with the added implication that informal sector activities are "traditional" or "transitional" in contrast to the "modern" formal sector; 2) the tendency to group all activities of the informal sector into one category and to neglect the considerable heterogeneity and complexity within the sector; and 3) the focus of attention on relatively static characteristics of the informal sector rather than on the linkages between formal and informal sectors and the associated dynamism

261

of the latter. These are not however necessary components of an approach using the informal sector concept. As Portes and Walton have pointed out, the informal sector should be seen as "an integral component of peripheral capitalist economies" (1981:104-105). Definitions which describe the informal sector as traditional or transitional are

> based on a static conceptualization of the informal economy as formed by those enterprises now in existence. Such activities might well disappear, but will give rise to new ones. The empirical evidence points to the capacity of the informal sector to constitute and reconstitute itself in response to changing conditions in the. . . economy (Portes and Walton 1981:83).

By using a definition of the informal sector as encompassing "all income-producing activities outside formal sector wages and social security payments" (Portes and Walton 1981:87), it is possible to approach the informal sector as a heterogeneous and dynamic set of activities that are linked to and affected by changes in the formal sector of the economy. Such a definition includes both the self-employed non-wage or family labor recognized in Hart's original definition as well as those who are employed at below minimum wages and with no social security protection. It is thus possible to recognize that informal sector firms themselves sometimes hire wage labor, but that such laborers have none of the protection associated with wage labor in formal sector firms, as well as to recognize that some of what appears to be "self-employment" turns out to be disguised wage labor in the form of commission selling or dependent selling (Bromley 1978:1165-66).

In examining informal sector commercial activities in the Nigerian city of Ilesha, I am concerned both with the heterogeneity of the sector and with the changes taking place within it. Not all those employed in the informal sector are among the "poorest of the poor"; rather, there is considerable income range. In addition, there is evidence that in Nigeria, formal sector workers may have as a goal the accumulation of sufficient savings to move into informal activities as small entrepreneurs (Peace 1979). Accounting for the dynamism of the informal sector requires examining both the strategies engaged in by the urban population as they seek out income-earning opportunities and the ways in which those opportunities are shaped by changes in the formal sector of the economy. For example, the construction of a new formal sector industry may lead to a situation where self-employed producers of that product are unable to compete, or where they become incorporated as piece workers for the large industry. On the other hand, other industries may lead to new opportunities, especially in distribution, for those in a position to take advantage of them. The situation to be considered here is of the latter type, where the construction of a brewery has helped to reshape the opportunities open to traders. By noting the heterogeneity within the informal sector, we are able to see how some well-placed individuals within it can take advantage of new opportunities.

In considering these issues in the Nigerian context, I will stress that urban market traders, selling both agricultural and manufactured commodities, form a major group within the informal sector. Furthermore, I will suggest that these traders and others engaged in informal sector commerce are more likely to be truly self-employed than seems to be the case in Latin American informal sector commerce (Portes and Walton 1981:101-103; Babb, this volume).

II. THE URBAN ECONOMY

The city of Ilesha is a Yoruba city in Southwestern Nigeria having an estimated population of over 200,000 [2]. Within the context of Southwestern Nigeria, it may be considered a medium-sized city, much smaller than the dominant cities of Lagos and Ibadan, but sharing many characteristics with the neighboring cities of Ile-Ife and Oshogbo, both located about twenty miles from Ilesha (Trager, in press). In the past, Ilesha was the capital of a kingdom which extended for a radius of 15-20 miles around the city (Peel 1983). Today it is primarily a commercial center for the surrounding region (Trager 1981a).

Yoruba cities have been described in the literature as "agro-towns," large, densely-populated settlements the majority of whose residents are engaged in agricultural activities (Ayeni 1981:248; Lloyd 1973). In the past, farming was the major occupation of males; however, women have long been active in market place trade and continue to be so today. Furthermore, men have now moved into a variety of occupations such as contracting, trade, and services, so that such occupations now predominate for both males and females. These occupations include a wide variety of trading
263

enterprises, both inside and outside the market place; services such as mechanics, photographers, seamstresses and tailors; and small-scale manufacturing and processing, such as goldsmiths, furniture makers, and bakeries. Nearly all of these are small enterprises, usually with few or no employees or apprentices (Ministry of Trade, Industries and Cooperatives 1979).

Formal sector employment has been very limited in Ilesha. There are several banks, two government hospitals, and an increasing number of educational institutions. [3] Commercial enterprises providing consumer goods are almost entirely in the informal sector; for example, no supermarkets or department stores have been established. One or two car dealerships and building supply companies are exceptions. Similarly, wholesale distribution is largely carried out by small enterprises, with the exception of those companies engaged in cocoa exporting and several warehouses that distribute some manufactured goods to retail traders. Furthermore, until very recently, there has been no formal sector manufacturing in the city. This has now changed, however, with the establishment of a brewery in 1978 and several other smaller industries around the same time.

The brewery is the most significant of these new establishments. It is one of a number that have been established in Nigeria in recent years, some of which are privately owned and others of which are owned by state governments. Beer has been viewed as an excellent focus for investment; a 1976 bank publication pointed out that there was inadequate beer production capacity to meet increasing demand and stated that "it can be safely asserted that demand prospects for beer are among the brightest in the country" (Standard Bank Nigeria Ltd. 1976:15). Planning for the brewery in Ilesha began in 1970, when several local businessmen met to consider jointly investing in such a project. The lead was taken by one man who had started out as a cocoa buyer and transporter in the 1930s. He investigated various possibilities for industries and decided that a brewery would be best. After a number of years, and some difficulties, he and the others in the group were able to get loans from several banks and from the state government and to arrange technical assistance from a German firm. The brewery opened in 1978. It has since doubled its capacity, and construction is now underway to double its size again. The brewery employs about 250 people on a regular basis and several hundred more as "casual workers" who work primarily in bottling and packaging. The top technical employees are German, while the manager and many of the employees are from Ilesha. Over the next several years, Nigerians are to be trained to replace the expatriate employees. The brewery employees are involved only in production. Distribution is not handled by the company but by distributors operating independently. As a result, although the brewery has had limited impact in terms of the actual numbers of people employed as regular workers, it has had substantial impact, as I shall argue below, on local commercial activity.

A. Informal Sector Commercial Activities

While a number of informal sector enterprises in Ilesha engage in manufacturing and services, commerce is the dominant activity. Of the small businesses surveyed by the Oyo State government in 1977, 59% were engaged in commerce (Ministry of Trade, Industries, and Cooperatives 1979). That is, in fact, only a small portion of those working in trade and commerce, as the survey omitted market place traders and others such as street vendors. Informal sector commercial enterprises share a number of general features. They are small in scale [4] and individually owned. Shops and stalls both inside and outside the market place are owned and run by single individuals. There is rarely a partnership, even between husband and wife or two women such as co-wives. Co-wives sometimes share a single stall in the market place but operate their businesses independently. Similarly, while a husband and wife may both be in retail trade, they sell different items and have separate shops at different locations. These businesses have few or no employees. In many cases, assistance is provided by children of the family, children of other relatives, and apprentices. A woman with a market place stall may take on a young girl who is the child of a poorer relative and train her, while also providing her room and board. Sometimes one or two employees are hired to help with the selling; this is especially true in the case of shops located outside the market place.

A final key organizational feature relates not to the structure of the enterprise but to its relationships with other enterprises and with customers. Personal knowledge and trust are key features of buying and selling (onibara) relationships

265

among market traders (Trager 1981b; compare Plattner, this volume and Acheson, this volume). Those in other types of informal sector businesses likewise need to establish relationships with suppliers and customers. As Berry shows in her study of mechanics in the neighboring city of Ife,

> In the highly competitive environment of the urban "informal" sector, . . . [one] needs to build up a clientele--a group of loyal customers who can be counted on it do business with him, time and again, rather than with his competitors (Berry 1983:6).

Despite these broad characteristics of informal sector commercial activities, considerable diversity exists within the informal sector of Ilesha. The heterogeneity of the informal commercial sector can be considered in terms of 1) locale of the enterprise; 2) type of commodity sold; 3) amount of starting capital; and 4) income.

There are three basic locales for commercial activity in Ilesha--the market places, retail shops outside the market, and along the streets by those who do not have fixed premises. Street vendors and those who sell in front of their houses have the lowest incomes and the lowest capital requirements. Selling goods ranging from cooked food to "provisions" (such as matches, sugar, tinned milk), they sell in the town center, in front of their houses, and as mobile vendors going from house to house. Few regulations control the activities of street vendors in Ilesha.[5]

Those operating fixed-premise retail shops outside the market place tend to be at the high end of the scale in terms of capital requirements and probable incomes. These shops line the main streets of the city. Most are small, consisting of a single room facing on the street with goods piled up inside and displayed in front; often, these shops are not much larger than market place stalls. Commodities sold in these shops are basically consumer goods such as cloth, patent medicines, hardware and building materials, and beer and soft drinks. Like market place stalls, these shops tend to specialize in one commodity type. Both men and women own and operate retail shops.

In contrast, the market places remain largely the domain of women [6], although a small number of men also sell there. In the market places, one finds the

266

largest variation in types of commodities sold and in capital requirements and income, ranging from very small-scale traders who are much like the street vendors to those operating as middlemen in the distribution of agricultural commodities. Capital requirements for entering trade range from lows of a few Naira in some agricultural commodities to highs of one hundred fifty Naira or more in manufactured commodities such as cloth. [7]

The daily market place is the site for the distribution and selling of all agricultural commodities entering Ilesha. Both wholesale and retail trade takes place, often handled by the same individuals. In addition, a large variety of manufactured goods is sold there, mainly on a retail basis. In addition to the daily market, a biweekly market attracts sellers from other towns and cities in the region, who are primarily engaged in the retail trade of manufactured goods. Market place trade is specialized by commodity with each trader selling only one commodity or commodity type.

B. Expansion and Change in the Informal Sector

The above description of the heterogeneous set of activities that make up the informal commercial sector in Ilesha can be used as the basis for an exploration of changes taking place in the sector. I will suggest that two types of change are taking place. On the one hand, an expansion in informal sector activities is occurring; on the other hand, changes in type of activity, especially in commodities being sold, are also occurring. The latter is mainly taking place outside the market place but involves people formerly based in the market. In this discussion I am concerned with changes that have taken place during the ten-year period, 1973-83. [8]

Expansion is evident in several of the arenas described above. This expansion involves both an increase in the numbers of people engaged in certain types of activities as well as in the space and time allocated to those activities. In 1973 the Ilesha market place had 1573 registered market stalls (Mrs. Daramola, personal communication, 26 July 1973); in 1983 this number had increases to 2,299, of which 2,137 were lock-up stalls and the rest open stalls (S.A. Sanni, personal communication, 4 June 1983). This 46% increase in the number of stalls was not the result of simply squeezing more stalls into the same amount of space. Rather, the space allocated to the market place

267

had been increased, by absorbing more of the palace land on which the market is located. [9] Furthermore, stalls have been constructed along the streets leading to the market place. In 1973 the road in front of the town hall and post office were free of stalls; today, these buildings are not visible from the street because of the stalls constructed there. In 1974 an open area across the street from the palace was designated an evening market to be used when the main market place was closed at night. Now, there are market stalls surrounding that open space, and it has become an active daytime market, with a majority of the stalls occupied by men selling manufactured goods such as cloth.

The biweekly big market day has expanded as well, in time and space as well as in numbers. Ten years ago those who came for the big market usually arrived the afternoon before; some would go around to Ilesha market traders to sell some of their goods in quantity rather than selling to retail customers the next day. In 1983, many traders not only arrived the day before but also set up their wares in the market for display to retail customers on that day. Whereas the big market was previously confined to the market place, with all open spaces being used for display of goods, it has now moved outside the market place to the adjoining streets, which become nearly impassable as traders set up temporary selling sites along and in the middle of the street.

Expansion in the numbers of street vendors has also occurred. In the town center, near the taxi and minibus stands, an increasing number of women are selling cooked food, while others are going around with various small manufactured items such as plastic sandals on a tray on their heads. It is however, very difficult to estimate the numbers of street vendors, especially those who sell from house to house. [10]

This expansion in market place trade and in street vending may well be the result both of overall population increase in the city and of the generally poor economic situation, in which more and more people are entering trade in an attempt to eke out a living, especially at the bottom end of the scale. In this respect, change in the Ilesha informal sector appears to be much like the situation described in cities elsewhere (e.g., Babb, this volume). However, the expansion described here does not constitute the totality of change in the Ilesha informal sector over

268

the past ten years. Other significant changes have occurred, especially in the retail shopping areas along the main streets, where we find changes in the commodities being sold rather than simply expansion.

The number of retail shops on the main shopping streets of the city remains roughly the same as previously, but the commodities sold in those shops have shifted. Most simply put, there has been an enormous increase in the number of places selling beer and soft drinks. Two surveys taken in 1977 provide figures for the number of beer and soft drink shops in that year, including wholesale and retail shops as well as "beer parlors"--small bars that usually serve food as well as drinks. The Oyo State Government counted 67 beer and soft drink shops (Ministry of Trade, Industries and Cooperatives 1979), while my own survey in a more restricted area of the city resulted in a count of 86. In contrast, in June 1983 licenses for selling beer had been given as follows: 450 with "off" licenses (to allow consumption off the premises) and 450 with "on" licenses (for consumption on premises) (S.A. Sanni, personal communication 4 June 1983). Of course, many places have both licenses, while there are certainly others with no license at all.

A more specific determination of the increase in number of places selling beer and soft drinks can be made by comparing the numbers on the two major streets of the city, where the vast majority of retail shops of all kinds are located. Table 1 shows the results of three counts on these two streets; depending on which of the 1977 counts is used, there were in 1983 somewhere between three and five times as many places selling beer and soft drinks as there were in 1977. At the same time, there has been a decrease in the number of shops selling other commodities, such as books and cloth.

What has generated this shift in commodities within informal sector commerce in Ilesha? How is this change linked to other changes in the local urban economy, especially the establishment of the brewery? Who are the people involved; are they new entrants to informal sector commerce, or people previously selling other commodities? How have they been able to enter trade in these new commodities, and why have they done so? To attempt to answer these questions, it is useful to shift our focus from an examination of overall patterns to a consideration of some of those individuals whose activities are helping to generate those patterns. To

269

Table 1.   Beer and Soft Drinks Shops on Two Main
              Streets, Ilesha, 1977 and 1983

	August 1977*	December 1977	June 1983
Area 1	13	27	58
Area 2	15	31	93
Total	28	54	151

* based on Oyo State survey (Ministry of Trade,
Industries and Cooperatives 1979); the other two
surveys are counts that I made.

do this, I will briefly consider the cases of three women engaged in informal sector commerce who have begun to sell beer since the opening of the brewery.

C. Three Cases

The three cases to be discussed all concern women who have moved into beer distribution in the past five years. Two of them have been engaged in commerce in Ilesha for many years; the third has only recently returned to Ilesha. In order to understand their current place in the Ilesha informal sector, it is necessary to consider their past activities; their position in the overall structure described earlier has enabled them to move fairly rapidly into a new commodity which is widely perceived as lucrative.

Case 1. The first case is that of one of the yam traders mentioned in the introduction. In 1973-74 she was a leading yam trader in the Ilesha market place, engaged primarily in long-distance yam trade. Unlike smaller-scale yam traders in Ilesha, she bought in large quantity directly from farmers and had yams available for sale throughout the year. Early in the yam season, she traveled to rural areas 20-30 miles from Ilesha to purchase her supply. Later, she and another trader went to an area about a hundred miles away where they both had regular suppliers among the farmers; they would buy enough yams between the two of them to fill a lorry. Still later in the year, they went even further from Ilesha to obtain yams, again buying directly from the farmers. Each sold their yams on a wholesale basis to other traders in Ilesha, as well as selling to retail customers. At times, they also took some of their produce to Lagos for sale.

At the time, this woman had one young baby and several older children. The baby and a girl to care for her accompanied her on yam-buying trips. The other children stayed in Ilesha, with her husband and his other wife and children. The husband owned one of the numerous small book shops along one of the main shopping streets. He had opened that shop in 1956, after having been a tailor for some years. For some time he continued on as a tailor while also selling books, and finally in 1968 he settled on books exclusively. Like the other bookstore owners in the area, he relied mainly on sales of school books and supplies to children, as books were not provided by the schools. In addition, he had a farm in the small town outside Ilesha where he was born, but had others

271

working on the farm for him.

Today, the husband still has his bookstore, even
though schools are now supposed to supply books so
there is no longer the assured demand for them.   His
wife, however, is no longer buying and selling yams in
the market place.   Instead, she has a shop about a half
mile down the road from her husband's store, where she
is selling beer and soft drinks by the case.   She
opened her shop in late 1982 and has considerable
stock, including Trophy, the brand brewed in Ilesha,
and several other brands.   She retains her stall in the
market but spends little time there; she gets some
income from the sales of the younger women who have
replaced her and who are using her stall for yam trade.
In part, this is a normal transition to a more
sedentary occupation as one gets older.   But in the
past, she would have continued to be at her stall in
the market, supervising the sale of yams even if she
didn't buy them herself. Or she might have moved to
another commodity in the market place such as cloth, if
she had the capital.   Instead she has moved to a new
commodity outside the market place and has begun to
establish herself there.

Case 2.   The second case is that of the woman who
was the head of the yam traders' association in 1973-
74.   In Yoruba market places, all commodity sellers
have associations headed by a woman called the iyalode
or olori.   Among the yam traders in Ilesha, this is a
particularly important position as yams constitute the
staple and preferred food in the area.   Unlike the
first woman, this woman did not travel to farms to buy
yams, but instead she had several women working with
her who did that.   She also bought yams from traders
who transported large quantities of yams from regions
north of Ilesha for sale in Ilesha.   Like the first
trader, much of her trade was wholesale, selling to
smaller-scale traders in the market.   But she also sold
on a retail basis, and she had regular customers among
women who sold cooked food and among suppliers to local
schools and hospitals.   There is no doubt that she was
not only one of the most important but also one of the
most successful yam traders in Ilesha, although like
any good Yoruba business woman, she was extremely
reluctant to provide any details regarding her
finances.   Some measure of her success may be judged by
the fact that she owned her own two-story house,
although she lived at her husband's house.   She was
also unusual among traders in having a bank account.
Her husband was, and still is, the owner of a small

272

transport business, first owning several lorries, and then buses, for transporting people between Ilesha and Ibadan.

Today, this woman is distributing beer. She buys cases of beer from the larger distributors [11] who buy directly from the breweries and stores the cases at home. Then, rather than selling in a shop like the first woman, she has a van and driver which she uses to take beer to smaller towns in the region, mainly in neighboring Ondo state. There, she sells to people with small shops and beer parlors. She has been selling beer for two or three years and is no longer selling yams at all. According to her, there was too much "wahala" (problems) in yam trade. Whatever the real reason, she has clearly made a major shift, not only in terms of moving from one commodity to another, but also in terms of the organization of trade and the people she deals with.

Case 3   The third case is that of a woman who did not live in Ilesha ten years ago, although Ilesha is her hometown. She provides an example of another way in which women have entered beer trade. She is the owner of a beer parlor, essentially a shed with three enclosed sides and a curtain in the front and some tables and benches inside. Here she serves drinks-- beer and soda--and cooked food that she herself prepares. Before her return to Ilesha several years ago, she lived in a number of Nigerian cities, as she was following her husband who was in the military. He is retired now and teaches at a college in Ibadan, but she decided to return to Ilesha. She first opened her beer parlor in the front room of her small house, which faces one of the main streets. About six months later, she built the shed in front of the house. There she prepares cooked food and visits with the customers who stop by. She also has a young girl working for her who hawks some of the food around the town. The young girl is, in other words, one of the many street vendors described earlier; she is not operating independently but is hired by another person in the informal sector. With the cooked food vending, the beer parlor owner has a source of income outside the shop itself.

These cases indicate some of the changes taking place in the activities of individuals employed in informal sector occupations and show that it is possible for those with access to adequate resources to move into new areas of trade. For the two former yam traders, beer distribution represents a very different

273

sort of commodity involving different distribution and supply networks. Yet in moving from one commodity to another they have been able to maintain their positions as trade intermediaries. Their earlier role in the informal economy as major yam traders has provided the economic base from which they were able to move into beer distribution. The resources available to them included not only capital, but also personal ties with others, such as those in the transport business, who are important in distribution of both yams and beer. More generally, the business knowledge acquired in long-distance yam trade no doubt is valuable in commerce in other commodities as well. The third woman has moved into beer selling in a rather different way, one which perhaps demands less knowledge of the local commercial scene. Although she began her business simply by selling beer from her house, she was able in a short time to build a shed and to hire a young girl to help sell cooked food. This again suggests the possibility of some success in acquiring capital and changing the dimensions of one's own business, even if only on a small scale.

D. The Brewery and Informal Sector Commerce: Linkages

Although the brewery employs relatively few people, it has had considerable impact on the local economy by helping to shape the kinds of opportunities available. While there were beer and soft drink sellers in Ilesha previously, their numbers have increased dramatically in recent years. In the past, beer and soft drink sellers in Ilesha had to obtain goods from distributors coming from Ibadan and Lagos. Now, Ilesha traders have local access to beer and the local brand tends to predominate in their shops. Those I have discussed buy from larger distributors who own trucks and get their supply directly from the breweries. With local supply, transport costs are reduced. The traders are likely to have personal ties with those distributing the local brand, ensuring access to regular supply. Furthermore, some have direct access to brewery employees and/or management, and may obtain some of their supply through those ties. [12]

Individuals such as the three women described above remain in the informal sector as intermediaries in the distribution of consumer goods. They, like other small retail shopowners, are independent entrepreneurs. They have perceived opportunities in beer distribution and have had the resources to take advantage of those opportunities. Their earlier activities have provided

274

the personal and financial resources necessary, and the opening of the brewery has helped create opportunities in which they were able to use those resources. Those operating small shops and beer parlors are not dependent sellers, nor are they commission sellers. They are, rather, essentially independent operators, who themselves may have others working for them. Like the motor mechanics in Ife described by Berry, they may be termed "petty capitalists" (1983:15).

Not all of those operating in the informal sector are independent entrepreneurs. Others are employees or apprentices. In the cases discussed above, both the beer parlor owner and the woman who distributes beer to other towns have an employee. Such employees are dependent on informal sector entrepreneurs for their livelihoods, generally receiving low wages or, in the case of apprentices, no wages in return for training. Those who are employees and apprentices tend to have establishment of their own small businesses as their goal (cf. Berry 1983); whether that is a real possibility is an open question, given the expansion in numbers entering informal sector trade and the relative lack of resources available to those employed for low wages in the informal sector. [13]

In Ilesha at present, the self-employed continue to predominate. Most of them, such as the majority of market traders, own and operate their own businesses with no employees or apprentices. A relatively small number, mainly those at the higher income end with shops outside the market, have one or at most two employees. For those who are self-employed, the establishment of new industries such as the brewery helps to create new opportunities in commerce. The evidence suggests that, as long as the industries do not themselves carry out distribution, many will perceive those opportunities and attempt to move into them. At least some, such as the women discussed in the cases above, will do so successfully.

III. CONCLUSIONS

In this paper, I have used a definition of the informal sector that is broadly inclusive of a range of commercial and manufacturing activities that are generally small-scale and outside formal sector wages and social security payments. Within this broadly-defined sector, there is considerable heterogeneity and complexity. In focusing on the commercial economy of Ilesha, I have noted that nearly all of it is within

275

the informal sector. Some basic organizational features tend to be widely shared by informal sector commercial enterprises in the city. They are small-scale, largely individually-owned businesses with few or no employees. Nevertheless, there is considerable diversity among these enterprises. An important differentiating feature is the amount of capital required for entering trade in a particular commodity, ranging from very small amounts for street vendors and some types of market place traders to substantial amounts for those selling manufactured goods both inside and outside the market place. There is also an important distinction to be made between those who are self-employed and those who are employees in informal sector commercial enterprises.

Within the informal sector, I have emphasized the important place of market place trade and the role of market place traders. Such traders are often excluded from studies of the informal sector, [14] perhaps because market trade is viewed as a "traditional" economic activity carried out by "petty traders" whose role in internal distribution is largely ignored (Trager 1976-77). Market place trade, like other informal sector activities, is a dynamic arena, with traders moving from one commodity to another as opportunities and resources change. That dynamism now extends outside the market place, as women who have long been traders in the market are entering retail trade in other commodities sold in other locales. The activities of three individuals have been described in some detail. Such a focus allows us to examine changes in the activities of individuals within a larger context of change and shows that what may initially seem unlikely--a movement from yam trade to beer distribution--is not so. [15]

Informal sector activities need to be seen as fully part of the modern urban economy. They are not traditional or transitional, and they are not disappearing. Rather, as we have seen, they are expanding, and there is, in fact, some encouragement for that expansion from urban authorities, as is seen in the addition of land to the market place. Trade and commerce have long been important in Ilesha and other Yoruba cities. But their current dynamics are shaped by contemporary economic processes, not by the fact that these are "traditional" activities. Changes in the larger economy and especially in the formal sector are closely linked to changes in informal activities. I have suggested that two types of change are

276

occurring--expansion in the numbers engaged in informal sector commerce, and movement into specific new commodities. In this connection, I have argued that the opening of the brewery in Ilesha has had considerable impact, not at the level of generating formal-sector employment, but in its effect on informal sector distributive activities. The effects of a new formal sector industry may be quite diverse, depending on the type of informal sector activity affected (Stark 1982:414-415). For example, if there were a local home-beer brewing industry in Ilesha, the establishment of breweries would no doubt have eliminated some of that activity. In this case, however, since the formal sector industry does not carry out its own distribution, the brewery has helped to create additional occupational possibilities in informal sector commerce.

Some discussions of formal-informal sector linkages imply that the former largely determines the latter. I would argue, rather, that it is only one of several important forces helping to shape informal sector activities, in conjunction with other forces. For example, in Nigeria, analysis of change in the rural economy, where agriculture has stagnated in recent years (Watts and Lubeck 1983:118), may well contribute to an understanding of the move from trade in agricultural commodities to trade in manufactured goods.

At the same time, it is important to examine not only the macroeconomic level of the effect of one sector on another but also to consider the role of individual participants in each sector and their decisions and strategies. The recognition of the heterogeneous nature of the informal sector aids in doing this. By considering the position of an individual and his/her access to resources--both financial and personal--we are better able to understand how individuals respond to opportunities and constraints that arise. The constant shaping and reshaping of the informal sector results not only from changes in the larger economy but also from the ways in which particular individuals respond, and in the process, themselves generate changes. To emphasize a simple example: The opening of more beer parlors may be due to availablility of--not to mention demand for-- beer. But the beer parlor owner who then hires a girl to be a street vendor of cooked foods is helping to affect still further the shape of informal sector commerce.

In Ilesha, and more generally in Southwestern Nigeria, distributive activities have remained largely the domain of the small-scale informal sector entrepreneurs. Large companies have rarely moved into distributive activities; it is significant that the brewery has not undertaken the distribution of its beer. Perhaps this is due to the recognition by large-scale firms such as the brewery of the strength and vitality of the small-scale trade sector and of that sector's ability to carry out effective distribution throughout the region. Perhaps it is due as well to the historical and cultural context in which small-scale commerce has long been seen as a route to success, [16] and where formal-sector employees are likely to have as a goal the establishment of their own small business. As O'Connor has suggested,

> There are fundamental differences between precolonial cities...,where petty trade and crafts form the historic basis of the urban economy and where the "formal sector" may even remain peripheral, and those cities where the latter developed first and an informal sector has emerged dependent upon it. Contrasting historical processes in two cities may have produced a similar numerical balance between the sectors, yet the relationships between them will differ greatly (1983:141).

In this context, those engaged in informal sector trade have considerable political influence and importance; market women have long been recognized as a force to be reckoned with in Nigerian politics. As local urban economies have changed and as formal sector industries have been encouraged, these traders have not been marginalized. Rather, they continue to be central to distribution in nearly all commodities. While it is possible that eventually informal sector commerce in Ilesha will become more dependent on the formal sector, at present such direct dependence--as opposed to the links discussed earlier--has not emerged. In this regard, current processes of change in the informal sector of Yoruba cities are substantially different from those processes elsewhere, such as in Latin America (e.g., Babb, this volume) and even elsewhere in Africa (e.g., Gerry 1979). In other words, the overall character of informal sector activities in a city like Ilesha is shaped not only by the linkages to formal sector change and by the role of individual participants but also by a historical and cultural context in which small-scale commerce has long been dominant in the urban economy.

ACKNOWLEDGMENTS

The data considered here derive from my study of the
Ilesha market and its surrounding rural hinterland in
1973-74; data on commercial activity outside the market
collected in 1977 and 1983; and interviews in 1983 with
traders and others.   I would like to acknowledge
support for the 1973-74 research from a Fulbright-Hays
Doctoral Dissertation Research Grant and the University
of Washington Department of Anthropology.   Travel to
Nigeria in 1983 was supported by the University of
Wisconsin-Parkside Committee on Research and Creative
Activity.   I would like to express my thanks to Mr.
E.A. Ifaturoti, Dr. Lawrence Omole and Mr. A.A. Akinola
for information regarding the Ilesha brewery and to
Florence Babb, Bruce Fetter, Gerald Greenfield, Stuart
Plattner, Richard Rosenberg, and Constance Sutton for
comments on an earlier draft of this paper.

NOTES

1.   In contemporary Yoruba orthography, the preferred
      spelling is Ilesa; however, for ease of
      publication, I am using the alternative spelling
      of Ilesha.

2.   The last published Nigerian census is that of
      1963, at which time the population of Ilesha was
      160,000.   Estimates of current population and of
      population growth rates are quite variable; some
      have suggested growth rates of around 8 percent a
      year.   Occupational data are also unavailable; the
      1963 census gave figures for Ilesha Division,
      including both rural and urban areas, as follows:
      54% of males--farmers; 40% of females--
      salesworkers; 41% of females--"inadequately
      described occupations" (Nigeria 1963; see also
      Trager, in press).

3.   The number of secondary schools has increased from
      12 in 1974 to 47 today, as a result of Oyo State
      Government policies on free secondary education.
      There is also a new state teachers college.

4.   Although, as we shall see, there is considerable
      diversity within the informal sector, there is no
      clear dividing line that would distinguish "small-
      scale" from those that are "intermediate" in scale
      (O'Connor 1983:142).

279

5.   Since this was written, Nigerian government policy toward street vendors and other informal sector enterprises has changed, with an order in late August 1984 to remove "nonpermanent structures" (e.g., stalls) from city streets and other efforts at urban clearance.

6.   The market place is historically the domain of women in Yoruba society. Beliefs and institutions recognize women's importance in the market; for example, the traditional head of the women in Ilesha (a chieftaincy position) is considered the head of the market.

7.   These figures refer to data collected from market traders in the early 1970s, who had begun their businesses still earlier. Capital requirements today would be higher, especially in manufactured goods. N1 = U.S.$1.50 approximately.

8.   During that period, the national economy of Nigeria has undergone considerable change, with a boom period in the mid 1970s due to increased oil revenue and a subsequent period of austerity as those revenues declined. (See Zartman 1983 for a discussion of these changes). This paper recognizes the importance of change in the national economy but focusses on local-level change.

9.   The Ilesha market was established on its present site in 1959 by taking some of the land surrounding the palace of the Owa (king) of the city.

10.   An ongoing research project on street foods in Ife being conducted by O.O. Kujore and others at the University of Ife should contribute to our knowledge in this area. Cooked foods are particularly important as many Yoruba households buy all or portions of at least one meal per day.

11.   Larger distributors own trucks and buy cases of beer directly from the brewery. Further investigation of their links both to the brewery and to the retail sellers is needed.

12.   For example, a daughter of the woman in case 2 works as a clerk at the brewery.

13.   Portes (1983) suggests that in Latin America two

different classes exist within the informal sector
--the "informal petty bourgeoisie" and "informal
proletariat," i.e., those owning informal sector
businesses and those employed in them.

14. Despite a considerable literature on urban markets
and traders, many studies of the informal sector
ignore those selling in the market place (e.g.,
Sethuraman 1981).

15. An advantage of considering the diverse activities
described as being within the informal sector is
that such a perspective leads to considering
jointly people and activities which might
otherwise be seen as separate. Another approach
would be to focus on the distribution channels of
specific commodities such as beer (cf. Dannhaeuser
1983, this volume). This would aid in
understanding linkages within the levels of trade
of a single commodity, but might also cause us to
view beer and yams as two very different
commodities with no links between them.

16. As we have noted, the key backer of the brewery
began his own business career as a small-scale
trader and transporter. Stories of such successes
are well-known and form cultural models, although
it is also recognized that few achieve the great
wealth of such individuals.

REFERENCES

Acheson, J.
   1984   The Social Organization of the Maine Lobster
           Market. 1984 Proceedings of the Society for
           Economic Anthropology, Markets and
           Marketing. (This volume)

Ayeni, Bola
   1981   Spatial Aspects of Urbanization and Effects
           on the Distribution of Income in Nigeria. In,
           The Political Economy of Income Distribution
           in Nigeria, H. Bienen & V.P. Diejomaoh, eds.
           pp.237-268. New York: Holmes & Meier.

Babb, Florence E.
   1984   Marketers in the Economy: Work, Dependency,
           and the Informal Sector in Peru. 1984
           Proceedings of the Society for Economic
           Anthropology, Markets and Marketing.

Berry, Sara S.
  1983   From Peasant to Artisan: Motor Mechanics in a
          Nigerian Town. Boston University, African
          Studies Center, Working Paper No. 76.

Bromley, Ray
  1978   Organization, Regulation and Exploitation in
          the So-called 'Urban Informal Sector': The
          Street Traders of Cali, Columbia. World
          Development 6:1161-1171.

Bromley, Ray and Chris Gerry, eds.
  1979   Casual Work and Poverty in Third World
          Cities. Chichester: John Wiley.

Dannhaeuser, Norbert
  1983   Contemporary Trade Strategies in the
          Philippines: A Study in Marketing
          Anthropology. New Brunswick: Rutgers
          University Press.

  1984   "Urban Market Channels Under Conditions of
          Development: The Case of India and the
          Philippines", Society for Economic
          Anthropology 1984 Proceedings, Markets and
          Marketing. (This volume)

Gerry, Chris
  1979   Small-scale Manufacturing and Repairs in
          Dakar: A Survey of Market Relations within
          the Urban Economy. In Casual Work and
          Poverty in Third World Cities, Ray Bromley
          and Chris Gerry, eds. pp. 229-250.
          Chicester: John Wiley.

Hart, Keith
  1973   Informal Income Opportunities and Urban
          Employment in Ghana.Journal of Modern African
          Studies 11:61-89.

I.L.O.
  1972   Employment, Incomes and Equality: A Strategy
          for Increasing Productive Employment in
          Kenya. Geneva: International Labour Office.

  1974   Sharing in Development: A Programme of
          Employment, Equity and Growth in the
          Philippines. Geneva: International Labour
          Office.

Lloyd, Peter
1973   The Yoruba: An Urban People In Urban
        Anthropology, A. Southall, ed. pp. 107-123.
        New York: Oxford University Press.

McGee, T.G.
1976   The Persistence of the Protoproletariat.
        Progress in Geography 9:3-38.

Mazumdar, Dipak
1976   The Urban Informal Sector. World Development
        4:655-679.

Ministry of Trade, Industries, and Cooperatives, ed.
1979   Directory of Business Enterprises in Oyo
        State, Nigeria. Ibadan: Caxton Press.

Moser, Caroline O.
1978   Informal Sector of Petty Commodity
        Production: Dualism or Dependence in Urban
        Development? World Development 6:1041-1064.

Nigeria
1963   Nigeria Census.

O'Connor, Anthony
1983   The African City. New York: Africana
        Publishing Company.

Onokerahoye, A.G.
1977   Occupational Specialization by Ethnic Groups
        in the Informal Sector of the Urban Economies
        of Traditional Nigerian Cities: The Case of
        Benin. African Studies Review 20:53-69.

Peace, Adrian
1979   Choice, Class and Conflict: A Study of
        Southern Nigerian Factory Workers. Atlantic
        Highlands, NJ: Humanities Press.

Peattie, Lisa R.
1980   Anthropological Perspectives on the Concepts
        of Dualism, The Informal Sector, and
        Marginality in Developing Urban Economies.
        International Regional Science Review 5:1-31.

Peel, J.D.Y.
1983   Ijeshas and Nigerians: The Incorporation of a
        Yoruba Kingdom 1890s-1970s. Cambridge:
        Cambridge University Press.

283

Plattner, Stuart
  1984   "Equilibrating Market Relationships", 1984
          Proceedings of the Society for Economic
          Anthropology, Markets and Marketing. (This
          volume)

Portes, Alejandro
  1983   Latin American Class Structures: Their
          Composition and Change During the Last
          Decades. Paper presented at the Third
          U.S./U.S.S.R. Conference on Latin America.

Portes, Alejandro and John Walton
  1981   Labor Class and the International System. New
          York: Academic Press.

Roberts, Bryan
  1978   Cities of Peasants. London: Edward Arnold.

Santos, Milton
  1979   The Shared Space: The Two Circuits of the
          Urban Economy in Underdeveloped Countries.
          London: Methuen.

Sethuraman, S.V.
  1981   The Urban Informal Sector in Developing
          Countries: Employment, Poverty and
          Environment. Geneva: International Labour
          Office.

Sinclair, Stuart W.
  1977   Ease of Entry into Small Scale Trading in
          African Cities: Some Case Studies from Lagos.
          Manpower and Unemployment Research 10:79-90.

Smith, Carol
  1981   What is the "Informal Sector" and How Does it
          Affect Peripheral Capitalism? Paper presented
          at conference on New Directions in Theory and
          Methods of Immigration and Ethnicity
          Research, Duke University, May 15-17, 1981.

Standard Bank Nigeria Ltd.
  1976   The Nigerian Beer Market. Quarterly Bulletin
          1, 3:11-15.

Stark, Oded
  1982   On Modelling the Informal Sector. World
          Development 10:413-416.

Steel, W.F.
　　1976　Empirical Measurement of the Relative Size
　　　　　　and Productivity of Intermediate Sector
　　　　　　Employment: Some Estimates from Ghana.
　　　　　　Manpower and Unemployment Research 9:23-31.

Trager, Lillian
　　1976-77 Market Women in the Urban Economy: The Role
　　　　　　of Yoruba Intermediaries in a Medium-Sized
　　　　　　City. African Urban Notes 2, part 2:1-9.

　　　1981a　Yoruba Market Organization--A Regional
　　　　　　Analysis. African Urban Studies 10:43-58.

　　　1981b　Customers and Creditors: Variations in
　　　　　　Economic Personalism in a Nigerian Marketing
　　　　　　System. Ethnology 20:133-146.

　in press Contemporary Processes of Change in Yoruba
　　　　　　Cities. In Class, Ethnicity and Lifestyles in
　　　　　　the City: International Perspectives, P.J.M
　　　　　　Nas and Aidan Southall, eds.

Watts, Michael and Paul Lubeck
　　1983　The Popular Classes and the Oil Boom: A
　　　　　　Political Economy of Rural and Urban Poverty.
　　　　　　In The Political Economy of Nigeria, I.
　　　　　　William Zartman, ed. pp. 105-144. New York:
　　　　　　Praeger Publishers.

West Africa
　　1983　Africa's "twilight zone" entrepreneurs. 24
　　　　　　October 1983:2469-2470.

Zartman, I. William, ed.
　　1983　The Political Economy of Nigeria. New York:
　　　　　　Praeger Publishers.

MIDDLEMEN AND "MARGINAL" WOMEN : MARKETERS AND DEPENDENCY IN PERU'S INFORMAL SECTOR

Florence E. Babb, Department of Anthropology, University of Iowa

Like other underdeveloped countries, Peru is experiencing rapid urbanization and growth in the informal sector at the same time that capitalist expansion is occurring. As a general process, this has been explained in terms of labor migration to cities where capital-intensive industrialization offers formal sector employment to only a minority of workers (Portes and Walton 1981). Small-scale urban marketing is one of the chief ways that both long-term residents and migrants are carving out a living in third world cities.

This paper begins with an examination of some frameworks for the analysis of petty commerce, then considers how well they account for the changing relation of marketers in the Peruvian economy. I will suggest a need to examine the social relations of marketing and the internal differentiation of market traders. To understand this process we will need an approach which takes into account the linkage of formal and informal economic sectors and the way that small-scale marketing is conditioned by the wider capitalist society.

I. APPROACHES TO URBAN MARKETING IN THE THIRD WORLD

Earlier discussions of petty marketers and street vendors in third world towns and cities commonly emphasized either traditional economic elements in the urban setting which were, perhaps, destined to disappear (Bohannan and Dalton 1962), or the resiliency of traders and their auspicious role in development (Tax 1953, Dewey 1962, Geertz 1963, Belshaw 1965). The proliferation of urban traders in underdeveloped areas has made the first view untenable; that is, marketplace commerce is no dying tradition. The second view has held forth in the form of studies of entrepreneurial activity among small-scale marketers (Davis 1973, Beals 1975).

This latter approach makes little qualitative distinction between the economic sphere in which small marketers participate and the larger capitalist economy. Rather, a continuum is suggested by the often-used term "small-scale" and "large-scale." Marketers in small-scale enterprises are viewed as having at least the potential for increasing the scale of their activities, even if the possibility is sometimes slight (Roberts 1975). Behind this approach is the assumption that the same economic forces condition the work of petty marketers and large entrepreneurs. Some researchers have predicted that with adequate support small producers and sellers will expand and hasten development; this has, for example, characterized the research and policy orientation of the International Labour Office (ILO) (Moser 1978).

In recent years, however, researchers have been more impressed by the structural constraints on urban marketers and street vendors and they have advanced analyses to account for the persistent poverty of these workers in dependent capitalist economies (Schmitz 1982; Moser 1980). It is to these analyses that I now turn my attention. In general terms, we may discern two emerging schools of thought, referred to as the informal/formal sector analysis and the petty commodity production analysis, though there are areas of convergence which I will note.

The informal/formal sector analysis came into use in the 1970s when Hart (1973) and others pointed to the differences found in these economic sectors in third world cities. In contrast to the capital-intensive, wage-earning formal sector, the informal sector was characterized by self-employment, easy entry, reliance on indigenous resources, and labor-intensive technology. Studies using this framework contributed importantly to our understanding of little-known economic activities and social groups.

Some critics, however, have argued that the informal/formal sector framework represents dualist thinking which obscures the interlinkages between the sectors. According to these critics, the inability of small-scale marketers to expand is precisely because of their dependent relationship in the dominant capitalist economy. Some researchers (e.g., contributions to Bromley 1978; Bromley and Gerry 1979) have used the concept of petty commodity production to locate the place of petty producers and traders at the margins of capitalist economies, but integrated within them as providers of surplus. Following Marx (1967: 761-762), the petty commodity mode or form of production is characterized by an incomplete separation of producers

288

from the means of production. Such an analysis has been used by Cook and Diskin (1976) in their study of peasant producer-sellers in Mexico, and by other researchers examining rural societies.

This analysis has also been found useful in research on third world cities, where, rather than diminishing, petty production and trade are often thriving (e.g., Gerry 1978, 1979). Informed by dependency theory, researchers attribute this persistence to the distorted process of capitalist development in third world countries. Instead of a western pattern of growth whereby an increasing number of workers are drawn into the industrial labor force, the capital-intensive sector employs only a limited number of people. The urban poor, often migrants from rural areas, have little alternative but to enter such marginal[1] occupations as petty manufacturing and trading.

The strength of the petty commodity analysis lies in its recognition of the distinct structural features of the small production and commerce sector, and its attention to the way this sector is conditioned by its subordinate position in the wider capitalist society. For the analysis of marketers and street vendors, it provides a framework for locating their work in the total production process and for assessing the productive component of marketing itself.[2] Once we understand the productive role of marketers, who locate, sort, clean, preserve, and often process the goods they sell, it is possible to examine the mechanisms by which surplus value is transferred from the sector in which small traders operate to the capitalist sector; this occurs when items are sold at low prices to consumers, keeping down the cost of reproducing the nation's labor force and thus contributing to the accumulation of capital. Such an analysis can account for the persistence of petty production and commerce in dependent economies, and for the frequent inability of these small-scale sellers to expand--their efforts ultimately subsidize the capitalist sector.

In Caroline Moser's (1978) review of the debate that emerged between advocates of informal sector analysis and their critics who proposed the petty commodity production analysis, the theoretical adequacy of the former is questioned. In particular, she challenges the assumption that the relationship of the informal and formal sectors is benign, and the policy implications this has when efforts are made to increase ties across sectors. For Moser, the relationship is exploitative and further integration of the informal sector in the dominant economy will mean further subordination. Writers like Moser and Alison Scott (1979) have called for closer examination of economic activities in the informal sector, to develop a more sophisticated analysis of the differentiation within this sector, where the apparently self-employed may actually be disguised wage laborers working as commission-sellers, outworkers and the like.

On the other hand, some followers of the debate have been less certain of the advantages of the petty commodity analysis. Long and Richardson (1978) consider the merits and limitations of both the informal sector approach and the petty commodity approach. While they credit the latter with overcoming some of the difficulties of a descriptive, dualist view, they remain dissatisfied with the attention given in petty commodity analysis to processes internal to the subordinate economic sector. Specifically, they emphasize the importance of economic strategies at the household level in shaping relations with the capitalist sector. Their critique may stem in part from their own research among some particularly entrepreneurial individuals who have managed to get ahead. In the end, however, they express the point made by Moser (1978) that there is a need for closer examination of differentiation and social relations among those in petty production and commerce.

In the last few years, there seems to be widespread acceptance of the informal/formal sector terminology, even among researchers persuaded of the validity of criticisms which have been raised. For example, in Helen Safa's (1982b) recent collection on third world urbanization, the editor and a number of contributors (McGee 1982, Remy 1982, Peattie 1982) use the terms in a critical, dynamic way. Safa (1982a: 7) writes: Contrary to earlier notions regarding the separate and discrete nature of the formal and informal economies, the yare now generally recognized as strongly interdependent, with the formal sector dependent on the informal for goods, services and cheap labor, and the informal dependent on the formal for a good portion of its clientele, income, and a source of new income-generating activities. ...[The informal sector's] resilience and strength prove its capacity to constantly transform itself in its subordination to the dominant capitalist sector.

290

Portes and Walton (1981) go so far as to judge the informal/formal sector approach a welcome replacement for views of the urban working poor influenced by the excesses of dependency theory. However, they themselves adopt a world systems perspective which places capital accumulation at the center of analysis, and emphasize the linkage of economic sectors. They (ibid.: 86) are critical of the concept of petty commodity production, while applying many of the insights arising from that conceptualization of urban workers. It is true, as they say, that as originally formulated by Marx, simple, or petty, commodity production was understood as a transitional form; but researchers such as Bromley and Gerry (1979) and others have modified the concept to bring it into line with the current situation in the third world. It is well known that under dependent capitalism the urban poor are proliferating in the areas of petty production and commerce, and this poses no problem for analysts wishing to use the concept.

As the discussion over the informal sector and petty commodity production and commerce has advanced, some central issues have emerged. From the literature of the debate, and particularly the Marxist contribution, I have become increasingly convinced of the importance of examining the labor process and social relations of marketing--noting internal differentiation--and locating the place of small marketers in the wider capitalist economy. Given the broad recognition of these questions in much of the literature today, I am content to use the concepts of petty commodity production and informal sector in what follows.[3]

II. THE CASE OF PERU

There was some optimism during the early years of Peru's recent military government (1968-80) that economic development would soon be underway. During those first years of General Juan Velasco Alvarado's government, land reform and expropriations of foreign industrial interests were enacted. The reorganization and state control of the productive sectors was not matched in the areas of distribution, but the military's desire to secure an adequate and cheap food supply for urban Peru made this a significant element in domestic policy. In 1970, an agency, the Empresa Pública de Servicios Agropecuarios (EPSA), was created to control the marketing of basic foodstuffs, and in 1972 the production and marketing of all agricultural products came under state control. A Ministry of Food was established in 1974 to regulate prices on a regional basis.

The optimism was short-lived, however; since the transfer of power to General Francisco Morales Bermudez in 1975 and the return to civilian government under Fernando Belaunde Terry in 1980, Peru has confronted a rapidly worsening economic situation. By the mid-1970s, Peru was experiencing the negative effects of a mounting international debt and International Monetary Fund (IMF) demands for austerity measures. With the military government turning its attention to capital-intensive industrial growth, and welcoming the return of foreign capital, there was a lack of concern for providing employment opportunities in the expanding cities. As a consequence, an increasing number of people have entered the impoverished petty commodity sector to carve out a living.[4] While these may often be highly motivated individuals, it appears that collectively they are rarely able to improve their condition and most remain among the highly visible urban poor.

Many writers have commented on the growing population in the cities of Peru of those dedicated to petty production and commerce. Few, however, have focused their research on the social conditions and employment of this part of the urban population. Anthropologists have generally directed their investigations to the rural area where agriculture remains the predominant form of livelihood, and economists and political scientists have looked primarily to the "modern" or capital-intensive sector. There are a few exceptions, though, and I will turn to them.

It is not surprising that the two areas of Peru for which we have the most information about petty production and commerce include the nation's capital and largest city, Lima, and the large commercial center in the sierra, Huancayo, and its environs. Both are growing urban areas with strategic roles in the nation's economy.

Huancayo, in the Mantaro Valley in central Peru, has been investigated by a team of researchers under the direction of Norman Long and Bryan Roberts. Their focus has been on small-scale local enterprises in relation to national economic and political development (Long and Roberts 1978). They emphasize the importance of viewing individuals at the local level as actors,

292

and change as deriving from the periphery as well as the center in Peru. This perspective is a corrective to views of small producers and marketers as passive victims of externally generated change; however, I wonder if Roberts (1975: 89) goes too far when he states that "the small enterprise, not the large, is the active agent of capitalist penetration in Peru." Significantly, the individuals studied by Long and Roberts were not the predominantly female market sellers, but the mostly-male entrepreneurs in independent businesses.

In Lima, where migrants are estimated to make up half the population, a number of writers (e.g., Doughty 1970; Mangin 1970) have considered the social and economic experience of this population through the use of case studies. Patch's (1967) study of La Parada, Lima's market district, is well-known for its rich description of the lives of residents in the area, but disappointing in its attention to the market itself.

Alison Scott's (1979) writing on Lima's informal sector is among the first to examine systematically the characteristics of the working poor in Peru. Using the petty production model, Scott argues that the self-employed/wage labor distinction which is basic to that model (as well as to the informal sector model) is not clear-cut and must be examined more closely. For example, artisans involved in petty manufacturing frequently lose their independence when confronted with large-scale industrial competition, and fall into dependent relationships with merchants who offer credit in return for output at a fixed price (ibid.:113-114). In the commercial sector, many workers who have the illusion of self-employment are really commissioned piece-wage laborers (ibid.: 119). Scott (ibid.: 123) notes that this sector may have proliferated in Lima because of its autonomous role under capitalism, or because it is actually promoted as an indirect source of surplus.

Jorge Osterling and several Peruvian colleagues have undertaken an investigation of Lima's street vendors, who have been the focus of considerable governmental concern in recent years. The expansion of petty commerce is located within the terms of the informal sector debate (Osterling 1981; Osterling, Althaus, and Morelli 1979; Osterling and Chàvez de Paz 1979), and the researchers point to internal differentiation in this sector, calling for more attention to social process in future studies. In shorter articles,

Grompone (1981) traces the growth of petty commerce in Lima to the contradictory, and uneven, development of capitalism in Peru, and Zamolloa (1981) notes the large number of dependent sellers working for wages or on consignment, and the majority of poor women sellers.

Several studies have focused on the particular experience of women in Lima's informal sector. As in many other third world cities, in Lima women predominate in informal activities. Female migrants outnumber males in the city, and while the majority find employment as domestic servants, petty commerce is the second most common occupation for women in urban Peru. Research in this area is only slowly beginning to appear as the results of a broad study on Lima's working women are published (Mercado 1978; Bunster 1982; Bunster and Chaney, forthcoming). So far, the findings from these studies have suggested that despite women's resourcefulness in making a living in the market at the same time that they meet family responsibilities, these women are marginalized as a consequence of their sex and class status and of Peru's distorted development.[5]

III.   ANDEAN WOMEN IN PETTY COMMERCE

In the remainder of this paper I will discuss my own research on marketers in a highland city in Peru in light of some of the insights about the informal sector which were mentioned earlier. Specifically, I will be interested to examine the increasing number of marketers and street vendors and the role they play in the economy; the labor process of marketers; the social relations of marketers and internal differentiation; and the link of petty commerce with the dominant capitalist economy.

In contrast to most studies of informal sector activity which have been carried out in major urban centers, my research has been in a provincial city of some 45,000 residents;[6] even so, I have discovered evidence of many of the same phenomena that others have described for larger cities in my own field research in the north-central Andes of Peru. My research was undertaken in Huaraz, the administrative and commercial capital of the department of Ancash. This city of Quechua-Spanish speaking people has seen steady population growth and renewed urbanization since an earthquake destroyed much of the downtown area in 1970. Huaraz has three indoor markets, two of them constructed in the 1970s, and a large sprawling open-air market; many street sellers now fill the major streets as well. Women outnumber men in the markets, making up almost 80 percent of all sellers. Men tend to be located in the sale of manufactured goods and in larger-scale retail or wholesale trade. Women are principally concentrated in the retail sale of fruits and vegetables and cooked foods. There is considerable overlap, however, in the area of men's and women's trade.

Since the mid-1970s, as Peru's economic crisis has deepened, more people have entered commercial activity in Huaraz. By my own count, in 1977 there were close to 1200 sellers in the city, and by 1982 the number had risen to almost 1600. Marketers themselves explain this phenomenon as a strategy for diversifying household economies in difficult times.

My research in Peru has benefited from studying marketing over a period of time, from 1977 to the present. During my major fieldwork in 1977 I witnessed the introduction of national austerity measures, and a return visit in 1982 allowed me to follow the effect of "economic packages" (devaluation of the currency and rising prices) on petty commerce.

Despite the often long hours and hard work of daily sellers from Huaraz and periodic sellers from the surrounding valley, these marketers commonly experience a marginal livelihood.[7] The vegetable and fruit sellers who comprise almost half of all marketers in the city (and among whom 92 percent are women) often earn less than US$.50 daily according to my interviews and observations. This is about half the daily wage of male agricultural laborers. Yet few alternatives exist in Huaraz, since there is little industry and jobs in administrative offices go chiefly to middle class employees. Among young women, petty commerce is generally preferred to domestic service for the degree of independence and flexibility it offers. Women with family responsibilities appreciate marketing for the way it may be integrated with childcare and other domestic activities. Men may value the status of having their own business, even if that business is typically precarious.

Undifferentiated accounts of commercial intermediaries in Peru fail to recognize the particular features conditioning the work lives of small retailers. Although Huaraz marketers, like marketers elsewhere, are integrated in the capitalist economy,

295

their relationship to it is rarely that of entrepreneurs or petty capitalists. After my field research in 1977, I concluded that the marketers could best be conceptualized within the framework of petty commodity production and trade (Babb 1981). The same analysis which sheds light on the situation ofpetty producer-sellers and petty manufacturers, could illuminate petty marketers like those in Huaraz. While only a minority of sellers take to market the product of their own fields or manufacture, as a group they add value to the goods they buy from producers and wholesalers, thereby extending the production process into the marketplace. The work contributed by marketers before their goods are ready for sale ranges from a fairly simple cleaning of fruits and vegetables, to the preparation of complete meals for consumption on-the-spot, to the confection of clothing and craft items. We may add to this work the time consuming process of buying up supplies, then transporting and preserving them until the time they are sold.

In my view, it is important to see the direct connection between the production and distribution of goods in this unified process. Though the production may begin in other hands, retailers are "finishers" inasmuch as they complete the preparation of goods and make them available to consumers. Huaraz marketers are busy as they sell, many of them readying more items for sale. The work of others is less visible, for it takes place at home before they leave for the market. For example, sellers of poultry buy live chickens which they must attend to at home, and sellers of flour take grains to local mills, before they are ready for sale. Vendors of tamales go through the steps to prepare these snack foods in their kitchens, then bundle them on their backs for sale in the streets.

In contrast to a far smaller number of large wholesalers, chiefly men whose profits are high, we have seen that the earnings of small retailers are typically very low. Under the recent military government, basic food prices were controlled at the regional and national levels. Since 1980, controls have been lifted from all but a few food items, but marketers' earnings remain low. This seems due to the expanding number of sellers in Peru, and their willingness to work for very little reward. Given their lack of alternatives, many are satisfied to have a small amount of food left over to take home at the end of the day--or enough money to buy some--and indeed measure their success this way.

In 1982, I returned to Huaraz and found that it was truly the exceptional marketer whose business had expanded in recent years. In one case, a man with more capital and higher education than most marketers had used earnings from a successful fruit drink stand to open a small restaurant. In another case, a childless couple had expanded their cosmetics trade from a portable stand to permanent glass display cases in a choice market location (rumors circulated about their black market connections). In any event, these successes were rare.

While reinterviewing a number of the sellers I knew from five years before, I was not surprised to discover that in many cases their level of business was contracting. The majority described the hardships they had experienced, and this was all too obvious from their declining health and impoverished appearance. In a number of cases, marketers rented smaller spaces to sell, offered fewer items, and, increasingly, their market incomes needed to be supplemented by additional family resources. I located a few women who had given up marketing altogether and had turned to work as maids in local hotels, bakery assistants, and other service sector jobs; surely there were many more who left petty commerce during this period--even as others began marketing for the first time. In general, it seemed that petty marketers were frequently unable even to reproduce their present conditions.

On further investigation, I found evidence to suggest that the autonomy of these workers in petty commerce may be undergoing a process of erosion. Already in 1977, I questioned whether small retailers could accurately be defined as independent, within the terms of the petty commodity production model. It appeared to me that their subordinate relation to wholesalers, on whom they were generally dependent for the extension of credit, was enough to cast doubt on the view of petty traders as autonomous. Furthermore, differentiation was evident among small retailers, with some sellers employing others to work for them. Examples include a food stall operator who hires an elderly woman as assistant on a regular basis, and a seller of ground garlic and chili peppers who occasionally hires another woman to peel garlic for her on a piecework basis. It should be noted that although in both these examples wage labor is employed, only in the first does this contribute to a process of capital accumulation.

Five years later, I was able to observe some changes in Huaraz. Not only had the total number of marketers and street vendors in the city increased substantially, but my interviews suggested that there was a greater number of dependent sellers--wage employees and commission-sellers. Particularly striking were the expanded number of street vendors selling ice cream, candy, prepared drinks and the like from carts, by day and by night; a large number, if not the majority, of these sellers are wage workers (some of whom hire up to a half dozen sellers). For example, sellers of emolientes (hot syrupy drinks) may be paid on a weekly or monthly basis to sit with carts at busy streetcorners, while the owners of the carts (often former marketers) stay home.

So far, we have examined instances of emerging inequalities within the informal sector. It is apparent that while the majority of marketers in Huaraz are experiencing difficult times, and some are going through a process of subordination, other marketers are doing the subordinating. Whether through hard work, luck, or some other advantage, a small number of individuals have indeed managed to accumulate capital and then to augment their advantage in the commercial sector. Differentiation among retailers may result in the formation of a market hierarchy--unequal relations in the economic process among informal sector participants.

However, a number of the small sellers of ice cream and candy seen in the streets of Huaraz are in dependent relationship to much larger interests in Peru's formal sector. Sellers of D'Onofrio ice cream novelties are supplied with refrigerated barrows and items to sell at prices set by the national company. As commission-sellers, their earnings and the conditions of their work appear similar to those sellers of traditional raspadillas (flavored ice cream treats), yet the latter are either independent sellers or working for others within the informal sector.

Furthermore, many marketers in Huaraz travel regularly to the coast to obtain manufactured goods directly from factories. These individuals sometimes receive goods on contract, then return to sell in Huaraz until it is time to pay off debts and replenish their stock. Other sellers obtain these same goods from wholesalers with whom they do business regularly. In this way, the numerous sellers of clothing, plastic kitchen utensils, mattresses, and other household items

298

are linked closely to the formal sector. Of course, even those sellers who appear "independent" are connected to the formal sector through their relation to formal sector consumers of their goods.

My impression that in some measure marketers, especially small-scale female sellers, are losing control over their work process was corroborated by marketers themselves. Even those who retain a degree of autonomy over their work agreed that marketing is increasingly controlled by more powerful interests. They testifiy to the many ways that marketers may be disguised wage laborers, when they work as commission-sellers, piecework wage-earners, and outworkers for other marketers or larger firms. Although this small study carried out over a five year period is not sufficient to document a process of subordination to the wage form, or proletarianization, the evidence lends support to the view that this is occurring.

Finally, let us turn our attention to the situation of Huaraz marketers in the context of Peruvian market sellers and street vendors more generally, and consider their relation to the national political economy. I have tried to show that in Huaraz marketers, whether independent or dependent sellers, generally have low earnings and barely manage to get by. Through a combination of numerous market fees and not infrequent fines, the earnings of marketers are further reduced and go instead to support the municipal government. From what is known about other Peruvian cities, especially Lima, the situation appears similar, although the erosion of marketers' autonomy may be more advanced on the coast than in the sierra.

Critics of the distribution process in Peru sometimes suggest that the problem lies in the chain of intermediaries which raises prices to consumers. However, it should be clear that the petty retailers who sell to the public are hardly the culprits they are depicted as being. Indeed, by working hard for little reward they actually hold down prices to a more tolerable level. This, we have seen, lowers the cost of reproducing the labor force and so contributes to the accumulation of capital at the national level. Moreover, with unemployment running high in Peru, small traders are able to make a living and offset a potentially greater economic problem.

Under the present terms of underdevelopment in Peru, marketers would seem to fill an important role--even if they themselves are rarely satisfied with the circumstances of their work. It may appear surprising then to discover that for the last decade the Peruvian government has launched a campaign against small marketers (Babb 1982a). Using the slogan "from the field to the pot", the stated goal has been to eliminate the "bad merchants" and "evil intermediaries" who are responsible for the economic ills in Peru. While the history of the campaign cannot be traced here, it is notable that a number of well-publicized producer and wholesaler markets in Lima have met with limited success, and a short-term producers' market in Huaraz received little support from consumers or even producers. My view is that rather than actually eliminate retail marketers, the government is using them as a scapegoat for the deeper economic troubles the country faces. They are certainly a highly visible and vulnerable group, but they have not hesitated to protest when local or national government has sought to curtail their activity.

IV.   CONCLUSIONS

My emphasis on the contribution of marketers in the Peruvian economy is not intended to suggest a need for policy to strengthen petty commerce in the informal sector, or to create stronger ties between the informal and formal sectors. We have seen that the integration of these sectors is already strong within the capitalist system which gave rise to them, and which depends for its reproduction on the surplus transferred from the informal to the formal sector. If any policy direction is implied in the paper it would have to be one calling for substantial structural change in the Peruvian economy and society.

However, my modest objective here has been to demonstrate that many of the insights of the informal sector analysis and the petty commodity analysis can shed light on small-scale marketing in urban Peru. I have suggested that attention to the labor process and social relations of marketers, as well as linkages with the wider capitalist economy, can show why marketers so rarely accumulate capital themselves and instead contribute to the accumulation of larger interests--in Peru, and perhaps in other areas of the third world. In short, the best insights of the last ten years can guide us in the direction of a political economy of petty commerce.

300

ACKNOWLEDGMENTS

I am grateful to Stuart Plattner, Lillian Trager and Johanna Lessinger for their thoughtful criticisms of this paper as presented at the 1984 meeting of the Society for Economic Anthropology. Field research in Peru was supported in 1977 by a State University of New York Grant-in-Aid (awarded to William W. Stein) and in 1982 by a travel grant provided by the organization Perú Mujer, for which I am most indebted. Above all, I wish to express my thanks to the marketers of Huaraz, Peru, for without their cooperation and friendship this research would have been impossible.

NOTES

1. The context in which I discuss marginal occupations and marginal workers should make it clear that I do not refer to a residual category set apart from the dominant economy. Rather, I refer to occupational sectors and individuals that, however vital they are to the economy, are located in a subordinate relationship to the dominant capitalist sector.

2. For further discussion of the productive aspect of marketing and an application of this analysis to the case of Huaraz, Peru, see Babb (1982b).

3. Trager's work (this volume), like mine, points to the importance of examining differentiation in the informal sector, and linkages between the informal and formal sectors. However, in her study of urban marketing in Nigeria she cautions against overemphasizing the links to the formal sector. In part, the difference in our analyses may stem from Trager's special interest in how some self-employed individuals are able to take advantage of new economic opportunities and my own interest in the general process of subordination of marketers to larger commercial interests. Another important factor underlying our different conclusions may be, as Trager notes, the diversity found in informal sector activity throughout Africa and Latin America.

4. Reliable information on this population is generally unavailable. However, Osterling and Chávez de Paz (1979:185) estimate that in Lima, street vendors alone (i.e., not including market sellers) make up ten percent of the population of over four million

301

people. And the findings of Esculies Larrabure et al. (1977:181) suggest that small marketers carry out 95 percent of retail commerce in Lima and 99 percent in Peru as a whole. See also Scott (1979) for a discussion of petty production and commerce in Lima.

5. Though my purpose here is not to elaborate on the cross-cultural research on women in the informal sector, this is a central concern in my own research, and I would note in passing the paucity of studies of women in urban commerce. Though it is frequently recognized that women play a significant, and often preponderant, role in commerce, systematic investigation has barely begun (Arizpe 1977; Hansen 1980; Nelson 1979; Trager 1976-77; Babb, forthcoming).

6. Trager (1976-77) has called for more studies of women's marketing in medium-sized cities in West Africa. I would argue for the same in Latin America.

7. There is, perhaps, a marketers' culture characterized by proclamations of hard financial times. A Huaraz marketer is likely to say, "How much do I earn? Better to ask how much I lose!" This reflects the frustration of sellers who in fact do lose from time to time, and who have been undergoing real hardship since the mid-1970s. But sellers must of course earn something or they would stop selling. See Babb (1981) for more discussion of marketers' earnings in Huaraz.

8. I thoroughly agree with Lessinger (this volume) when she calls for more discussion of political mobilization among urban marketers. Like the Indian market traders she describes, marketers in Huaraz have organized to defend their interests and to protest the growing number of restrictions placed on their trade. See Babb (1981) for further discussion of the activity of Huaraz marketers' unions and their response to rising market fees, restricted areas for selling, and other controls imposed by the city government.

REFERENCES

Arizpe, Lourdes
    1977   Women in the Informal Labor Sector: The

Case of Mexico City, <u>Signs</u> 3(1):25-37.

Babb, Florence E.
    1981   Women and Marketing in Huaraz, Peru: The
                Political Economy of Petty Commerce.   Ph.D.
                dissertation, State University of New York
                at Buffalo.

    1982a   E c o n o m i c   C r i s i s   a n d   t h e   A s s a u l t   o n
                Marketers in Peru. <u>Working Papers on Women
                in International Development</u>, Working Paper
                No. 6. East Lansing, Michigan: Michigan
                State University.

    1982b   Marketers as Producers: The "Hidden" Labor
                Process of Workers in Petty Commerce.
                Paper presented at the Annual Meeting of
                the American Anthropological Association,
                Washington, D.C.

    n.d.   Women in the Marketplace: Petty Commerce
                in Peru, forthcoming in <u>Review of Radical
                Political Economics</u> 16(1), spring 1984.

Beals, Ralph L.
    1975   <u>The Peasant Marketing System of Oaxaca,
                Mexico</u>. Berkeley: University of California
                Press.

Belshaw, Cyril S.
    1965   <u>Traditional Exchange and Modern Markets</u>.
                Englewood Cliffs, N.J.:   Prentice-Hall.

Bohannan, Paul J. and George Dalton, eds.
    1962   <u>Markets in Africa</u>.   Evanston,   Illinois:
                Northwestern University Press.

Bromley, Ray, ed.
    1978   The Urban Informal Sector: Critical
                Perspectives, special issue of <u>World
                Development</u> 6(9-10).

Bromley, Ray and Chris Gerry, eds.
    1979   <u>Casual Work and Poverty in Third World
                Cities</u>. New York: John Wiley and Sons.

Bunster, Ximena
    1982   Market Sellers in Lima, Peru: Talking
                About Work, in <u>Women and Poverty in the
                Third World</u>. Edited by Mayra Buvinic and
                Margaret A. Lycette. Baltimore: Johns

Hopkins University Press.

Bunster, Ximena and Elsa M. Chaney
    n.d.   Working Women in Lima. New York: Praeger,
                forthcoming.

Cook, Scott and Martin Diskin, eds.
    1976   Markets in Oaxaca. Austin: University of
                Texas Press.

Davis, William G.
    1973   Social Relations in a Philippine Market.
                Berkeley: University of California Press.

Dewey, Alice
    1962   Peasant Marketing in Java. New York: Free
                Press.

Doughty, Paul L.
    1970   Behind the Back of the City: "Provincial"
                Life in Lima, Peru, in Peasants in Cities.
                Edited by William Mangin.   Boston:
                Houghton Mifflin.

Esculies Larrabure, Oscar, Marcial Rubio Correa, and
Veronica Gonzalez del Castillo
    1977   Comercialización de Alimentos: Quiénes
                anan, Quiénes Pagan, Quiénes Pierden.
                Lima: Centro de Estudios y Promoción del
                Desarrollo (DESCO).

Geertz, Clifford
    1963   Peddlers and Princes. Chicago: University
                of Chicago Press.

Gerry, Chris
    1978   Petty Production and Capitalist Production
                in Dakar: The Crisis of the Self-Employed,
                World Development 6(9-10):1147-1160.

    1979   Small-Scale Manufacturing and Repairs in
                Dakar: A Survey of Market Relations Within
                the Urban Economy, in Casual Work and
                Poverty in Third World Cities. Edited by
                Ray Bromley and Chris Gerry. New York:
                John Wiley and Sons.

Grompone, Romeo
    1981   Comercio Ambulante: Razones de una Terca
                Presencia, Quehacer 13:95-109.

Hansen, Karen Tranberg
  1980   The Urban Informal Sector as a Development Issue: Poor Women and Work in Lusaka, Zambia, Urban Anthropology 9(2):199-225.

Hart, Keith
  1973   Informal Income Opportunities and Urban Employment in Ghana, Journal of Modern African Studies 2(1):61-89.

Lessinger, Johanna
  1984   "Nobody Here to Yell at Me," Job Security and Political Activism Among Urban Retail Traders in South India. Paper presented at meeting of The Society for Economic Anthropology, Davis, California.

Long, Norman and Paul Richardson
  1978   Informal Sector, Petty Commodity Production, and the Social Relations of Small-Scale Enterprise, in The New Economic Anthropology. Edited by John Clammer. New York: St. Martin's press

Long, Norman and Bryan R. Roberts, eds.
  1978   Peasant Cooperation and Capitalist Expansion in Central Peru. Austin: University of Texas Press.

McGee, T.G.
  1982   Labour Mobility in Fragmented Labour Markets, the Role of Circulatory Migration in Rural-Urban Relations in Asia, in Towards a Political Economy of Urbanization in Third World Countries. Edited by Helen I. Safa. Delhi, India: Oxford University Press.

Mangin, William, ed
  1970   Peasants in Cities. Boston: Houghton Mifflin.

Marx, Karl
  1967   Capital, Vol. 1. New York: International Publishers.

Mercado, Hilda
  1978   La Madre Trabajadora: El Caso de las Comerciantes Ambulantes. Serie C, No. 2. Lima: Centro de Estudios de Población y Desarrollo.

Moser, Caroline
    1978   Informal Sector or Petty Commodity
                Production: Dualism or Dependence in Urban
                Development? World Development 6(9-
                10):1041-1064.

    1980   Why the Poor Remain Poor: The Experience
                of Bogotá Market Traders in the 1970s,
                Journal of Interamerican Studies and World
                Affairs 22(3):365-387.

Nelson, Nici
    1979   How Women and Men Get By: The Sexual
                Division of Labour in the Informal Sector
                of a Nairobi Squatter Settlement, in Casual
                Work and Poverty in Third World Cities.
                Edited by Ray Bromley and Chris Gerry. New
                York: John Wiley and Sons.

Osterling, Jorge
    1981   La Pobreza Urbana a la Luz del Sector
                Económico Informal Urbano: Una Perspectiva
                Transcultural, Socialismo y Participación
                16:71-84.

Osterling, Jorge, Jaime de Althaus, and Jorge Morelli
    1979   Los Vendedores Ambulantes de Ropa en el
                Cercado: Un Ejemplo del Sector Económico
                Informal en Lima Metropolitana, Debates en
                Antropología 4:23-41.

Osterling, Jorge and Dennis Chávez de Paz
    1979   La Organización de los Vendedores
                Ambulantes: El Caso de Lima Metropolitana,
                Revista de la Universidad Católica 6:185-
                202.

Patch, Richard
    1967   La Parada, Lima's Market, American
                Universities Field Staff Reports, West
                Coast of South America Series 14(1,2,3).

Peattie, Lisa R.
    1982   What is to be Done With the 'Informal
                Sector'? A Case Study of Shoe
                Manufacturers in Colombia, in Towards a
                Political Economy of Urbanization in Third
                World Countries. Edited by Helen I. Safa.
                Delhi, India: Oxford University Press.

306

Portes, Alejandro and John Walton
1981   Labor, Class, and the International System.
         New York: Academic Press.

Remy, Dorothy
1982   Formal and Informal Sectors of the Zaria,
         Nigeria Economy: An Analytic Framework
         with Empirical Content, in Towards a
         Political Economy of Urbanization in Third
         World Countries. Edited by Helen I. Safa.
         Delhi, India: Oxford University Press.

Roberts, Bryan R.
1975   Center and Periphery in the Development
         Process: The Case of Peru, Latin American
         Urban Research, Vol. 5. Edited by Wayne A.
         Cornelius and Felicity M. Trueblood.
         Beverly Hills: Sage.

Safa, Helen I.
1982a   Introduction, in Towards a Political
         Economy of Urbanization in Third World
         Countries. Edited by Helen I. Safa.
         Delhi, India: Oxford University Press.

1982b   Towards a Political Economy of Urbanization
         in Third World Countries. Delhi, India:
         Oxford University Press.

Schmitz, Hubert
1982   Growth Constraints on Small-Scale
         Manufacturing in Developing Countries: A
         Critical Review, World Development
         10(6):429-450.

Scott, Alison MacEwen
1979   Who Are the Self-Employed? in Casual Work
         and Poverty in Third World Cities. Edited
         by Ray Bromley and Chris Gerry. New York:
         John Wiley and Sons.

Tax, Sol
1953   Penny Capitalism: A Guatemalan Indian
         Economy. Smithsonian Institution, Institute
         of Social Anthropology, No. 16.
         Washington, D.C.: U.S. Government Printing
         Office.

Trager, Lillian
1976-7   Market Women in the Urban Economy: The
         Role of Yoruba Intermediaries in a Medium-

Sized City. <u>African</u> <u>Urban</u> <u>Notes</u>, Women in Urban Africa, Part 2, Vol. II(3).

1984   From Yams to Beer in a Nigerian City: Expansion and Change in Informal Sector Trade Activity. Paper presented at meeting of the Society for Economic Anthropology, Davis, California.

Zamalloa, Edgar
  1981   Comercio Ambulatorio: Mito y Realidad, <u>Debate</u> 8:39-42.

**NOBODY HERE TO YELL AT ME: POLITICAL ACTIVISM AMONG
PETTY RETAIL TRADERS IN AN INDIAN CITY**

Johanna Lessinger, Columbia University, New York

1. INTRODUCTION

The concept of an informal sector is becoming
extremely valuable in the study of petty trade and
marketing.   At the same time, a number of new questions
are raised which need further examination.   One such
problem is that of political activism among traders--a
question which some writers have tended to ignore or
downplay.

Recent theoretical discussion of the informal sector
has broadened our understanding of urban marketing by
showing that trade need no longer be studies in
isolation.   Trading can now be seen as one of a range
of urban occupations, all sharing certain important
characteristics.   At the same time, the informal sector
model forces us to examine traders within the larger
context of an urban class structure, while specifying
their relationships to the city, national and world
economies.   From this perspective city marketing can be
understood not as an urban holdover of peasant activity
but as a characteristic form of urban economic behavior
given new meaning by its larger context.

Urban marketing is not just one among many kinds of
informal sector work, but is one of the most prevalent
forms.   Kowarick (1979:76) calls it "archetypal" of the
economic strategies, ranging from shinning shoes to the
establishment of small backyard factories, which allow
the urban poor to survive in highly stratified cities
offering little permanent wage work in industry or
elsewhere in the formal sector.   Like other informal
sector jobs, trading is small-scale self-employment
within a sphere which is dependent upon, and subsidiary
to a dominant capitalist economy.   In addition trading
is poorly paid and potentially insecure work.   It is
often a source of temporary employment for individuals
trying multiple job strategies over a lifetime.
(Equally, many enter trading after having tried other
kinds of informal sector work.)   Marketing is usually
carried out by an isolated worker or by a single
household, rather than by people organized into a
larger unit.

Within the realm of informal sector jobs, however,

petty trading seems to attract particularly large numbers of workers, a trend which Babb suggests elsewhere in this volume. Perhaps trading, although it does not offer better financial returns than other kinds of informal sector jobs, offers greater job security and better working conditions under certain circumstances -- a point which will be further elaborated later.

Another question raised by the use of the informal sector model is the ambiguity of the actual class position occupied by petty traders. In terms of Marxist theory, traders are not proletarians selling their labor but are fledgling members of the petty bourgeoisie. Bromley, (1982:65) for instance, emphasizes the self-employment of petty traders, their substantial personal autonomy of action, and their chances for upward social mobility. These attributes are accompanied, he believes, by a developing petty bourgeois political consciousness.

In contrast, many writers view traders as being progressively proletarianized by the forces of capitalist development, a point stressed by Babb (this volume). She and others note the kinds of economic dependence marketers fall into, a dependence which takes the form of indebtedness to suppliers or money lenders, of commission sales or of selling which is actually a form of disguised wage work (MacEwan Scott, 1979; Davies, 1979). Moser (1980) compares trading to petty commodity production and points to a more general dependence on the capitalist sector.

A further argument for the proletarianization of traders lies in the fact that the formal and the informal sectors are never wholly distinct. MacEwan Scott (1979) argues convincingly that the informal sector itself is frequently highly segmented, that it is often hierarchical, and that within it a number of contradictory relations of production exist. Work histories show that people frequently move in and out of a variety of jobs along an employment continuum ranging from industrial wage work to various forms of informal sector work. In this situation the same household often contains both proletarian wage workers and informal sector workers. Ramaswamy (1983), for instance, cites Indian examples of this phenomenon. Gerry (1979:246-247) resolves the apparent paradox posed by informal sector workers' class relations by suggesting that capitalist transformation is constantly pushing such workers toward one of two poles --

310

proletarianization or membership in the petty
capitalist class.

A question immediately raised by Gerry's formulation
is the role of political activism in defining the
emergent class status of informal sector workers.
Whether marketers take part in overt political activity
or not, they are linked to a national political system
just as they are enmeshed in a national economy.
Students of urban marketing have then to ask what kinds
of political activity traders engage in and how this
activity affects their economic and class relations.

Many of those writing about political activity among
the urban poor have disparaged its extent and its
effectiveness. Deriving their analyses from Latin
American data, social scientists such as Nelson (1979),
Roberts (1968, 1978) and Cornelius (1974) stress the
parochial, fragmented and ephemeral quality of
political resistance among local groups of the urban
poor. All note the tendency of cooptation and vertical
patron-client ties to undermine any wider, class-based
efforts at mobilization. Roberts (1968:201 and
1978:155) specifically blames economic competition and
striving for mobility among informal sector workers for
this state of affairs. Bromley (1982:65-66) cites an
"intensely competitive, individualist mentality" plus
the vulnerability and isolation of those working in the
streets as barriers to political involvement and
protest. These rather bleak viewpoints portray
informal sector workers as either mired in a petty
bourgeois mentality engendered by self-employment and
the illusion of prosperity, or else rendered
politically helpless through economic marginality,
isolation and the fragmentation of the work process. A
useful corrective is offered by the work of Velez-
Ibanez (1983). While acknowledging the reality of
cooptation and the inevitable "failure" of political
protest among such marginal groups, Velez-Ibanez
(1983:241-242) points out that the experience of
collective protest and resistance can itself strengthen
and change those engaged in it. These changes, small
in themselves, thus have important implications for the
long-range development of class alignments and class
consciousness among the urban poor. Such changes also
indicate that capitalist penetration not only isolates
and alienates workers, but also provokes their
resistance.

Difficult as political mobilization is for informal
sector workers to achieve, it does occur. The argument

311

presented here is that market traders, among the whole range of informal sector workers, may have certain built-in advantages in their work situations and their relations of production which favor the growth of political activism. Furthermore, it is suggested that traders' ability of organize in defense of their livelihood may be one of the features which makes petty trade an attractive choice among the selection of informal sector jobs open to the urban poor. [1] Finally, I suggest that once such organizing occurs, it becomes an important factor in determining where, along the continuum of available jobs and class relations, individual workers will end up. More important, such political potential becomes a material force in shaping the emergent class status of those in the informal sector.

Conflicts overselling locations and rights to selling space are endemic wherever marketing and petty trading occur (McGee and Yeung, 1977). In many parts of the world petty traders are involved in a de facto seizure of selling space, and when such seizure is contested the issue becomes a major point of class conflict. In fact, in many parts of the world there is a distinct parallel between the formation of squatter residential settlements and the formation of what might be called "squatter markets" whose personnel have illegally occupied vacant land, not to build houses but to establish market places. Both kinds of squatting provoke direct confrontation with sectors of the urban bourgeoisie. Capitalist development is usually thought of as shaping petty market trade through the goods and credit available and the spread of competition. Yet the conflicts surrounding squatter markets may be another, and equally critical, form of capitalist impact on marketing systems.

There are, of course, dangers in generalizing too widely from a single ethnographic case. Nevertheless, I would like to show the kinds of conditions making it possible for market traders in a large Indian city to organize effectively and to engage in extensive political opposition, despite their seemingly petty bourgeois economic activities. Furthermore, I argue that the process of political mobilization itself does a great deal to create a working-class consciousness, reenforcing the proletarianization created by traders' existing social ties and the relations of production arising from their work. Such material suggests that if the urban poor are, in fact, moving among a variety of jobs in both the formal and informal sectors, market trading and its specific conditions offer this group of urban workers unusual opportunities for politicization and the development of class consciousness.

The conditions which pave the way for such political mobilization include:

1. Cities whose rapid population expansion helps to make petty retail trade comparatively secure in terms of income and steady employment. This security in comparison to other types of jobs makes trading an attractive occupation, drawing in workers from other occupations and swelling the numbers of traders and market places. Such security makes trading an occupation worth defending through political means, and the ability to organize becomes an important component of job security.

2. The ability of traders to monopolize the sale of particular kinds of goods such as fresh foodstuffs because their sale is too risky and labor-intensive to involve the formal sector. This kind of monopoly gives traders a potent political weapon if they should decide to strike.

3. A consciousness which stresses the individual autonomy of the trader. Although, as has been pointed out, many traders actually operate under a system of disguised wage work or commission selling, while others are dependent on suppliers or moneylenders, the absence of daily supervision, harassment and extraction from ever-present employers is important in allowing traders to organize and to seek outside political support. This aspect of what some might call petty bourgeois consciousness can have its uses in the political mobilization of traders, and should be distinguished from individualism.

4. Relations of production and social relations surrounding marketing which create a physical concentration of traders and impose on them a high degree of cooperation. Unlike many other informal sector workers, traders are often concentrated, cheek by jowl, in congested market places. This concentration, often essential to the market's economic functioning, demands a high degree of cooperation to keep

313

the market operating smoothly. In these respects petty traders' work relations often resemble those of industry more closely than those of other informal sector workers. Traders' cooperation is reenforced by extensive ties of kinship, marriage or common birthplace, since success in marketing commonly attracts kin or neighbors. Plattner (1978) in discussing kin-based social networks among Mexican traders, believes that the "closed" nature of the occupation reflects its general desirability. Both the physical concentration and obligatory cooperation among traders also helps foster a kind of patron-client tie which binds the personnel of an entire market place, not just selected individuals, to a politician or political party.

5.   Conflicts between traders and the authorities which can be perceived clearly by participants as instances of class conflict. Disputes over the right to sell on vacant or public land are particularly clear examples, but official complaints that markets are dirty, unhealthy or unsightly can also be seen as aspects of class conflict. Disputes which threaten to eradicate traders' livelihood in marketing are most likely to mobilize traders.

6.   The existence of a political culture which legitimates popular protest and offers some avenues for conflict resolution. As Portes and Walton (1976), Gutkind (1973) and Sandbrook (1977) all point out, the political potential of workers has to be judged against the background of the local political culture. Does that culture offer ideological justification for protests from below? Does it offer mechanisms for the resolution of market disputes, for instance through the formation of patron-client ties between political parties and markets?

Many of these conditions seem to have been met in the retail marketing system of Madras City. There the result is a long-drawn out cycle of political protest on the part of retail traders which has served to define for them a class identity which is more proletarian than bourgeois. The conditions which have created this situation are not unique, either to Madras or to India. Rapid rural to urban migration,

314

overcrowding, the growing value of urban real estate and city authorities who vacillate among venality. Inefficiency and a desire to promote the interests of the middle classes can be found in almost any city.

II. MADRAS CITY

Madras City, located in the South Indian state of Tamilnadu, was founded by European merchants and developed by the British as the regional capital of what was then Madras Presidency. The colonial pattern, which established a few major cities in India with economic dominance over the surrounding agricultural countryside, has not been appreciably altered in South India by the area's slow post-Independence industrialization. Under British rule, Madras City acquired several textile mills, a port, and a regional railroad repair workshop. It was also a major administrative and service center, providing government offices, colleges and universities, hospitals, banking and trading facilities to the surrounding hinterland. Today, it has added a truck factory (built with British capital), an enormous movie industry, and a number of small industries making shoes, cement, chemicals, bicycles and some electronic goods. Its dangerous and antiquated port is declining under competition from more modern ports and the collapse of the colonial-era agricultural trade with Burma and Sri Lanka. Madras remains one of India's major cities, with a population of over 3 million. The city and its hinterland, however, are somewhat peripheral to India's major industrial development, which is concentrated hundreds of miles away in the north of the country.

The profoundest effect of recent economic changes in the area has been the transformation of agriculture, which now receives major capital investment from the rural elite and from an urban professional class. The capitalization of agriculture, most striking in the 20 years of "green revolution" in the state's Thanjavur District, has affected other parts of Tamilnadu State as well. Electrically-powered irrigation, chemical fertilizers and pesticides and new seed varieties have increased the yields of traditional grain and pulse crops. These same changes have also vastly increased the acreage planted in fruit and vegetables intended for urban consumption, while an improved road network has facilitated the movement of these crops to city wholesale markets.

If these changes have brought new prosperity for

315

rural elites and profitable investments for urban professionals, they have also increased unemployment and landlessness among agricultural laborers, artisans and small tenant farmers. These rural poor have been rendered superfluous by changes in the rural economy, and they have made up much of India's vast post-World War II migration into cities. Madras, for instance, increased from a population of 1 million in 1941 to 3 million in 1971. Without skills, literacy or adequate contacts, these migrants can rarely obtain highly-prized work in the city's formal sector. Instead, they find work in small backyard factories or in the service sector, both of which in Madras are virtually coterminous with the informal sector.

A portion of this wave of immigrants moves into petty retail trading, of which the largest branch is the retail selling of fresh fruit and vegetables in dozens of retail market places scattered around the city. This kind of trade in fresh food items is critical in supplying the urban population with the major items of its diet. Local markets, with anywhere from 10 to 250 male and female traders, are located in both residential and business districts. Such markets are housed either in pre-1947 market buildings, city- or privately-owned, or in flimsy, home-made shelters on street corners and pieces of vacant land. The latter are all technically illegal under city laws against encroachment on city or private property. It is this kind of market, formed spontaneously through accretion or through prearranged occupation, which I call a "squatter market." Sarin (1979) has described a parallel phenomenon in the newer city of Chandigarh, and the process is probably taking place in other Indian cities as well. In Madras the distinction between legal and illegal selling is somewhat blurred, in that the busier legal market places have commonly run out of space, and have illegal adjuncts in the form of overflow crowds in the streets outside. Citywide, the trend is toward the growth of new market places and the recruitment of new traders to serve a growing population. Such growth makes this kind of produce trading one of the most frequently available types of informal sector work.

A. Marketing and Marketers in Madras

A variety of characteristics make this kind of produce trading attractive to rural migrants of both sexes in Madras. The work itself is available year round and offers a daily income, however small.

Inexperienced individuals can (and usually do) begin to trade on a very small scale and then work their way up, but the business retains a great degree of flexibility, so that those who have temporary reverses can reduce the scale of their operations without leaving the market place altogether (McGee, 1971). Such trading requires little initial capital, since wholesale suppliers will provide goods on credit and social networks are particularly useful in helping the newcomer find a selling spot in an established market place, where kin frequently claim the right to introduce a relative. An unexplored aspect in the attraction of migrants into petty trade may lie in the work's social aspect, offering among other things the potential for political organizing.

First generation rural migrants to the city make up 54% of the retail traders interviewed, while the bulk of the other 46% are the children or grandchildren of similar migrants who came to Madras from the villages of Tamilnadu and the adjacent state of Andhra Pradesh. Patterns of chain migration ensure that most market places have at their core groups of relatives or fellow villagers who have migrated in pursuit of work opportunities suggested or even arranged for them by previous migrants.

Many of those in Madras who come to retail trading do so after trying a variety of other urban informal sector jobs first. Aside from those who had worked as rural artisans or agricultural laborers, the largest category have worked as domestic or shop servants, as coolies (day laborers), as itinerant hawkers selling goods door to door from baskets, as cart vendors working on commission for wholesale merchants, as truck or rickshaw drivers, as tea stall proprietors, or as assistants to another retail trader. A small but significant number of male traders actually combine formal sector work with part-time trading, using selling spots initially established by their wives or inherited from their parents. A few other men indicated that they had abandoned certain kinds of formal sector employment (such as temporary factory work or dock work) for the relatively greater security of trading.

It is this kind of financial security which traders emphasized repeatedly in interviews when asked why they had gone into trading. Some said that "Any fool can learn this work", while others emphasized the advantages of a virtually assured daily income, however

317

small. Comments such as "At least this way you can eat regularly" were frequent. An equally common theme in these interviews was that of personal autonomy. "There's nobody here to yell at me," said a former domestic servant of her present marketing. Traders vividly recalled the unfairness, maltreatment or humiliations they had experienced in other jobs, and they welcomed their present jobs which, if exhausting, at least allowed them to arrange their own work schedules, to make their own decisions and to evade direct personal exploitation.

The profit levels of retail trading are modest and do not permit everyone to accumulate capital, but the earnings are marked by consistency for those willing to invest long hours of their own labor in the distribution process. Traders estimate that they make a 10% profit on goods bought on credit from the wholesale merchants who supply them. Retail earnings range from a minimal four rupees a day to a high of Rs. 40, with most averaging Rs. 10-15 a day. [2] These earnings compare favorably with the daily two to three rupees a coolie can earn, the five to six rupees a day a rickshaw puller can hope to earn, or the Rs. 150 a month a low level clerk or female grade school teacher can hope for. These profit levels enable a certain number of retailers in the busy markets to go beyond the usual unpaid family labor to hire assistants -- boys or young men [3] who will work for a few months for one or two rupees a day while amassing capital to start their own retail business, gaining experience and building the needed social networks. For a handful of male retail traders there is one additional avenue to major capital accumulation: if they are able to combine daily retail trading with contract sales to the kitchens of restaurants or institutional canteens, they may earn enough to buy a house, some cows, or a rickshaw to lease out.

This means that every retail market contains within it a small number of very successful traders, whose outside contracts have placed them squarely in the petty capitalist class, who own investment property and hire others on a regular basis. The bulk of the market is made up of those less prosperous who nevertheless are able to rent a room or hut in a slum, are able to hire occasional help to supplement the labor of their families and who eat regularly as long as they are not overtaken by illness or family disaster. A smaller number of traders, generally single women or old people, live on the brink of destitution, earning only

318

enough to keep total starvation at bay. One of the important aspects of market politicization is that it is able to overcome many of the internal divisions engendered by these differences in wealth and status within a competitive market place. It was noticeable during the course of field work that those markets which had the greatest internal conflict were those which had not yet encountered external bureaucratic foes, suggesting that external opposition forces the development of internal unity.

It is evident that much of the ordinary retailer's prosperity and earning ability depends on the kind of daily sales turnover possible. This, in turn, depends on the acquisition and retention of a good selling location. Good sales in "hot" or busy market places -- the ambition of every trader -- are possible only in markets located where large crowds of buyers will pass every day. In pursuit of good selling spots, traders flock to major intersections and to central facilities like temples, shopping areas, bus stands or railway stations. Unfortunately, these are also the areas most highly prized by bourgeois property owners, for essentially the same reasons. Clashes are almost inevitable. Thus the necessity grows for the most prosperous market places to defend their selling locations through political organization.

B.   Disputes and Squatter Markets

Amidst this competition for space, it is the busiest Madras markets, located either wholly or partially on "illegal" or contested sites, that become the focus of disputes. Those which attract little trade and thereforeremain within the boundaries of market buildings, or on land which nobody else wants to claim, are likely to be untroubled. Thriving markets, on the other hand, which recruit new traders regularly, bring in crowds of customers and contribute significantly to the economic health of a neighborhood, are always the focus of complaints. Local homeowners, and many of the officials to whom they complain, condemn the markets as noisy, smelly, dirty and a nuisance, a process which Sarin (1979) also details for the Punjabi city of Chandigarh. More forceful opposition, in the form of attempted eviction, comes from land owners who want to oust the market in order to construct offices, apartments or shops in the space.

Even before property owners begin to apply pressure, the illegal status of a great many traders leaves them constantly prey to police threats and demands for bribes and protection money. This kind of abuse is apparently endemic in Indian cities. Jain (1980:30-31) reports it as a major source of difficulty for female traders in the Gujarati city of Ahmedabad. In Madras, if such bribery demands remain modest, a group of traders tends to reach an accommodation and to pay off individual policemen privately. Such demands are likely to escalate over time, however, and traders eventually must seek political protection.

A far more serious form of trouble comes when the police, usually acting on the basis of complaints, raid a market with the aim of dislodging it. Traders are arrested and fined, their goods and equipment are confiscated or destroyed. A good market is hard to dislodge, and traders usually reassemble the next day, but full-fledged raids are costly and disruptive and keep entire neighborhoods on edge for weeks. Few retailers are so prosperous that they can afford to miss days of work, pay large fines or lose the goods, equipment and selling spots in which their slender capital is invested.

From the early 1960s onward, traders in Madras have responded to this situation by forming market associations. According to the recollections of older traders, the first of these associations was formed in that period at the suggestion of a local Congress Party "social worker" (party organizer), who suggested to a group of harassed traders that an association, under Congress Party protection, might halt police raids. This successful solution seems to have been taken up by other markets so that by the early 1970s, when this research was done, eight of the eleven market places studied had associations, complete with elected officials. Each association was allied with one or another of the two major parties in the city. Of these, the Congress-0 Party was a local faction of the ruling national Congress Party and it formed a powerful opposition in Madras City government and in the Tamilnadu state government. The ruling Dravida Munnetra Kazhagam or DMK was a local nationalist party which dominated both the city government and the state legislature. Through these parties market associations sought mediation and protection when disputes over selling space arose, as they did with great regularity.

In allying themselves as the clients of political parties and local politicians, the market associations were following a time-honored tradition in India, through which most formal voluntary associations, from women's groups to trade unions, seek political party sponsorship. For the poor, such alliances provide access to badly needed resources. Wiebe (1975:45), for instance, describes how Madras slum communities get water pipes and electric lines through such political patronage. For the city's market associations the relationship brings mediation of disputes and a certain limited immunity from arrest. In return, traders and their families are expected to vote for the party, and for the particular politician-patron, at election time. In addition, market associations have a more general obligation to display emblems of party loyalty, to close down if their party should announce a citywide strike and to honor party notables at annual functions.

In Madras, however, traders seem to have carried the relationship several steps further. Some associations were no longer simply the passive recipients of favors, but were actively making demands on the parties and on the city government generally. These demands offered a potential challenge to some of the accepted power and property relationships in the city. The market associations, and the disputes they were involved in, can be traced through three stages of development.

In the first stage, traders were apparently simply grateful for temporary mediation efforts which took the pressure off them for varying periods. Thus prominent local political brokers would arrange a settlement whereby traders were immune from arrest if they limited their operations to a single designated selling spot, and promised to give up such "low" behavior as quarreling and fighting. Over time these paternalistic arrangements inevitably broke down. In fact they carried the seeds of their own destruction, because a market where traders had immunity from arrest inevitably attracted more vendors, and the market's swollen size meant a renewal of official pressure for its removal.

As conflict continued, marking a second stage, traders began to use protest methods drawn from both the Gandhian and trade union traditions. Some markets asked customers to sign petitions attesting to the market's economic importance to its neighborhood. Some staged protest marches to the city hall or to the homes of prominent political figures. Although some of these marches apparently involved a humble plea for intercession and protection by the powerful, others were described as more militant, "with banners and slogans." Some associations closed their markets briefly, using a short strike to dramatize their demands. Others fought back against police raids, a situation designed to send shivers through city officials always nervous about the threat of urban unrest. In one case angry vendors besieged a police station where market leaders were being held under arrest. The crowd dispersed only when promised the release of the market leaders and a settlement negotiated by local political brokers. In another case, rioting went on for many hours, and the accidental arrest of middle-class passers-by by overzealous police did nothing to lessen the local scandal and uproar. In this case too there was a hasty official effort to mediate the case.

By the early 1970s several markets had reached a final stage where initiative in the conflict had been reversed. In preparation for local elections the two major parties were actively wooing the support of certain market associations. The associations, in their turn, were asserting themselves through more extensive demands. No longer content to ask for short-term immunity from arrest, some groups were now insisting that the association be given legal title to the market selling location. Two markets successfully demanded the erection of brick market buildings to replace home-made thatch shelters. Furthermore, these markets wanted control over the allocation of space in the new buildings, once completed. Such demands were radical because they challenged the exclusive right of the city's property-owning elite to control construction and the subsequent use of prime real estate.

Strong market associations, able to sustain long-term struggle and to make such demands on city officials, grow out of the extensive cooperation and interdependence which exist among traders. This does not mean that such markets are devoid of competition and interpersonal conflict. They are not. It simply means that these market associations are able to mute or resolve such internal problems. They do so by threatening sanctions such as fines or expulsion and by constantly invoking the need for unity in the face of external threats.

In the first instance, cooperation among traders who are potential competitors is built upon the social ties which bring kin, affines, fellow-villagers and close friends to sell near each other in the same market place. These ties are not enough, however, to hold an entire market place together over a long period of time, particularly when every busy market attracts non-kin and relative strangers. Another and equally extensive form of cooperation develops as marketers work together, often in difficult circumstances. Thus traders will share and adjust their selling space to accomodate each other, will cooperate in building a common roof over adjacent stalls or in hiring transport to move their goods from the central wholesale market. They join the same rotating credit associations, hire each others' sons and nephews, cooperate to keep the market clean and try to smooth over each others' quarrels. They join forces to repel would-be traders trying to use scarce market space without the sanction of those already there. When a destitute vendor dies, others contribute money for funeral expenses.

Market-wide solidarity built up through day-to-day cooperation in mundane matters is sometimes severely tested in the acute stages of political struggle. Thus Pannagal Park market, after years of battling city authorities, had finally gotten the city to legalize its existence and to build it a brick market building, complete with running water, a latrine, and electric light. It was clear, however, even before the traders moved into their prized building, that it contained far too few stalls to house the actual number of vendors in the market. At the critical moment, when the traders were going to move in, the city demanded that the market association exclude the "surplus" traders. The association instead negotiated a compromise. Each stall in the new building was divided in two, and the latrine was also turned over to selling space. Most importantly, richer traders occupying multiple stalls in the old market were persuaded to accept only a single stall apiece in the new building. This arrangement, which penalized the better-off, enabled the last of the poor betel and flower sellers to be crammed into the cherished new building which symbolized the culmination of years of struggle.

This incident also suggests the pressures which keep market leaders from being wholly coopted by the political parties with which the market associations ally themselves. Although market leaders often increase their wealth, prestige and influence by becoming the clients of individual party functionaries, they lose legitimacy with their fellow-traders as soon as they are seen to abandon the interests of the market as a whole. Once a market leader is unable to mobilize

323

his followers to vote or to engage in symbolic displays of party loyalty, he becomes far less useful to the party which once extended patronage to him. In the Pannagal Park case cited above, the market leaders each "owned" several stalls in the old market, and they were obligated to take the lead in sacrificing selling space in order to avoid bitter accusations of bribery and corruption and consequent loss of influence.

C. Political Culture

Various writers have suggested that the ability of the urban poor to organize political resistance is dependent not only on their own social and structural characteristics, but on the political environment in which they must exist. Not only the existing level of political repression but also the role of the specific political culture, which shapes the issues, debates and strategies of local political activism, determines how and where political resistance will emerge. In Madras, market associations are able to incorporate and make use of elements in the national and regional political culture which stress populism. Traders have identified and seized upon strands of a shared ideology, common to both the DMK and the Congress Party, in waging disputes with officialdom and the city's elite. This ideology has become a material force in traders' resistance.

Since its founding in 1949, the DMK has been many things to many people, and it has stressed a variety of ideological issues, reflecting its mixed class base. At certain the party has advocated a virulent regional and ethnic chauvinism, embodying the aspirations of a NonBrahmin professional and landowning elite. At other points it has elaborated an emotionally powerful populism which has been incorporated into a number of the state's agrarian struggles (see Sivertsen, 1963; Beteille, 1971). This populism, in particular, has been fervently absorbed by large numbers of the urban poor. The cornerstones of DMK populism are support for the poor and downtrodden, an advocacy of the rights of the "common man," particularly Untouchables and the urban poor, and an opposition to caste distinctions which create privileges for Brahmins and oppression for Untouchables. In addition, the DMK has done a great deal of grassroots organizing, and its local party offices (or "circles") and reading rooms may well have been one model for the formation of market associations.

In Tamilnadu, the local faction of the Congress

Party is controlled by the rural and urban bourgeoisie, but its ideology has been strongly shaped by contact with its DMK rival, as Barnett (1976) points out. Congress continued to attract votes from the urban poor in a city like Madras because it has an historical association with Gandhi and the independence movement, and because it has adopted some of the populist political idiom of its rival to offset its bourgeois class identification. Probably the most important aspect of Congress ideology to filter down to the city's working class is the legitimacy of popular resistance to illegitimate authority.

It is these ideas, present in the ideologies of both parties, which retail traders stress in talking about themselves, about their political protests, and about their demands on city officials and politicians. They speak repeatedly of their poverty and of their struggles to make an honest living. They talk about "those rich ones, going by in their cars", who want the markets removed. They indicate their need for solidarity, saying, "We poor people must help each other. Who else will help us?" They insist that politicians with claims to legitimacy as representatives of the people must help them, because their protests and their demands are just, and eventually unstoppable. This appeal to populist ideology has certainly moved local politicians to intervene in market disputes, because the traders are widely seen as justified in trying to protect their modest livelihood. Although political figures obviously want to forestall dreaded urban rioting and unrest, their public statements on the occasions of market disputes stress the need for reconciliation because the traders' demands for selling space are reasonable and legitimate.

In presenting themselves as paradigmatic of the urban working poor, the "common man" or woman of Tamil political symbolism, retail traders have obliged the major parties to take their demands seriously, even to court their support. Like rickshaw drivers, another highly visible occupational group, market retailers have become emblematic of the urban poor whose political allegiance each party is anxious to attract. This does not mean, of course, that traders have automatic access to everything they demand. As land becomes scarcer and more valuable in an expanding city, the stakes in every dispute will grow larger. Nevertheless traders have proven their ability to work together, as traders rather than as individual

325

entrepreneurs, within a set of political ideas which legitimate their activities. This gives them a certain freedom to organize -- a freedom lacking to the inhabitants of many other third world cities.

There are, of course, definite limitations on the kind of political mobilization described here, and it would be wrong to imply that these traders are in the vanguard of any kind of radical social change. Although they see the world in terms of an opposition between rich and poor, they do not have a class analysis which explains why the world is so divided. These traders have not envisioned a radically different social order, simply one in which they themselves would suffer fewer impositions, just as the DMK and Congress parties with which they have had the greatest contact stress the amelioration of particular social disabilities but avoid analyzing class oppositions. This framework, if retained, may pave the way for eventual competition between market places, or may hinder the future formation of citywide traders' organizations. Such a vision could also undercut the creation of ties between traders and other working-class groups and organizations. The present forms of patronage-based political incorporation, linking each market separately to a sector of its chosen party to receive rewards in proportion to the vigor of its protests, suggest endless possibilities for cooptation.

At the moment, however, the effect of these disputes has been to create among traders for the first time a group identity based on occupation which overrides internal differences of wealth. In the process traders have identified themselves symbolically with the urban poor in order to wring major concessions from the city's bourgeoisie. Nor is this likely to be a temporary phenomenon, since urban growth and the increase in informal sector trade are ongoing processes in Madras. A built-in part of the process seems to be political conflict about the right of markets to exist. As some markets reach (temporary) accommodation with the city, the cycle of conflict is likely to break out in other markets, engaging an ever-renewed stream of migrant traders. Inevitably these clashes of economic interest between property owners, the city and petty traders will keep class antagonism, protest and political organizing alive. In such a situation, the ability of people to select, remake and mold to their own ends elements of existing political ideology should not be underestimated.

326

III   CONCLUSION

I have presented here a case in which the development of regional capitalism and urbanization have touched off widespread political organizing among market traders in one Indian city.   The material suggests several points of relevance to the study of marketing in many other third world cities.

In the first place, it seems clear that conflict over selling space closely parallels the more familiar squatter movements for the seizure of housing and land. Thus market disputes too need to be analyzed as a major focus of urban protest and politicization.   In identifying disputes between petty traders and local property owners or authorities, the "neat and clean" argument so frequently used to condemn petty trade should be recognized for what it is -- an aspect of class conflict.   Alongside such disputes are others over control of urban real estate, which are also frequently cloaked under objections about market sanitation or safety.

What are needed now are comparative studies of market conflict which define the circumstances under which traders organize or fail to organize.   Babb (this volume), for instance, has indicated that the Peruvian petty traders she studied, although extensively harassed by the authorities, had not developed group strategies of resistance.   In examining such situations, it is useful to ask whether the ability of traders to organize in defense of their jobs forms one of the attractions drawing workers into this kind of informal sector work.

The material presented here strongly suggests that it is wrong to categorize all informal sector workers as incapable of effective political action.   At a time when the complexity of the informal sector itself is increasingly understood, it is also important to recognize the political dimension of informal sector work.   Political activism, or its potential, has an immediate relevance to the class position of informal sector workers and to their relationships with other classes.   This is particularly true if, as Gerry (1979) suggests, that class status is still emergent, rather than firmly fixed.   Thus capitalist penetration may push some informal sector workers into the petty bourgeoisie, or create relations of production which isolate and atomize workers.   Yet for many informal sector workers such as petty traders undergoing

327

proletarianization, the relations of production reenforce this process by encouraging cooperation and resistance while keeping alive a sense of oppression and class-based resentment.

ACKNOWLEDGMENTS

This paper is based on field research carried out in 1971-73 in Madras City with the aid of a National Science Foundation grant. The work involved interviews with 85 fresh produce wholesale merchants in the city's central wholesale market and with 250 produce retail traders located in 11 market places scattered around the city. In addition, large numbers of clerks, market collectors, farmers, supply agents, laborers and politicians connected with the markets were interviewed. I am grateful to Florence Babb, Eva Friedlander, Betty Levin, Frances Rothstein, Nina Schiller, Ida Susser and Joan Vincent for reading and commenting on earlier versions of this paper.

NOTES

1. There are, of course many other reasons for the popularity of petty trade as an occupation, among them the small amount of initial capital needed, the accessibility of selling space through horizontal social networks and flexibility in the scale of trading. The political aspect, however, should not be overlooked.

2. The exchange value of the rupee at the time of the research was about $.15 U.S. However, its local buying power is indicated by the fact that a kilo of cheap rice (enough to feed an adult for a day) could be bought for two rupees. Extremely poor women in the city estimated that they needed a minimum of four to five rupees a day to provide food, cooking fuel and shelter for a household of two adults and several children.

3. Women as well as men enter the produce retail trade, although never in as large numbers. However prevailing cultural norms severely limiting the interaction of men and women serve to marginalize women traders. Among other things, women cannot hire men or boys unless these are also close relatives, and women or girls are never hired, even by other women.

REFERENCES CITED

Barnett, Marguerite Ross
   1976   The Politics of Cultural Nationalism in
           South India. Princeton: Princeton
           University Press.

Beteille, Andre
   1971   Caste, Class and Power. Berkeley:
           University of California press

Bromley, Ray
   1982   "Working in the Streets: Survival Strategy,
           Necessity or Unavoidable Evil?"   in
           Urbanization in Contemporary Latin America.
           A. Gilbert, J. Hardy and R. Ramirez eds. pp.
           59-77, Chichester: John Wiley and Sons Ltd.
Cornelius, Wayne
   1974   "Urbanization and Political Demand Making:
           Political Participation Among the Migrant
           Poor in Latin American Cities" in American
           Political Science Review, Vol. 68, No. 3,
           pp. 1125-1146.

Davies, Rob
   1979   "Informal Sector or Subordinate Mode of
           Production?   A Model in Casual Work and
           Poverty" in Casual Work and Poverty in Third
           World Cities.   R. Bromley and C. Gerry eds.
           pp. 87-104, Chichester: John Wiley and Sons
           Ltd.

Gerry, Chris
   1979   "Small-scale Manufacturing and Repairs in
           Dakar: A Survey of Market Relations within
           the Urban Economy" in Casual Work and
           Poverty in Third World Cities.   R. Bromley
           and C. Gerry eds., pp. 229-250, Chichester:
           John Wiley and Sons Ltd.

Gutkind, Peter
   1973   "From the Energy of Despair to the Anger of
           Despair: The Transition from Social
           Circulation to Political Consciousness Among
           the Urban Poor of Africa" in Canadian
           Journal of African Studies, Vol. 7, pp. 179-
           198.

Jain, D., N. Singh and M. Chand
   1980   Women's Quest for Power. Sahibabad,

Ghaziabad District, U.P.:   Vikas Publishing
House.

Kowarick, Lucio
    1979   "Capitalism and Urban Marginality in Brazil"
            in Casual Work and Poverty in Third World
            Cities. R. Bromley and C. Gerry eds., pp.
            69-85, Chichester: John Wiley and Sons Ltd.

MacEwan Scott, Alison
    1979   "Who Are the Self-Employed?" In Casual Work
            and Poverty in Third World Cities. R.
            Bromley and C. Gerry eds., pp. 105-129,
            Chichester: John Wiley and Sons Ltd.

McGee, T. G.
    1971   The Urbanization Process in the Third World.
            London: G. Bell and Sons Ltd.

McGee, T.G., and Y.M. Yeung
    1977   Hawkers in Southeast Asian Cities. Ottawa:
            International Development Research Centre.

Moser, Caroline
    1980   "Why the Poor Remain Poor: The Experience
            of Bogota Market Traders in the 1970s" in
            Journal of Interamerican Studies and World
            Affairs, Vol. 22, No. 3, pp. 365-387.

Nelson, Joan
    1979   Access to Power: Politics and the Urban
            Poor in Developing Nations. Princeton:
            Princeton University Press.

Plattner, Stuart
    1978   "Occupation and Kinship in a Developing
            Society" in Human Organization, Vol. 37, No.
            1, pp. 77-83.

Portes, A. and J. Walton
    1976   Urban Latin America: The Political
            Condition from Above and Below. Austin:
            University of Texas Press

Ramaswamy, Uma
    1983   Work, Union and Community: Industrial Man
            in South India. Bombay: Oxford University
            Press.

Roberts, Bryan
    1968   "Politics in a Neighborhood of Guatamala

330

City" in <u>Sociology</u>, Vol. 2, No. 2, pp. 105-203.

1970   "Urban Poverty and Political Behavior in Guatemala" in <u>Human Organization</u>, Vol. 29, No. 1, pp. 20-28.

1978   <u>City of Peasants: The Political Economy of Urbanization in The Third World</u>. Beverly Hills: Sage Publications.

Sandbrook, Richard
   1977   "The Political Potential of African Urban Workers" in <u>Canadian Journal of African Studies</u>, Vol. 11, No. 3, pp. 411-433.

Sarin, Madhu
   1979   Urban Planning, Petty Trading and Squatter Settlements in Chandigarh, India" in <u>Casual Work and Poverty in Third World Cities</u>. R. Bromley and C. Gerry eds. pp. 133-160; Chichester: John Wiley and Sons Ltd.

Sivertsen, Dagfinn
   1963   <u>When Caste Barriers Fall</u>. Oslo: Universitets Forlaget.

Vélez-Ibanez, Carloa
   1983   <u>Rituals of Marginality</u>. Berkeley: University of Carolina Press.

Wiebe, Paul
   1975   <u>Social Life in an Indian Slum</u>. Durham: Carolina Academic Press.

PART FOUR

MARKETS IN HISTORICAL PERSPECTIVE

PART FOUR

MARKETS IN HISTORICAL PERSPECTIVE: INTRODUCTION
Frances F. Berdan

The states and empires of early history hold a particular fascination for students of economic exchange systems. These early systems are at the same time familiar and exotic, close and remote. In bold outline, many ancient economic institutions resemble modern forms, and have been given names familiar in modern usage: markets, taxes, foreign trade. Urban centers and peasants are mentioned; money, credit and interest are at times suggested.

Yet on close inspection the economic features of early states take on different hues from those of the twentieth century. These very differences between ancient and modern have inspired vast researches into the nature of early state economies. One incentive for this research has been the variety of questions that can be posed when a historical posture is assumed. These include questions relating to the origins of markets or taxes, processes of economic change in the context of state-building, economic correlates of imperial expansion, and relationships between early non-industrial production and the mechanisms that moved materials from hand to hand.

While studies of historical states have a special potential for answering such questions, they also entail special problems. Evidence, whether archaeological or ethnohistorical, is characteristically incomplete, and often ambiguous or even contradictory. Theoretical approaches and models, designed to enhance the descriptive or explanatory value of fragmentary data, have been mired in endless argument and debate. The resulting reconstructions of these early state and imperial economies have therefore undergone continual readjustments in interpretation as the collection and use of data have become more refined, and as theoretical approaches have become more sophisticated.

Evidence, approach, results. These are the three keys in reconstructing ancient economic systems. Refinements in these key areas are a hallmark of the three articles in this section, all focusing on market systems of early states and empires.

335

In Chapter XIII,Frances Berdan relies almost exclusively on documentary evidence for reconstructing the market structure of imperial Aztec Mexico. After weighing the evidence, she contends that the detailed descriptions of the largest of the Aztec markets are not usefully applied to other markets of the realm. In other words, Berdan questions the use of data from a singular context (such as descriptions of the large Tlatelolco marketplace) to devise generalizations. By approaching the problem of market types from a "compromise model" analysis, she proposes that marketplaces in different niches of the imperial realm responded differently to imperial conquest and its economic and political consequences. Her four types of markets, metropolitan, urban specialized, provincial and extra-empire, and borderland, all made variable adjustments to conditions of local ecology, demography, and dynamic economic and political forces. The result of considering a variety of factors in market variation leads Berdan to conclude that the metropolitan, urban specialized and borderland markets demonstrated strong adaptations to an expanding city and empire, the provincial and extra empire markets exhibited much less transformation as a result of those centralized political and economic forces.

Richard Blanton, in Chapter XIV,brings comparative evidence to bear on broad historical/processual questions. He is particularly concerned with the relations between production and market areas, and the manner in which territorial and political segments are linked economically. By carefully analyzing the core zone and periphery production and distribution systems of prehispanic Mesoamerica, China and pre-industrial Europe, Blanton suggests pre-conditions for capitalism that were present in Europe but absent in Mesoamerica and China. While approaching the broader problem from a specific question, "Would Mesoamerica have developed capitalism in the European fashion had not its historical trajectory been interrupted by European conquest," Blanton arrives at more general conclusions concerning the influence of large-scale economic organizations on rural production and market development - how these may inhibit or promote the move to capitalist production. He concludes that Mesoamerica was much like China, with a well-developed market system and highly intensive core zone agricultural production. Europe, in contrast, had a somewhat more flimsy market structure, and less intensive core zone agricultural production. Along with a seasonally-available labor supply, Europe really

336

had few structurally inhibiting factors for the development of capitalism. On the other hand, China and Mesoamerica had such well-entrenched production and distribution systems that the impetus for change was weak, and unlikely. Here, the comparative method, carefully applying comparable evidence, had yielded intriguing results.

Timothy Earle, in Chapter XV, asks the mystifying question, "Where were the markets in the prehispanic Inca State?" His results derive from the more specific question, "How was the organization of production affected by political changes associated with imperial conquest?" His evidence is based on archaeological recovery of household-level products; his initial goal is to gain a measure of degree of household consumption of different types of commodities as an indication of market development. On the basis of his archaeologically-recoverable materials, Earle devises a scheme for relating production locales with consumption locales, and concludes that most of the commodites consumed by the households, notably subsistence products, could have been produced locally, requiring no elaborate exchange institution such as a market. Some products, however, would have entered regional trading, such as certain lithics, ceramics and metals, and occasional markets, perhaps associated with regular religious events, could have provided the arena for these exchanges. And some few items, such as exotic ceramics and shell, traveled great distances, and might have been in the hands of long-distance professional traders. In all, however, Earle concludes that market development in the Inca realm was certainly less than in Mesoamerica during the same period, and questions the frequent assumption that markets are a "rather automatic adjunct to the development of complex state and imperial organizations." He also concludes that there is at this point a lack of evidence for increasing regional and long-distance exchange following Inca conquest. Because of its rather unusual exchange design, the Inca case should be considered carefully by theoreticians.

In these articles there are no broad typologies or idealized models, but rather a desire to extract, from the detailed archaeological and ethnohistoric record, a more precise understanding of the market milieu of early historic societies. With Berdan we see an interplay of ecological, demographic, economic, and political forces yielding specifically adaptive market forms. With Blanton we find carefully constructed

337

comparisons designed to reveal patterns of process and change in economic production and distribution. And with Earle we find the detailed application of material data to yield a better understanding of economic responses to state and imperial growth. While each of these studies focuses on a particular part or parts of the world, they emphasize the value of careful use of evidence, present interesting approaches to some fundamental questions, and offer results that might usefully serve as hypotheses for testing in other parts of the world.

MARKETS IN THE ECONOMY OF AZTEC MEXICO

Frances F. Berdan, California State University, San Bernardino

The great urban marketplaces of Aztec Mexico:[1] they were crowded, well-regulated, and stocked with wares from all corners of the imperial domain. They were a clearing-house for specialized and exotic products, an arena for wealthy merchants testing their astuteness, a hub of social activity and the latest news and rumor. The grandest of these marketplaces was the one at Tlatelolco, sister-city to the Aztec capital of Tenochtitlan. The Spanish conquistadors marveled at this market's orderly arrangement and noisy business, its overwhelming size and variety of wares on display (Diaz del Castillo 1956: 218-219; Cortes 1977: I: 257-259; Anonymous Conqueror 1971: 392-394). In the mid-sixteenth century, elderly Nahua informants recalled this same marketplace, recounting the special merchandise and moral virtues of selected marketplace sellers (Sahagun 1950-82, Book 9: passim). Indeed, the several documentary descriptions of this most splendid of all Aztec marketplaces are rich in detail and color, although sometimes offering only fleeting glimpses of marketplace rules, procedures and organization.

Much of what is understood about the Aztec market system in general has derived from Spanish sources that document these major urban marketplaces. But these were rather extraordinary markets. They provisioned a large and rather special population: a concentration of nobles with exclusive noble needs, a ruler's splendid household,[2] enclaves of immigrants, headquarters for professional merchants, a heavy concentration of specialized producers.[3] They were located at the center of imperial power, toward which voluminous tribute flowed, and from which haughty merchants trekked on their dangerous yet profitable journeys.

But what of the smaller marketplaces of the imperial realm? More distant from the center of imperial power, serving smaller and more homogeneous populations, seeing caravans of professional Aztec merchants only occasionally, did these marketplaces carry the same range of goods as their urban counterparts? Were they subject to the same types of regulations? Did they respond in the same fashion to imperial expansion as did the urban marketplaces?

339

There has been a recognition that "centralized" and "provincial" markets were distinctive, even distinctive types (Kurtz 1974).[4] Not all marketplaces were mirror images of the one at Tlatelolco; each played a somewhat dissimilar role in the overall imperial economic system. Indeed, the many markets of the imperial domain responded quite differently both to local conditions and to the variable fortunes and accompaniments of the expanding Aztec state. Urban or rural, central to political power or peripheral, within the bounds of the empire or beyond, marketplaces made varying adjustments to the structure and activities of the Aztec conquest state. The conditions underlying these differing responses, and the varying appearance of marketplaces in different niches of the realm, provide the focus for this article.

I. THE AZTEC IMPERIAL STRUCTURE

The years 1430-1519 saw the growth and expansion of Aztec military power throughout much of central Mesoamerica. In 1430, the three city-states of Tenochtitlan, Texcoco and Tlacopan formed a Triple Alliance, a powerful coalition for conquest of regions beyond their localized domains in the Valley of Mexico. By 1519, the imperial Aztec domain contained some 38 culturally-distinct and geographically diverse provinces.[5]

The growth of this empire was accompanied by a dramatic increase in the rate of urbanization and an intensification of occupational and regional specialization. It also saw an increasing consolidation of power and resources in the hands of the Triple Alliance rulers (especially the Tenochtitlan ruler), and an enlargement of the nobility "class" along with a concentration of social and economic perquisites in the hands of this elite.

While the administration of this expanding empire required an increasingly complex bureaucratic structure, the conquered provinces remained only loosely attached to their conquerors. Regional and provincial city-state rulers, after being conquered by the Triple Alliance, were frequently maintained in their traditional positions. In essence, the imperial administration was characterized by little more than the establishment of certain high-ranking Aztec officials (usually tribute collectors) in the provinces, and the imposition of special tribute levies. More rarely, a province might be required to

340

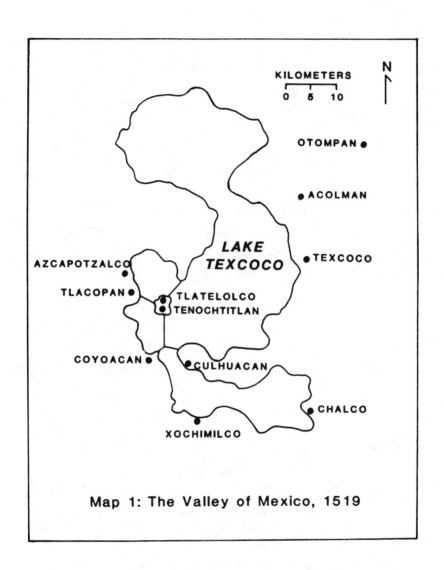

KILOMETERS

0   5   10

N

OTOMPAN ●

● ACOLMAN

LAKE
TEXCOCO

● TEXCOCO

AZCAPOTZALCO
●

TLACOPAN ●

TLATELOLCO
TENOCHTITLAN

COYOACAN ●

● CULHUACAN

● CHALCO

XOCHIMILCO ●

Map 1: The Valley of Mexico, 1519

Map 1.   The Valley of Mexico, 1519.

support an Aztec military garrison, provision an Aztec
army traveling through its territory, or adhere to
special market requirements. In general, the local and
regional social, economic and political structures in
the provinces remained essentially unchanged by the act
of Triple Alliance conquest.

Much of the military effort of the empire was
expended in reconquering rebellious provinces,
especially during the first two decades of the
sixteenth century. Indeed, Moctezuma II (1502-1520)
spent much of his reign reconquering territories
initially subdued by his energetic predecessor,
Ahuitzotl (1486-1502).[6] In this loosely-organized
and oftimes unstable political environment, the
sixteenth-century empire maintained its paramount
position through frequently reaffirmed military
dominance,[7] and through strategies aimed at
controlling the economic resources of its tenuous
realm. Beyond direct control of land and labor, these
strategies involved the imposition of tribute levies
and the regulation of foreign trading enterprises. The
impact of military expansion and imperial policy on the
structure of marketplace exchange was generally
indirect and, indeed, quite uneven throughout the
empire's broad sphere of influence.

A.   Variation in Markets and Trade

On close inspection, the numerous markets of Aztec
Mexico exhibit considerable variation, representing
special adaptations to local environments, geographical
situation, and imperial forces. These market
variations can be grouped into several useful
categories: metropolitan,[8] urban specialized,
provincial/extra-empire, and borderland markets.

1.   Metropolitan markets

The Aztec metropolitan market is exemplified by the one
at Tlatelolco, indeed a market in a class by itself.
It served perhaps 20,000-25,000 persons daily, and on
every fifth day, "market day,"[9] an estimated 40,000-
50,000 persons participated in the market (Anonymous
Conqueror 1971: 392).[10]

Marketplace judges and supervisors carried heavy
responsibilities and had extensive authority in this
market: they heard cases of dispute or theft, summarily
sentenced violators, and perhaps could regulate

342

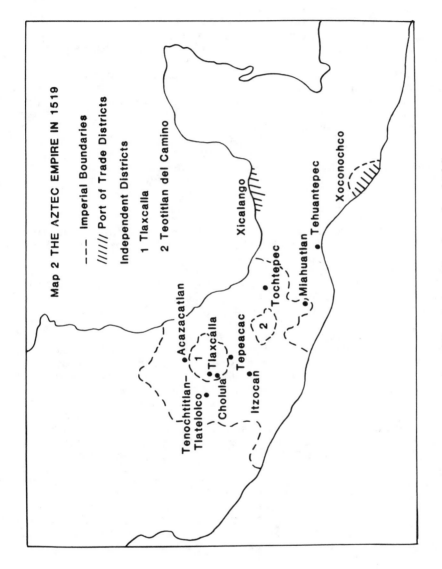

Map 2. The Aztec Empire in 1519.

prices [11] and oversee exchange activities in general (AGI Audiencia de Mexico 68; ENE: 15: 164; Diaz del Castillo 1956: 216; Cortes 1963: 73: Sahagun 1950-82, book 8: 67, 69). It is possible that these overseers were also high-ranking merchants, or <u>pochtecatlatoque</u> (Sahagun 1950-82, book 8: 67).[12] Other officials were stationed at strategic entrances to the market, especially where the canoes were unloaded, to collect a tax levied on market vendors. Supposedly the taxes were assessed individually, and on a daily basis - this may in fact have been the case in this huge and highly diversified metropolitan market. Apparently the right to tax, and the tax itself, belonged to the ruler (Cortes 1977: 263; Torquemada 1969: II: 560; Duran 1967: I: 180).[13] In addition to this obligation, the "market folk" were also obligated to supply war provisions - this may have taken the form of a special purpose levy in kind - foodstuffs are the only provisions mentioned (Sahagun 1950-82, book 8: 69).

Of all imperial markets, this one exhibited by far the widest range of wares for sale, and the greatest diversity of buyers and sellers. The vendors exhibited local lacustrine products along with distant tropical luxuries. In fact, the entire empire and beyond was the hinterland for this active market: cacao beans came from as far as Guatemala, chiles from Oaxaca and the northern Gulf Coast, and cotton cloaks from the remotest corners of the empire. A full range of daily subsistence needs could be served by a visit to this market, including a choice among at least 27 varieties of chiles,[14] 15 types of maize,[15] five grades of cotton,[16] and 10 regional varieties of fancy gourd bowls [17] (Sahagun 1950-82, book 10: 65-78). Feathers from every imaginable bird were available, as well as tropical fruit delicacies, and an extensive menu of prepared tamales. Beyond subsistence, albeit different standards of subsistence for nobles and commoners, a dazzling array of exotic tropical products and exquisite works of metal or feather art could be viewed and purchased (viewed by all, but conspicuous use of such luxuries was restricted to persons of elite standing). Obviously, the full range of Aztec persons, from a ruler with his palace of thousands, to a commoner's small household, could be provisioned through this single "primate" market.

Tlatelolco was officially a conquest of the greatest power of the Triple Alliance, Tenochtitlan. Conquered in 1473, mid-way in the empire's history, the annexation of Tlatelolco to Tenochtitlan included not only lands and subjects, but especially control over the prized marketplace, valued at more than a hundred towns [18] (Alvarado Tezozomoc 1975: 396; Hicks n.d.a.). This conquest also channeled the loyalties and energies of the far-ranging professional merchants (pochteca or oztomeca) to the service of the Tenochtitlan ruler, for there were significant concentrations of such merchants in Tlatelolco barrios (calpulli).[19]

These professional merchants (in their many "guises") were purveyors of some goods in the Tlatelolco market (Sahagun 1950-82, book 10: passim). They specialized in items of high value and prestige: gold, decorated cloaks, feathers, cotton, cacao and slaves (ibid: 59, 61, 63-64, 75). They ranged from the principal merchants (ueicapan tlacatl) who dealt in fine, decorated cloaks, to the wealthy slave dealers (tecoani) to undistinguished pochteca (dealing in gold and feathers) and oztomeca (providing bulky goods from markets in the tierra caliente, such as cotton and cacao). These merchants, having traveled to distant markets to obtain such luxuries (or having commissioned other merchants to do so for them), would certainly frequent the most urban of all marketplaces, with its great concentration of potential noble buyers. And, importantly, their activities forged a link among markets within and beyond the imperial domain.

Also providing links with outlying markets were the tlanecuilo, or regional merchants.[20] The objects of their trade were, for the most part, a far cry from the luxury wares purveyed by the guild merchants: cacao, maize, amaranth seeds, chili, tortillas, wheat, [21] sandals, cotton, palm fiber cloaks, painted gourd bowls, cane carrying baskets, turkey and salt (ibid: 65-94). Five of these items included distinguishable regional varieties, some coming from the distant reaches of the empire and beyond. It is significant that in all but one case (wrinkled chia), whenever regional varieties are mentioned, so also are the tlanecuilo. It may have been their special efforts which supplied the urban dwellers with such a remarkable assortment of consumer goods. Many varieties of cacao, maize, chili, cotton and gourd bowls would have been either imported from long distances by individual merchants, or would have worked their way through successive regional marketplaces to finally reach Tlatelolco. In most cases, there would have been a combination of possibilities. For example, cacao and cotton were imported by oztomeca (guild

345

merchants), retailed by <u>tlanecuilo</u> and reportedly marketed by the field owners themselves.[22] Invariably, the owners, workers or manufacturers of a given product are listed as also selling that item in the Tlatelolco marketplace; only in these few cases are full-time merchants also mentioned. Why they are involved with these particular goods is somewhat mystifying. The five items from broadly diverse regions are understandable - the <u>tlanecuilo</u> gained economically by transporting and selling them, especially in the urban marketplace. By expending this effort, the value of the item increased: this served as their means of livelihood. Of the remaining items, only the palm fiber cloaks may have required the services of <u>tlanecuilo</u> for reasons of distance. The others may have been in sufficiently great demand in the urban environment to support specialized retailers.[23]

2. Urban Specialized Markets

The Tlatelolco market dwarfed the markets of the neighboring lakeside cities, even those of Tenochtitlan itself. Cortes was so awed by the sight of the Tlatelolco market that he barely, and most superficially, mentioned the other markets of the island sister-cities. "The city has many squares where markets are held, and trading is carried on" is all he says (1977: I: 257). The Anonymous Conqueror, somewhat more observant, offers that "aside from this large plaza [Tlatelolco] are others, and markets in which are sold food, in various parts of the city" (1971: 394).[24] This comment suggests that some of the markets in the surrounding urban area may have been specialized. The very size and density of Tenochtitlan (150,000-200,000 persons spread over more than 12 square kilometers) would make the establishment of food markets throughout the city highly practical, and these markets may have sold nothing else. Foods were also available in the large markets of the region's second city, Texcoco (Alva Ixtlilxochitl 1965: 243). With a population of some 30,000 inhabitants (Sanders, Parsons and Santley 1979: 198), this city had extensive marketplaces, the major market being held every fifth day, with ordinary markets (undoubtedly emphasizing utilitarian goods) held daily (<u>ibid</u>: 175; Cortes 1977: I: 248; Torquemada 1969: II: 559). This and other urban markets would have displayed a wide variety of goods - luxury and utilitarian, local and exotic. Nonetheless, some of these markets became known for

346

their specialized offerings. Acolman was famous for its dogs; Texcoco for cloth, ceramics and fine gourds; Otompan and Tepepulco for turkeys; Azcapotzalco for slaves [25] (Duran 1967: I: 180-181; Motolinia 1971: 375-376; Alva Ixtlilxochitl 1965: 151).

The fame of the Acolman dog market continued well into the Colonial period:

> It was established that dogs were to be sold in the periodic market at Acolman and that all those desirous of selling or buying were to go there. Most of the produce, then, which went to the tianguiz consisted of small- and medium-sized dogs of all types, and everyone in the land went to buy dogs there--as they do today, because at this time the same trade is carried on. One day I went to observe the market day there, just to be an eyewitness and discover the truth. I found more than four hundred large and small dogs tied up in crates, some already sold, others still for sale. When a Spaniard who was totally familiar with that region saw [my amazement], he asked, "Why are you astonished? I have never seen such a meager sale of dogs as today! There was a tremendous shortage of them!" (Duran 1971: 278).

It seems that these specialized markets were established through administrative policy, apparently for the regulation of traffic in these important goods:

> In this land the sovereigns had set up a regulation regarding the markets: they were to take the form of fairs or markets specializing in the selling of certain things. Some markets, therefore, became famous and popular for these reasons: it was commanded that slaves were to be sold at the fair in Azcapotzalco and that all the people of the land who had slaves for sale must go there and to no other place to sell. The same can be said of Itzocan. Slaves could be sold in these two places only (Duran 1971: 277-78).

However strong the intent of the administrative policy, it does not seem to have been rigidly carried out. Some historical sources tell us that slaves could be sold in any market, and on a daily basis (Motolinia 1971: 371; AGI Patronato 184 #2). Furthermore, the Tlatelolco market offered all the goods listed for specialized markets, including slaves (Diaz del Castillo 1956: 215-217; Cortes 1963: 72-73; Sahagun

347

1950-82, book 8, 67-69). Some markets may have become renowned for their available range and quality of specific wares, but it is doubtful if the selling of these types of goods was restricted to those markets alone. However, the specialized markets would have served as reliable sources of certain items of generally low demand which may not have appeared regularly at other markets. This especially applied to elite items of somewhat occasional purchase: dogs, turkeys, and slaves.

Other surrounding markets also came to emphasize particular specialties, but more from local availability of certain products than from administrative edict. For example, nearby Coyoacan carried a wide range of wood products and, interestingly, these products were sold by "wood dealers" (quauhnecuillo) rather than "sellers" or "makers," as was most of the other merchandise (Anderson, Berdan and Lockhart 1976: 138-149). These regional merchants may have marketed wood products in fairly sizable lots, also carrying them to other nearby markets on a staggered weekly schedule. Indeed, since their taxes seem to have covered monthly or annual attendance at the market, it may be assumed that these retailers followed a relatively consistent and well-entrenched market schedule. Aside from regional merchants, professional merchants (oztomeca) and "makers of things" also sold in this market, as they did in the Tlatelolco market.[26]

Many of these urban centers were also renowned craft centers: for example, Xochimilco for lapidary work, Azcapotzalco for gold and silver work, and Tlatelolco for featherwork. Yet, interestingly, the Azcapotzalco market was known for slaves not silver, and the Xochimilco market did not seem to have any special attraction. Perhaps in so dense an urban agglomeration, with many cities and even more markets, there was no particular advantage in matching market craft specialization with community specialization in production of crafts.

Several Valley of Mexico urban centers were also important headquarters for professional merchant guilds.[27] These merchants traveled great distances throughout the empire and beyond, invariably carrying items high in value and low in bulk. While the primary destination for their merchandise would have been the Tlatelolco market, many may have traded their wares in the markets of their home-city, thus diversifying the

348

market offerings of these cities.

Little is known of the administrative regulations placed on these markets, but they were probably less rigid than those of the Tlatelolco market. Surely the vendors of these markets were taxed. And, as at Tlatelolco, the tax probably belonged to the local ruler (tlatoani). For Coyoacan, the only other market for which such detailed data is extant, the tax was clearly the property of the ruler. Unlike tax collection in Tlatelolco, the Coyoacan market payments were made monthly or annually, and by groups rather than individuals (ibid.). This may reflect the smaller and more intimate nature of a peripheral urban market.

These urban markets derived their specializations from the subsistence requirements of a highly concentrated urban populace (e.g., the Tenochtitlan food markets), from economic forces reflecting a need for reliable supplies of elite consumables (e.g., the Azcapotzalco slave market, the Acolman dog market, and the turkey markets), or from the production of locally-available goods (e.g., the Coyoacan wood market). In essence, the Tlatelolco metropolitan market was encircled by a zone of smaller, in many cases specialized markets. These markets could have served as intermediate steps in the transference of certain goods from region to region; this is documented for the turkeys of Otompan and Tepepulco, who were carried from these markets to the metropolitan market (Torquemada 1969: II: 559).[28]

3. Provincial and Extra-empire Markets

Beyond the great urban agglomerations of the Valley of Mexico, smaller markets served as hubs for lively regional and inter-regional exchange. Trade in these markets was stimulated by a variety of factors, including localized production of specific products; location along busy commercial routes; the imposition of tribute by an imperial, regional or local rulership; and the direct intervention in market activities by political decree. In all, these "outlying" markets exhibited generally similar characteristics regardless of the dominant or conquering power - thus I have grouped Aztec provincial markets with those external to the empire. Indeed, the Aztec imperial structure was a rather superficial overlay of more ancient city-states and kingdoms; Aztec tribute demands were built on, even relied on, antecedent market networks. While in some few cases the Aztec rulership directly interfered with a market's functioning, this was rare. On the whole, provincial markets do not seem to have suffered severe or sustained disruption from the act of Aztec conquest.

The offerings of many of these marketplaces reflected the local ecology, emphasizing production specialties of the immediate vicinity (PNE:IV, V, VI: passim). However, some of them also exhibited goods transported from great distances. The market at Tepeacac, for example, while providing locally-produced agricultural products, highlighted woven cloth and clothing. This was the case even though the raw cotton was obtained from as far as 120 kilometers away. Reportedly the people of Tepeacac journeyed this distance to the tierra caliente to obtain the cotton; the women of Tepeacac then wove that cotton into cloth, proceeding to sell it in the market (PNE:V: 40-41). This same Tepeacac market also served as a distribution point for salt, which was not native to the region but obtained from a distance of 72 kilometers (PNE:V: 40). People from as far away as 96 kilometers trekked to this market for their salt provisions, undoubtedly also attracted there by its wide range of available goods, including an abundance of maize (PNE:V: 41, 83, 150, 157, 162). Such a broad service area is somewhat unusual, the more typical service area for a large regional market (involving these types of goods) being between 38 and 58 kilometers (PNE:V: 3, 88, 122, 131, 150; VI: 36, 126, 130, 143).

The localized availability of key subsistence goods seems to have stimulated inter-regional exchange and particularly the development of professional traveling merchants at a regional level. Salt, cotton and cacao were especially subject to transport over long distances. Both individual householders and merchants might travel over 200 kilometers for salt or cotton (PNE:IV: 204), and an undetermined distance for cacao. Merchants were particularly active in carrying salt and cotton, products which were bulky and not widely produced (PNE:IV: 122, 181, 204; VI 78, 85, 112, 164, 241; Sahagun 1950-82, book 10:84). When individual peasant householders were involved, they were the ones who typically journeyed to the source of the salt, cacao or cotton; the producers of these commodities seem not to have transported their products[29] (e.g., PNE:IV: 67, 98, 103, 107, 113, 181, 223; V: 30, 130, 157, 162; VI: 4, 31, 85, 143, 164, 225, 230). This is to be expected, given the great demand, limited supply and hence high value placed on these special commodities. Given this, it may also be expected that trade in those goods would be of particular interest to professional merchants. Indeed, for Tlatelolco, Sahagun (1950-82, book 10:84) says that the salt retailer (<u>iztanecuilo</u>) "sets out on the road, travels with it, goes from market to market..." The somewhat surprising anomally is cacao: while regional merchants were active in this trade, more commonly individual householders in the provinces may have trekked to the <u>tierra caliente</u> to secure this prized item (PNE:V: 181-182, 175; VI: 131, 136, 164, 321).

Trade in these high-demand commodities was frequently intertwined. For example, the people of Teotitlan del Camino, external to the Aztec domain, manufactured <u>huipiles</u> (women's shifts) and sold them to merchants who carried them to Guatemala, Chiapas, Suchitepeques and Xoconochco. There they exchanged the huipiles for cacao, which the people of Teotitlan lacked. Nor did the people of Teotitlan grow their own cotton for their extensive <u>huipilli</u> manufacture; this they obtained from the distant Tehuantepec area (PNE:IV: 107). While the "type" of merchant involved in this intricate web is not specified, they were probably non-guild regional merchants, given the relative ease with which they would have necessarily crossed and recrossed Aztec imperial boundaries.[30]

For all those goods, salt, cotton and cacao, the householders exchanged small surpluses of their subsistence production. This included both raw materials and manufactured items: maize, beans, chile, chia, fish, vegetables, fruits, honey, pinole, gourd bowls, mats and cloaks (PNE:V: 157, 182-183; VI: 126, 131, 136, 164, 165, 261, 321). Likewise, full-time merchants trafficked in these more generally produced goods. However, whenever salt, cotton or cacao were exchanged for one another, merchants rather than peasant householders were most likely to be involved in the transaction (PNE:IV: 241, 246; VI: 112).

Regional merchant activity in outlying areas was extensive and lively. An excellent example comes from within the bounds of Aztec military control.[31] Miahuatlan in the Zapotec area became an entrepot for the distribution of salt, brought there from Tehuantepec nearly 200 kilometers away. The full-time merchants who engaged in this distribution also dealt in fish, maize, chile and cotton, carrying these goods from marketplace to marketplace in the Miahuatlan area (PNE:IV: 122). But the grandest marketplace of the region was at Miahuatlan, where a great <u>tianguiz</u> was

351

held weekly (in conformity with the Spanish calendar), and reputedly everything was bought and sold there (PNE:IV: 126). The full-time merchants hailed from surrounding communities as well as from Miahuatlan itself: Coatlan merchants specialized in the salt trade; merchants from other unspecified communities dealt in cochineal [32] (PNE:IV: 126, 136), and the commercial entrepreneurs from Miahuatlan itself specialized in amole, used for cleaning clothes (PNE:IV: 126). These merchants were regionally-based, and not the guild-organized pochteca from the Valley of Mexico who primarily specialized in the trading of exotic luxury goods. Such regional professional merchants probably provided the backbone of the marketplace exchange system in the provinces; still, as in Tlatelolco and Coyoacan, the majority of the vendors were those who sold small lots of their own surplus production.

Markets that came to be known for specialized goods transported from great distances were usually those located along busy commercial routes. Major provincial trading centers such as Tepeacac and Acazacatlan may have served as "gateway communities" which are

> ...generally located along natural corridors of communication and at the critical passages between areas of high mineral, agricultural, or craft productivity; dense population; high demand or supply for scarce resources; and, at the interface of different technologies or levels of socio-political complexity. They often occur along economic discontinuities in the free movement of merchandise. The function of these settlements is to satisfy demand for commodities through trade and the location of these communities reduces transportation costs involved in their movement (Hirth 1978: 37).

Tepeacac has already been mentioned as a trading center for cotton cloth and salt - it was located on a major commercial route from the highlands to the tropical lowlands. Acazacatlan, north and east of the Valley of Mexico, was likewise situated on an important trade route, again from highlands to lowlands - this highland market seems to have specialized in selling cotton and, to a lesser extent, salt (Saindon 1977: 46). In addition to the forces for "economic discontinuity" mentioned by Hirth, these communities and others like them also sat at the juncture of ethnic and linguistic

352

boundaries (Gerhard 1972: 278, 390).

A notably special case representing "gateway" attributes was the market at Itzocan which specialized in slaves, perhaps by imperial decree (Duran 1967: I: 180-181). Itzocan was located at the confluence of two major north-south trade routes. These were routes heavily traveled by Valley of Mexico professional merchants, and the wealthiest of these merchants dealt in slaves. The Itzocan market, located not quite mid-way between the Valley of Mexico and the merchant outpost of Tochtepec, may have been frequented by these professional slave merchants.

As in the great urban centers of the Valley of Mexico, the major markets of "outlying areas" corresponded roughly to seats of local dynastic rulership (tlatoani centers). This, however, was not a perfect correspondence, since many towns lacking rulers nonetheless had active and lively markets (Smith 1979, Hicks n.d.b.). Frequently, as in provinces of the Aztec empire, the local ruler and his subjects answered to a more powerful sovereign and were required to satisfy imperial tribute demands on a regular or special-purpose basis.

It is specifically documented that a province gave in tribute those goods readily available to it (Duran 1967: II: 168, 255, 321; Zorita 1963: 117; Sahagun 1950-82, book 8: 53-54; PNE:IV: 48, 248-249: VI: 108-109, 205, 285). Since many goods were demanded in tribute that were not actually produced within the province, it is likely that the mechanisms by which those goods worked their way into the province were more ancient than the imposition of tribute. These mechanisms, in fact, comprise a complex array of economic transactions in the provincial areas. The major means by which goods entered a province from beyond its boundaries fall into three categories: (1) individual commercial effort whereby local householders journeyed across provincial boundaries to obtain needed goods; (2) individual commercial activities of the producers of those goods in extra-empire regions, themselves carrying the goods into the Aztec province; or (3) the activities of professional merchants, also traveling across provincial borders. Each of these processes was present and lively in the provinces. By whatever means, the extensive regional market network characteristic of highland Mexico served as the focal point for this exchange activity, and would have allowed goods to flow from nonconquered areas into

353

conquered provinces. From the point of view of the conquerors, the conquest of a single province allowed the empire to obtain through tribute not only locally-produced goods, but also goods which had traditionally passed into the region through the more ancient market network. From the point of view of the provincial commoners, they probably undertook marketplace activities much as they had prior to imperial conquest.

For the local householder or petty trader, the boundaries of the empire were seemingly quite fluid and permeable. For the Aztec state-sponsored professional merchant, however, trade across imperial boundaries was a risky business (Berdan 1983). To facilitate the activities of these professional merchants, with their expensive luxury wares, certain entrepots emerged which I call borderland markets.

4. Borderland Markets

Borderland markets, on the geopolitical fringes of major city-states or empires, seem to have been especially subject to state interest and state-control. These markets, whether through administrative decree or commercial convenience, especially catered to the state-level professional merchants. Cholula was probably the most famous of these markets. An important merchant and pilgrimage center, it was strategically (and rather dangerously) situated on the border between the habitually warring states of Tlatelolco/Huexotzinco and the Triple Alliance. Throughout the fifteenth and early sixteenth centuries, Cholula waffled between its own independence and its allegiance to hostile neighbors, nonetheless retaining its reputation as a major merchant and market center.[33] It appears that Cholula functioned quite in the spirit of a neutral or quasi-neutral port of trade - professional merchants who invited assassination by entering hostile territory could safely exchange their exotic wares in this "no-man's land."

As for Tlaxcalla, arch-enemy of the Aztecs, their market was reported by Cortes (1977: 210; Gibson 1952: 15) as displaying gold, silver, precious stones, and feather ornaments - all of this quite contrary to their own professed poverty. This market, like several within Aztec imperial bounds, may have performed a "borderland function" for Tlaxcalla.

Nearby Tepeacac also may have served a similar

354

purpose. By Aztec imperial order, when Tepeacac was conquered it was required to hold a market on a designated day. A wide variety of luxury goods, including rich cloaks, stones, jewels, feathers of different colors, gold, silver (and other metals), skins of jaguars and ocelots, cacao, rich loin cloths and sandals were to be sold in this market (Duran 1967: II: 62).[34] Given the types of goods to be available (luxuries), it is probable that the Valley of Mexico professional merchants frequented the Tepeacac market. It may well have been under the state's watchful eye for purposes of making these tropical or specialized luxury wares more readily available to those merchants. Likewise, merchants from other parts of the empire, and perhaps beyond, may have had access to the offerings of this market.[35]

Another interesting example was the market at Cohuaxtlahuaca in present-day Oaxaca. Professional merchants from several Valley of Mexico cities frequented this market before its conquest by the Triple Alliance, obtaining gold, feathers, cacao, fine gourd bowls, clothing and thread made from rabbit fur (Duran 1967: II: 185). It was conquered by Moctezuma I, at which time Cohuaxtlahuaca was on the fringes of Aztec expansion (Kelly and Palerm 1952: 291-295).

Borderland markets such as these were of particular interest to imperial and city-state rulers. Their very location allowed luxury goods to travel across otherwise hostile and perhaps closed borders. While petty traders could cross such borders with little difficulty, state-sponsored professional merchants were too often flagged as political agents to travel easily in enemy territory (Berdan 1983). The assurance of a lively luxury trade in borderland markets provided these merchants with an appropriate and safe setting for their entrepreneurial efforts.

II. FACTORS IN MARKET VARIATION

Juan de Torquemada, in 1615, saw fit to "reduce all [the markets] to those of the city of Mexico [Tenochtitlan]; because you will see that through these it is possible to understand the markets of all the other parts of the land" (1969: 555).[36] Yet the markets of "all the other parts of the land" did not so precisely mirror one another. While they all conformed to some staggered scheduling, the larger markets also met daily. While most markets carried a sufficiently

355

broad range of goods to satisfy local needs, some catered to buyers from great distances. Such markets specialized in certain desired goods, such as dogs, turkeys or slaves; or they were entrepots for professional long-distance merchants with their luxury wares; or they attracted buyers for their wide selection of products - from maize to jade. On the other hand, some markets had regular, predictable deficiencies of key products, such as salt or cotton (Berdan 1980:39).

Metropolitan, urban specialized, provincial/extra-empire and borderland markets all contributed to provisioning the people of Aztec Mexico at prescribed, desired or feasible standards of living. Yet each made its contribution in a unique way. Many factors, ecological, demographic, economic and imperial contributed to a market's unique character.

Ecologically, the markets of the realm tended to respond to local product availability. This tendency was particularly noticeable in markets relatively unaffected by the forces of urban growth and imperial power; that is, the provincial and extra-empire markets. Markets situated in strategic geographic locations, especially between highland and lowland regions, often augmented their local offerings with distantly-produced commodities.

The great urban concentrations of the Valley of Mexico had somewhat different market needs than the small communities of the hinterland. The metropolitan and urban markets responded to sheer size by offering great quantities and variety. But these markets also served a somewhat different clientele than the outlying markets: especially large numbers of nobles with expensive tastes, and concentrations of craft artisans with needs for special raw materials and outlets for their finished products. The number and diversity of consumers probably exerted an influence measured in degree rather than kind: the metropolitan market always had an abundance of exotic wares, the small provincial market may only occasionally have seen such luxuries; the metropolitan market displayed a wide array of foodstuffs, the small provincial market may have had regular deficiencies in some subsistence products.

The markets of the Aztec realm also responded differently to the economic needs and requirements of Triple Alliance military expansion. The imposition of

356

tribute on conquered provinces tended to "solidify" long-existing market relations, in that tribute demands frequently called for goods available only through market networks. The activities of Valley of Mexico professional merchants were encouraged by the Aztec state, not only through state-sponsored trading (and spying) missions, but also through the regulation of certain markets at borderlands - regulations particularly favorable to merchants' trade in luxuries. The interest of the Aztec state in market activities waned with distance from the centers of imperial power. Exceptions to this involved centers with strategic access to trade routes (such as gateway communities), locales controlling resources perceived by the imperial powers as critical, or unstable borderlands.

All the markets of the realm made varying adjustments to local ecology, demographic changes, and economic-political forces. The provincial and extra-empire markets adapted primarily to their local ecological settings, with variations deriving from geographic situation, especially along trade routes, localized availability of key products, and the nature of tribute demands. The metropolitan, urban specialized and borderland markets exhibited strong adaptations to the demographic, economic and political demands of an expanding city and empire. As the fate of the empire changed, so too did the nature of these markets.

Acknowledgements

An earlier version of this paper was read by Richard Blanton, Timothy Earle, Frank Salomon, and Kathleen Truman. Their valuable comments are greatly appreciated.

Notes

1. Use of the term "Aztec" has become somewhat problematical in recent research, since none of the central Mexican groups seem to have referred to themselves by that name. "Aztec" and "Aztec empire" are most appropriately used in reference to a political-military alliance of three major city-states in the Valley of Mexico (Tenochtitlan, Texcoco and Tlacopan), the empire including considerable ethnic variation and political "disunity" within these imperial bounds. When discussing individual cultural groups or political

entities, I will refer to them by specific names.

2. The grandpalace of Moctezuma II (1502-1520) was
    said to house artisans and servants, nobles and
    government officials, along with the ruler's
    numerous wives and children. Cortes speaks of 300
    men to look after the royal aviary and another 300
    to care for birds of prey and zoo animals
    (1977:I:266). To this he added over 600 nobles who
    were present at Moctezuma's palace every day, the
    servants of these nobles overflowing two or three
    palace courtyards. Bernal Diaz del Castillo
    (1956:211) estimates that over 1000 dishes of food
    and 2000 containers of cacao were served to the
    ruler's unnumbered palace guards. To these must
    be added vast numbers of artisans, laborers (such
    as masons and carpenters), government officials,
    and entertainers.

3. Calnek (1976: 289-291) emphasizes the cosmopolitan
    character of Tenochtitlan-Tlatelolco, with its
    large complement of immigrant, specialized, and
    transient (especially market-day) populations.

4. Kurtz (1974) distinguishes between "peripheral" and
    "transitional" market types, the latter emerging as
    a result of the urbanization process.

5. This is the total from the Codex Mendoza. The
    Matricula de   Tributos contains 33 provinces
    (it   is presumed that some pages have been lost),
    and the Informacion of 1554 (Scholes and Adams
    1957) lists 36 provinces. For a fuller discussion,
    see Berdan 1976.

6. Conrad and Demarest (1984) make this very clear.
    For a detailed account of Aztec conquests achieved
    by each ruler see especially Kelly and Palerm 1952.

7. In addition to direct conquest and reconquest,
    Aztec military might was verified at special
    ceremonies. Rulers of enemy or potentially
    rebellious city states were invited to
    Tenochtitlan, under the tightest security, to
    witness mass human sacrifices and receive exquisite
    gifts from the Tenochtitlan ruler - all designed to
    unnerve and humiliate the kingly guests.

8. Hicks (n.d.a.) also uses this term, although to
    refer to the entire market complex serving
    Tenochtitlan-Tlatelolco.

358

9. Numerous sources mention that every five days (one Aztec week) a major market was held, displaying a wide variety of both utilitarian and exotic wares (Las Casas 1967:I:366; Duran 1967:I:178; Motolinia 1971:375). This was the case throughout the empire. In some districts, such major markets were held at intervals of twenty days (one Aztec month), though the five day interval was more common (Motolinia 1971:375). In the major centers, markets were held daily, but these daily markets offered primarily utilitarian goods (Las Casas 1967:I:366; Motolinia 1967:375).

10. More extravagantly, and probably unrealistically, Cortes estimates the scale of activities in the Tlatelolco market at more than 60,000 buyers and sellers daily (1977:257).

11. The matter of price regulation is hotly debated, this suggestion deriving from only one source (Fray Bernardino de Sahagun who mentions fixed pricing twice). This issue has been discussed by Carrasco (1983) and Calnek (1978), to name but two of the major contributors to the debate. Given the possible unfavorable reputation of some merchants (see note 20), the regulation of prices may refer less to actual price fixing than to a more generalized control over suspected shady dealings.

12. Diaz del Castillo records the presence of three judges, assisted by numerous supervisors who apparently wandered about the market, inspecting merchandise and methods of sale. Cortes, however, viewing this same market, states that ten to twelve judges were present, along with numerous inspectors.

13. Duran, however, also mentions that the tax was divided between the ruler and the community. This is unlikely in the case of conquered Tlatelolco, although Duran may be alluding to the "division" of that market among the Tenochtitlan ruler's trusted advisors and captains. Cortes admits he did not know in the specific case of Tlatelolco, but opts in favor of the ruler, since he had seen the rulers of other districts control the market tax.

14. This includes 20 types distinguished by physical characteristics, and seven by region. It includes only the "good" products, not the "stinking, sharp to the taste, evil-smelling, spoiled..." ones

359

(Sahagun 1950-82, Book 10: 68).

15. Seven varieties are distinguished by physical properties (mainly color), eight by region. It is not clear in the text if these overlap (e.g., if the varicolored maize is also the maize from Chalco). In addition, Sahagun includes maize from Tlaxcala and Michoacan, avowed enemies of the Aztecs. I have included these in the regional types, although their appearance in the market may be a post-conquest phenomenon. On the other hand, the emperor Moctezuma ate from bowls produced in Cholula, an on-again, off-again enemy.

16. These are definitely ranked as to quality, the irrigated varieties being the most highly valued, followed by that from the "hot countries," from the west, from the northern desert lands, and finally from the Totonac country (northern Gulf Coast).

17. This includes bowls from Tlaxcala, Huexotzinco and Michoacan, all historic enemies of Tenochtitlan. If Cholula pottery bowls could enter the empire, perhaps these could also.

18. This supposedly refers to the value of the market tax assessed vendors. The Tenochtitlan ruler (tlatoani) did not claim all this potential wealth for himself, but divided it among his advisors and military officers, much as he would a conquered town with its fields. The precise nature of this division is nowhere recorded.

19. Not long after the conquest of Tlatelolco, Ahuitzotl (1486- 1502) lavished special attention and privileges on the professional merchants in what was clearly a mutually beneficial relationship. On many expeditions, the merchants acted as state emissaries or spies for the Mexican ruler (see Berdan 1978).

20. The tlanecuilo are translated as "retailer" or "dealer" by Anderson and Dibble (Sahagun 1950-82, Book 10, passim). A term referring to swindling or fraudulent dealings is presented as the first option for tlanecuilo in Molina's sixteenth-century dictionary (1970:127v.).

21. Wheat is the only non-indigenous item listed by Sahagun for the tlanecuilo.

360

22. This was probably rare in the case of tropical products. Numerous examples (PNE vols. IV, V, VI: passim) indicate that purchasers of these products traveled to the sources of production rather than the producer marketing his goods in highland towns.

23. Sahagun (1950-82, book 10:91) also describes peddlers (tlacocoalnamacac) in the Tlatelolco market: these were retailers of an assortment of apparently unrelated wares.

24. Translation by the author.

25. These were not slaves in the classic Western sense of the term. In Aztec Mexico, a person could become a temporary slave more or less voluntarily by such means as punishment for theft, offering oneself as gambling stakes, or a "welfare" alternative to poverty. These persons, or better, their labor potential, could be bought and sold in markets, although it was required   that the transaction always take place before witnesses.

26. The documents containing this information derive from the mid-sixteenth century. While this market may have felt some Spanish influence, on the whole the Spaniards were disinterested in such markets and effected little change (see Berdan 1980 and Gibson 1964:352-353).

27. In addition to Tenochtitlan and Tlatelolco, merchant guilds were established in Uitzilopochco, Azcapotzalco, Quauhtitlan, Texcoco, Uexotla, Coatlichan, Otompan, Chalco, Mixcoac and Xochimilco. For a discussion of the role of these guilds in the Aztec economy, see Berdan 1978.

28. Torquemada is referring to a Colonial situation, and undoubtedly speaking to pre-Spanish antecedents. He mentions that many of the "birds" in these markets were turkeys, although most were chickens, a Spanish introduction.

29. This   is   despite Sahagun's statement that the owners of cacao groves and cotton fields sold their products in the Tlatelolco market (1950-82, book 10: 65, 75). Salt was sold in that market by both producers and retailers - transportation would have posed few problems, since salt was produced in several locations within the Valley of Mexico, and the extensive lake system allowed transport by canoe.

30. If this indeed reflects a pre-Colonial pattern, the merchants would have had to cross through the Aztec-controlled provinces of Cohuaxtlahuacan and Coyolapan, and into the Aztec province of Xoconochco (and out again, of course).

31. For other examples, see Berdan 1975 and Carrasco 1971: 63-64.

32. This specialization may, to some extent, reflect the strong Spanish interest in cochineal. Still, high demands for salt and amole reflect pre-Spanish patterns; this market was probably transformed slowly under Colonial rule. The Miahuatlan Relacion Geografica is dated 1580.

33. Duran (1971:278) states that "In...Cholula, it was ordered that the merchandise must consist of jewels, precious stones, and fine featherwork." Although the hand of a political power is at work here, it is not specified which power (Aztec? Cholula? Tlaxcala?). Also, the types of items available strongly suggest a guild-merchant clientele.

34. The tribute from the province of Tepeacac includes no such goods (Matricula de Tributos 1980: 38-39).

35. There is no definitive record of state-sponsored merchants from non-Aztec controlled city-states being allowed to traffic within the bounds of the empire. However, at a borderland (and gateway) market like Tepeacac, it may have in fact been common practice.

36. Translation by Michael Smith 1979:111.

References Cited

AGI (Archivo General de las Indias, Sevilla), Audiencia de Mexico 68
    1533-1571   Cartas y expedientes del Presidente y Oidores de Mejico.

AGI, Patronato 184, no. 2
    1525   Carta de Rodrigo de Albornoz a S. M. dando cuenta de las conquistas que estaba haciendo Cristobal de Olid...

Alva Ixtlilxochitl, Fernando de
   1965   Historia Chichimeca. Mexico: Editora
              Nacional

Alvarado Tezozomoc, Fernando
   1975   Cronica Mexicana. Mexico: Editorial
              Porrua.

Anderson, Arthur J. O., Frances Berdan and James
Lockhart
   1976   Beyond the Codices: the Nahua view of
              Colonial Mexico. Berkeley: University
              of California Press.

Anonymous Conqueror
   1971   Relacion de algunas cosas de la Nueva
              Espana y de la Gran Ciudad de Temestitan
              Mexico; escrita por un companero de
              Hernan Cortes. In Coleccion de
              Documentos para la Historia de Mexico, J.
              C. Icazbalceta, ed., vol. I: 368-
              398.

Berdan, Frances F.
   1975   Trade, Tribute and Market in the Aztec
              Empire, Unpublished Ph.D. dissertation.
              The University of Texas at Austin.

   1976   A Comparative Analysis of Aztec Tribute
              Documents. In Actas del XLI Congreso
              Internacional de Americanistas, vol. II:
              131-142. Mexico.

   1978   Ports of Trade in Mesoamerica: a
              reappraisal. In Thomas A. Lee Jr. and
              Carlos Navarrete (editors), Mesoamerican
              Communication Routes and Cultural
              Contacts: 187-198. Papers of the New
              World Archaeological Foundation, number
              40. Provo, Utah.

   1980   Aztec Merchants and Markets: local-level
              economic activity in a non-industrial
              empire. Mexicon, vol. II, no. 3:37-41.

   1983   The economics of Aztec luxury trade and
              tribute. Paper presented at the
              conference, The Aztec Templo Mayor,
              Dumbarton Oaks, Washington, D.C.

363

Calnek, Edward
1976   The internal structure of Tenochtitlan.
            In The Valley of Mexico, Eric R. Wolf,
            ed., pp. 287-302.   Albuquerque:
            University of New Mexico Press.

1978   El sistema de mercado de Tenochtitlan.
            In Economia politica e ideologia en el
            Mexico prehispanico. Pedro Carrasco and
            Johanna Broda, eds. Mexico: Editorial
            Nueva Imagen.

Carrasco, Pedro
1971   Los Barrios Antiguos de Cholula.   In
            Estudios y Documentos de la Region de
            Puebla-Tlaxcala, vol. III: 9-88. Puebla,
            Mexico.

1983   Some theoretical considerations about the
            role of the market in ancient Mexico. In
            Economic Anthropology: topics and
            theories, Sutti Ortiz, ed.   Lanham:
            University Press of America and Society
            for Economic Anthropology.

Conrad, Geoffrey W. and Arthur A. Demarest
1984   Religion and Empire: The dynamics of
            Aztec and Inca expansionism. Cambridge:
            Cambridge University Press.

Cortes, Hernan
1963   Cartas y Documentos. Mexico: Editorial
            Porrua.

1977   Fernando Cortes: His Five Letters of
            Relation to the Emperor Charles V, 1519-
            1526. Transl. and Ed. by F. MacNutt.
            Glorieta, New Mexico: The Rio Grande
            Press, Inc.

Diaz del Castillo, Bernal
1956   The Discovery and Conquest of Mexico. A.
            P. Maudslay, trans. New York: Noonday.

Duran, Diego
1967   Historia de las Indias de Nueva Espana e
            Islas de la Tierra Firme. Mexico:
            Editorial Porrua. 2 vols.

1971   Book of the Gods and Rites and the
            Ancient Calendar. Trans. by F.

364

Horcasitas and D. Heyden.   Norman:
University of Oklahoma Press.

ENE (Epistolario de Nueva Espana)
    1939-42   Francisco de Paso y Troncoso, ed. Mexico.
                 16 vols.

Gerhard, Peter
    1972   A Guide to the Historical Geography of
                 New Spain. Cambridge: Cambridge
                 University Press.

Gibson, Charles
    1952   Tlaxcala in the Sixteenth Century.
                 Stanford: Stanford University Press.

    1964   The Aztecs under Spanish Rule. Stanford:
                 Stanford University Press.

Hicks, Fred
    n.d.a.   First Steps Toward a Market-integrated
                 Economy in Aztec Mexico. Paper presented
                 at the conference, The Early State and
                 After, Montreal, 1983.

    n.d.b.   La Posicion de Temazcalapan en la Triple
                 Alianza. Forthcoming in Estudios de
                 Cultura Nahuatl.

Hirth, Kenneth G.
    1978   Interregional Trade and the Formation of
                 Prehistoric Gateway Communities.
                 American Antiquity 43 #1: 35-45.

Kelly, Isabel and Angel Palerm
    1952   The Tajin Totonac. Part 1: History,
                 Subsistence, Shelter and Technology.
                 Smithsonian Institution Institute of
                 Social Anthropology Publication No. 13.
                 Washington: U.S. Government Printing
                 Office.

Kurtz, Donald V.
    1974   Peripheral and Transitional Markets: the
                 Aztec case. American Ethnologist 1, no.
                 4:685-705.

Las Casas, Bartolome de
    1967   Apologetica Historia Sumaria. Mexico:
                 Universidad Nacional Autonoma de Mexico.

Matricula de Tributos
1980   Facsimile edition of the Matricula de
            Tributos, with commentaries by Frances F.
            Berdan and Jacqueline de Durand-Forest.
            G r a z :   A k a d e m i s c h e   D r u c k   u .
            Verlagsanstalt.

Molina, Alonso de
1970   Vocabulario en Lengua Castellana y
            Mexicana. Mexico: Editorial Porrua.

Motolinia, Toribio (de Benavente)
1971   Memoriales, o Libro de las Cosas de la
            Nueva Espana y de los Naturales de ella.
            Mexico. UNAM, Instituto de Investigaciones
            Historicas.

PNE (Papeles de Nueva Espana)
1905-1906 Francisco del Paso y Troncoso (editor).
            Madrid: Sucesores   de   Rivandeneyra.
            Vols. IV-VI.

Sahagun, Bernardino de
1950-82   Florentine Codex: General History of the
            Things of New Spain. Translated by
            Arthur J. O. Anderson and Charles E.
            Dibble.   University of Utah and School of
            American Research, Santa Fe.

Saindon, Jacqueline
1977   Cotton Production and Exchange in Mexico
            1427-1580, M.A. Thesis in Anthropology,
            Hunter College, The City University of
            New York.

Sanders, William T., Jeffrey R. Parsons, and Robert S.
Santley
1979   The Basin of Mexico: ecological processes
            in the evolution of a civilization. New
            York: Academic Press.

Scholes, F.V. and E.B. Adams
1957   Informacion sobre los Tributos que los
            indios pagaban a Moctezuma, ano de 1554.
            Documentos para la Historia del Mexico
            Colonial, vol. 4. Mexico.

Smith, Michael E.
1979   The Aztec marketing system and settlement
            pattern in the Valley of Mexico: a

central place analysis. <u>American Antiquity</u> 44: 110-124.

Torquemada, Juan de
1969   <u>Los Veinte i un Libros Rituales i Monarchia Indiana</u>. 3 vols. Mexico: Editorial Porrua.

Zorita, Alonso de
1963   <u>Life and Labor in Ancient Mexico</u>. Benjamin Keen, transl. New Brunswick, N.J.: Rutgers University Press.

COMMODITY EXCHANGE AND MARKETS IN THE INCA STATE: RECENT ARCHAEOLOGICAL EVIDENCE

Timothy Earle, Department of Anthropology, UCLA

Did markets distribute commodities in the prehispanic Inca state? This question is basic to evaluating the proposed relationships between markets and complex, nonindustrial sociopolitical formations, of which the Inca state, existing as it did down to the historic period, represents a crucial example. Various authors have proposed that markets either caused state formation because of a need for centralized regional management (Sanders 1956; Adams 1966) or were used by states to facilitate finance (Brumfiel 1980). In the Inca case, however, historical researchers have argued that markets did not exist (Murra 1980 [1956]; LaLone 1982). Is this possible?

To evaluate these issues, I will present some recent archaeological research that has focused on the economic organization in the Mantaro Valley, Peru during the late prehistoric periods (Earle, et al. 1980). The Mantaro Valley, in Peru's Central Highlands, is a high (3200-4000m) but agriculturally rich basin (Fig. 1). In the end of the Late Intermediate Period (Huanca II phase, A.D. 1250-1460), the local population of the region around Jauja was organized as complex chiefdoms (Earle, et al. 1980; LeBlanc 1981). Towns, such as Hatunmarca and Tunanmarca, contained several thousand habitation structures and probably had populations over 10,000. Smaller settlements, such as Umpamalca, appear to have been politically subservient to these larger centers. All settlements were located in fortified, hilltop positions and the political organization was apparently fragmented into local, competing groups. In terms of internal organization, a social elite was distinguished, and leaders were particularly important in regional warfare.

In the Late Horizon (Huanca III, A.D. 1460-1532), the region was conquered by the Inca state and incorporated as an important agricultural district into the state's staple finance system (Earle and D'Altroy 1982). The state constructed the administrative center of Hatun Xauxa along the main north-south road that ran through the valley. The local settlement pattern dispersed into smaller settlements, such as Huancas de la Cruz and Chucchus, many of which were located at

369

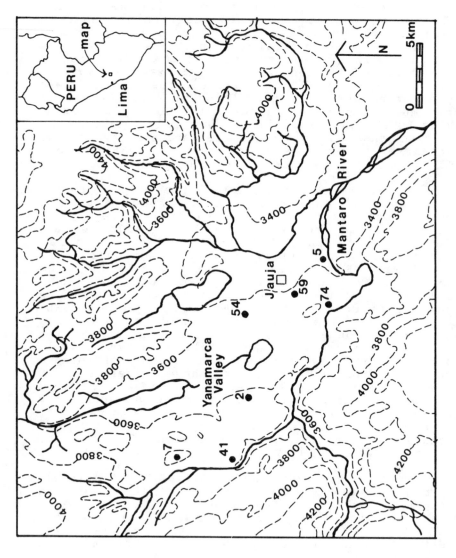

Figure 1. Map of the Upper Mantaro research area. Sites shown are as follows: 2, Hutunmarca; 5, Hatun Xauxa; 7, Tunanmarca; 41, Umpamalca; 54, Marca; 59, Huancas de la Cruz; 74, Chucchus.

lower elevations probably to emphasize maize production desired by the state. Some town size settlements, such as Hatunmarca and Marca, dominated the settlement system. Traditional leaders became important both as local chiefs and as low level state officials responsible for organizing state corvèe labor (D'Altroy 1981).

In 1982 and 1983, the Upper Mantaro Archaeological Research Project investigated changes in the local economy from stateless society (Huanca II) to state (Huanca III). To do this we excavated in six sites-- Hatunmarca, Tunanmarca and Umpamalca for Huanca II and Hatunmarca, Marca, Huancas de la Cruz and Chucchus for Huanca III. In all sites, we excavated 31 patio groups that represented householding units. Both elite and commoner patio groups were chosen for excavation.

The goal of this research was to document the degree of economic specialization in the settlements and how the pattern of specialized production was related to social stratification. We wanted to see how the organization of production was affected by the dramatic sociopolitical changes coming with imperial conquest. An additional element of this research was to document the extent of exchange in household products.

To investigate the importance of markets in the Inca case we must define operationally what a market is. Discussions of markets are broadly scattered through the anthropological literature, as for example in Polanyi (1957), Dalton (1961), LeClair (1962), Schneider (1974:242-243), Beals (1975:9-12), and LaLone (1982:300-301). The most basic definition of a market is the situation or context in which a supply crowd (sellers) and a demand crowd (buyers) meet to exchange goods and services.

This general definition of market implicitly includes all forms of exchange, but the notion of market has usually been limited to conditions where the "market principle" is operating. The market principle refers to the way supply and demand conditions determine "price" which in turn determines production and consumption decisions. The market principle, however, is not something that can be said to be present or absent. Rather it governs all exchange systems to some degree, and so we need a set of quantitative measures that describe the degree of market involvement for any society. Belshaw offers the following seven variables describing market systems:

371

1) the impersonality or otherwise of the interaction of buyers and sellers...

2) the systematization of exchange values (that is, prices), so that we may see whether and how they affect one another;

3) the degree to which buying and selling of specific goods and services are specialized functions;

4) the range of goods and services for which buying and selling are conventionally valid;

5) the degree to which exchange transactions enter into the stages of production from raw resources to consumable product or service;

6) the degree and nature of competition in buying and selling.

7) the degree to which buying and selling may be differentiated through the interposition of a medium of exchange... [1965:8-9]

The degree to which markets can be said to exist in any society can be measured by evaluating these seven characteristics of exchange.

Measurement of all characteristics outlined by Belshaw is impossible in archaeology where exchange events and price fluctuations cannot be observed directly. To operationalize Belshaw's list for archaeology, three measurable variables can be used to evaluate market involvement:

1) the importance of specialized institutions of production and exchange divorced in their operations from other institutional relationships;

2) the development of a medium of exchange to facilitate the systematization of exchange values;

3) the percentage of goods utilized by a household that are obtained by exchange.

First, specialized institutions of exchange can be recognized by their explicit and dominant function to handle exchange, in contrast to more general purpose

372

institutions in which exchange may be imbedded. This definition includes two types of exchange institutions: (1) the site specific marketplace, as represented by the bustling peasant markets, and (2) a "site free" market that includes a collection of specialized exchange houses, such as stores, agencies, auction houses and the like (LeClair 1962; Dalton 1961). The special function of these exchange institutions is important because it implies that nonexchange relationships, such as kinship and political ties, will not unduly constrain choice.

In the Inca state, specialized exchange institutions appear to have been of limited importance. Both Murra (1980 [1956]) and more recently LaLone (1982:301-309) have argued convincingly that marketplaces were rare or absent in the core of the empire. Early observers rarely mention marketplace gatherings. Rather, marketplaces were described only in the northern region of the empire (now Ecuador) where they existed prior to Inca conquest and continued under Inca rule (Salomon 1978), or in the core region after Spanish conquest where they were developed by the Europeans (LaLone and LaLone 1979). Similarly, other specialized exchange institutions appear to have been largely absent in the core region. The main exception was the entrepreneurial traders who brought in goods from beyond the state's controlled territory (Rostworoski 1970, 1975). The mechanism by which these long-distance exchange goods were distributed within the empire is not known, however, and it seems likely that the state itself handled distribution (Earle 1983).

Despite this general conclusion that specialized exchange institutions were rare or nonexistent in the Inca empire, exchange events may well have taken place within the broader context of other institutional gatherings. (As we know from many tribal societies, such as the Trobriand Islands [Malinowski 1922; Uberoi 1962] and the New Guinea Highlands [Pospisil 1963], ceremonies gather people from different local communities and thus create opportunities for exchange.) In essence, any gathering of people from ecologically different zones creates a pseudomarket. In the Inca empire, large gatherings of people from different ecological zones were probably associated with the annual calendar of ceremonies that took place at least monthly in the public squares (Rowe 1946:308-312). Today, in Peru, as elsewhere in Latin America, the market cycle is closely coordinated with the religious calendar of fiestas (Valcarcel 1946:480). In

373

the Mantaro Valley, for example, annually all potting villages come to sell ceramics in a special ceramics market that fills the central plaza of Orcotuna. This ceramics festival is held in early September on the day of the town's patron saint.

Archaeologically, evidence for marketplace exchange in the Andes is at best only suggestive. Marketplaces can be identified archaeologically as centrally located open spaces with unrestricted public access often associated with small-scale craft workshops and retail storage facilities (see Millon [1964:351] for the Teotihuacan example and Blanton [1983:54] for Monte Albán). In Peru, open centrally located plazas characterize large settlements during much of prehistory. For the Mantaro Valley, as an example, the Late Intermediate Period and Late Horizon towns of Tunanmarca and Hatunmarca were organized around central open spaces with special, nonresidential buildings. The Inca administrative centers in the Central Highlands were clearly built around large open plazas. At Huánuco Pampa, buildings were laid out around a plaza of 19.2 ha. with roads entering at each corner and with the ceremonial platform (ushnu) at the center (Morris and Thompson 1970); at Pumpu a similar layout defines a 16.9 ha. plaza (LeVine, personal communication). Although most researchers have assumed that these plazas served for state and community ceremonies, their multifunctional use as marketplaces in association with large, periodic gatherings should not be dismissed without careful consideration. When Pizarro arrived at the administrative center of Hatun Xauxa in the Mantaro Valley, Estete reported the following gatherings:

"se juntaban cada día en la plaza central cien mil personas, y estaban los mercados y calles del pueblo tan llenos de gentes, que parecia que no faltaba persona.   [Estete 1947:341]

[each day 100,000 persons gathered in the main plaza and the markets and streets of the town were so full of people that it seemed everyone was there]. [LaLone 1982:303]

LaLone (1982:303-304) cautions that this observation is not typical and probably represents a gathering in support of the Inca army; however, it seems plausible that such periodic gatherings would have served as a context or a pretext for exchange, although closely tied to nonmarket activities.

As discussed below, much better evidence for specialized institutions of production exist for the Andes. Although full documentation cannot be presented here, some level of village craft specialization has been documented for chert blades, cooking pots, and spinning in the Mantaro. The concentration of production in particular villages and the general distribution of finished goods to all villages argue for some exchange in these craft items.

The second characteristic of market is the presence of a medium of exchange. A medium of exchange, such as the cowrie shell money of Africa or the early currencies of China, facilitates exchange by providing a store of value between exchange events and by creating a simplified system of values used to calculate equivalencies. The systematization of exchange value implied by a medium of exchange is basic to the market principle that requires production distribution and consumption decisions to be based on an evaluation of comparative costs and benefits.

Evidence for a medium of exchange in the Andes under the Inca is very limited and most historians argue that the empire's economy used no monetary system (Einzig 1948:190-91). Although Jose de Acosta (1954 [1590]:91) mentions the use of coca as a medium of exchange and Cobo (1979 [1653];34) mentions maize as a generalized medium, any form of money was clearly limited in use when compared to the currency systems of the Old World or the commodity monies of the Aztec. In our archeological research, no artifacts were recovered that conformed to the expectations for a medium of exchange -- restricted availability and standardized form that permits easy division into accounting units (see Earle 1982). For example, although metal objects were recovered repeatedly from excavations, common types such as discs or pins were highly variable. This contrasts with the presence of copper "money" in coastal Peru and Ecuador where it was probably involved in long-distance entrepreneurial trade (Shimada 1984). Of course negative evidence is always inconclusive as perishable goods such as textiles or maize may have served as an exchange medium.

The third characteristic associated with markets is the range of goods and services exchanged. This characteristic can be quite easily operationalized in archaeological research by analyzing the percentage of goods and services consumed by a family that were obtained through exchange. Here we can consider two alternative idealized models that represent the ends of a spectrum. At one end is Sahlins's (1972) Domestic Mode of Production, in which each household is economically generalized and self sufficient. It produces all that it uses, and exchange outside the family is nonexistant. At the other end of the spectrum is the modern market system in which household members exchange their labor for cash which is then used to purchase all desired goods and services in the market place.

Although consistent quantitative work on this subject has not been done, an easily measurable and comparable indicator of household dependency on exchange is desirable for evolutionary studies on the development of economic systems. By imposing such a simple measure, I might appear to be denying the different ways that societies can institute the exchange process. In fact that is precisely what I propose at least for archaeological cases where exchange mechanisims are not directly visible, but I would probably be more aggressive and propose that the behavior of exchange is ultimately more important than the ideology of its institutionalization. Polanyi's (1957) now classic typology of reciprocity, redistribution, and market exchange has proven analytically difficult if not impossible to apply. For example, the "redistributive" financial system of the Inca empire was built on an explicit ideology of reciprocity (Wachtel 1977), and market exchange is often associated with strong reciprocal bonds as in the pratik relationship in Haitian markets (Mintz 1961; Plattner, this volume).

For cross-cultural and cross-time studies of economic processes, I believe that a simple measure of exchanged commodities as a percentage of total household consumption is probably a good reflection of market development. This can be operationalized in the following way. For any archaeological assemblage, materials can be identified as to source and classified as to local (<10 km from source), regional (10-50 km), or long-distance (<50 km). These distances are not chosen arbitrarily, and they will vary somewhat according to a society's settlement density and organization. The ten kilometer separation between local procurement and regional exchange is based on 1 1/2 times the distance between contemporaneous communities in the Yanamarca Valley where our sites are located. Local procurement (<10 km) therefore presupposes the possibility for direct access to a desired resource or the exchange for the commodity with a neighboring family or community. The resource comes either from your community's territory or the territory of a directly bordering group. The organzational complexity of such exchange would be the simplest possible. Regional exchange (10-50 km) presupposes exchange across several communities. Without the close social and economic contacts that can exist locally, economic decisions involving production and distribution can be expected to take on the characteristics of a market principle as volume increases. The upper limit on this region (50km) is set for the Mantaro by the naturally defined river valley and by its ethnically homogeous population (the Huanca). Long-distance exchange (>50km) presupposes exchange across multiple ethnic groups and natural regions. As volume expands, the opportunities for entrepreneurial traders increase and the market principles would affect many decisions with regard to goods traded.

For purposes of the present analysis, three types of goods are distinguised for analysis -- subsistence products, craft goods, and wealth items. As we will see, these categories show considerable differences in their frequency of exchange.

Subsistence products are primarily foods, items that must be procured frequently and used daily by all households. Food products are represented in our archaeological collections by macrobotanical and faunal remains recovered systematically by screening and water flotation. Although these data have not heen fully analyzed for the 1982 and 1983 seasons, some patterning is evident. The vast majority of all foods -- including highland tubers, maize, quinoa, llamas, and quinea pigs -- could easily have been produced within the site catchment of the sites studied. In an earlier study, Hastorf (1983) has shown that plant remains recovered from a site reflect the agricultural potential within the site's catchment. Because variation in diet among sites mirrored the immediate local potential for food production, exchange would have been comparatively minor. Foods that were not immediately available to a settlement represented a small part (apparently less than 10%) of the diet. Regional exchange of food is suggested primarily by occurences of maize and deer. Some sites, such as Umpamalca, had more maize than would be expected based on available farming land (Hastorf 1983:292). Although all sites were within deer's ecological range, they

377

TABLE 1. Percentages of Lithic Materials According to
          Distance of Procurement.

Period	<10km (%)	10-50km (%)	>50km (%)	N (kg)
Huanca II	78.8	21.2	trace	863.8
Huanca III	86.0	14.0	trace	1236.3
Total	83.0	17.0	trace	2100.0

were probably extirpated close to settlements and thus may have been obtained by exchange with less populated locales. These foods, i.e. maize and deer, appear to have been restricted mainly to elite households. Based on available data, there is no observed change in the frequency of regionally traded foods from Huanca II to Huanca III. Foods obtained from long-distances (>50 km) were limited to trace occurrences of aji (Hastorf 1983) and shellfish. Most shell recovered by the Upper Mantaro Archaeological Research Project served decorative rather than dietary uses; however, mussels coming in from the coast (about 250 km distant) may have been eaten. During the two seasons, mussel shells were recovered from 11 of 1520 excavated good context proveniences. This is a very low recovery rate (1/138; .007) and would have contributed little to the diet. An increase in occurrence is seen from Huanca II (1/790; ,001) to Huanca III (1/73; .014).

The craft goods recovered in our excavations included a variety of tools and utensils made from stone and ceramics. Used in food preparation and manufacturing, these tools must have seen daily service. A wide range of tools used for cutting, grinding and pounding were manufactured from stone, and the properties of particular stone materials made them desired and traded.

As can be seen clearly in Table 1, although most lithic materials (83%) were obtained locally, a significant amount (17%) was obtained through regional exchange. Most important in this exchange were chert and phyllite. It should be emphasized, however, that the distances involved were relatively short (all being obtained from less than 16 km). Only a trace amount (really only a handful of obsidian flakes) was obtained through long-distance exchange.

Particularly interesting, there is no evidence for increasing regional exchange with the imposed peace of the Inca state. Quite the contrary. Regional exchange, especially in phyllite, seems to have decreased with an overall change from 21.2% to 14.0% of the lithic assemblage (see Table 1).

The red cherts were used for flake tools and blades. The chert was procured from a large quarry site (56 ha) located within the research area. From the quarry, prepared chert cores (with very little natural cortex) were taken to a nearby settlement such as Umpamalca where blades were manufactured for exchange. At

379

TABLE 2.   Ratio of Red Chert to Volcanics as related
            to Distance From the Chert Source

Site	Ratio (c/v)	Distance (km)	Weight (kg.) Red Chert	Volcanics
Umpamalca	6.8	3.2	43.7	6.4
Tunanmarca	1.1	5.0	6.8	6.0
Hatunmarca (Huanca II)	0.9	7.6	7.1	7.6
Hatunmarca (Huanca III)	1.7	7.6	25.8	15.6
Marca	0.2	12.8	3.2	20.0
Huancas de la Cruz	0.1	15.3	0.4	3.3
Chucchus	0.0	16.0	0.1	13.1

Umpamalca, blade manufacture is documented by a high ratio of blade cores and debris to finish blades. At other, more distant settlements, used blades are found but chert manufacturing debris is comparatively rare. This pattern of manufacture suggests village level specialization for exchange at sites such as Umpamalca.

For the red chert, a clear relationship exists between frequency of occurrence and distance from source. The ratio of chert to volcanic material (which is a locally available substitute) decreases significantly with distance from the chert source (Table 2).

The decay in frequency with distance from source is characteristic of exchanged materials (Renfrew 1977) and probably represents costs associated with transportation. This downward sloping curve is a special case of the classic "demand curve." As the "price" of the chert increases with distance, consumers shift to less desirable but less costly locally available materials and the demand for the good declines.

The second regionally traded lithic material was phyllite derived from hills along the eastern edge of the Mantaro Valley. The phyllite, used primarily as grinding slabs, was found commonly at all sites excavated. Table 3 presents the available data on its occurrence. Any fall off with distance was quite subtle and the pattern is not statistically significant. More importantly, certain sites and especially elite patios contain an unusually large amount of phyllite that we interpret as indicating some special activity at these locations. The lack of fall off in the abundance of phyllite probably reflects the limited local substitutes for whatever particular function it served.

Obsidian, dispite its unusual cutting properties, was not traded in significant quantities. This is suprising with a major obsidian source located less than 150 km to the south (Burger and Asaro 1977). The frequency of obsidian increases very slightly from Huanca II to Huanca III collections. This very low level of obsidian trade contrast to Mesoamerica where it was traded widely from Formative times and was involved in specialist manufacture (Spence 1981).

Ceramics were exchanged in a pattern similar to that for lithics. Several ceramic forms, including cooking

381

TABLE 3.   Ratio of Phyllite to Other Ground Stone as
            Related to Distance from the Phyllite Source

Site	Ratio (p/o)	Distance (km)	Weight (kg.) Phyllite	Other
Umpamalca	0.67	15.3	67.3	101.1
Tunanmarca	0.31	16.0	82.2	266.5
Hatunmarca II	0.59	12.8	8.5	14.3
Hatunmarca III	0.44	12.8	66.8	133.4
Marca	0.73	6.5	147.7	202.5
Huancas de la Cruz	2.93	6.5	4.4	1.5
Chucchus	0.66	6.5	15.1	22.9

Micro Bibli. →

jars, storage jars and serving bowls, were commonly used by the Huancas, and several special items were exchanged regionally. For the analysis presented here, the ceramics have been divided into five general classes:

1. Local ceramics include the types Base Clara, Huanca Red, and various plain wares which were common on all sites. Vessel forms included various large storage jars, bowls, and miniatures. Local manufacture of these types is documented by the consistent recovery of production waste (wasters). Although wasters are recovered from all our large sites, some level of village specialization and local exchange is indicated by the comparatively high frequency of wasters at Huanca II site of Umpamalca and the Huanca III site of Marca (Costin 1984).

2. Regional ceramics include Base Roja and Huanca Polished. These styles were most commonly large jars that were probably used for storage. The paste and tempers of these styles are distinctive from the local ceramics and appear to be identical with ceramics found in the Mantaro Valley near Huancayo, about 40 km to the south of our research area (D'Altroy and Costin 1982).

3. Micaceous Self Slip is a distinctive plainware primarily used for cooking jars. The paste is highly micaceous, unlike the more common, local wares. The forms are standardized and may well have been produced by ceramic specialists for a broad regional demand (Hagstrum 1984). Manufacturing techniques were simplified so as to lower cost. We feel that this is good evidence for production for exchange; by lowering production costs, the ceramics can compete regionally with local products despite the transport costs involved. Although this ware is quite common at our sites, we have no conclusive evidence for its local manufacture and it may have been procured in regional exchange.

4. Inca ceramics are found on Huanca III sites where they represent a significant percentage (13%) of the assemblage. The vessel forms include various storage jars (arybolloids), dishes, and other special pieces. In general,

383

TABLE 4.   Percentages of Ceramic Materials According
               to Distance of Procurement.

Period	<10km (%)	10-50km (%)	>50km (%)	? (%)	N
Huanca II	67.2	6.2	.5	4.19	1465
	MSS=22.0				
Huanca III	53.1	5.1	.3	1.6	1380
	MSS = 22.2				
	Inca = 17.7				
TOTAL	60.4	5.7	0.4	2.8	2845
	MSS = 22.1				
	Inca = 8.6				

the Inca forms appear to replace locally produced forms. The ware is distinctive from the other wares and at present we are not sure where it was manufactured. Petrographic analysis shows that the ceramics were produced within the Mantaro; Inca ceramics from other nearby administrative sites (Tarmatambo and Acostambo) were made with distinctive clays and tempers (D'Altroy and Costin 1982, Costin, personal communication). The Inca ceramics show both high standardization and high labor investment (Hagstrum 1984). This combination of attributes is quite unusual. The standardization suggests specialization, but the high labor investment per item suggests a nonmarket distribution system in which competition and the need to minimize production costs were not operative. Is this an archaeological example of state, bureaucratic inefficiency? In all probability, the Inca ceramics were produced in the Mantaro and distributed regionally by the state.

5. Exotic ceramics include unique wares that were apparently traded into the Valley from a long distance (>50km). Isolated pieces, mostly bowls, have been identified as from Tarma, from the North Coast (Chimu), and from other unknown locaations. Inca style ceramics with distinctive nonlocal pastes represent less than 1% of all Inca pieces; these unusual pastes were probably also traded into the region. Exotics were somewhat more common in elite patios and decreased somewhat from Huanca II to Huanca III.

The pattern of ceramic procurement summarized by distance from source is seen in Table 4. Definite local ceramics were most common (60.4%) in the assemblage. Regional ceramics werea small, but consistent component (5.7%). Long-distance ceramics were rare (0.4%). Ceramics that came either from local or regional sources, i.e. the Micaceous Self Slip (22.1%) and Inca (8.6%), were of considerable importance; although the origin of these ceramics is not known, they were apparently produced by specialists and obtained through exchange. In sum, although local procurement of ceramics dominated this sphere of the economy, there is considerable evidence that specialists and exchange existed. These specialists were apparently producing for somewhat different "markets"/patrons -- Base Clara for local exchange, Micaceous Self Slip for local and regional exchange, and Inca for state controlled regional distribution.

Evidence for change from Huanca II to Huance III is remarkably limited. Regional and long-distance exchange remained either stable or may have decreased slightly. The only important change was of course the introduction of Inca ceramics (0-17.7%) that provides probable evidence for a state organized production and regional distribution system. Again, the state is considered to have been responsible because of the comparatively high degree of standardization and labor costs in the manufacture of the Inca vessels.

Wealth items include artifacts that were used primarily for personal adornment or other special functions. Such items were probably obtained only occasionally and kept for a long time. Those recovered in our excavations included special items made of metal, shell and stone. These items were comparatively rare and recovered from only a small fraction of all excavated proveniences. Their rarity contrasts with the general occurrence of subsistence and craft goods.

Metal objects were an important commodity traded in the Andes. From our 1982 and 1983 escavations, 181 items were recovered from 2062 excavated proveniences. Copper, silver, lead, and gold are all represented (Earle 1983), and they were fashioned into a broad range of utilitarian objects (needles, chisels, axes, weights, knives) and decorative objects (pins, discs). The Mantaro region contained large ore deposits of all these metals, but, because mines were located more than 10 km from the sites, metals must have been obtained through some regional distribution system. Interestingly, metal objects from throughout the region are formally very similar and it is likely that they were made in a relatively few locations.

Evidence for long-distance exchange in metals presents an interesting shift accompanying Inca conquest. In a qualitative analysis of material components of our metals, the copper is seen frequently mixed with either arsenic or tin to produce a bronze (Howe 1983). During the pre-Ince period, coppers often contained arsenic; because arsenic copper ores are available in the Upper Mantaro, these metals would appear to have been obtained regionally. During the Inca period, the coppers contain tin which is not available regionally but must have been obtained long distance from southern Peru or Bolivia.

Shell, used primarily as beads, was an uncommon but consistent item exchanged prehistorically. In all, shells (other than mussel) were recovered from 43 of 1520 analyzed excavated proveniences (1/35; .028). Several species were used but all would have involved long-distance exchange. Most of the species came from along the Peruvian coast, at least 250 km distant; a few examples of Spondylus sp. indicate trade with Ecuador (1500 km); some landsnails were probably derived from the tropical forest, 50 km to the east.

Based on the frequency of shell, a possible shift in long-distance trading may be observed. During Huanca II (prior to Inca conquest), shell was found 19 of 790 excavated proveniences (1/42; .024); during Huanca III (the Inca period), occurrence increased to 24 of 730 excavated proveniences (1/30; .033). This is further evidence of increased long-distance trade under the Inca, although amounts of goods remained quite limited.

Stone was also used for several nonutilitarian forms including beads, pendants, unmodified crystals, discs, and figurines. The majority of these items (89.9%) were made of materials, such as steatite, mica, quartz and phyllite, that are available regionally but not locally. No long-distances materials were recovered in these collections, although lapis lazuli beads were found in an early historic burial excavated in 1977. In all, the stone "goodies" are quite rare. They increase in occurrency somewhat from Huanca II (18/899 proveniences; .020) to Huanca III (39/1075; .032) contexts. All wealth objects, including the stone items, were concentrated in elite patios.

SUMMARY AND CONCLUSION

The archeological evidence in the Mantaro Valley suggests a consistent, but comparatively low volume of exchange. For subsistence goods, evidence for exchange is very little, and communities (and perhaps even households) were largely generalized, self-sufficient units. For craft goods, the evidence for exchange is much stronger (cf Table 5). About 15% or more of both lithics and ceramics apparently came in from greater than 10 km and particular communities were specialized in craft production. Certain ceramic vessel types appear to be the product of craft specialization. Specifically, manufacture of Micaceous Self Slip was

TABLE 5. Summary of rough percentages of materials, based on weights, according to distance from source. In parentheses are the changes from Huanca II to Huanca III.

	Local < 10 km (HII-HIII)	Regional 10-50 (HII-HIII)	Long-distance > 50 (HII-HIII)
Food Goods	90%[1]	10%[1]	trace
Lithics	83% (79-86)	17% (21-14)	trace
Ceramics	60% (67-53)	6% (6-5)	0.4 (0.5-0.3)
	0-50 km = 31 (22-40)		
Metals	0	80%[1] (100-70)	20%[1] (0-30)
Shell	0	0	100%
Stone goodies	9% (22-4)	90% (78-94)	0

[1]
 At present, these figures are estimates of magnitude.

both standardized and cost minimizing, characteristics that we interpret as appropriate for a market distribution system. Other craft products were apparently distributed locally, although particular communities emphasized the manufacturer of one or more crafts. During the Inca period, the state may well have been directly involved in both production and distribution. For wealth goods, items were quite rare but were obtained through regional or long-distance exchange. Some items obtained from long-distance (aji and mussel, obsidian, and tin and shell) increase to a small extent following Inca conquest.

Did markets exist in the prehistoric Andes? To some degree they probably did. Community level specialization and local and regional exchange especially in craft goods are clearly demonstrated. The range of goods traded and the volume involved is quite restricted in comparison with Mesoamerica, for example, and the lack of evidence for exchange in food products suggts a high degree of local economic autonomy. This picture fits with the lack of evidence for market place exchange (at least on a regular basis not associated with ceremonial occasions) and for a medium of exchange.

Perhaps the most important conclusion from our data is the clear lack of evidence for increasing regional and long-distance exchange following Inca conquest. Exchange at the regional level was restricted but still important in Huanca II. In Huanca III, regional exchange (with the exception of Inca ceramics which we conclude was produced and distribution by the state) remained constant or decreased. A small increase in long-distance trade items may indicate either state administered exchange in wealth and/or entrepreneurs. In general, exchange seems to be much less than would be expected given the imposed peace of the empire and it would seem to be manipulated by the state.

In support of the historical studies by Murra (1980 [1956])and LaLone (1982), market involvement in the Andes during the pre-Inca and Inca periods appears to have been comparatively restricted. Without specialized exchange institutions, without a medium of exchange, and without extensive exchange in goods, the market principle would have affected production and consumption decisions in a comparatively narrow range of economic activities.

How can it be that exchange and the developments of

389

markets, so commonly associated with states (Claessen 1978), could be of such limited importance in the Inca state? To understand this problem, the place of markets in state societies requires careful consideration. Markets, of course, provide two linked but analytically separate function -- horizontal and vertical economic integration (Mintz 1959).

Horizontal integration involves exchange between local groups and households who are to some degree specialized, often because of underlying differnces in the environment. In the Andes, the necessity for exchange was limited by the relatively high degree of local environmental diversity that permitted access to many resources within a limited territory. Local subsistence economies varied, but little need for exchange existed beyond the local community.

As is evident from the Central Andes, the horizontal function of markets was not necessary for state formation and did not necessarily increase following the imposed regional integration of a state. In the Inca case, the separation of communities economically and politically was an explicit goal of the state to minimize the horizontal ties between local population that might be used in revolt against the state.

Instead of allowing or encouraging the development of a regional market systems, theInca encouraged community self-sufficiency. Where high resource diversity permitted direct access to the range of desired gods, community economic independence can be seen as an outcome of the local ecology. Where diversity was more limited, however, the Inca state extended community access by granting rights to lands in more distant ecological zones. This "archipelago model" of diverse resource exploitation and economic integration within the extended community has been described by John Murra (1972). I add only that it was not necessarily an ancient Andean tradition as much as it was an explicit state policy to isolate local populations to increase their political dependency.

The Inca state, in addition, maintained the ability to control intercommunity transportation of goods within the empire on which market system would have depended. The road system was state property and movement was carefully regulated by facilities along the road and at bridges (cf D'Altroy 1981). In addition llama herds, used in caravans as the only nonhuman beast of burden, were nominally the property

390

of the state. This would have severly limited any bulk movement of goods by individual entrepreneurs not working under direct state contract.

Vertical integration involves the movilization of locally produced subsistence goods needed by the state to support the nonproducing sector of the society, such as state officials, military, and religious personnel. In many states, markets may play a role in state finance whereby wealth goods used as payment by the state are converted into needed subsistence goods (this had been argued by Brumfiel 1980 for the Aztec case). Markets in these situations may well have existed prior to state formation, and were then used as a critical element in state finance.

As the Inca case shows quite clearly, however, markets are again not strictly necessary for the vertical integration on which states depend. Another alternative, developed by the Inca and other agriculturally based states, is staple finance (Polanyi (1968; Earle and D'Altroy 1982). In these centrally managed state economies, staple goods were collected either as a percentage of production or as the produce from special lands farmed as part of corvée labor obligations. The staples collected in central warehouse facilities were then paid out to state personnel who could use them directly for personal support or barter them in a market or other context for desired goods. The state, by mobilizing and distributing basic subsistence goods, acted as a market replacement in its support of state personnel without direct access to staples.

A whole class of archaic states were financed not primarily through markets but by mobilizing and distributing needed products to specialist personnel. Most primary states, such as in Mesopotania, Egypt, Indus, China, and the Andes, seem to have emphasized local staple finance without significant market development in their earliest stages. In these cases, states depended on ownership of improved agricultural land with irrigation and terracing. Markets, at least initially, were evidently peripheral to state finance.

As I have argued at length elsewhere (Earle 1983), the development of markets in many states comes well after state formation and appears as part of a shift to wealth finance, using currency or other money-like commodities, which permit more central control and greater managerial flexibility. To the degree that the

391

state actively encouraged and controlled long-distance exchange in special products including metal and shell, wealth may have acted as an alternative to staple goods in the Inca state (D'Altroy and Earle, 1985). This could explain the increase in long-distance exchange that accompanied the Inca expansion into the Mantaro Valley.

In sum, it may be inappropriate to speak of the Andean world as marketless as specialization and exchange in certain products, especially craft goods and wealth objects, clearly were established. The development of a market principle, however, was apparently quite restricted because the range of goods being produced for exchange was not large. Rather than markets, local communities were largely generalized and self-sufficient, and the state depended on control of land and the distribution of its "surplus" for institutional finance.

ACKNOWLEDGMENTS

CathyCostin and Glenn Russell have generously provided the ceramic and lithic data on exchange in the Mantaro Valley. They and Francis Berdan have read earlier versions of this paper and offered valuable criticisms. The Mantaro Valley research reported here was supported by a grant from National Science Foundation (BNS82 03723). Figure 1 was drafted by Eliza Earle. Thank you all for your help.

REFERENCES

Acosta, J. de
    1954   [1590] Historia natural y moral de las
            Indias. Biblioteca de Autores Espanoles 73.
Adams, R.
    1966   The evolution of urban society. Chicago:
            Aldine

Beals, R.
    1975   The peasant marketing system of Oaxaca,
            Mexico. Berkeley: University of California
            Press.

Belshaw, C.
    1965   Traditional exchange and modern markets.
            Englewood Cliffs, N.J.: Prentice-Hall.

Blanton, R.
    1983   Factors underlying the origin and evolution
            of market systems. In Economic
            Anthropology: topics and theories.
            Monographs in Economic Anthropology I Sutti
            Ortiz, ed. Lahnam, MD: University Press of
            America and Society for Economic
            Anthropology. pp.51-66.

Burger, R., and F. Asaro
    1977   Análisis de rasgos significativos en la
            obsidiana de los Andes Central. Revista del
            Museo Nacional, Lima 43:281-325.

Brumfiel, E.
    1980   Specialization, market exchange, and the
            Aztec state: a view from Heuxotla. Current
            Anthropology 21:459-478.

Claessen, H.J.M.
    1978   The early state: a structural approach. In
            The early state, edited by H. Claessen and
            P. Skalnik, pp. 533-596. The Hague:
            Mouton.

Cobo, B.
    1979   [1653] History of the Inca empire,
            translated by R. Hamilton. Austin:
            University of Texas Press.

Costin, C.
    1984   Specialization in ceramic production among
            the late prehispanic Huanca. Paper
            presented at the Annual meeting of the
            Society for American Archaeology, Portland,
            OR.
Dalton, G.
    1961   Economic theory and primitive society.
            American Anthropologist 63:1-25.

D'Altroy, T.
    1981   Empire growth and consolidation: the Xauxa
            region of Peru under the Inca. Ann Arbor:
            University Microfilms.

D'Altroy, T., and C. Costin
    1982   Producción de cerámica durante el Horizonte
            Tardío en el Alto Mantaro. Unpublished ms.
            submitted to the Instituto Nacional de
            Cultura, Lima.

393

D'Altroy, T., and T. Earle
    1985   Staple finance and wealth finance in the
            Inka political economy. Cur̲r̲e̲n̲t̲
            Anthropologist. (in press)

Earle, T.
    1982   The ecology and politics of primitive
            valuables. I̲n̲ C̲u̲l̲t̲u̲r̲e̲ a̲n̲d̲ e̲c̲o̲l̲o̲g̲y̲, edited
            by J. Kennedy and R. Edgerton, pp. 65-83.
            Special Publication of the American
            Anthropological Society 15.

    1983   Specialization and the production and
            exchange of wealth: the Hawaiian chiefdoms
            and the Inca state. Paper presented at the
            XI International Congress of Anthropological
            and Ethnological Science. Vancouver, May.

Earle, T., T. D'Altroy, C. LeBlanc, C. Hastorf, and T.
LeVine
    1980   Changing settlement patterns in the
            Yanamarca Valley, Peru. J̲o̲u̲r̲n̲a̲l̲ o̲f̲ N̲e̲w̲ W̲o̲r̲l̲d̲
            A̲r̲c̲h̲a̲e̲o̲l̲o̲g̲y̲ IV (1).

Earle, T., and T. D'Altroy
    1982   Storage facilities and state finance in the
            Upper Mantaro Valley, Peru. I̲n̲ C̲o̲n̲t̲e̲x̲t̲s̲ f̲o̲r̲
            p̲r̲e̲h̲i̲s̲t̲o̲r̲i̲c̲ e̲x̲c̲h̲a̲n̲g̲e̲, edited by J. Ericson
            and T. Earle, pp. 265-290. New York:
            Academic Press.

Einzig, P.
    1984   P̲r̲i̲m̲i̲t̲i̲v̲e̲ m̲o̲n̲e̲y̲. London: Eyre and
            Spottiswoode.
Estete, M.
    1947   V̲e̲r̲d̲a̲d̲e̲r̲a̲ r̲e̲l̲a̲c̲i̲ò̲n̲ de l̲a̲ c̲o̲n̲q̲u̲i̲s̲t̲a̲ d̲e̲l̲ P̲e̲r̲u̲
            y̲ p̲r̲o̲v̲i̲n̲c̲i̲a̲ d̲e̲l̲ C̲u̲z̲c̲o̲ [1534], by F. Jerez.
            Biblioteca de Autores Espanoles 26.

Hagstrum, M.
    1984   The technology of ceramic production of
            Huanca and Inca wares from the Yanamarca
            Valley, Peru. C̲e̲r̲a̲m̲i̲c̲ N̲o̲t̲e̲s̲ 3. (in press).

Hastorf, C.
    1983   Prehistoric agricultural intensification and
            political development in the Jauja region of
            Peru. Ann Arbor: University Microfilms.

Howe, E.
    1983   Metales provenientes del alto Mantaro: un

analisis preliminar. Report submitted to
the Instituto Nacional de Cultura, Lima.

LaLone, D.
1982   The Inca as a nonmarket economy: supply on
command versus supply and demand. In
Contexts for prehistoric exchange, edited by
J. Ericson and T. Earle, pp. 291-316. New
York: Academic Press.

LaLone, D., and M. LaLone
1979   Trade and marketplace in the Inca realm.
Paper read at the 43rd International
Congress of Americanists, Vancouver B.C.

LeBlanc, C.
1981   Late prehispanic settlement patterns in the
Yanamarca Valley, Peru. Ann Arbor:
University Microfilm.

LeClair, E.
1962   Economic theory and economic anthropology.
American Anthropologist 64:1179-1203.

Malinowski, B.
1922   Argonauts of the Western Pacific. London:
Routledge.

Millon, R.
1964   The Teotihuacan mapping project. American
Antiquity 29:345-352.

Mintz, S.
1959   Internal market systems as mechanisms of
social articulation. In Proceedings of the
1959 Annual Spring Meeting of the American
Ethnological Society, pp. 20-30. Seattle:
University of Washington Press.

1961   Pratik: Haitian personal economic
relations. IN Proceedings of the 1961
Annual Spring Meeting of the American
Ethnological Society, pp. 54-63. Seattle:
Washington University Press.

Morris, C., and D. Thompson
1970   Huánuco viejo: an Inca administrative
center. American Antiquity 35:344-362.

Murra, J.
1972   El control vertical de un máximo de pisos

ecologicòs en la economía de las sociedades andinas. In Visita de la provincia de León de Huánuco, Tomo II, edited by J. Murra, pp. 429-476. Huánuco, Peru: Universidad Hermilio Valdizan.

1980   [1956] The economic organization of the Inka state. Greenwich, Conn.: JAI Press.

Polanyi, K.
1957   The economy as instituted process. In Trade and market in the early empires, edited by K. Polanyi, C. Arensberg, and H. Pearson, pp. 243-270. Glencoe: Free Press.

1968   Primitive, archaic and modern economies: essays of Karl Polanyi, edited by G. Dalton. Garden City, N.Y.: Doubleday.

Pospisil, L.
1963   Kapuuku Papuan economy. New Haven: Yale University Press.

Renfrew, C.
1977   Alternative models for exchange and spatial distribution. In Exchange systems in prehistory, edited by T. Earle and J. Ericson, pp. 71-90. New York: Academic Press.

Rostworowski de Diez Canseco, M.
1970   Mercaderes del valle de Chincha en la epoca prehispanico: un documento y unos commentarios. Revista Espanola de Antropologia Americana 5:135-177.

1975   Coastal fishermen, merchants, and artisans in pre-Hispanic Peru. In the Sea in the pre-Columbian world, edited by E.P. Benson, pp. 167-188. Washington, D.C.: Dumbarton Oaks Research Library and Collections.

Rowe, J.
1946   Inca culture at the time of Spanish conquest. In Handbook for South American Indians, Vol. 2, edited by J. Steward, pp. 183-330. Washington, D.c.: Smithsonian.

Sahlins, M.
1972   Stone age economics. Chicago: Aldine

Salomon, F.L.
  1978   Ethnic lords of Quito in the age of the
          Incas. Unpublished Ph.D. dissertation,
          Department of Anthropology, Cornell
          University. Ann Arbor: University
          Microfilms.

Sanders, W. T.
  1956   The central Mexican symbiotic region: a
          study in prehistoric settlement patterns.
          In Prehistoric settlement patterns in the
          New World, edited by G. Willey, pp. 115-127.
          New York: Wenner-Gren Foundation.

Schneider, H.
  1975   Economic Man. New York: Free Press.

Shimada, I.
  1984   Llama and cash flow on the prehispanic
          Peruvian coast. Paper presented at the 49th
          Annual Meeting of the Society for American
          Archaeology. Portland, April.

Spence, M.
  1981   Obsidian production and the state in
          Teotihuacan. American Antiquity 46:769-788.

Uberoi, J.P.S.
  1962   Politics of the Kula ring. Manchester:
          Manchester University press.

Valcarcel, L.
  1946   Indian markets and fairs in Peru. In
          Handbook of South American Indians, Vol. II,
          edited by J. Steward, pp. 477-482.
          Washington, D.C.: Smithsonian.

Wachtel, N.
  1977   The vision of the vanquished. (trans. by B.
          and S. Reynolds) Hassocks, Sussex:
          Harvester Press.

Gilberto
Rodriguez
for. de Cateuraco
de Veracruz.

398

A COMPARISON OF EARLY MARKET SYSTEMS

Richard E. Blanton, Department of Sociology-Anthropology, Purdue University

I. INTRODUCTION

Archaeological research in Highland Mexico is uncovering a trend that existed during the latter Postclassic (i.e. during the last few centuries prior to the Conquest) toward an increasing commercialization of society (Blanton et al. 1981, 1982; Finsten 1983). This has prompted the hypothetical question: could this heightened degree of commercial orientation have produced an independent development of European-style capitalism? Of course we will never know since European expansion terminated the aboriginal developments, but it might be possible to answer this question partially by placing the Mesoamerican economies in a comparative perspective with Europe, where capitalism did flourish, and with other areas where it did not. China is often discussed in this kind of comparative exercise since it was highly commercialized but did not develop as a capitalist economy (i.e. with capitalist industry). The failure to develop capitalism in China is usually attributed to the depressing influences of its centralized and unified imperial structure on commercial activities (cf. Elvin 1973; Jones and Woolf 1969; Wolf 1982;267,8). Wallerstein (1974:348), for example, argues that "...capitalism as an economic mode is based on the fact that the economic factors operate within an area larger than that which any political entity can totally control" (cf. Elvin 1973:177; Wolf 1982:269). [1]

Would an imperial structure have depressed economic development in Mesoamerica as it did in China? It seems unlikely. Gary Feinman and I (Blanton and Feinman 1984) have argued that prehispanic Mesoamerica had been a kind of world-system that Wallerstein (1974:15-17) calls a "world economy", i.e. a world-system lacking a unified imperial structure. Thus in this sense it was more analogous to Europe than to China, although not by any means identical in form to either area. Even if Mesoamerica had been analogous to Europe in its macroregional organization, however, there is no guarantee that it would have been the site of an independent birth of capitalism. Here I argue that to pursue this question in more depth it is necessary to explore how activities in the "world-system" arena were linked up to rural market development and peasant production.

II. ECONOMIC ORGANIZATION OF THE HIGHLAND MEXICAN CORES

In Medieval Europe, regional power and posperity were almost always linked to an export orientation. Until later industrial times this often involved the cloth trade: As Esther Goody (1982: 9) puts it, "the history of the northern-European cloth trade is entwined with political history". Related sources of power and prosperity were involvement in long-distance trade and international finance (Venice, Genoa, Amsterdam, or London, for example). Thus it must have come as somewhat of a surprise to the early Spanish to find that the Valley of Oaxaca, long renowned as the most powerful core zone of the Southern Highlands of Mesoamerica, lacked a major long-distance trade market (although others were present in what is now the state of Oaxaca, in politically more marginal zones), nor was the Valley known as an exporter of craft goods, cloth or otherwise. Instead, these Spaniards comment on the fact that the valley was capable of producing primarily one thing in abundance: food (Cortès 1971:269; Duràn 1951:243).

If we look at the Late Postclassic history of the Valley of Mexico (a region better documented for this period than Oaxaca), we can perhaps understand how a core zone could have become so strongly oriented to food production. During these last years of the Postclassic there had taken place a tremendous buildup of agricultural facilities, including irrigation and other water-control projects, swamp drainage, terracing, and the contruction of the famous chinampas ("floating gardens"), over thousands of hectares (Armillas 1971; Sanders, Parsons, and Santley 1979:222-281). Associated with these activities, labor-intensive farming techniques were adopted, involving elaborate soil preparation, various kinds of fertilizing, and the growing of two or three crops per year ("...No chinampas are rested for more than 3 to 4 months of the year", according to Sanders 1965:44). It would be difficult to overemphasize the importance of this set of changes. This was one of the most thoroughgoing rural transformations in the history of any Mesoamerican region.

At the same time, the expansionist Aztec state was bringing into the region from more agriculturally marginal zones an abundance of tributary imports, virtually all of which were manufactured goods (as opposed to raw materials) (Berdan 1975:112). As both Litvak (1971:118) and Brumfiel (1976, 1980) have suggested, these goods could have "flooded" the market, reducing the prices of non-food items. One can surmise that a reason for the development of this tributary flow was to encourage a transformation of rural work-time in the Valley of Mexico away from craft production and toward food production by, in effect, exporting labor-intensive craft activities to peripheral areas (especially weaving, judging from the tremendous quantities of cloth received as tribute) (cf. Blanton and Feinman 1984). Brumfiel (1976:223) suggests that "...the ultimate effect of circulating tribute goods in the market system would be to create a situation which would encourage the rural populace to become specialized food producers." This process would account for some of the region's growing commercialization since families which devoted more work-time to specialized food production would correspondingly become more dependent on the market system for goods they no longer produced domestically.

I do not mean to imply that the scenario sketched above has been domonstrated to everyone's satisfaction. More research is needed on the interrelationships among the key variables: agricultural development (and the forces driving this development, which included a rapidly growing urban population and a powerful expansionist state), the transformation of rural work-time, rural commercialization, and commodity flows. And such research will be productive not only in the Valley of Mexico, but in other highland Mesoamerican core zones as well, such as the Valley of Oaxaca, where, as I noted, food production seems to have been so important. And would this pattern have characterized the earlier Classic Period, or does it pertain primarily to the more commercialized Postclassic developments? While admitting that more work is needed, I think the information now available is consistent with the following set of hypotheses: 1) An increase in the urban population of a core zone is supported energetically primarily by agricultural intensification in the surrounding rural area. Families in this rural zone commit more work-time to agricultural production, and are thus less self-sufficient in production of other goods; 2) Craft production for this growing rural (as well as urban) market is increasingly exported away from the most desirable agricultural land surrounding the core-zone cities, and toward more distant and more agriculturally marginal localities, resulting in a pattern of specialization by territorial segments linked together by the state, via its tribute flows, and by an expanding market system (for example, the growth of maguey and nopal production in the agriculturally marginal northern Valley of Mexico(Berdan 1982:25)). Sanders and Price (1968:188-193) identify this zone of linked territorial segments as the "Central Mexican Symbiotic Region".

One of the most interesting features of this pattern is that some of the categories of craft production that could be so economically and politically important in the European cores (e.g. weaving) were instead apparently tending to become delegated to peripheries. Admittedly, some categories of craft production developed in the core cities (cf. Calnek 1975), but by and large these involved the production of goods for internal elite consumption or state use, rather than for "competitive export", if I may call it that, of utilitarian commodities, in the European fashion.

III. CHINA BY COMPARISON

Although on a larger scale, an analogous pattern emerged as a consequence of the agricultural revolution in south-central China after the 8th century A.D. This involved a reorientation of core-zone rural labor (especially to wet rice cultivation), using intensive techniques that involve virtually constant labor inputs year-round (thus, as Elvin notes, wiping out rural unemployment) (1973:122, Chapter 9). As would be expected, this reorientation of rural labor-time to agricultural specialization was to produce an increasing dependence on market systems and an attendent commercialization (Skinner 1977:233; discussions of the commercial revolution can be found in Twitchett 1966; Ma 1971; Shiba 1975; Elvin ibid.: Chapter 12). And as the most desirable core-zone land was converted to food production, other production was increasingly pushed out to peripheral settings, resulting in the same kind of territorial specialization that was beginning to characterize Central Mexico. Whole regions or sub-regions became strongly identified with particular specializations (cf. Dietrich 1972; Elvin ibid.: 163, 168, 213, 282; Shiba 1975; Sun 1972:72, 83). And more was involved than just elite goods, as lower-order goods were also increasingly moved long distances from points of production to points of consumption.

As this kind of specialization developed in China, the various territorial segments were integrated into the emerging market system by means of merchant intermediaries who transferred products from these areas to the market systems and urban centers of the core zones (Elvin ibid.: Chapter 16; of this, more below).

IV. EUROPE BY COMPARISON

We think of Europe today in some of the same terms I have described above: Intensive production involving territorial specializations (industrial areas, wine-growing areas, etc.),linked together by means of a complex economic system. But historically Europe was actually quite different. Much of the territorial specialization that now characterizes Europe came about after the commercial and agricultural revolutions that followed the transformation to capitalist production (i.e. during and after the 17th and 18th centuries) (Jones 1977; Kriedte 1981:30). Previously, and even to a great extent now, European regions, even those that were the economically and politically important cores, retained rather generalized production bases, involving both food production as well as artisanal production for internal consumption or export (or things like wine-making or the herding of animals).

Why did the European cores resist specialization (at least until quite late)? Probably the most important single factor can be found in the nature of European agriculture, which tended to be less intensive than the Mexican and Chinese core-zone cultivation discussed above, and, of particular importance for our purposes here, employed rural labor more seasonally, leaving a relative abundance of underemployed labor-time during agriculturally slow periods (Kriedte 1981:14; Mendels 1972:242) (this was especially true of the agriculture of the north; Mediterranean cultivation was more balanced due to the combination of grain-growing with vines and olives (Braudel 1972:429)). This need not imply that European agriculture was characterized by excess labor overall. In fact, during peak agricultural periods labor shortages were common, and labor-saving technology that helped to relieve these seasonal bottlenecks was an important feature of agricultural development in Europe (Collins 1969).

This European agriculture is associated with the kind of peasantry that anthropologists often think of as "typical" (e.g. Wolf 1969), that is, a peasantry

403

retaining a high degree of household self-sufficiency and producing some artisanal or other kind of product for the market only as a supplement to household income (e.g. as described by Everitt 1967a and Thirsk 1961). It is expected that this situation would have resulted in a relatively retarded development of rural market systems by comparison with Mexico and China where peasant production had been more specialized and market-oriented. For example, whereas in China goods produced for the market often had to travel long distances from the point of production to the point of use, by means of intermediaries, in Europe peasants were more often able to exchange what they produced for what they needed directly in local markets or fairs.

The relative simplicity of European market systems will be difficult to demonstrate, however, since there are so many methodological obstacles to any measurement of rural commercialization, especially in the context of cases known only historically or archaeologically But the values given in Table 1 provide support for the hypothesis. While the numbers of persons per rural market are suprisingly similar for all these cases (5,000 to 10,000 or so), there are some drastic differences in average area serviced by rural markets, with the Chinese and Mexican values smaller than the European--thus the European populations in question would, on average, have to travel further from house to market-place. However, this may be due primarily to higher population densities in the congested rural core-zone populations in China and Mexico rather than indicating greater commercialization.

The most convincing evidence is to be found in the frequency of market-days. Presumably, market-day periodicity can serve as a measure of market dependence, since families more dependent on the market would require more frequent trips for market transactions. Another way to look at it is to say that market places experiencing increased traffic can most effectively respond to that demand by adding new market days (Skinner 1963:15-16).

The highland Mexican pattern in the cores was a five-day sequence (10, 15, and 20-day intervals were usually found only in more marginal localities), while the Chinese pattern in the most densely populated cores was normally somewhere between a 3 and a 5-day periodicity; the standard for rural European markets was a 7-day interval, which I interpret as evidence for weaker commercialization (references for this discussion are found in Table 1).

Another imporant indicator of the relatively weaker commercialization of rural Late Medieval Europe is the fact that even until late (i.e. in many areas until the 19th century) fairs contined to be an important context of commercial transactions; since they convene even less frequently that periodic markets they are a good indicator of poor rural demand (as Braudel (1982;93) put it: "...the fair is an archaic form of exchange.") I have not been able to find much evidence of the use of fairs as contexts for commercial activities either in traditional China or prehispanic Mesoamerica, although they did exist, at least in China. Where fairs are mentioned for China, the references are most often to temple fairs, which are really religious festivals (e.g. Skinner 1963:38). Commercial fairs may have existed in Mesoamerica (Feldman 1978:14), but there is no indication that they existed in great numbers as they did in Europe.

I conclude that Medieval Europe was unlike prehispanic Mexico or traditional China. Europe was in general less commercialized (at least at the level of rural market systems), its cores were less specialized for high-intensity food production, and these same cores exhibited an interdigitation of artisanal or other kinds of production activities with food production, rather than the extreme territorial specializations that characterized the Central Mexican Symbiotic Region and south-central China. And the European cores had more seasonal underemployment of labor than was present in the other two areas.

V. CONCLUSION

I started out trying to decide whether or not aboriginal developments in highland Mexico might have produced an independent evolution of capitalism. At this point I think I would have to conclude that this would have been highly unlikely since in so many ways Mexico seems to have been evolving in a manner analogous to the Chinese pattern. But why would the pattern necessarily be associated with a failure of capitalist development? Obviously this is an extremely complex issue not resolvable here, but I do think that the broad characteristics I have mentioned may be pertinent to such an inquiry, even though they are usually overlooked in such comparisons.

Capitalist production is initiated once merchant

405

Table 1. Comparison of Preindustrial Rural Market
          Systems (a)

	Periodicity	Avg. Person/ Market	Avg. Km2/ Market
Mexico (1) (16th century Valley of Mexico)	5-day(b)	8-10,000(c)	80 (c)
Premodern China (2)	3-5 day(d)	7,000 (e)	50 (f)
England (3) (16th and 17th centuries)	7-day	6-7,000	121-202 (g)
Généralité of Caen (1725) (4)	7-day (h)	9,000	172

(a)   Ideally this would be a comparison of what
        Skinner (1963) called "standard markets" (rural
        markets "which meet all the normal trade needs
        of the peasant household"). While the market
        information presented for the Valley of Mexico
        and two European regions in this table pertain
        primarily to rural markets, they do not pertain
        strictly speaking to standard markets alone,
        but instead include some higher-ranking
        markets. A definitive cross-cultural
        comparison of standard markets has yet to be
        accomplished.

(b)   This was changed to a 7-day cycle after the
        Conquest.

(c)   These are rough estimates that will be
        modified, probably downward, once it is
        possible to identify with greater security
        markets that are the equivalent of standard
        markets, and to eliminate those that have
        higher ranks. I calculated this figure on the
        basis of population data for the Late
        Postclassic Valley of Mexico found in Sanders,
        Parsons, and Santley (1979: Chapter 6,
        passim).

(d)   6, 10, or 12-day cycles were found only in marginal areas.

(e)   South-central, excluding areas of least commercialization. Rozman's (1973:127) higher values (11,000-12,000) are for China as a whole, which would include some less commercialized areas (cf. Rozman 1982:Chapter 5)

(f)   Modal size for standard markets.

(g)   South-central, excluding areas of least commercialization.

(h)   A minority (19%) had frequencies greater than 7 days.

(1)   Based on a preliminary estimate made by Frances Berdan (personal communication) that there may have been roughly 100 market places in the Valley of Mexico by the end of the Late Postclassic. Previous discussions of the Valley of Mexico market system refer to a smaller number of market places, probably because they included only markets in places that also had administrative functions, overlooking the numerous localities that had small markets but no administrative importance (cf. Bray 1972a:919, 1972b:165; Gibson 1964; Sanders 1965:71; Smith 1979).

(2)   Skinner 1963: 10-16, 33.

(3)   Everitt 1967b (cf. Rozman 1976:Chapter 5)

(4)   Braudel 1982:47 (cf. Rozman 1976:Chapter 5)

(Table 1. continued)

entrepreneurs begin to intervene directly in the process of production, thus deriving profit from both production and circulation. Why this should have happened in Western Europe -- with increasing frequency after the 15th century or so--is not well understood, as is discussed at length by Braudel (1982). But viewed from the perspective I have developed here (focusing on rural markets and rural production), Europe would seem to have had at least two distinct advantages over Mesoamerica and China:

1) Even in its core zones, Europe had a relative abundance of rural labor-time available for new kinds of production activities, and to "fund" a new round of production intensity. And the earliest form of large-scale capitalist industry, the Verlagssystem, or putting-out system, emphasized the use of rural labor (a recent discussion of this so-called protoindustrialization is found in Kriedte, Medick, and Schlumbohm 1981). Mexico and China appear to have been singularly lacking in seasonally underemployed rural labor in their corresponding cores.

2) A second advantage could have come from Europe's relatively poorly developed rural market system. One way to view this is to see the Chinese market system as having been so efficient that merchants did not find it necessary to organize production--they could make ample profits from circulation alone and so did not need to intervene in production (e.g. Elvin 1973:274; Goody 1982:34). Perhaps, but I suggest that an even more important point is the fact that the European system was so simple that it could be more easily reorganized by capitalists. In the more complex rural economies like China's, production units, and those who linked these units to the national markets, were so highly specialized, organized, and entrenched that they created obstacles to change. This kind of institutional complexity and conservatism was precisely the reason why the early capitalists bypassed the European urban guilds in setting up their new enterprises--the guilds were highly organized and were able to resist merchant attempts to expand production and to impose control over the production process (cf. Kriedte 1981:21, 22; Weber 1978:1330-1331). Capitalist ventures were most successful when they constituted the introduction of a new kind of production to an area, such as occurred with the spread of silk production during the 16th century in places such as Genoa and Venice; as Braudel (1972:431) pointed out, " ...their

vitality at the end of the century is in marked contrast to such old manufacturing centers as Florence, where the ancient arts of luxury woollen and silk cloth manufacture were to some extent suffering from old age, some say 'petty-mindedness'". English wool cloth manufacture stands as a major example of this general process. After the fourteenth century England ceased exporting raw wool to be worked into cloth by Flemish towns, and instead began producing its own cloth--a new (for England), and to say the very least, highly successful industry. (Braudel (1982: 253-4) makes a similar observation concerning early capitalist agriculture: "It was no accident that the new farming ventures were so often launched on wasteland or woodland. It was better not to upset existing land systems and customs.")

There is no question but that in traditional China there was a considerable amount of institutional complexity surrounding rural production and marketing (e.g. Sun 1972 concerning the social organization of weaving), and this would have had the same depressing effect on change as occurred among the European guilds. Elvin (1973: 283) discusses an example of what may have come the closest in rural China to a "putting-out system", the rural silk industry. Even in this case, however, silk production "account houses" issued silk to households for weaving, but "...the account houses were divorced from actual production by one and sometimes two levels of so-called 'management contractors'" (ibid.). As Elvin expresses it, putting-out endeavors such as this constituted "'progress', but...the methods of organization tended to separate those in commerce from those in production." (ibid.: 284).

Sun (1972: 103) relates an example of a failure of a silk-reeling factory that nicely sums up the difficulties of establishing capitalist industrial production in China (although it is not an ideal example for my purposes since it occurred in an urban rather that rural setting): "The first steam filature...was set up...in Shanghai in 1862, but the venture was unsuccessful and the plant closed down in 1866...The failure of this early filature has usually been attributed to lack of technically-trained labor, and to the obstructions raised by traditional "middlemen" who feared the competition of the new industry." Other factors were related to the failure, but is notable that both a lack of labor and a rigid market framework were prominently noted.

409

This discussion begs many questions and is far from definitive. It also suffers from operating at such a high level of generalization that it ignores what may be crucial details. Some areas of Western Europe, for example, including the Low Countries and Eastern Norfolk, were becoming quite intensively cultivated in Late Medieval times (Campbell 1983, Slicher Van Bath 1963: 177-180). But these strategies diffused slowly, so that it is still safe to say that overall the transformation of European agriculture did not occur until during and after the period of protoindustrialization and early industrialization (Jones 1965).

My goal has not been to do a detailed comparison of these three areas; it has been limited to making the argument that in understanding the failure of capitalist development in China or in other similar situations it is not sufficient to refer only to the depressing influences of centralized bureaucratic states or world empires. It is necessary, instead, to show how these larger-scale organizations influence rural production and market development, and how this organization, in turn, inhibits or promotes the transition to capitalist production.

ACKNOWLEDGMENTS
I was aided in the preparation of this paper by comments from Frances Berdan, Gary Feinman, Laura Finsten, Steve Kowalewski, and Jackie Saindon. I also benefited from an important personal communication on Valley of Mexico markets by Frances Berdan, and by references I encountered while reading Scott Cook's Peasant Capitalist Industry (1984). I received some useful references on Chinese agriculture from Greg Veeck. All errors and misinterpretations are my own.

NOTES

1. Max Weber (1966, 1978) provided what still stands as the most complete--and widely repeated--discussion of the differential growth of capitalism. In contrast with the just-mentioned authors who paid most attention to scale and degree of centralization of political formations, Weber considered a multiplicity of factors, especially those in the realm of religious belief and religious organization, as well as the degree of rationality in administration, legal codes, and methods of capital accounting, and the presence or absence of

410

what he terms a rationalistic economic ethic. The discussion that follows is restricted to a much narrower range of variables.

REFERENCES CITED

Armillas, Pedro
1971   Gardens on Swamps. *Science* 174:653-661.

Berdan, Frances
1975   Trade, Tribute and Market in the Aztec Empire. Ph.D. Dissertation, University of Texas at Austin.

1982   *The Aztecs of Central Mexico: An Imperial Society.* New York: Holt, Rinehart, and Winston.

Blanton, R., S. Kowalewski, G. Feinman, and J. Appel
1981   *Ancient Mesoamerica: A Comparison of Change in Three Regions.* Cambridge: Cambridge University Press.

1982   Monte Albán's Hinterland, Part 1: The Prehispanic Settlement Patterns of the Central and Southern Parts of the Valley of Oaxaca, Mexico. Ann Arbor: University of Michigan Museum of Anthropology Memoirs 15.

Blanton, R., and G. Feinman
1984   The Mesoamerican World-System. *American Anthropologist* 86 (3):673-682.

Braudel, Fernand
1972   *The Mediterranean and the Mediterranean World in the Age of Philip II,* Vol. 1. New York: Harper and Row.

1982   *Civilization and Capitalism, 15th-18th Centuries, Vol. 2: The Wheels of Commerce.* New York: Harper and Row.

Bray, Warwick
1972a   "Land-use, settlement pattern and politics in prehispanic Middle America: A review. In *Man, Settlement, and Urbanism.* P.J. Ucko, et al., eds. pp. 909-926. London: Duckworth.

1972b   "The city-state in Central Mexico at the

time of the Spanish Conquest." Journal of
Latin American Studies 4(2): 161-185.

Brumfiel, Elizabeth
1976   Specialization and Exchange at the Late
        Postclassic (Aztec) Community of Heuxotla,
        Mexico. Ph.D. Dissertation, The University
        of Michigan.

1980   "Specialization, market exchange, and the
        Aztec state: a view from Huexotla".
        Current Anthropology 21(4):459-78.

Calnek, Edward
1975   Organización de los Sistemas de
        Abastecimiento Urbano de Alimentos: El Caso
        de Tenochtitlan. In Las Ciudades de América
        Latina y Sus Areas de Influencia a Través de
        la Historia. J. E. Hardoy and R. P.
        Schaedel, eds. Pp. 41-60. Buenos Aires:
        Ediciones A.I.A.P.

Campbell, Bruce
1983   Agricultural Progress in Medieval England:
        Some Evidence From Eastern Norfolk.
        Economic History Review 36 (1):26-46.

Collins, E.J.T.
1969   Labour Supply and Demand in European
        Agriculture 1800-1880. In Agrarian Change
        and Economic Development: The Historical
        Problems. E. L. Jones and S. J. Woolf, eds.
        Pp. 61-94. London: Methuen.

Cook, Scott
1984   Peasant Capitalist Industry. Lanham,
        Maryland: University Press of America.

Cortés, Hernan
1971   Letters From Mexico. Translated and edited
        by A. R. Pagden. New York: Orion Press.

Dietrich, Craig
1972   "Cotton culture and manufacture in early
        Ch'ing China." In Economic Organization in
        Chinese Society. W. W. Willmott, ed. Pp.
        109-36. Stanford: Stanford University
        Press.

Durán, Fray Diego
1951   Historia de las Indias de Nueva Espana.

412

Mexico: Editorial Nacional.

Elvin, Mark
    1973   The Pattern of the Chinese past. Stanford:
            Stanford University Press.

Everitt, Alan
    1967a   "Farm Laborers". In The Agrarian History of
            England and Wales. Joan Thirsk, ed. Pp.
            396-465. Cambridge: Cambridge University
            Press.

    1967b   "The Marketing of Agricultural Produce." In
            The Agrarian History of England and Wales.
            Joan Thirsk, ed. Pp. 466-592. Cambridge:
            Cambridge University Press.

Feldman, Lawrence
    1978   Moving Merchandise in Protohistoric Central
            Quauhtemallan. In Mesoamerican Communication
            Routes and Cultural Contacts. Thomas Lee,
            Jr., and Carlos Navarrete, eds. Pp. 7-18.
            New World Archaeological Foundation Papers
            40. Provo: New World Archaeological
            Foundation.

Finsten, Laura
    1983   The Classic-Postclassic Transition in the
            Valley of Oaxaca, Mexico: A Regional
            Analysis of the Process of Political
            Decentralization in a Prehistoric Complex
            Society. PhD. Dissertation, Purdue
            University.

Gibson, Charles
    1964   The Aztecs Under Spanish Rule. Stanford:
            Stanford University Press.

Goody, Esther
    1982   Introduction. In From Craft to Industry:
            The Ethnography of Proto-Industrial Cloth
            Production. Esther Goody, ed. Pp. 1-37.
            Cambridge: Cambridge Papers in Social
            Anthropology 10.

Jones, E. L.
    1965   Agriculture and Economic Growth in England,
            1660-1750. Agricultural Change. Journal of
            Economic History XXV (1): 1-18.

    1977   "Environment,   Agriculture,   and

413

Industrialization in Europe." <u>Agriculture</u>
<u>History</u> 51(3): 491-502.

Jones, E.L. and S. J. Woolf
  1969   Introduction: The Historical Role of
            Agrarian Change in Economic Development.
            In <u>Agrarian</u> <u>Change</u> <u>and</u> <u>Economic</u>
            <u>Development:</u> <u>The</u> <u>Historical</u> <u>Problems.</u>
            E.L. Jones and S. J. Woolf, eds. Pp. 1-
            21. London: Methuen.

Kriedte, Peter
  1981   The Origins, the Agrarian Context, and the
            Conditions in the World Market. In
            <u>Industrialization</u> <u>Before</u> <u>Industrialization:</u>
            <u>Rural</u> <u>Industry</u> <u>in</u> <u>the</u> <u>Genesis</u> <u>of</u>
            <u>Capitalism.</u> Peter Kriedte, Hans Medick, and
            Jurgen Schlumbohm, eds. Pp. 12-37.
            Cambridge: Cambridge University Press.

Kriedte, Peter, H. Medick, and J. Schlumbohm, eds.
  1981   <u>Industrialization</u> <u>Before</u> <u>Industrialization:</u>
            <u>Rural</u> <u>Industry</u> <u>in</u> <u>the</u> <u>Genesis</u> <u>of</u> <u>Capitalism.</u>
            Cambridge: Cambridge University Press.

Litvak King, Jaime
  1971   <u>Cihuatlán</u> <u>y</u> <u>Tepecoacuilco:</u> <u>Provincias</u>
            <u>Tributarias</u> <u>de</u> <u>México</u> <u>en</u> <u>al</u> <u>Siglo</u> <u>XVI.</u>
            Mexico City: Universidad Nacional Autónoma
            de México. Instituto de Investigaciones
            Historicas.

Ma, Laurence J.C.
  1971   <u>Commercial</u> <u>Development</u> <u>and</u> <u>Urban</u> <u>Change</u> <u>in</u>
            <u>Sung</u> <u>China</u> <u>(960-1279).</u> University of
            Michigan, Michigan Geographical Publications
            No. 6.

Mendels, Franklin
  1972   Protoindustrialization: The First Phase of
            the Industrialization Process. <u>The</u> <u>Journal</u>
            <u>of</u> <u>Economic</u> <u>History</u> XXXII: 241-261.

Rozman, Gilbert
  1973   <u>Urban</u> <u>Networks</u> <u>in</u> <u>Ching</u> <u>China</u> <u>and</u> <u>Tokugawa</u>
            <u>Japan.</u> Princeton: Princeton University
            Press.

  1976   <u>Urban</u> <u>Networks</u> <u>in</u> <u>Russia,</u> <u>1750-1800,</u> <u>and</u>
            <u>Premodern</u> <u>Periodization.</u> Princeton:
            Princeton University Press.

414

1982   _Population_ _and_ _Marketing_ _Settlements_ _in_
        Ch'ing _China_. Cambridge: Cambridge
        University Press.

Sanders, William T.
   1965   The Cultural Ecology of the Teotihuacan
        Valley. Mimeo, Pennsylvania State
        University.

Sanders, William T., and B. Price
   1968   _Mesoamerica_: _The_ _Evolution_ _of_ _a_
        Civilization. New York: Random House

Sanders, William T., J.R. Parsons, and W. Santley
   1979   _The_ _Basin_ _of_ _Mexico_. New York: Academic
        Press.

Shiba, Yoshinobu
   1975   "Urbanization and the Development of Markets
        in the Lower Yangtze Valley." In _Crisis_ _and_
        Prosperity _in_ _Sung_ _China_. J.W. Haeger, ed.
        Pp. 13-48. Tucson: University of Arizona
        Press.

Skinner, G. William
   1963   "Marketing and Social Structure in Rural
        China: Part I." _Journal_ _of_ _Asian_ _Studies_
        XXIII: 3-43.

   1977   "Regional Urbanization in Nineteenth-Century
        China." In _The_ _City_ _in_ _Late_ _Imperial_ _China_.
        G.W. Skinner, ed. Pp. 211-249. Stanford:
        Stanford University Press.

Slicher Van Bath, B.H.
   1963   _The_ _Agrarian_ _History_ _of_ _Western_ _Europe_:
        _A.D._ _500-1850_. London: Edward Arnold.

Smith, Michael
   1979   "The Aztec marketing system and settlement
        pattern in the Valley of Mexico: a central
        place analysis." _American_ _Antiquity_ 44(1):
        110-25.

Sun, E-Tu Zen
   1972   Sericulture and silk textile production in
        Ch'ing China. In _Economic_ _Organization_ _in_
        Chinese _Society_. W.E. Willmott, ed. Pp. 79-
        108. Stanford: Stanford University Press.

Thirsk, Joan
    1961   Industries in the Countryside. In _Essays in the Economic and Social History of Tudor and Stuart England_. F.J. Fisher, ed. Pp. 70-88. Cambridge: Cambridge University Press.

Twitchett, Dennis
    1966   The T'ang market system. _Asia Minor_ XII(i): 202-248.

Wallerstein, Immanuel
    1974   _The Modern World-System: Capitalist Agriculture and the Origins of the European World-Economy in the Sixteenth Century_. New York: Academic Press.

Weber, Max
    1966   _General Economic History_. New York: Collier Books.

    1978   _Economy and Society: An Outline of Interpretive Sociology_. 2 Volumes. Guenther Roth and Claus Wittich, eds. Berkeley: University of California Press.

Wolf, Eric
    1969   _Peasants_. Englewood Cliffs: Prentice-Hall.

    1982   _Europe and the People Without History_. Berkeley: University of California Press.

NOTES ON CONTRIBUTORS

ACHESON, JAMES M. (Ph.D., University of Rochester, 1970) Professor of Anthropology, University of Maine, Orono, Maine. He has done extensive fieldwork in the Tarascan area of Mexico and with fishermen along the New England coast. In 1974-75 he served as Social Anthropologist for the National Marine Fisheries Service in Washington, D.C.

APPLEBY, GORDON (Ph.D., Stanford, 1978) Rural Sociologist, Planning Unit, Organization pour la Mise en Valeur du Fleuve Gambie (O.M.V.G.). An economic anthropologist working in development whose interests focus on practical applications of social science theory and methods.

BABB, FLORENCE E. (Ph.D., SUNY-Buffalo, 1981) Assistant Professor of Anthropology, University of Iowa. She has carried out fieldwork among Peruvian market women in 1977, 1982, and 1984. At present she is writing a book on the political economy of women's market activity in Peru.

BERDAN, FRANCES F. (Ph.D., Texas-Austin, 1975) Professor of Anthropology, California State University, San Bernardino. Her research has focused on the Aztec economic system, central Mexican codices, and Nahuatl language documentation in colonial Mexico.

BLANTON, RICHARD E. (Ph.D., Michigan, 1970) Professor of Anthropology, Purdue University. An archaeologist who has worked on the evolution of prehispanic civilizations in the valley of Mexico and Oaxaca in the central and southern highlands of Mexico.

BYRNE, DANIEL J. (M.A., U.C. Irvine, 1985) He is beginning dissertation research on regional trade networks in West Africa.

COOK, SCOTT. (Ph.D., Pittsburgh, 1968) Professor of Anthropology at the University of Connecticut. His research interests have focused on simple commodity production and capitalist development in the Oaxaca Valley, Mexico. He has published a number of articles and books on these topics.

417

DANNHAEUSER, NORBERT (Ph.D., U.C. Berkeley, 1973) Associate Professor of Anthropology, Texas A & M University. His current research interests are on traditional and modern markets in South and Southeast Asia and the cultural ecology of aquaculture.

EARLE, TIMOTHY. (Ph.D., Michigan, 1973) Associate Professor of Anthropology, University of California, Los Angeles. His archaeological and historical work has dealt with Polynesian chiefdoms and Andean states. He has published a number of books on prehistoric economics.

LESSINGER, JOHANNA. (Ph.D., Brandeis University, 1977) Affiliated with the Research Institute for the Study of Man, New York City. She is currently engaged in research on Indian immigrant entrepreneurs in New York. Her previous work was concerned with urbanization, petty trade, and women's roles in India.

PLATTNER, STUART. (Ph.D., Stanford University, 1969) Associate Professor of Anthropology, University of Missouri-St. Louis. He studies economic behavior in markets, and he has done research in southern Mexico and in the middle western United States.

SKINNER, G. WILLIAM. (Ph.D., Cornell, 1954) Professor of Anthropology, Stanford University. His research interests are focused on Chinese society in China and Southeast Asia. His most recent book is The City in Late Imperial China.

SMITH, CAROL A. (Ph.D., Stanford University, 1972) Associate Professor of Anthropology, Duke University. Her research has focused on economic and political relations in western Guatemala. She is presently writing about petty commodity production, Latin American urbanization patterns, and class/ethnic struggle in Guatemala.

TRAGER, LILLIAN. (Ph.D., University of Washington, 1976) Associate Professor of Anthropology, University of Wisconsin-Parkside. Her research interests focus on markets, the urban informal sector and rural-urban linkages in Nigeria and the Philippines.